Law for Student Police Officers

JONATHAN MERRITT

LearningMatters

First published in 2007 by Learning Matters

British Library Cataloguing-in-Publication Data
A catalogue record for this book is available from the British Library.

ISBN 978 1 84641 038 3

Cover design by Topics – The Creative Partnership
Cover photograph by kind permission of Fouad Bechwat
Project management by Deer Park Productions, Tavistock
Typeset by Pantek Arts Ltd, Maidstone, Kent
Printed in Great Britain by Bell & Bain Ltd, Glasgow

Learning Matters
33 Southernhay East
Exeter EX1 1NX
Tel: 01392 215560
info@learningmatters.co.uk
www.learningmatters.co.uk

Law for Student
Police Officers

Contents

To my wife Dawn, with love
'…with all its sham drudgery and broken dreams it is still a beautiful world.'
Desiderata

Acknowledgements

I would like to thank everyone who has had the remotest link with this project but must keep this section within bounds. I would like to thank all who provided material, ideas and direct support and also those who, wittingly or unwittingly provided inspiration or assistance to my efforts. In no particular order then I would like to thank De Montfort Department of Law staff Professor Richard Ward, Professor Michael Hirst, Professor Richard Card, Kath Shorrock, Pat Hirst, Tim Hillier, Lynne Ross, Gavin Dingwall, also Annette Crisp of Health and Life Sciences. I would like to thank Castle College staff Sarah Dennis and Rob Bowes for their support during my time there. I would also like to thank PC Kevin Priest, PC Ed Watkins, Sgt James Pidgeon, Sgt John Coxhead, PCSOs Dawn Merritt, Sally Wiggington, Catherine Nightingale and Paul O'Dwyer for technical information and inspiration given. Can I thank my parents Peter and Marjorie Merritt and my big brother Neville and his family for supporting me and my efforts unswervingly and with love. Thanks are also due to Jonathan Harris and Dee Bettaney of Law Matters for their help and understanding, also Jeremy Stein. Errors and omissions of course remain mine and mine alone. Any suggestions for inclusion or amendment will always be gratefully received via the publisher.

Foreword

I am pleased to write this foreword to *Law for Student Police Officers*. Its author, Jonathan Merritt, has considerable first-hand experience of police training as well as 12 years' experience teaching criminal law. He was course leader of one of the first foundation degrees in policing and has been at the forefront in the national development of foundation degrees in criminal justice. The primary aim of this book is to support probationary constables and students on foundation degree and NVQ courses in policing, criminal justice and community justice. The author is obviously very well qualified to write it.

The text has been written with IPLDP and the Home Office 'Learning Requirement' firmly in mind. It seeks to go further in terms of analysis than traditional police training manuals but carefully avoids going into deeper water than is required for its intended readership. One of its attractions is the frequent reference to the context within which policing is set. With its focus on the ethos and methodologies inspired by IPLDP and the analysis which it provides, the text is a valuable and innovative addition to the ranks, sitting as it does between those textbooks which are akin to undergraduate law books and the basic 'need to know' definition books for police officers which exist.

As one would expect, the contents concentrate on criminal law; all the major offences and all the offences most commonly committed are covered, as are police powers. Commendably, it also deals, to the requisite extent, with the law of criminal evidence, with relevant areas of the civil law and with sentencing. The last of these is novel for a book aimed at the intended market, but it is important that those involved in the criminal justice system understand why a particular sentence is passed once a case is out of their hands.

A distinguishing feature of the text is that it is geared to the learning needs of its readers. Each section sets out a clear statement of 'aims and objectives' at the start and the subject matter is punctuated by 'revision' boxes, 'knowledge check' or test exercise boxes and research activities. Where appropriate the text includes pointers and suggestions for reflection.

This book will appeal not only to the market referred to above but also to Police Community Support Officers who want advanced reading and to experienced officers who want a quick refreshment of basic knowledge.

I congratulate Jonathan Merritt on this book. I am pleased to commend it to the range of readership to which I have referred.

Richard Card
Emeritus Professor of Law
Formerly Head of De Montfort Law School
De Montfort University, Leicester

Table of statutes

Table of cases

Introduction – How to use this book

Police training, National Occupational Standards and recognised qualifications

Up until relatively recently the arduous training that a police officer must go through in England and Wales could produce a very well-trained police officer but it did not count towards any nationally recognised qualification. There was a need to respond to this almost unique state of affairs. In a drive to professionalise the police service the Home Office, Skills for Justice (the national training organisation for justice-sector workers) and the training staff of many of the police forces have established what might be described as a core curriculum for a patrol officer. This currently centres around 22 National Occupational Standards (NOS). These types of standards exist in many professions from nursing to care to custody, security, construction and so on. The 22 NOS are constantly under review by Skills for Justice; the current titles of those NOS are found at Appendix 1 to this volume, together with a further set which have been developed to apply to the Police Community Support Officer (PCSO). This volume would also therefore constitute advanced reading for PCSOs in training and for their continuous professional development (CPD) as well. In fact many of the NOS are the same for a student police officer.

Each chapter begins with a section that indicates to you which of the 22 NOS the chapter addresses in terms of the legal knowledge required. As the NOS require competence in the workplace to be 'passed' by the student, the information in this book cannot provide more than underpinning knowledge. There follows an example from Chapter 2, 'Human rights':

Underpinning knowledge towards Patrol Officer NOS:

1A1, 1A2, 1A4, 1B9, 2A1, 2C1, 2C2, 2C3, 2C4, 2G2, 2G4, 2H1, 2H2, 2I1, 2I2, 2J1, 2J2, 2K1, 2K2, 4C1

and PCSO NOS:

1A1, 1A4, 1B11, 2A1, 2C1, 2C2, 2C3, 2C4, 2C5, 2J1, 2J2, 2K1, 4C1

For further information on these NOS, which are also Policing Level 3 and 4 NVQ unit titles, refer to Appendix 1 to this volume.

In many police forces the student officers training now leads to a foundation degree and/or the achievement of the Level 3 and Level 4 National Vocational Qualification (NVQ) in Policing. More detail about these NVQs can be found by accessing the websites detailed in Appendix 1 and listed at the end of this chapter. In summary, 11 of them equate to the NVQ Level 3 and the remaining 11 to the NVQ Level 4 qualification. Level 3 is nominally equivalent to studying at A-level in school or college. Level 4 is equivalent to studying for a degree.

Whether the NVQs are delivered as separate qualifications or are embedded within a foundation degree, the level is that broadly of an undergraduate studying a traditional degree although the assessments may be very different and much more vocational. This mirrors moves in other UK professions in the same vein; nurses and probation officers are examples. Indeed some foreign countries have gone further and require their applicants to be full university graduates before they are considered for recruitment to the police.

Foundation degrees are two-year degrees designed with considerable employer input. They are very vocational in nature and lead to a university award. Graduates either receive the designation FdA (Foundation Degree – Arts) or FdSc (Foundation Degree – Sciences) and may use these letters after their names. Kent Police produced the first graduates of this method of police training in association with University College, Christchurch. Nottinghamshire and Leicestershire Police operate a similar training scheme through Castle College, Nottingham and De Montfort University, Leicester.

This book and recent developments in police training

This book was written with a primary purpose in mind, to support the learning required by student officers under the new Initial Police Learning and Development Programme (IPLDP). Almost all police forces no longer send their recruits to regional training centres. Most police forces train their officers either in-house, at a local further education college or a university. Some use a mixture of all three approaches. The thinking behind this is partly to help address discrimination. Some potential recruits, such as single parents or the members of certain religious and cultural groups, would find the traditional 12–14 week residential course some distance from home an absolute bar to joining. It was considered that a more local approach would help the new police officers embed themselves in and become aware of the concerns of their local community in all its diversity. Recently there have also been some real concerns, highlighted by some highly controversial TV documentaries, about the phenomenon of the so-called 'canteen culture'. This can, at its worst extremes, result in the reinforcement of racist, sexist and homophobic attitudes. This phenomenon has in the past been noted particularly in enclosed training environments in a variety of sectors, not just the police service.

Learning police law with this book

The legal knowledge required of a patrol officer is arguably greater now than it ever has been. The criminal law is growing ever more detailed with new Acts and other legislation adding layer upon layer of complexity. The training of police officers has always contained relevant statute law (the **Theft Act 1968, Sexual Offences Act 2003**, etc.) and Statutory Instruments (SI) such as the **Road Traffic Regulations** of various years. This new form of training requires officers to think much more on a par with lawyers however. Legal training requires these professionals to know the law as it is stated in the most recent of court cases as well. This can be markedly different to what is stated in the statute. For example the meaning of the word 'appropriation' in Section (shown as s) **3 Theft Act 1968** and 'intention' in a range of offences has changed dramatically due to cases such as **R v Gomez (1996)** and **R v Matthews and Alleyne (2003)** respectively.

It is important to remember that winning a court case depends not solely on whether the Crown Prosecution Service (CPS) lawyers, those acting for the police, can present a case without flaws. It also depends on whether the police officers gathered the evidence lawfully or made a lawful arrest, for example. Put bluntly, if the police constable does not know the law as interpreted by case law as well as statute when making that arrest, outside a kebab shop on the high street at 9 p.m. there is almost nothing the CPS lawyer can do to rectify mistakes made. Put another way, if the PC makes a fundamental error through lack of knowledge then the case may not continue or may fail at court. With this in mind the effect of case law is considered essential and has been described in appropriate detail throughout this book as well as the statute law itself.

Testing your knowledge and revising

From the paragraphs above you will see that important cases and statutory provisions are shown in bold in the text. This is to show that you especially need to remember them and use them in a particular way. When you answer a question you need to support your answer with the appropriate case or statute as 'authority'. The technique can be demonstrated by looking at an example from one of the many 'knowledge checks' or test exercises which are used in this book. These can either be self-test exercises for students or tutors can use them to set exercises for the class. An example is shown below adapted from Chapter 9, 'Property offences'. The associated answer is also shown below. These answers are, however, usually found at the end of the relevant chapter.

Knowledge Check 1

PC Gregory attends the Saver-Save Supermarket just outside of town having received information about a shoplifter. Has theft or any other offence occurred in the following scenario?

A man came to the information desk with four items of clothing still with labels attached and asked for a cash refund, he has a receipt for £98.96. A store detective is suspicious and stops him at the exit after he has received his refund, the receipt looks to him like a photocopy cut down to size. A store colleague confirms the man took the items from the shelf and has not been through a checkout.

The answer is at the back of the chapter.

Answer – Knowledge Check 1

The first stage is to set out the key elements of the **s.1 Theft Act 1968** definition: dishonestly, appropriate, property, belonging to another, intention to permanently deprive. Assuming the receipt is a forgery and ignoring any non-theft offences for now, there appears to be little doubt in relation to the elements of dishonesty, property belonging to another and intention to permanently deprive. Turning to appropriation, this is covered by **s.3 Theft Act 1968** and is satisfied by an assumption of the rights of the owner, *any* right according to **R v Morris (1983)**. Appropriation would still take place even if it was with the consent of the owner per **R v Gomez (1993)**. Thus when the cashier at the information desk freely handed over the £98.96 the man appropriated it. In fact arguably the man appropriated the clothes when he took hold of them from the shelf. Taking hold of any item in a shop is usurping one of the rights of the owner. He did not of course intend to permanently deprive the clothes, however.

Do not worry, the aim of this book is to enable you to discuss legal issues with as much confidence as this eventually but you are not expected to do so yet. The knowledge check is merely an example of one of the ways knowledge is tested in this book. It is also an example of how to use case law and statute in an answer of this type. We also utilise multiple-choice questions were appropriate.

One of the advantages of legal textbooks like this one is that they do not just have a contents page and an index to help you find your way around. They also have a Table of Statutes and a Table of Cases. These will be found towards the front of any legal text and this one is no exception. With these tables you can go straight to the act and section or case that you need explanation for, wherever it is found in the book.

There has also been every effort to place signposts throughout the book to highlight the essential points for revision purposes. These 'Revision boxes' look like this one, taken from Chapter 6, 'Violence and intimidation':

REVISION

Battery requires:
- ✓ Intentional or reckless
- ✓ Application of unlawful force to another
- ✓ Consent can render force lawful, the validity of consent depends though on:
  - – how useful or worthwhile the activity is;
  - – accepted 'norms' of public morality;
  - – the severity of the injury.

You will notice that wherever possible, the information is arranged in 'threes'. There is research which indicates that the brain can recall information in sets of three better than in other combinations; you might want to take that into account when revising for important tests and exams.

Examinations were invented by the ancient Chinese about the same time as they also invented the wheelbarrow. Not everyone is convinced of the merits of unseen exams against a time limit and would even argue that the wheelbarrow was the better invention of the two. Nevertheless the best compromise in any course of study is probably a range of coursework, exam, research and practical exercises testing a range of different skills. With this in mind not all the exercises designed to test your knowledge as you move through this book take the form of knowledge checks. In many cases an activity is presented. These might be ideas for role-plays or presentations or research activities to help you reinforce what you have learnt. These are some examples, the first is from Chapter 5, 'Police organisation':

ACTIVITY

You may have noticed whilst on holiday in France or Spain for example, or whilst watching US crime dramas or real crime shows on television that there are a variety of law enforcement agencies at work in each of these countries. Do some research on the internet. Some of these agencies such as the Federal Bureau of Investigation (FBI) in the USA and the French *Police Nationale* have national jurisdiction. Does the UK have a crime-fighting organisation with such jurisdiction? What are the advantages and disadvantages of separate local forces by comparison?

This is a research activity designed to make you think a bit more about what you are reading and to explore the topic more widely and in a bit more detail. Another example follows, taken from Chapter 1, 'Basic legal concepts':

ACTIVITIES

---

1 Write brief notes analysing:

   (a) The difference between direct intention and oblique intention using appropriate case law.

   (b) When a person may be judged reckless as opposed to grossly negligent, again using decided cases.

2 Have a discussion with a colleague, or even a family member unconnected with your studies, around the following scenario. Greg decides to demonstrate his prowess at taekwondo by aiming a kick to strike the air exactly 2 centimetres from Don's nose. What liability in terms of guilty mind do you think Greg has? (You'll find explaining the legal principles to someone else actually cements your understanding: some studies indicate 95 per cent retention by this method.)

This book, your learning and 'learning styles'

You will see that the exercises above are a mix of traditional and non-traditional learning activities. Making brief notes on a topic from memory has long been a good way of finding out what you really remember about it without the unnecessary pressure of a timed test scenario. The idea of you, even though you are new to the subject, explaining a technical issue to an interested lay person is a relatively new learning technique. Again this comes from taking a fairly scientific approach to the way we learn. We all have different learning styles. Some of us learn best visually, by being taught the traditional way with a teacher or trainer in a classroom situation. Others learn better by doing, known as 'kinaesthetic' learning.

Much of the time it depends on what we are doing, as well as how we learn. No one would try to learn to drive a car by classroom teaching alone and no one would successfully learn higher-level maths with counting-bricks. There are many different learning styles, and ways to find out what yours are. It is very likely that your trainers will try to find out what these styles are early on in your service. You could look up sources on the web or find a written work like *The manual of learning styles* by Honey and Mumford. In a Harvard style reading list or bibliography like those used in this book this would appear like this:

Honey, P and Mumford, A (1992) *The manual of learning styles*. Maidenhead: Peter Honey.

You could use this reference to make a search of a local library or a college or university one. You do not have to be enrolled on a course to use any library for reference purposes so you could do this before you start your official training if you wanted to make a head start.

Learning outcomes

As we learn, it is very important that we know what it is we should expect to have achieved by the end of each learning or research session. Modern teaching methods recommend that 'learning outcomes' should be very evident on training materials, lesson plans and even displayed in the classroom. Learning outcomes are what exactly we should know or be able to do if the teaching has been successful. Following this way of thinking, in this book, at appropriate points, boxes appear which set out what you should know or be able to do by the end of the section. An example follows from Chapter 6, 'Violence and intimidation', the section on Homicide:

By the end of this section you will be able to:

- evaluate the definition of and major case law on murder;

- explain the difference between voluntary and involuntary manslaughter;

- utilise relevant case law and statute to answer short-answer questions on topics in this area.

The words used are quite specific. 'Evaluate', 'analyse' and 'explain' require quite high-level understanding. By contrast, words like 'list', or 'state' do not require much more than being able to recite facts. 'Describe' requires a level of understanding somewhere in between. It is important to recognise therefore what the section sets out to do. If it states in the 'outcomes' box that you should be able merely to list the differences between two sets of facts, do not be concerned that you cannot analyse or evaluate these facts from what you have read. If, however the text states that you should be able to analyse the issues after you have read the section but you feel you could only list them, you probably need to go over the material again.

Do not think of the concept of 'evaluation' as particularly offputting. We all do this as part of our everyday lives. If we pick up a cheap tin of baked beans in the supermarket we consider its cheapness at the same time as we compare the likely quality of its contents with that of a tin from the leading brand. This comparison of the good and bad points of something is 'evaluating' it.

Reflecting on your learning

Modern police officers need to be able to 'think outside the box' to be able to see how their actions have wider implications and side effects. They also need to be able to consider, throughout their careers, how well they deal with incidents and people, what they are good at and which skills need further development. To this end modern police training is designed to encourage student officers to reflect on issues and their own performance. Where appropriate this book includes pointers on this and suggestions for reflection. There is an example below from Chapter 5 'Police organisation':

⑦ *Consider for a moment how much you really know about policing in the UK. Is the law the same in Scotland and Northern Ireland? How many police forces are there? Are they all county based? How much intelligence information about an individual could you obtain if they had just moved into your area? Continue to think about these issues as you read on.*

And another example, in a slightly different vein, from Chapter 3:

⑦ *Think about the community you have been allocated to police. Is it sensible to talk only about geographically defined communities or are there several communities in the same place? These could identify with each other by virtue of common ethnicity or sexuality, for instance. Remember this non-geographical approach to defining communities when making SOLAP or reflective entries.*

The reference to 'SOLAP' is particularly important. This document was developed to form part of IPLDP training. The initials stand for *Student Officer Learning Assessment Portfolio*. Put simply it is to record evidence of the officer's learning, primarily on duty and 'on the job'. This is a very effective method of recording vocational training but in some respects does not cater for the new approaches described above. Those approaches, which require the officer to widen their horizons and think about the wider impacts of what they are doing, as well as ways in which their skills could be developed. Again there are parallels in other professions. A teacher has to think and learn in this way and, like a police officer, cannot be observed by an assessor during all of every workday. Teacher training has long utilised a form of reflective journal, a kind of diary which focuses on wider issues, what went well and what did not go so well in each prominent experience at work.

Some police forces have utilised the idea of a reflective journal or learning diary to augment the SOLAP. This is to add the reflective element necessary for effective study at Level 4 and especially on foundation degree programmes. The hints and tips towards a reflective entry like the ones you see represented above appear throughout this book to give student officers and trainers some ideas as to what these entries might be centred on. They are by no means prescriptive and are intended as ideas to stimulate debate and thought.

Research and further reading

Towards the very end of each chapter information is provided to stimulate further research into the relevant topic. It may be that student officers will have gained all that they require to know about the subject from reading the chapter itself. If interest to pursue the subject further is sparked, however, research suggestions are made such as the one below taken from Chapter 3:

Suggested research

There have been a number of high profile murders where the victim has been black since Stephen Lawrence. Visit the Home Office website **http://police.homeoffice.gov.uk/community-policing/race-diversity/stephen-lawrence-inquiry** to view the legacy of the enquiry into Stephen Lawrence's murder. Research other more recent murders such as Damilola Taylor and Anthony Walker. Consider what lessons have been learnt and what work still has to be done with respect to the development of police powers and investigation in the light of those cases.

There is also the important point that modern police training can form the basis of further higher-level study to bear in mind. This book is designed to assist IPLDP training but it could also be used as introductory reading for a 'top-up' year towards a Bachelor of Arts degree. These are regularly found as follow-on study from a foundation degree. Higher-level policing NVQs exist up to Level 5 in addition and could be used as an alternative route to further relevant study. In this context these research ideas could be very useful to prompt ideas for study at these higher levels.

With the same ideas in mind, further, optional reading is provided at the end of each chapter. Books and other works are listed alphabetically in the traditional Harvard style. This style would be useful to copy when producing your own bibliographies at the end of your longer written pieces of work where required. The books, journal articles and web-sites are listed in sections to let you know how best they can assist your study. Examples below come from Chapter 9, 'Property offences':

Further reading

Further detailed discussion of all the topics in this chapter can be found by reading:

Card, R, Cross, R and Jones, P (2006) *Criminal law*, (17th edn). London: Butterworths.

Elliott, C and Quinn, F (2006) *Criminal law*, (6th edn). Harlow: Pearson.

English, J and Card, R (2005) *Police law*, (9th edn). Oxford: Oxford University Press.

Heaton, R (2001) *Criminal law*, (3rd edn). London: Butterworths.

Useful websites

Home Office strategies to target the market in stolen goods:

www.crimereduction.gov.uk/burglary/burglaryminisite07.htm

The Law Commission:

www.lawcom.gov.uk

The Crown Prosecution Service:

http://cps.gov.uk

Legislation:

www.opsi.gov.uk

Case law and legislation databases:

www.westlaw.com* (an educational case law and statute database)

www.lexis-nexis.com* (an educational case law and statute database)

www.pnld.co.uk* (a police service specific database of case-law and statute)

* Likely to be available through the virtual learning environment (VLE) which supports your course/training.

Continuous professional development

To conclude, it is probably a good time to talk about where your training should take you after you have been confirmed as a police officer. Traditionally that has been at the two-year point after you were recruited. That may not always be the case as forces are considering the benefits of giving some form of credit or APEL (Accreditation for Prior Experience and Learning) for relevant training and experience. It may be that prior service in the military police, as a PCSO or special constable (to name but three examples) may, in time, be something which would shorten that two-year period, as could study on a relevant pre-entry degree or other programme. Further consultation and probably pilot schemes will be needed before these APEL schemes are widespread, however.

In general it is becoming ever harder to sustain the argument that the training of a police officer stops, other than specialisation training and legal updates, at the end of the initial two-year period. No other profession takes this approach and almost all insist on formal recorded CPD (continuous professional development) as a condition of continuing practice. The solicitor's profession is an example of this. Further NOS are being constantly developed and reviewed by Skills for Justice to build a framework for the training and development of police officers throughout their careers. Many police officers as individuals have always taken further training seriously, whether that be for promotion exams, by taking degrees or masters' programmes in their own time or by attending internal training events and national seminars as regularly as possible. The Skills for Justice framework merely allows for this to all fit together in a more co-ordinated fashion. To learn more about Skills for Justice and the 'Integrated Competency Framework' you could visit **www.skillsforjustice.com** and see for yourself how your training could develop over your service in the police force.

Last of all, good luck in your training and career; it is hoped that this book will have been a help to you. Comments and suggestions are always welcome, if you feel that an aspect of the book is particularly worthwhile or could be developed, please contact the publisher.

Further reading

For a discussion about learning styles:

Honey, P and Mumford, A (1992) *The manual of learning styles*. Maidenhead: Peter Honey.

A title to further develop awareness of learning in the workplace:

Kolb, A (1984) *Experiential learning: Experiences as the source of learning and development*. New Jersey: Prentice-Hall.

The following works explore the ideas around reflecting and developing as a practitioner in a range of professional fields:

Megginson, D and Whitaker, V (1999) *Cultivating self-development*. London: Institute of Personal Development.

Moon, JA (1999) *Reflection in learning and professional development*. London: Kogan Page.

Mumford, A (1999) *Effective learning, management shapers series*. London: Institute of Personal Development.

Murdock, A and Scutt, C (1997) *Personal effectiveness*. Oxford: Butterworth/Heinemann.

Nortledge, A (1983) *The reflective practitioner, how professionals think in action*. London: Temple Smith.

Useful websites

www.skillsforjustice.com

www.ncalt.com (police-restricted site developed as a virtual learning environment for student officers)

OCR versions of the L3 and 4 Policing NVQs:

www.ocr.org.uk/qualifications/OCRNVQLevel3inPolicing.html and **www.ocr.org.uk/qualifications/OCRNVQLevel4inPolicing.html**

1   Basic legal concepts

(?) *Remember this symbol indicates that the material might be useful for your Student Officer Learning and Assessment Programme (SOLAP) portfolio or any attached reflective practice record you are required to make.*

Underpinning knowledge towards Patrol Officer NOS:

1A1, 2C1, 2C3, 2C4, 2G2, 2G4, 2H1, 2H2, 2J1, 2J2, 2K2, 4C1

and PCSO NOS:

1A1, 2C1, 2C3, 2C4, 2C5, 2J1, 2J2, 4C1

For further information on these NOS, which are also Policing Level 3 and 4 NVQ unit titles, refer to Appendix 1 to this volume.

Actus reus and *mens rea*

The 'guilty act'

By the end of this section you will be able to:

- use the term *actus reus* to describe the relevant part of a crime;

- describe the different ways an *actus reus* can occur;

- analyse problem *actus reus* issues in criminal law scenarios.

The goal is to study individual offences and apply that knowledge to scenarios to determine what crimes might have been committed. Before we can do that we have to understand what component parts crimes have and what relationship each part has to each other. This is rather like the fact that you would need to know the purpose and description of woodwork tools before you could attempt to make a chair. Similarly it would be necessary to understand how a piece of gym equipment functions before using it to work out on.

Criminal offences potentially have both a physical element and a mental element. All have the physical part, that is: hitting, killing, stabbing, taking, destroying, driving and so on. Most also have an accompanying mental state, for example intention, recklessness, carelessness, negligence even 'wilful blindness'.

A conviction for some criminal offences can be obtained just for doing the physical element, although these are the minority. Driving too fast on a road is an example of this; we call this speeding and the criminal law is not interested in whether this was intentional or resulted from a lapse of concentration. We will consider this further in the 'Strict liability' section.

The physical element is called the *actus reus* (guilty act) and the mental element is called the *mens rea* (guilty mind). Be careful about the use of the word 'act', however; some types of *actus reus* do not involve acts at all but rather failing to act as we shall see in the next section.

Connecting the *actus reus* to a *mens rea* can be a very important issue as well. For example, if a man walks towards a woman and head-butts her, this could be one of two things.

(a) he has intentionally committed a serious assault on her;

(b) he tripped and as he fell his head came into contact with hers.

Both examples contain the same act which could be an *actus reus*, a blow to the head of the victim. But only a) describes an accompanying *mens rea* which could result in a conviction for assault; b) could simply be an accident.

REVISION

✓ *Actus reus* means 'Guilty act'
✓ *Mens rea* means 'Guilty mind'

Actus reus – some more complex issues

Students should try not to be put off by the use of Latin terms, they are declining dramatically in number in law generally and the remainder actually do help as a label as we will discover.

An *actus reus* can be one of three things:

- A **positive act**, i.e. 'doing' something. Examples include strangling someone, kissing someone you should not (yes – believe it or not in certain circumstances!), setting fire or growing something you should not (e.g. a cannabis plant).

- An **omission**, perhaps better understood as failing to do something. This could be failing to feed a child, check the health of a seriously ill patient in your care or close a watertight external door on a ship.

- A **state of affairs**. This would not require the accused to have done anything or omitted to do anything, he or she simply is found to be in a certain set of circumstances. This might include being an illegal immigrant or being drunk and in charge of a bicycle in the street.

Positive acts are relatively straightforward both in terms of recognising them in ordinary police work and in terms of answering exam and assignment questions. The more difficult areas are the omissions and states of affairs.

(?) *When you are filling out your SOLAP or any associated reflective diary remember to make links with the criminal law study you have done.*

Omissions

Generally English law does not require people to act to help others, whatever the moral position might be. Otherwise consider what would happen if, as a civilian, you passed a burning house in the street. You know the fire brigade will not get there in time to save the occupants. If the law required you to act you would have to run into the house and try and save the victims to avoid prosecution. Some jurisdictions, such as France, do place these duties on ordinary people in certain circumstances. Some of the photographers first on the scene at Princess Diana's crash in the underpass in Paris were investigated for the offence of failing to summon assistance.

Under English law however, there are only really four situations when people are required to act and will be guilty of an omission if they do not:

- When the victim is a **dependant** or in another **'special relationship'** with the accused. This could be an adult relative with severe learning difficulties in the care of the accused for example.

  A leading case in this area is **Gibbins v Proctor (1918)**. A couple intentionally withheld food from a child with the result that the child died. They were guilty of murder.

- When the accused has **created a dangerous circumstance and failed to rectify it.** This might be when a couple go to a hay barn for illicit sex and the man knocks over a gas camping light, setting fire to the hay. He runs from the scene leaving the woman to be trapped and killed by the fire without summoning assistance.

  An example in case law would be **R v Miller (1982)**. Miller was a squatter who fell asleep on a mattress in the squat. By definition the property did not belong to him. Miller's cigarette set fire to the mattress but he awoke and discovered the fire. Mysteriously however, he simply went to another room where he found a mattress which was not on fire and fell asleep on that. Miller was found guilty of reckless criminal damage by omission.

- When there is a **contract to act** and the accused did not do something he or she should have done. This might be an employment contract, for example a teacher's, which would include the requirement to act to keep pupils safe while in the teacher's charge. This contractual duty was the central issue in **R v Pittwood (1902).** Pittwood was employed to raise and lower a railway crossing barrier; he went to lunch leaving it up. As a result a man driving a horse and cart across the railway crossing was killed. Pittwood was convicted of manslaughter.

- When the accused voluntarily **assumes responsibility** for the victim but **fails to carry through the obligation**. For example in **R v Instan (1893)** a niece agreed to care for her aunt but then failed to feed her properly.

  Perhaps the most harrowing example of this though is **R v Stone and Dobinson (1977).** Stone and Dobinson were a cohabiting couple. The sister of one of them, Stone, came to live with them. Between them, Stone and Dobinson had learning difficulties, sight and hearing problems and the need for a social worker to visit their son to contend with. The sister, Fanny, was anorexic, became ill and died from malnutrition and infected bedsores. This was unsurprising as she had lain in her own faeces and urine for some time in a bed in her part of the house.

Fanny was an adult but both accused had assumed a voluntary duty to her. They had done this by putting food out for her and making feeble attempts to summon medical assistance. They had failed to notify the social worker of Fanny's plight. Both accused were convicted of what was then known as reckless manslaughter.

REVISION

✓ An *actus reus* can occur through:
  – an act;
  – an omission;
  – surrounding circumstances.

✓ An *actus reus* by omission only occurs when there is a duty to act:
  – when the victim is dependant;
  – when the accused creates the danger;
  – when there is a contract;
  – when responsibility is voluntarily assumed.

Work through the following examples before continuing with your reading to consolidate your learning.

Knowledge Check 1

You are a Custody Sergeant. You are considering whether to charge the following people. You need to form a view before you consult the CPS staff based at your station. Write down whether, in each case, the *actus reus* of the crime of homicide is present.

1. Kat is a nurse and is walking down the road after work. She sees a drunk obviously fighting for breath and clutching his chest by the roadside. She does nothing to help him and he dies.

2. Imran has a friend staying with him whom he knows is diabetic. He does not know anything about the correct treatment for diabetes but vaguely remembers that sugar is connected to the condition in some way. Imran's friend appears to be going into some kind of fit then into a deep sleep. Imran leaves a cream cake next to his friend and goes to bed. In the morning his friend is dead.

3. Bob is a university tutor, who is walking along the canal bank to work one day when he notices one of his students, who is 20 years of age, is in the water having presumably fallen in. The student is waving frantically and appears not to be able to swim. Bob is late for work and is unsure whether or not he is the subject of a prank at this stage. He leaves the scene doing nothing to help. The student is genuinely in distress and drowns.

In your answer assume that all you are concerned about is the actus reus *of the crime. Exercises to test your understanding of* mens rea *will follow. Remember also that there may be no clear answer and that responses qualified with for instance 'it maybe that...' or 'it could be argued...' are quite acceptable.*

Now you can check your answers at the end of the chapter.

State of affairs

As we have said, sometimes the *actus reus* of a crime can come from the state of affairs that the defendant finds themselves in.

Consider for example the crime of being drunk in charge of a motor vehicle. A person may commit this whilst sleeping off his night's excesses on the back seat of the car. If the person is over the limit and has the means to drive the car, he or she contravenes **s. 4 Road Traffic Act 1988**. The accused would not be *acting* or *omitting to act*. The *actus reus* would be found in the surrounding circumstances. There are some surprisingly harsh examples in case law as well. In **R v Larsonneur (1933)** and **Winzar v Chief Constable of Kent (1983)** the common factor was that the accused was placed in the circumstances which were the *actus reus* of the offence by police officers. In **Larsonneur** the accused was brought to the UK handcuffed to a police officer having been deported from Eire. She was banned from being in the UK under immigration legislation that existed at the time and was prosecuted for being here. In **Winzar** the accused was removed from a hospital by police officers who were called because he was drunk. They removed him to their car. As a result of this change of location it was possible to prosecute him for being drunk in a highway, contrary to **s. 12 Licensing Act 1872**.

You will see that most crimes which rely on surrounding circumstances or states of affairs are also strict liability which will be covered later in this chapter.

The guilty mind

By the end of this section you will be able to:

- use the term *mens rea* to describe the state of mind relevant to the crime;
- describe the different types of *mens rea* in the types of crimes a patrol officer is likely to come across most often;
- analyse problem *mens rea* issues in criminal law scenarios.

As we have said, this is known in criminal law as *mens rea*. There are several states of mind which, when accompanied by a defined *actus reus*, constitute a crime. To give an example, put simply, murder requires the killing of a human being with *intention* to do so or at least *intention* to commit grievous bodily harm (GBH). If the *mens rea*, the intention, is not there, even if another state of mind, like recklessness, exists murder definitely is not the correct crime to charge the accused with.

Intention

Intention has a strict legal meaning; what we must not do is confuse the concept with that of 'motive'. If the accused kills his brother, it matters little whether it was done out of revenge, under an abnormality of mind like a delusion, because the brother is terminally ill and requests to die or to collect on life insurance taken out on his life. The point is that a person was intentionally killed. The factors outlined above are states of mind but would not have any bearing on the conviction itself, only the amount of time spent in custody as a result of the killing.

The classic definition in case law is found in **R v Mohan (1976)**. The accused was attempting to evade capture when he ran over and killed a policeman. His defence rested on what he was trying to do at the time. If his intention was to escape and the death was almost a 'by-product' of that action then he would be innocent of murder. If his intention was to kill or cause grievous bodily harm he would be guilty of the crime. The court found that intention should have a narrow meaning as a person's 'aim or purpose'. Mohan's aim or purpose was to cause serious harm at the very least so he was guilty of murder.

Oblique intention

There are times when there is no clear 'aim or purpose' but the accused has done something which they must have foreseen would be virtually certain to break the law. For instance, dropping a kerbstone from a road bridge onto passing vehicles or behaving dangerously with a loaded firearm whilst drunk. The question for many years was whether 'foresight of virtual certainty of a prohibited consequence' or similar wording was the same thing as intending that consequence. Throughout a variety of cases through the 1970s and 1980s there were differing outcomes on this point. What seems to be settled is that it can extend to situations where a jury can 'feel sure that death or serious bodily harm was a virtual certainty ... and the defendant appreciated that such was the case'. This was in part the judgement in **R v Woollin 1998**. In the Court of Appeal case of **R v Matthews and Alleyne (2003)** however, it was held that foresight of virtual certainty does not equal intention but is something from which a jury can infer that intention is present. It is *evidence* of intention, in other words. The accused Matthews and Alleyne threw a person into a watercourse knowing he could not swim and he drowned (see also Chapter 6, 'Violence and intimidation').

REVISION

✓ Intention means a person's 'aim or purpose' (R v Mohan 1976).

✓ Oblique intention means that a jury can infer direct intention was present from the fact that a person foresaw a prohibited consequence (death, damage etc.) was virtually certain (R v Matthews and Alleyne 2003).

Recklessness

Again there was some debate for many years in academic circles and legal practice as to what this word actually meant. Specifically the question was: reckless as to whose standard? That of the accused or that of the reasonable man (represented in effect in the court room by the jury or magistrates)? In law actions which are judged against the standards the accused set himself concern *subjective* standards. Those actions which must be judged against the standards of the reasonable man must meet an *objective* standard. Basically, subjective tests take into account what the accused was actually thinking whereas objective tests look at what the accused ought to have thought according to reasonable standards. This test is the harder of the two to satisfy.

REVISION

✓ Subjective tests look at whether the accused met his or her own standards or what was in his or her own mind.
✓ Objective tests consider whether the accused met the standards of the 'reasonable man'.
✓ The 'reasonable man' is represented in the courtroom by the jury or the magistrates.

That debate is largely settled now by **R v G and Another (2003)**. This criminal damage case concerned minors and decided that only subjective recklessness was sufficient to warrant criminal liability. This type of recklessness was defined in **R v Cunningham (1957)**. The accused broke into a gas meter to steal the money which had been inserted through the coin-slot which activated pre-payment meters at the time. The gas used then was coal gas which is potentially lethal if breathed in quantity (as opposed to North Sea gas which is non-toxic and found in domestic supplies today). The damage to the meter caused a leak which in turn caused **Cunningham's** prospective mother-in-law to be seriously ill. **Cunningham's** actions were held to be 'deliberate risk taking'. This phrase is still used to describe subjective recklessness.

(?) *If you arrest someone for reckless criminal damage, consider making reference to the above discussion when you record it in your SOLAP or learning diary.*

Negligence and gross negligence

Negligence is in fact a civil standard and very few criminal offences require it as a *mens rea*. It is important to understand it however, so that gross negligence is easier to follow as a concept.

In essence, since the case of **Donoghue v Stevenson (1932)**, the first true negligence case, it has been possible to sue in the civil courts for compensation if it can be shown that the defendant owed the claimant a duty of care, that duty was breached and foreseeable loss ensued. This will be discussed further in Chapter 20.

The criminal law is only concerned if the negligence can be termed *gross*. Gross negligence is only relevant for involuntary manslaughter studied in Chapter 6 under homicide. The difference between ordinary negligence and gross negligence was summed up in **R v Bateman (1939)** in that gross negligence is 'more than a mere matter of compensation...'. In other words, if compensation does not seem to be an appropriate remedy the acts complained of may be construed as gross negligence. Such acts could be if a doctor injects the wrong drug into a patient killing him, a teacher allows a boy in his charge to drown on a school trip or an electrician leaves faulty domestic wiring which kills an occupant of the home. A prosecution can follow allowing for punishment of the individual and encouragement to others to take more care. This does not preclude a separate civil suit to recover compensation for the estate of the deceased.

The full definition of gross negligence is found in **R v Adomako (1994),** discussed more fully in Chapter 6. The act must involve a breach of a duty of care (note the similarity with civil negligence thus far), the breach however must also cause death and be grossly negligent.

> **REVISION**
> ✓ Subjective recklessness is 'deliberate risk taking' (R v Cunningham 1957).
> ✓ Gross negligence is a breach of a duty of care which causes death. This breach must be grossly negligent (R v Adomako 1994).
> ✓ Gross negligence is negligence that is more serious than compensation will remedy (R v Bateman 1939).

Knowledge, reasonable belief and wilful blindness

Knowledge is implied in some statutory offences, for example in **Sweet v Parsley (1970)** it was held that it was possible for the word 'knowingly' to be read into an offence which existed at the time concerning 'management of premises used for the purpose of smoking cannabis'. Without doing this the offence would have been one of *strict liability* (see later in this chapter). This would have been most undesirable as any landlord of, say, student digs could be liable for this offence where the tenants behaved in this manner, even if the landlord had never visited the premises.

In some offences the requirement of knowledge is expressly required. For example, in the offence commonly called handling stolen goods contrary to **s. 22 Theft Act 1968**, discussed further in Chapter 9. It is required that the accused handled the goods 'knowing or believing' them to be stolen. Belief is stronger than suspicion and also 'wilful blindness' neither of which will suffice in this offence although in others, confusingly, wilful blindness will be the same thing as knowledge. In short, wilful blindness is a deliberate failure to find out certain information because that information might make it clear to an accused that they have committed an offence. An 'ostrich putting its head in the sand' approach, you might say.

Reasonable belief is a key feature of the **Sexual Offences Act (SOA) 2003.** For many years under the **Sexual Offences Act 1956** sexual intercourse with a girl under 16 was a strict liability offence and it mattered not if the accused genuinely had no idea that the girl in question was under the legal age of consent. The accused would be convicted in these circumstances. The **SOA 2003** reduced the harshness of this position by allowing the accused a defence, provided the victim is 13 or over if they held 'reasonable belief' that the victim was over 16. Put another way, the court might be prepared to give someone the benefit of the doubt in some cases but would not be able to if the victim were any age up to and including 12. The reasoning being presumably that such a situation would stretch credulity in the extreme. Reasonable belief is an objective standard as opposed to *honest* belief and will be discussed at greater length in Chapter 6.

> **REVISION**
> ✓ Knowledge can be implied or expressly required in an offence.
> ✓ Wilful blindness is deliberately not finding something out.
> ✓ Reasonable belief is taking an *objective* view about what is believable. Honest belief is often insufficient as a person may honestly believe something but no reasonable person would.

You may find it helpful to complete the following exercises to consolidate your learning.

ACTIVITIES

---

1. Write brief notes analysing:
    (a) The difference between direct intention and oblique intention using appropriate case law.
    (b) When a person may be judged reckless as opposed to grossly negligent, again using decided cases.

2. Have a discussion with a colleague, or even a family member unconnected with your studies around the following scenario. Greg decides to demonstrate his prowess at taekwondo by aiming a kick to strike the air exactly 2 centimetres from Don's nose. What liability in terms of guilty mind do you think Greg has? (You'll find explaining the legal principles to someone else actually cements your understanding, some studies indicate 95 per cent retention by this method.)

The remaining sections in this chapter deal with the relationship between *mens rea* and *actus reus*. Firstly, under strict liability we look at offences which do not need a *mens rea* for a conviction. Next, we consider to what extent the *mens rea* and *actus reus* need to happen at the same time or 'contemporaneously'. Finally, the extent to which *mens rea* can be transferred from one victim or subject to another is discussed.

Strict liability

By the end of this section you will be able to:

*   demonstrate an understanding of the difference between strict liability and fault based liability;

*   describe the common features strict liability offences have;

*   analyse situations were *mens rea* may be 'read in' to an offence which does not require a guilty mind expressly.

Put simply, strict liability refers to law where liability can be imposed on someone without them being held to be at fault, i.e. morally to blame. There are examples of this in civil law, in contracts and torts like negligence for instance. What concerns us here is to decide which *crimes* are strict liability. Obviously if no *mens rea* need be proved it makes them harder to avoid committing and easier to prove in court. Take for example speeding. Those of us who drive know that there are limits to the speed we may drive at on a public road. It will not avail us at all to argue that we did not notice that the speed had increased to an illegal level or that we drove at such a speed to escape a vehicle 'tailgating' at an unacceptably close distance. All that is required is for the driver to be driving a mechanically propelled vehicle on a public road at a speed over the limit for that road. In other words, all that is required is the *actus reus*.

We have already mentioned the offence of driving or attempting to drive whilst unfit through drink or drugs contrary to **s. 4 Road Traffic Act 1988** in the context of 'state of affairs' crimes. It is also true to say this is a strict liability crime. Whether or not the accused intended or was reckless as to becoming unfit is not relevant, all that is required is that the *actus reus* can be proved. This could be by a constable witnessing a man who was, in the constable's opinion, drunk (the only issue upon which a constable may be an expert witness ironically; on all other matters a constable must be a witness of fact only). If that man is sitting in his car on a road with the keys in the ignition, on confirmation by a breath test the offence may be charged. If it transpires that someone 'spiked' this person's drink with strong alcohol without their knowledge this will not affect the conviction, only possibly, the sentence, but even this is unlikely. The same reasoning may be applied to a range of motoring offences. Driving whilst uninsured for instance, contrary to **s. 143 (1) and (2) Road Traffic Act 1988** is a further example of a strict liability offence. This offence requires a conviction were a person 'uses...a motor vehicle on a road or other public place, unless there is in force...such a policy of insurance...as complies with the Act' (see Chapter 19, 'Roads policing'). If you drive a car under the impression that your husband had insured it but in fact he never got round to it and lied to you that he had, you will have committed the offence even though you could not possibly have known that you were breaking the law.

There are a number of non-traffic examples of strict liability criminal offences such as non-payment of a television licence and various health and safety law violations. The main offences a patrol officer is likely to encounter are to do with roads policing, however.

Some offences are strict liability in respect of one issue but not all issues in the offence. **Section 5 Sexual Offences Act 2003** (see Chapter 7) for example, outlines the offence of rape of a child under 13. The strict liability is in respect of the age. It will be no defence to say that the accused thought the child to be older. The penetration must still be intentional, however.

The main purpose of this section is to explain the rules and conventions around strict liability offences rather than to outline them all. This is because it is more important that student officers learn to recognise strict liability offences and can do so as new legislation is passed throughout their working lives. New laws arrive on the desks of lawyers, judges, magistrates and police officers with a certain amount of guidance material but ultimately how the law will work in practice is laid down as cases are decided and form a body of case law. Strict liability offences are not always 'labelled' as such but they have certain features in common, the main ones being:

- Low 'moral stigma' – it could be argued that it is fundamentally unjust to brand someone a criminal when they have committed the act but lack the moral culpability. It is sometimes necessary to do this for practical reasons, for example (as discussed below) when it would be virtually impossible to secure a conviction if *mens rea* had to be proved. For this reason Parliament is normally only comfortable with creating strict liability offences if the stigma, or level of public disapproval of someone carrying such a conviction, is relatively low. The moral stigma that would be carried by someone with a speeding conviction would be quite low compared with say a conviction for rape which would be extremely high.

There are exceptions to the above reasoning but it is safe to adopt as a general rule. For example, the moral stigma attached to drink driving is relatively high now after many high-profile media campaigns and a general shift in public opinion. The offence remains one of strict liability and it is difficult to imagine how it might function if *mens rea* were included. It may be that some of the graphic road-safety advertising in the visual media on speeding may have a similar effect on the level of public disapproval of that offence over time.

- Impossible burden of proof – as mentioned above, if it were necessary to prove *mens rea* to secure a conviction for say, not wearing a seatbelt whilst driving, this would make an almost impossible job for the prosecution as all anyone need say is 'I forgot' or 'I didn't notice it was not on' to show they had no *mens rea*. Very few summons, or, more likely nowadays, fixed penalty notices could result in successful action leading to people largely ignoring the law. Strict liability offences tend to be ones therefore where *mens rea* would be very hard to prove.

- Regulatory nature – strict liability offences rarely concern great moral questions of our time, they tend to deal with technical matters such as the maximum gross laden weight permitted for a certain vehicle on a public road or the maximum safe working height of a crane on a construction site, for instance. It would be extremely unlikely that a new offence concerning the misuse of drugs or a new theft act would contain any strict liability.

These are the main issues then to look for to establish whether an offence is likely to be one of strict liability. It is quite possible however for an offence to be written into a statute or act of Parliament without any *mens rea* words used and for this to have happened quite by accident. Remember that these laws are written after debate by politicians, members of both Houses of Parliament who, in many cases will not be lawyers, and mistakes happen. Because they are not elected by the people, judges are understandably unwilling to rewrite or ignore the words of a statute even where a mistake appears likely to have been made in the drafting. A classic example of what this can lead to is the case of **Sweet v Parsley (1970)**. Sweet rented a property to students who regularly smoked cannabis there completely unknown to her as she did not reside there and rarely visited. When the tenants were prosecuted she was also proceeded against for being concerned in the management of premises which were being used for the purpose of smoking cannabis contrary to drugs legislation now repealed. There were no words in the relevant section of the statute like 'intentionally' or 'knowingly' so the court of first instance took this to be a strict liability offence.

The offence does not sit very well with the types of offences which are meant to be strict liability as we have discussed above. Consequently an appeal was heard by the highest appeal court, the House of Lords. The court decided that all criminal statutes were *presumed* to contain *mens rea* (and are therefore fault-based liability) unless there was clear evidence, that the offence was intended by Parliament to be one of strict liability. The three examples of the common features found in strict liability offences (described above) would be such evidence, it could be argued. Thus if a new offence was created to prevent dishonest activity of some kind such as deception (commonly described as fraud) but there was no mention of *mens rea* it could be argued that the words had simply been missed out. This is because it was neither an offence of low moral stigma, neither would it be unduly hard to prove *mens rea*, nor is it a regulatory offence. The court decided that the offence Sweet was charged with fell into a category where there was no clear evidence it should have been strict liability, *mens rea* was 'read in' by the judges, Sweet was found not to possess the requisite *mens rea* and found not guilty of the offence.

> **REVISION**
>
> Strict liability offences usually are:
>
> ✓ Crimes were no serious 'moral stigma' attaches to those that commit them.
> ✓ Crimes where the need to prove a *mens rea* would produce an impossible burden for the prosecution.
> ✓ Crimes of a regulatory or technical nature.
>
> Not all offences without *mens rea* words in them have been deemed to be deliberately strict liability crimes by the courts. In obvious cases of error judges could read the required words in to the statute (Sweet v Parsley 1970).

Knowledge Check 2

1. Write brief notes explaining the main difference between strict and fault-based liability.

2. Imagine you have been a police officer for some years. The law on homicide and on dog fouling have both changed since your initial training. You decide to research these by looking at the new statutes on the internet on the Parliament website. Consider whether:

    (a) Each is *likely* to be a strict or fault based liability offence.

    (b) The reasons why in each case.

    (c) The approach the courts would adopt if a statute had no words like 'intentionally' or 'recklessly' contained in it but only because of a drafting error.

Now you can check your answers at the end of the chapter.

(?) *A great many offences you come across in your first years of service will be minor and strict liability in nature. If you make record of, for example, having issued a Fixed Penalty Notice for a traffic offence in your SOLAP the entry will be more interesting and useful if you make reference to the preceding discussion.*

Contemporaneity

By the end of this section you will be able to:

- demonstrate what is meant by the 'Contemporaneity Rule';

- explain the courts' approach to cases where *actus reus* and *mens rea* have not happened simultaneously;

- analyse and utilise case law relevant to this topic.

Do not be put off by this term, it is in common use. Early in your service you will become familiar with the concept of 'contemporaneous note-taking', that is, notes taken at the same time as the speech is given.

The Contemporaneity Rule relates to the relationship between *actus reus* and *mens rea*. They must both happen satisfactorily if the crime is based on fault liability. They do not both happen satisfactorily if there is a time lag between one and the other. They do not happen *contemporaneously* in other words.

An example of this might be as follows. Imagine your tutor is driving home from a lecture. He runs over one of his students who steps into the road without warning. The student is killed instantly. It is only when the tutor looks under the car at the body that he recognises the most obnoxious and unpleasant student in his group who has made himself deeply unpopular with staff and students alike. If at that point the tutor thinks 'I am glad I have killed him, I hated him anyway', ignoring for the moment any traffic offence, he cannot be guilty of murder. He lacked any *mens rea* until after the deed was done. Whatever we may think of the morals of this man, the most heinous of crimes has not been committed. Conversely, if the tutor realised the identity of the student before he hit him (and failed to avoid him) there could be a *prima facie* (case to be answered) instance of murder because the *mens rea* would coincide with the *actus reus*.

This is a fairly simplistic example and the courts have been faced more than once with the situation where the strict application of the rule would have lead to an extreme example of injustice. In **Fagan v Metropolitan Police Commissioner (1969)** a rather bizarre set of facts was considered. A police constable signalled for Fagan to stop his car. Fagan did so but managed to park on the policeman's foot by accident. Understandably the police officer urged Fagan to remedy this situation quickly. Fagan's response was unsympathetic in the extreme, he locked the car and walked away leaving the unfortunate officer in that situation. Fagan was charged with an assault but the problem was when he committed the *actus reus* he lacked the *mens rea* because it was an accident. When he did have the *mens rea*, i.e. when he walked away, he had stopped committing the *actus reus* because he had already parked on the foot some period of time ago. This idea might be best understood by looking at the diagram of a time line below.

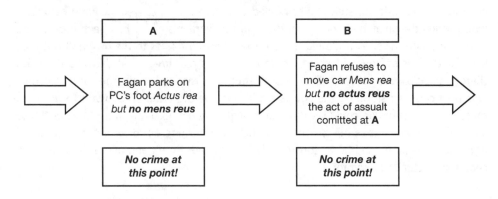

Diagram of chain of events in *Fagan v MPC*

There was at this stage in the argument a very real danger that Fagan would not be convicted of the assault despite there having been, on a common-sense view, 'criminal conduct'. This was not something the court was prepared to tolerate and a legal concept was developed in the case. The *actus reus* was treated as a 'continuing series of acts' such that the *actus reus* of the assault was held to be begun at point **A** in the diagram above and to continue until point **B** and beyond. This is of course not true in a real sense. If it were true then any attacker who shoots his victim with the bullet remaining inside that victim until removed an hour later by surgeons would be held to be shooting the victim continuously for an hour. The principle in **Fagan** might be described as a 'legal fiction'. It did at least enable a finding that there was an *actus reus* and *mens rea* at point **B** above. It might have been simpler to treat the assault as one committed by omission (see *Actus reus* section above) but the court chose not to approach the case in that way. A similar rationale had been used earlier in the murder case of **Thabo Meli v R (1954)**.

REVISION

✓ Contemporaneity means 'at the same time'.
✓ Where the *actus reus* and the *mens rea* do not coincide, the courts can treat the *actus reus* as one long series of acts (Fagan v MPC 1969, Thabo Meli v R 1954).

The doctrine of transferred malice/intent

By the end of this section you will be able to:

- demonstrate an understanding of transferred intent;

- apply appropriate case law to problem scenarios to establish whether or not intent may be transferred.

Sometimes the *mens rea* and *actus reus* do not happen together in the sense that they do not happen to the same person or thing. Imagine that a woman waits at home with a gun to shoot her husband as soon as he comes through the door. It is late at night and the hallway is in darkness. The front door opens and the woman fatally shoots the person standing there. Unfortunately she has failed to realise it his her well-meaning neighbour who pushed the unlatched door open thinking the woman's house had been broken into. In this situation, when considering murder the *mens rea* relates to the husband but there is no *actus reus* as he is not killed. There is no *mens rea* directed at the neighbour but there is an *actus reus* as he is killed. In both situations there is, on the face of it, no crime. This is of course a situation the courts could not tolerate either. If allowed to go unaddressed such a situation could lead to unjust acquittals. For example, if a protestor throws a petrol bomb at a line of police officers, all he would have to do to secure an acquittal for intentional assault would be to convince the jury he did not hit and injure the police officer he was actually aiming for.

To deal with this potential problem the courts have developed the 'Doctrine of transferred malice' (malice is sometimes referred to as 'intent'). A doctrine is merely a set of rules; the word is used in a religious context as well. The key is, however, that the crime that is intended must be the same as the one actually committed. This is illustrated by a pair of useful cases. In **R v Latimer (1886)** a blow was aimed at the intended victim with a belt, the blow missed and the belt struck a woman standing next to him, seriously injuring her. Latimer was charged with injuring the woman but, as in the hypothetical scenario above, on the face of it there is no *mens rea* directed at the woman. The court followed the Doctrine however, and transferred the *mens rea*, the intent, to the woman victim and Latimer was convicted.

In **R v Pembliton (1874)** however, the situation was a little different; the accused was fighting in the street and threw a stone at his opponents, he missed them and his stone broke a window. Pembliton was charged with intentional criminal damage of the window with the prosecution relying on the Doctrine to transfer the intent from the people to the window. The Doctrine has limits however, and it is not possible to transfer intent if the crime the accused sets out to do (in **Pembliton** that was assault) and the one which is ultimately committed (criminal damage) are different. Consequently Pembliton had to be found not guilty. The charge would have succeeded had the prosecution relied on reckless criminal damage which has clearly been committed in this case. This discussion underlines the importance of arresting for, charging and prosecuting exactly the right offence from the outset to the conclusion. There is more than one leading case where the outcome was undesirable because the prosecution was centred on the wrong charge, where the correct one would have succeeded with little difficulty.

REVISION

✓ The Doctrine of transferred malice/intent allows the *mens rea* to be transferred from the intended victim to the actual victim.

✓ This can happen where the crimes are the same (R v Latimer 1886), but not where they differ (R v Pembliton 1874).

Now check your learning on contemporaneity and transferred malice.

Knowledge Check 3

1. Why was there no 'contemporaneity' on the face of it, on the facts of **Fagan v MPC 1969**?

2. A lorry driver agrees to drive two illegal immigrants in his empty refrigerated truck through the UK border controls from a cross-channel ferry for a fee. He thought he had switched the refrigeration unit off but, because of a fault, the unit is full on. The immigrants freeze to death within an hour. The border is crossed without incident but the lorry is tailed by police. The lorry driver thinks his cargo is still alive but, rather than risk arrest, he leaps from the vehicle as it heads for a cliff edge on a hill road. The lorry bursts into flames on impact at the bottom of the cliff.

    If murder were charged, how might the courts apply the contemporaneity rule here?

3. Bob agrees to kill Sam for a fee of £4000. Bob sees a man who, from the description given to him appears to be Sam. Bob shoots and kills the man and collects the £4000 but is subsequently arrested. It transpires that the victim was not Sam at all but his older brother Steve who looks very like him.

    What charge would Bob face and how would the doctrine of transferred malice be relevant?

The answers are at the end of the chapter.

Causation

By the end of this section you will be able to:

* demonstrate an understanding of the difference between factual causation and legal causation;

* demonstrate an understanding of the concept of 'reasonable foreseeability' in legal causation;

* apply appropriate case law.

Causation is a separate issue but is often part and parcel of the *actus reus* of the crime. For instance, in actual bodily harm (ABH) it is essential to prove that the initial assault caused the ultimate ABH. Similarly in involuntary manslaughter the unlawful act or the gross negligence must have caused the death.

There are two types of causation however, *factual* causation and *legal* causation. Firstly it must be proven that the act or omission caused the outcome in fact. For example, consider the situation of a motorist running down a pedestrian who is standing in the road. If the pedestrian dies, not because he has been struck by the car but because of the massive heart attack he was in the early stages of having when crossing the road, then there is no factual causation upon which a charge of causing death by dangerous driving could rely. A more minor traffic offence might be provable though.

The test for whether factual causation can be found is often referred to as the 'but for' test. In the scenario above, could it be said that 'but for the actions of the motorist the pedestrian would still be alive?' The answer would have to be no, therefore there is no factual causation. The leading case in this area is **R v White (1910)**. White gave his mother poison but she died of natural causes before the poison could kill her and accordingly no chain of factual causation between his actions and her death could be proven. White had to be acquitted of murder. In addition the act or omission must be more than a minimal cause of the victim's death. This is known as the *de minimis* rule. In our scenario above, the sight of the oncoming car would probably not have done anything to reduce the strain on the victim's heart but arguably this was a relatively minor issue if he was already having a serious coronary episode.

REVISION
✓ Factual causation means there must be no other *factual* cause which could have resulted in the outcome (R v White 1910).
✓ Legal causation means there can be no other cause *in law* for the outcome.

Legal causation must also be proven, in other words the court must be satisfied that the outcome was caused by the accused in law. There are various different ways of looking at this issue. Firstly, to establish legal causation it must be shown that the actions of the accused were a substantial 'operating cause' of the outcome. In other words, even if other factors have intervened, the accused's actions are the substantial cause of the outcome. The case of **R v Smith (1957)** illustrates this. Smith stabbed a fellow soldier in a fight at an army base. Smith's victim was dropped by stretcher bearers twice and then misdiagnosed by the medical officer who treated him but failed to notice a life-threatening injury. Smith was convicted because although the stabbing itself was not fatal if properly treated, the stabbing was a substantial cause of the death.

Another way to look at these cases is to say that the actions of the accused will be the legal cause of the outcome unless there is a factor which intervenes which could not have been foreseen by the accused. This is a tough test to pass and in almost no decided cases have the courts allowed an acquittal when the accused alleges the intervening event was unforeseeable. It should be remembered that unforeseeable means not in the realms of all likely occurrences, not merely unlikely. To take a hypothetical example, a woman could be knocked unconscious by a mugger. The ambulance could break down and the woman could be forgotten in a trolley in a corridor in a hectic casualty department. By the time she is treated the clot on her brain could have proved fatal. The clot could have been removed if she had been treated in a timely fashion. None of these events is unforeseeable so is unlikely to break the chain of legal causation no matter what separate claim for civil damages against the hospital might be successful.

The line between what is foreseeable and unforeseeable might be better understood with reference to a pair of cases with similarities. In **R v Jordan (1956)** the victim was recovering from his injuries and was almost well again when the doctor gave treatment which in the words of the judge was 'palpably wrong'. The victim was allergic to certain drugs and the hospital was aware of this from his notes. The doctor administered these drugs through negligence and the victim died. This was held to be unforeseeable and to break the chain of causation. In **R v Cheshire (1991)** an argument developed in a fish and chip shop which culminated in the accused shooting his victim. The injuries were treatable but the victim died from complications associated with his tracheotomy tube. These complications were not unknown but were not spotted by the medical staff treating the victim. Undoubtedly this could be categorised as medical negligence but not of the same order as that in **Jordan.** There is a line of argument that **Jordan** is unlikely to be followed in later cases and certainly there are few if any authorities with a similar finding. It may be safe to at least start from the premise that if the accused started the chain of events it will take an intervening issue of some considerable magnitude before the courts will hold that the course of things has been altered. **R v Dear (1996)** has muddied the waters a little on this issue but some argue it may not be followed either. In this case a victim was slashed many times with a knife. His wounds had been treated but reopened, either by his actions, perhaps in a suicidal moment, or they reopened themselves and he failed to seek further treatment. In any event the court held that, as long as the accused's actions were a significant operating cause of the victim's condition, no intervening act would break the chain of causation no matter how unforeseeable that act was.

Many of the cases surround medical treatment after the attack. In contrast, **R v Pagett (1983)** concerns a police armed siege. Pagett, not being the most chivalrous of people, used his girlfriend as a human shield as he escaped, firing. The police fired back in self-defence and killed the girl. The police were held accountable in negligence but the death was held to be caused by Pagett himself. An analogy might be that he placed her in extreme danger and can no more be exonerated than if he had placed her against a bare electric wire. The electrician might be held negligent for leaving the wire bare but the accused would be liable for the death.

The 'egg shell skull' rule or principle

At first sight this principle may seem to run counter to the need for an intervening act to be unforeseeable to break the chain of causation. This rule is used when a victim is harmed more than might be foreseen in the ordinary course of things because of a certain weakness or extra vulnerability to harm that they might possess. The leading case on this is **R v Blaue (1975)**. The unfortunate victim was an 18-year-old girl who had refused Blaue's attentions so he stabbed her. She was a devout Jehovah's Witness and her beliefs precluded her from accepting a blood transfusion she needed to survive. She died and the accused contended that she was the cause of her own death even though he was indisputably the cause of her injury. The court considered however, that an accused must 'take the victim' as they find them, whether they have brittle bones, haemophilia, certain religious beliefs (the reasonableness of which the court will not inquire into), a thin skull or anything else which might turn a simple blow into a life-threatening injury. It will not be a defence for the accused to say he or she knew nothing about the condition and could not have foreseen it.

REVISION

✓ Intervening acts which are totally unforeseeable will normally break the chain of legal causation.
✓ The fact of a victim's particular vulnerability to attack will not break the chain of legal causation no matter how unforeseeable it is (R v Blaue 1975).

ACTIVITIES

Try the following scenario as a basis for group work:

PC David and PC Goldbloom are called to a house in Donchester. They find the victim of an attack, Linda, semi-concious. She was attacked by her husband and, although the injury was not that serious, she has been too afraid to look for her inhaler which she needs for her asthma. Linda dies in the ambulance en route to hospital.

Imagine you are the police officers discussing the appropriate charge with a CPS lawyer. There can be three 'parts' played in this activity therefore and it can be done sat down with a cup of coffee, or as formally as you like. What conclusion do you come to as a group?

Suggested research

In 1998 a reform to the law on assaults was proposed and an Offences Against the Person Bill was put out for consultation with police and other interested groups. How was it proposed that the *mens rea* and *actus reus* would be defined in this (never enacted) statute?

Further reading

For more in depth discussion and more case law on the topics in this chapter, student officers might consider reading from:

Card, R and English, J (2005) *Butterworths police law*. London: Butterworths.

Card, R, Cross, R and Jones, P (2005) *Criminal law*. London: Butterworths.

Useful websites

www.legislation.hmso.gov.uk (provides full text of statutes passed by Parliament as well as delegated legislation)

www.westlaw.com* (a legal database)

www.lexis-nexis.com* (a legal database)

www.pnld.co.uk* (a police service specific database of case law and statute)

* Likely to be available through the virtual learning environment (VLE) which supports your course/training.

Answers

Knowledge Check 1

1. At first sight this might seem like a similar situation to a doctor finding the drunk in this condition. The key to explaining the legal position (note we ignore the moral position completely) however, is to establish whether an act or an omission has led to the drunk's death. We can conclude that it was Kat's failure to help and therefore an omission.

    The next step is to check whether the omission falls within one of the few categories where English law imposes a duty to act. The nurse is in a different situation to a doctor in that there is no duty to act by virtue of the profession itself. Any duty could only arise from the employment contract the nurse is party to such as in **R v Pittwood (1902)**. It is unlikely that the contract imposes a duty to act when not at hospital premises and may even discourage such activity as the hospital's insurance may not cover acts done off duty. Arguably therefore no *actus reus* has occurred.

2. The question which matters is whether Imran has assumed a duty to care for his friend. This can happen through taking on the care of someone else such as another person's child at a birthday party or, as here, by making ineffectual attempts to help someone in trouble. It

could be argued that the law sees that the accused became aware of the need to take care and then abandoned the attempt which is felt to warrant criminal liability. The situation here is parallel to that in **R v Stone and Dobinson (1977)**. Imran begins to take care of his friend but falls below the standard of care required by such a degree that the criminal law is involved. The *actus reus* of the crime has occurred through Imran's omission.

3. There may well be a moral compulsion here to help but is there a legal duty? The tutor/student relationship is not like a teacher/school pupil one as the tutor is not caring for minors in his charge *in loco parentis:* in other words, in the place of the parents. If Bob was in this position then the closest analogy would be **R v Gibbens and Proctor (1918)**. There is no legal basis on which to impose a duty of care on Bob however as the student is an adult. There is no *actus reus* by omission here.

Knowledge Check 2

1. In all areas of law liability is based on fault or blameworthiness except where liability is strict and can be incurred purely by doing the prohibited act. In criminal law this means that whilst many crimes require both *actus reus* and *mens rea* for liability, such as murder, GBH, criminal damage or theft, some crimes only require the *actus reus*. These are strict liability crimes and include many road traffic offences such as speeding, not wearing a seatbelt, failing to insure your vehicle and other crimes like pollution of the environment and health and safety violations in the workplace. The presumption is that all crimes require *mens rea* but that presumption can be overturned if there is evidence Parliament intended liability to be strict **(Sweet v Parsley 1970)**.

2. (a) Murder is most likely to be fault based and dog fouling will be strict liability.

    (b) Murder is inevitably going to require fault-based liability; there are no reasons why this should be a strict liability offence. If this were so, any death in peacetime, caused by another would be categorised as the most heinous of crimes. This would include accidental deaths in car collision incidents and all deaths resulting from, say, complications during medical surgery. Such a situation would be an absurdity. Dog fouling on the other hand is much more likely to be a strict liability offence. The moral stigma attached to the offence is extremely low and the obstacle to a conviction faced by the prosecution were *mens rea* to be required would be enormous. Furthermore, the offence is of a relatively minor regulatory nature.

    (c) The courts would look at the nature of the offence and apply many of the points of reasoning discussed in (b) above. If the offence was one resulting in say a high moral stigma but the statute did not on the face of it require *mens rea* the courts may agree with the ruling in **Sweet v Parsley (1970)**. Such an approach was taken, in the latter years of the statute's life, towards certain sexual offences under the **Sexual Offences Act 1956** until the nature of the liability was clarified by introducing the concept of 'reasonable belief' in the **Sexual Offences Act 2003.**

Knowledge Check 3

1. The law requires *actus reus* and *mens rea* to occur at the same time or contemporaneously. In **Fagan v MPC 1969** the defendant parked on a policeman's foot by accident. At this point he had the *actus reus* of assault but not the *mens rea*. When Fagan decided not to remove the car, locked it and walked away, he possessed the *mens rea* but the *actus reus* happened in the past, even if recent past and was technically no longer operating. This anomaly was addressed by treating the *actus reus* as a continuing series of acts.

2. The contemporaneity rule would only need to be applied if the charge was one of murder. The *actus reus* is present when the immigrants die but the *mens rea* of murder is not present. When the lorry driver leaps from the vehicle, death or GBH must be intended or at least there must be foresight of virtual certainty of such. The *mens rea* is arguably present at this point but the *actus reus* is not as the immigrants died some time ago. This chain of events is analogous to **Fagan v MPC (1969)**. A court is likely to be able to conclude that the *actus reus* of killing the immigrants was a continuing series of acts here as well.

3. Bob could face a charge of murder. The *actus reus* happens in respect of Steve but the *mens rea* attaches to Sam. The Doctrine of transferred malice could be utilised to transfer the intent to kill from Sam to Steve as in **R v Latimer (1886)**.

2   Human rights

(?) *Remember this symbol indicates that the material might be useful for your Student Officer Learning and Assessment Programme (SOLAP) portfolio or any attached reflective practice record you are required to make.*

Underpinning knowledge towards Patrol Officer NOS:

1A1, 1A2, 1A4, 1B9, 2A1, 2C1, 2C2, 2C3, 2C4, 2G2, 2G4, 2H1, 2H2, 2I1, 2I2, 2J1, 2J2, 2K1, 2K2, 4C1

and PCSO NOS:

1A1, 1A4, 1B11, 2A1, 2C1, 2C2, 2C3, 2C4, 2C5, 2J1, 2J2, 2K1, 4C1

For further information on these NOS, which are also Policing Level 3 and 4 NVQ unit titles, refer to Appendix 1 to this volume.

Human rights in the UK

By the end of this section you will be able to:

- describe some fundamental human rights;
- explain the difference between civil rights and civil liberties.

The concept of fundamental human rights is perhaps hardest to grasp for those born and brought up within the United Kingdom as compared to almost any other country. This is a product of our history and the way that our constitution has developed over centuries. We are almost the only country that does not possess an overarching set of fundamental laws that cannot easily be changed by the government of the day. In most countries this set of laws is contained in a single document or set of documents and are held to be superior to those laws made in the country's parliament. There is even an international version, **the Universal Declaration on Human Rights,** adopted by the United Nations in 1948. With no global enforcement organisation as such however, this document remains an expression of collective goodwill and little more. It does however contain international agreement that human beings should be free from slavery **(Article 4)** and torture, cruel and inhuman punishment or degrading treatment **(Article 5),** to take two examples.

Hopefully nobody reading this book would have an issue with those basic rights. When, however, does police questioning technique step over into mental torture? An international court has ruled just that in relation to the UK security services. Is denying someone euthanasia cruel and inhuman? This question was before the courts in the famous case of Diane Pretty in 2001. These questions are rarely simple to address.

REVISION

✓ Human rights are fundamental overarching rules on the way that human beings should be treated by the state and other individuals.

✓ The UK does not have such rules set above national law.

To take an example at national level, in the United States even primary school children are taught about the US Bill of Rights and its place in the way the country is governed – specifically how it regulates the rights of an individual when faced by the power of the state. Some Bills of Rights, and the US version is one of them, also in practice safeguard the rights of the individual if they are infringed by another individual or corporation.

To further illustrate the point let us consider the right not to have to self-incriminate, often called the right to silence. This right is contained within the Fifth Amendment to the US Constitution. The first ten amendments make up the US Bill of Rights, which was ratified in 1791. This absolute right to silence, which cannot be legislated away by the US government, means that a person cannot be forced to say anything under questioning which would help the prosecution case.

It is often argued that if a person has nothing to hide, why would they keep anything from the prosecutors? There are two reasons arguably. Firstly the state, in this case the criminal justice system, has very large resources, it has enormous amounts of money, and huge organisations to do its work with many people employed in them. This mass weight of power is directed against every individual accused of a crime. The balance of power is overwhelmingly on the side of the state. To allow the state to draw an inference of guilt from the lack of answers to police questioning or to allow the prosecution to put people on trial again and again until they were found guilty would place even more power in the hands of the state. For this reason the Fifth Amendment does not allow the US government to do these things by placing a general burden of proof on the prosecution.

Secondly there are many reasons why, say, John Smith may not want to tell the police why he was in Elm Street at 1 am on 2 November 2006. One reason may be because he was a burglar but he could just as easily be returning to his wife and family after a rendezvous with his mistress. Reprehensible perhaps but the legal system does not allow for criminal charges to be brought for such behaviour.

In the United Kingdom, such rights as we have are best described as civil liberties rather than civil rights. This is because there is no concept of a fundamental set of laws which cannot be challenged in Parliament. The core of our parliamentary system is arguably the 'Doctrine of Parliamentary Sovereignty'. This means that Parliament has the right to 'make or unmake any law whatsoever'. Historically no one, not even the courts, have had the right to challenge an Act of the UK Parliament. By contrast the US Supreme Court does have the right to decide that an Act has no validity, reinforcing the point that US human rights are seen there as above the reach of the government except by a particular process.

Knowledge Check 1

1. Why are human rights considered necessary in a modern society?

2. How are human rights protected in an international sense?

3. What is the Doctrine of Parliamentary Sovereignty?

The answers are at the end of the chapter.

In the UK therefore rights have been said to be 'residual' in the sense that you can do anything you like as long as there is no law against it. You can therefore walk through the streets with a placard declaring your opposition to all wars and your commitment to peace. A large group of you doing so would break the law however, as you would need to seek the permission of a senior police officer under the **Police and Criminal Evidence Act 1984 (PACE)**. Furthermore, doing this in the middle of the road would cause an obstruction. If you went so far as to accuse a prominent local businessman of selling arms to foreign dictatorships without an export licence you might fall foul of the law of libel. This is of course assuming that it was not true.

REVISION

✓ Human rights are protected in different ways in different countries.
✓ In the USA the constitution allows the court to challenge laws made in the country's parliament.
✓ In the UK rights are best described as civil liberties rather than fundamental rights.

To go back to our example of the right to silence, there was such an absolute right but the UK government in 1994 legislated that an inference of guilt could be drawn by a jury if a person failed to mention something when questioned which they later relied on in court for their defence (**s. 34 Criminal Justice and Public Order Act 1994**).

(?) *You could make reference to this statutory provision when you make a SOLAP or reflective diary entry on any occasion you have given the caution on arrest or on reporting someone for summons.*

ACTIVITY

The caution now says:

> You do not have to say anything. But it may harm your defence if you do not mention now [when questioned] something which you later rely on in court. Anything you do say may be given in evidence.

Ask a colleague with long enough service to remember the old caution in place prior to 1994. Consider the wording of it. Did the change in wording mean the demise of the absolute right to silence in the UK?

Ironically, despite long opposition to the idea of a Bill of Rights with the same special ('entrenched') position as in the US, the UK made several moves towards safeguarding rights in this way in the latter half of twentieth century. Many of the countries given independence as the British Empire was wound down were given a written constitution; Ghana for example in 1957. Secondly, British lawyers were involved in drafting the **European Convention on Human Rights 1948 (ECHR)** (which has nothing whatsoever to do with the European Union). This document does not have the status of a national law in any of the countries that are a signatory to it. It is a treaty and binds those countries that have signed it to a code of conduct with respect to their citizens. Any infringement could result in a case being brought to the European Court of Human Rights (ECtHR) which sits in Strasbourg. This court is not part of the court system of the UK. It is not an appeal court like the Court of Appeal or House of Lords. In order to take a case to the ECtHR the applicant must first have exhausted all possible remedies in their own country. The issue at stake tends to be whether a fundamentally fair process was adhered to rather than simply challenging a guilty verdict. If the outcome favours the applicant there is no compulsion to reopen the case or change the national law which has been criticised. In practice though, one or both of these things happen because to ignore a judgment that the UK is breaching the human rights of its citizens puts the government in a very bad light. Additionally it makes it difficult for the government to criticise the human rights record of foreign countries should the need arise.

An example of a case which followed the process above is **Gregory v UK (1998)**. Gregory was accused of burglary. During his original trial the jurors passed a note to the judge saying to the effect that that one of the jurors was considered to be racist. Gregory was black. The judge had the option to discharge the jury but decided not to do so. Instead he issued a strong warning to the jury telling them to decide the case on the facts alone, not personal feelings. Gregory was convicted and took his case to Strasbourg. Surprisingly the ECtHR decided in favour of the UK, stating in effect that the judge had done enough to ensure a fair trial.

Many cases are quite controversial. One such is the case brought by the IRA because some of its unarmed members were shot dead in and around the forecourt of a petrol station in Gibraltar by undercover SAS soldiers. This incident was made (in)famous by the 'Death on the rock' television documentary. More recently **T and V v UK (1999)** was a case brought by the killers of James Bulger who were young children themselves. Their complaint was that they were juveniles tried in an adult court and therefore did not receive a fair trial. Secondly, they complained that their detention for an indefinite period at the discretion of the Home Secretary, a politician (common practice at the time for juveniles convicted of murder), was unlawful. The ECtHR agreed with them on both counts and the UK reviewed its procedures in both areas.

Knowledge Check 2

1. What is the European Convention on Human Rights?

2. Describe an ECHR case which concerns a racist jury.

3. What does 'entrenched' mean when used to describe a bill of rights?

The answers are at the end of the chapter.

In the half century or more since signing the treaty the UK has lost many cases against its citizens. It has arguably one of the worst records amongst the European nations who signed the treaty. Therefore for some years there has been pressure to create a system where UK citizens can bring human rights cases in UK courts without the need to go to Strasbourg with their case. During its first term of office the current Labour government proposed what became the **Human Rights Act 1998 (HRA).** This more or less brings the provisions of the **ECHR 1948** into UK law so that breaches of the Act can be dealt with in the High Court. This does not prevent an action being taken in the ECtHR after this process, however.

REVISION

✓ The European Convention on Human Rights is a treaty signed by the UK.
✓ The Human Rights Act 1998 brings the provisions of this treaty into national law in the UK.

The Act does not explicitly give individuals the right to sue other individuals, only 'organs of the state' like government departments and the police for example. Arguably, if a court refused to hear a case brought by an individual against an individual there could in theory be an action against the court as an arm of the state for failure to uphold the complainant's human rights. This has not been fully tested at law yet, however. Furthermore there is no provision for the court to 'strike down' legislation that is incompatible with the **HRA** as would be the case in the equivalent US process. Instead a 'declaration' may be made that the Act in question is incompatible and changes left to the government of the day.

A final point about the **HRA** is that it does not have any special status in law. It is not 'entrenched' like the US or even the old Soviet constitutions, changeable only by a special voting procedure. Consequently it could in theory be repealed by any future government and opposition politicians have recently voiced their intention to repeal some or all of its provisions once they take office. Whether a future government would ever risk the public relations effect of discarding an act designed to protect its citizens' human rights is a matter for debate of course. It is also difficult to dispute that having an 'entrenched' bill of rights does not prevent it being ignored or side-stepped by a government determined to do so, however democratic its credentials.

(?) *Before reading on consider how many of the occupational standards, designed for you to be assessed against as a competent patrol officer, these sections on human rights refer to. It would be a good idea if you made reference to the relevant human right when making SOLAP and reflective diary entries.*

What are your human rights?

By the end of this section you will be able to:

- list the human rights protected under the Human Rights Act 1998;

- analyse the different ways these rights impact on the police officer and the wider criminal justice system.

In the UK these are the rights set down in the **Human Rights Act 1998 (HRA)**. As we have already said, however, if the case fails in the High Court and Courts of Appeal it is still possible to take the case to the European Court of Human Rights under the **European Convention on Human Rights 1948 (ECHR)**. There is no guarantee that winning a case here will result in any action by the UK government; in practice however, it is highly likely to act. This action may not be to everyone's liking however; in a leading case on immigration it was held that the rules on males entering the UK from particularly the Indian subcontinent were not equal to those on females entering the UK from the same parts of the world. The UK government accepted this finding but responded not by relaxing the rules but by making them harsher in relation to both sexes.

How the **HRA** works is contained in the sections of the Act. The rights themselves form a schedule appended at the back of the Act. This schedule effectively reproduces the key articles of the **ECHR**. To most intents and purposes therefore, the police officer may treat the rights under both documents as the same.

ACTIVITY

Everyone seems to know they have human rights. Very often though, the rights that people speak of are not human rights at all. There is for example no explicit 'right to die'. The right of a woman to choose whether or not have her baby is not explicitly protected either.

Have a conversation with a friend, family member or colleague about what they think human rights are, then compare what they thought, and what you thought, with the following text.

The key articles are:

- Article 2 Right to Life

- Article 3 Prohibition of Torture

- Article 4 Prohibition of Slavery and Forced Labour

- Article 5 Right to Liberty and Security

- Article 6 Right to a Fair Trial

- Article 7 No Punishment Without Law

- Article 8 Right to Respect for Private and Family Life

- Article 9 Freedom of Thought, Conscience and Religion

- Article 10 Freedom of Expression

- Article 11 Freedom of Assembly and Association

- Article 12 Right to Marry

- *(Article 13 not incorporated in the Act)*

- Article 14 Prohibition of Discrimination

It is worth spending a few moments now considering how each of these could impact on a police officer's daily duties, the criminal justice system in its widest sense and society in general.

Article 2 Right to Life

Everyone has a right to live. This would not be contravened however, if the UK reintroduced the death penalty say, as life could be deprived under due process of law. Similarly the police, for example, could kill someone whilst quelling a riot or in self-defence or prevention of crime, providing this is proportionate to the threat the person posed when they were killed.

Article 3 Prohibition of Torture

Most people understand the notion of torture and would not support it. The inclusion of 'inhuman or degrading treatment or punishment', however, widens the prohibition and it would not be difficult to stray into this area in the treatment of detained persons. In **Price v UK (2001)** a thalidomide victim and wheelchair user was committed to prison for seven days for contempt of court. She was seriously disabled by her condition, was very cold and risked sores because she could not get to her bed and it was also too hard. The court was scathing of the British judiciary for committing her to prison without checking the facilities were adequate. In **Ireland v UK (1978)** the court had to consider the interrogation techniques used against IRA suspects by the British authorities. These techniques included hooding suspects, making them stand against a wall with limbs outstretched for long periods of time, subjecting them to intense noise, depriving them of sleep and feeding them bread and water. The ECtHR concluded these techniques fell short of torture but were a breach of **Article 3** as inhuman and degrading treatment.

Article 4 Prohibition of Slavery and Forced Labour

This prohibition would not be infringed by requiring prisoners to work in custody, the forced continuation of voluntary military service (i.e. a refusal to discharge a soldier on his or her request), forced labour during a major emergency or performing civic obligations. These situations are exempted. A case was brought by four sailors who were only 15 or 16 at the time their requests for discharge were repeatedly refused **(W,X,Y and Z v UK 1968)**. They lost their case, primarily because non-conscripted military service is exempted from **Article 4** but as a result Navy rules in this area were relaxed. This is an example of how **ECHR** cases can indirectly influence UK law.

Despite the exemption relating to prisoners, a case could arguably be brought by a prisoner in a police cell who was forced to clean floors for example, perhaps for being non-compliant. There is an implication that the actions of the authorities will be reasonable and that they will not be applied to persons who are not yet found guilty of an offence.

Article 5 Right to Liberty and Security

This right impacts directly on the duties of a patrol officer. It basically forbids the taking of liberty other than under due process of law. It also guarantees that a suspect must be 'informed promptly, in a language which he understands, of the reasons for his arrest and of any charge against him'. Furthermore, the right to a trial within a reasonable time, the right to challenge the lawfulness of detention and compensation if that challenge is successful are all covered by **Article 5.**

To be in breach of this article, the police need not be engaged in arbitrary night-time arrests 'Soviet-style'. A detention by a Police Community Support Officer in an area where detention powers are not yet authorised by the Chief Constable could be a breach. A stop and search under **Section 1 PACE 1984** could constitute a breach if there were not sufficient grounds for the stop. An unreasonable refusal of bail would also be challengeable under this provision.

The UK government has found itself having to defend its actions in respect of the prisoners in Belmarsh Prison held without trial as a result of increased fears of terrorism since 9/11. These detainees were held under the **Anti-Terrorism Crime and Security Act 2001**. The House of Lords ruled that the detainees were held in breach of their human rights and they were granted bail.

Article 6 Right to a Fair Trial

The main reason why there are worries about whether individuals can receive a fair trial in any society is because there is no 'equality of arms' between the state and the individual. This is to say that the state holds almost all the power, money and resources whereas the individual is seriously disadvantaged. One of the ways this imbalance is addressed in the UK is the fact that an arrested person is allowed access to a lawyer irrespective of their ability to pay. This right is enacted by virtue of **s. 58 PACE 1984.** This provision in the **ECHR** and now the **HRA** is arguably one of the reasons why state funding for legal services (formerly called Legal Aid) has not undergone the kind of sustained cost-cutting attack that funding for civil compensation claims has.

Article 7 No Punishment Without Law

The state is not allowed to administer punishment just because there is a majority opinion that certain activities are reprehensible. There must be a properly constituted law to underpin the state action. In **Welch v UK (1995)** a drug dealer was convicted and jailed. After his conviction confiscation legislation was introduced. Welch successfully argued that to apply this legislation to him would be a breach of **Article 7** because laws cannot normally be applied retrospectively. The ECtHR refused to accept this argument in **SW v UK (1995)** however, because this case concerned rape within marriage. This was not a crime until the case of **R v R (1991)** overturned years of House of Lords rulings and accepted that rape was possible within matrimony. The ECtHR felt that this change in the law was so foreseeable it was not a breach of the Convention to convict a man retrospectively for raping his wife even though at the time he did it he was not committing a crime.

Article 8 Right to Respect for Private and Family Life

Many cases in this area concern surveillance but could arguably apply to any unwarranted breach of privacy or confidentiality by an official such as a police officer. In **Halford v UK (1997)** the bugging of a telephone was held to be capable of being a breach of **Article 8**. Properly authorised telecommunications interception will normally not be a breach, of course. It remains to be seen whether the monitoring of emails by an employer looking for those not connected with an individual's employment is a breach. It probably will not be if the workforce is warned that monitoring could happen.

Articles 9 Freedom of Thought, Conscience and Religion

Detainees in police cells must be accorded proper facilities for the observance of their religious beliefs. Any diet would have to take account of prohibited foods to the devout, such as pork in relation to the Jewish faith and Halal meat if requested by a Muslim arrested person.

It is unlikely that the UK authorities would seek to outlaw a particular religious or political viewpoint but membership of groups which espouse these views (like the IRA) or promotion of the realisation of these views by violent means can and is rendered illegal by Parliament. The **Terrorism Act 2006** for example makes it illegal to 'glorify' terrorism. The grey area between voicing support for the aims of a terrorist group and glorifying the acts of that group is likely to generate **HRA** actions.

Articles 10 and 11 Freedom of Expression, Assembly and Association

These articles are dealt with here together as in practice they are often inextricably linked in public order situations. The problem with provisions like these is that the police are open to criticism whatever their actions. Consider a request under **PACE 1984** to hold a march in public by a group holding particularly objectionable views, perhaps deeply racist ones. If the police refuse permission they are accused of 'gagging' a section of the population. If they allow permission they are seen as supporting these views. Furthermore, they will inevitably be held responsible for the ensuing unrest if the march meets elements that disagree with the organisation's views.

In the US a similar provision to the one here on expression has been relied upon to legalise hardcore pornography on the basis that to ban it infringed on the film makers' freedom of expression.

In a society which values freedom of speech these issues will inevitably throw up heated debate. The key is that these rights are universal and not only available to those with an unblemished record or those that hold the majority viewpoint.

Article 12 Right to Marry

The right to marry and found a family has to a certain extent been a factor in the movement towards acceptance of same-sex legalised partnerships. The **Civil Partnerships Act 2005** accords same-sex couples with rights which come very close to those of married heterosexual couples.

There was some dissent when Prince Charles married Camilla Parker-Bowles from traditionalists who could not accept that the heir to the throne and the next head of the Church of England could marry a divorcee. No serious legal challenge was ever mounted but it is interesting to note that Prince Charles could have relied on **Article 12** should the legalities of his actions under the UK constitution have been questioned. Any law forbidding him to marry a divorcee could have been found incompatible with the **ECHR** in any such case.

Article 14 Prohibition of Discrimination

Tackling discrimination internally is probably one of the highest priorities in any of the UK police forces. There have been high-profile court cases such as the Stephen Lawrence investigation which have thrown this issue into sharp relief in recent years. The failure of the Metropolitan Police to properly investigate the racist murder of a black teenager led to the **McPherson Inquiry.** The findings of this caused the Metropolitan Police to accept publicly that they were 'institutionally racist'. In effect this meant that all police forces and large parts of the wider criminal justice system have been viewed in the same light rightly or wrongly.

Even more recently television programmes such as the 'Secret policeman' and one 'Dispatches' programme have highlighted ongoing problems with racism and sexism in UK forces.

These issues are by no means new and race issues were very important in the civil unrest experienced in Brixton, Toxteth and Wandsworth in the early to mid-1980s. The **Scarman Report** into the Brixton riots was critical of the police relationship with ethnic communities and was instrumental in the creation of **PACE 1984.** One can see the sensitivities towards the dress of ethnic minorities in the **Section 1** provisions around stop and search, permitting only the 'outer coat, jacket and gloves' to be searched in public. This recognises that some headgear has religious significance.

The **HRA** prohibition of discrimination is very wide and covers discrimination 'on any ground such as sex, race, colour, language, religion, political or other opinion, national or social origin, association with a national minority, property, birth or other status'. The most important words are arguably 'on any ground' with the remainder of the wording serving as examples. There is already much legislation on these issues. The **Sex Discrimination Act 1975** and **Race Relations Acts 1976** onwards cover discrimination including but not limited to the workplace. The **Rehabilitation of Offenders Act 1974** limits but does not entirely bar discrimination against ex-offenders. Moves towards further publication of paedophiles' details over and above connected with the punishment they have received for their crimes initially would probably be challengeable under **Article 14,** however.

The **Article 14** prohibition would apply to all actions of a police officer however, and not just to those acts done in the pursuit of a prosecution of an offender. The failure to respond promptly to a minor complaint because it was made by a member of the travelling community or a failure to adhere strictly to the permitted remit of a stop and search because the subject was an illegal immigrant would all create a basis for a legal challenge under the **HRA.**

(?) *No human right is more important than any other but discrimination within the police service and in its dealings with the wider public are certainly very topical and hotly debated issues currently. Consider how you could make SOLAP and reflective entries which highlight how you have attempted to uphold these fundamental rights whilst on duty.*

ACTIVITY

Organisations like Liberty and Charter 88 have long campaigned on the issue of human rights in the UK. Perform a web search and find out what these organisations have to say about the state of human rights. Consider – do you agree or disagree with what they have to say? What could be done to improve the situation? Have human rights 'gone too far', as some politicians and newspaper editors are quoted as saying?

You could take this activity a step further and prepare a short talk based on what you have discovered. Deliver the talk if you can find a willing audience. Just the preparation of it will help to embed your knowledge in any event. It may even form the basis of a presentation you are formally asked to do on your course.

REVISION

The key human rights are:
- ✓ Right to Life
- ✓ Prohibition of Torture
- ✓ Prohibition of Slavery and Forced Labour
- ✓ Right to Liberty and Security
- ✓ Right to a Fair Trial
- ✓ No Punishment Without Law
- ✓ Right to Respect for Private and Family Life
- ✓ Freedom of Thought, Conscience and Religion
- ✓ Freedom of Expression
- ✓ Freedom of Assembly and Association
- ✓ Right to Marry
- ✓ Prohibition of Discrimination

Knowledge Check 3

1. What is the relationship between the ECHR and the Human Rights Act 1998?

2. Describe a case brought under Article 3 – Prohibition of Torture.

3. PC Daley is approached by a group of foreign tourists who try to indicate that they have had their passports and money stolen. They speak no English and Daley assumes they are Eastern European economic migrants. Daley distrusts these people and walks away from them, refusing to deal with their complaint. When they follow her she shouts at them to go away and tells them they are not allowed to go around in a group as this 'harrasses people'. When they still do not disperse she slaps one of them hard in the face. Irrespective of any other laws and procedures which may have been breached, consider which of these individuals' human rights have not been adhered to.

The answers are at the end of the chapter.

Suggested research

Politicians have urged a review of the Human Rights Act 1998 over recent years. Use the internet and newspaper sources to find out which politicians are calling for these changes and their reasons.

Look up the Protocols and Articles 16–18 of the HRA 1998. These may have some bearing on your duties but were considered outside the scope of discussion of a book of this size.

Further reading

An easy introduction to the US style approach to a bill of rights is contained in:

Bachmann, S (1987) *US Constitution for beginners*. New York: Writers and Readers.

For more in-depth discussion and more case law on the topics in this chapter, student officers might consider reading from:

Fenwick, H (2000) *Civil rights: New Labour, freedom and the Human Rights Act* (Law in Focus). Harlow: Longman.

Leckie, D and Pickersgill, D (1999) *The 1988 Human Rights Act explained* (The Point of Law). London: The Stationery Office.

Ovey, C and White, R (2002) in Jacobs and White, *The European Convention on Human Rights*. (3rd edn). Oxford: Oxford University Press.

Wadham, J, Mountfield, H and Edmundson, A (2003) *Blackstone's guide to the Human Rights Act 1998*. (3rd edn). Oxford: Oxford University Press.

Useful websites

www.opsi.gov.uk/acts/acts1998/80042— d.htm (this should take you straight to the full text of the HRA 1998)

www.dca.gov.uk/peoples-rights/human-rights/faqs.htm (a useful introductory discussion of the HRA by the Dept. of Constitutional Affairs)

www.westlaw.com* (a legal database)

www.lexis-nexis.com* (a legal database)

www.pnld.co.uk* (a police service specific database of case law and statute)

* Likely to be available through the virtual learning environment (VLE) which supports your course/training.

Answers

Knowledge Check 1

1. In all modern societies the state holds the balance of power. It has great resources of money and manpower to use against the individual if it so wishes. Extreme examples of the abuse of this power would be Soviet Russia, Nazi Germany and Saddam Hussein's Iraq. There are of course documented examples of such abuses in nations that are democracies. Human rights are fundamental rights which in theory protect the individual from acts of abuse by the state. In some cases acts perpetrated by other individuals who do not work for the state are covered. The problem is often not with the existence of the right but whether or not it is enforced in any given nation's courts.

2. The United Nations Declaration on Human Rights 1948 is binding internationally. It lacks enforceability because it is merely a treaty and without any kind of fully functioning global government it is difficult to mount any kind of meaningful court or other action against offending states.

3. This doctrine exists uniquely in the UK. It means that 'Parliament has the right to make or unmake any law whatsoever'. In this context it makes it difficult, if not impossible, to have a set of unchallengeable rights set above national law as in, say, the USA.

Knowledge Check 2

1. The European Convention on Human Rights (ECHR) 1948 is a treaty signed by many European countries including the UK, who helped draft it. The Convention is enforced by taking cases to the European Court of Human Rights located in Strasbourg. Judgments of this court do not have the same force as those of a domestic court in the UK but in practice usually lead to compensation where appropriate and changes in the law. The ECHR was incorporated into UK domestic law by the provisions of the Human Rights Act 1998. Actions under the Treaty's articles can now be taken to the High Court.

2. Gregory v UK (1998) concerned a burglary trial of a black defendant. The jurors passed a note to the judge to the effect that one of their number held racist views. The judge had the option to discharge the jury but instead issued a strong warning to them to convict on the basis of fact not prejudice. Gregory was convicted and took his case to the ECtHR. The ECtHR determined that the Convention had not been breached in this instance.

3 'Entrenched', when used to describe a bill of rights, means that the document is considered to be a higher form of law which cannot be changed as easily as a regular Act of Parliament or whatever the term used in that country is for nationally agreed statutes. Usually a special voting procedure and a very high majority of votes are needed for change. This also means that any Acts of Parliament that are incompatible with an entrenched bill of rights are in many states struck down by the courts. The UK does not have such an entrenched bill of rights. The Human Rights Act is an Act of Parliament with in theory no special superior status.

Knowledge Check 3

1. The ECHR was incorporated into UK domestic law by the provisions of the Human Rights Act 1998. Actions under the Treaty's articles can now be taken to the High Court. The sections of the HRA deal with the workings of the Act. The ECHR is effectively reproduced as a schedule to the act. The terms are therefore effectively the same as those in the Treaty.

Either:

Price v UK (2001)

Price was a thalidomide victim and a wheelchair user. She was committed to prison for seven days for contempt of court. She was seriously disabled by her condition, was very cold and risked sores because she could not get to her bed and it was also too hard. The court was scathing of the British judiciary for committing her to prison without checking the facilities were adequate.

Or:

Ireland v UK (1978)

At the behest of the Irish government, the court had to consider the interrogation techniques used against IRA suspects by the British authorities. These techniques included hooding suspects, making them stand against a wall with limbs outstretched for long periods of time, subjecting them to intense noise, depriving them of sleep and feeding them bread and water. The ECtHR concluded these techniques fell short of torture but were a breach of Article 3 as inhuman and degrading treatment.

Or any case from research on Article 3.

2. PC Daley has breached at least the following articles:

Article 14 Prohibition of Discrimination:

Daley clearly has treated this group less favourably because of their nationality.

Article 11 Freedom of Assembly and Association:

There is no justifiable legal reason why this group should not be allowed to gather together; they are exercising a legal right to report a crime. If the group became aggressive or violent, Daley would be justified in telling them to disperse.

Article 7 No Punishment Without Law:

Daley's slap is arguably corporal punishment; this could not be applied unless there was a national law allowing for its administration. There is no such law and any such provision would probably fall foul of the Article 3 prohibition on degrading and inhuman treatment anyway.

3   Police powers under PACE 1984 and SOCPA 2005

(?) *Remember this symbol indicates that the material might be useful for your Student Officer Learning and Assessment Programme (SOLAP) portfolio or any attached reflective practice record you are required to make.*

Underpinning knowledge towards Patrol Officer NOS:

1A1, 1A4, 2A1, 2C1, 2C2, 2C3, 2C4, 2G2, 2G4, 2H2, 2I1, 2I2, 2J1, 2J2, 2K2

and PCSO NOS:

1A1, 1A4, 2A1, 2C1, 2C2, 2C3, 2C4, 2C5, 2J1, 2J2

For further information on these NOS, which are also Policing Level 3 and 4 NVQ unit titles, refer to Appendix 1 to this volume.

Some powers relate only to minor matters such as the issue of documentation, which can lead to fines and the seizure of vehicles, etc. The more potentially controversial powers that police officers have concern the deprivation of liberty, either to search and/or gather evidence or to deliver the person ultimately before a court of law. There are also specific powers attached to certain criminal offences such as the powers to search under the **Misuse of Drugs Act 1971** (discussed further in Chapter 8) and anti-terrorism legislation.

Most recently the general powers relating to the removal of liberty have been set down by the **Serious and Organised Crime and Police Act (SOCPA) 2005** which came into force on 1 January 2006. This statute is best understood in conjunction with the legislation which went before it. This is because to a certain extent it varies the powers contained in the preceding statute and much of it is still in force. This was the **Police and Criminal Evidence Act (PACE) 1984**. Statute is not the only source of police powers however, and some are derived from common law. This source has become less important and has gradually been almost completely replaced by statute.

What is often underestimated is the power of the ordinary citizen to deprive liberty. Without this, citizens' arrests would not be possible and, for instance, the store detective's job would be near impossible. The police officer's powers are best understood as an important extension of these 'any person' powers rather than a distinct set. These 'any person' powers need to be taken into account in any event as the police community support officer only has these powers to fall back on in situations were the power of detention is not available. It is important that PCSOs using this text as reading to enhance their skills understand their powers and further discussion of this point will be found in this chapter under the **Police Reform Act 2002** section and in Chapter 4. It is equally important that student police officers understand the limits to the powers of their PCSO colleagues. A key point is that legislative restraint on police powers is an important way to persuade the community that is being policed, that it is being policed fairly.

(?) *Think about the community you have been allocated to police. Is it sensible to talk only about geographically defined communities or are there several communities in the same place? These could identify with each other by virtue of common ethnicity or sexuality for instance. Remember this non-geographical approach to defining communities when making SOLAP or reflective entries.*

Powers under PACE and SOCPA 2005

By the end of this section you will be able to:

- evaluate the likely impact of breaches of PACE;

- describe in more detail the impact of SOCPA 2005;

- explain the main powers granted to police officers by this legislation.

You should note that references to constables and police officers in this section relate to anyone who is an attested constable whether special or regular. Regular police officers have constabulary powers 24 hours a day, seven days a week in England and Wales and associated coastal waters. Special constables have them whilst on duty only. There are also geographical limitations. Special constables' powers extend to the police area they operate in (such as a county) under **s. 30(2) Police Act 1996** and any coastal waters bordering on that. They have powers anywhere they are sent under a mutual aid scheme and in police areas that border on theirs. This is to prevent the ludicrous situation arising of a special constable chasing a suspect across a county boundary and losing his or her powers on the other side.

PACE and its associated codes are enormous pieces of legislation; the coverage here therefore is centred on what a student officer is likely to have to make a decision on without reference to higher authority. Consequently much more attention is focused on a stop-and-search situation than on a road check which requires authorisation. To do more than this would be outside the scope of this volume but it is intended that the basic syllabus for IPLDP is addressed.

It should be remembered that the real problem areas for police officers are when they have to make a decision whether to arrest, search or detain. If a warrant signed by a magistrate is in existence, such as an arrest warrant or a search warrant, and it relates to the person or premises in question then there is no need at this stage in an officer's training to be concerned about the legalities of it.

(?) *You may be asked to execute an arrest warrant quite early in your service: this activity is commonly used as a way to introduce the student officer to the realities of taking another person's liberty. Even if the power has been granted by a magistrate the arrest should still be carried out sensitively and professionally. A SOLAP or reflective entry on this could be enhanced by a brief discussion of the difference between arrests with or without warrants as outlined above.*

It is important to remember, however, that a breach of the provisions of **PACE** and sometimes its associated codes of practice is always serious. There are arguably four possible consequences of a breach. It could result in a criminal offence being committed by the officer. An obvious example would be that an arrest made on insufficient grounds could be termed an assault. A conviction of this sort would spell the end of an officer's career at the very least. Such a finding would probably lead to a compensation claim being laid in the civil courts which, if successful, would normally run into thousands of pounds. The chief officer of the police force concerned is not bound to pay these damages, there are rules about when an 'employer' (police authorities are treated in law as like an employer to a constable) has to pay an employee's compensation for him to a third party. This is covered in greater depth in Chapter 20. The police officer concerned could therefore find him or herself sacked and liable for compensation.

The second possible consequence is that the breach seriously compromises the investigation of the crime concerned. For instance, a failure to caution at the appropriate time does not affect the legality of the arrest but renders any subsequent confession inadmissible at court.

A failure to adhere to the codes can seriously undermine eye-witness evidence as well, which is unreliable at the best of times. The courts are rightly cautious about allowing this type of evidence. This is especially true if it is felt to have been tainted in some way by the way the police have handled the witness. The original Damilola Taylor murder trial in April 2002 was halted in part because of well-meaning but inappropriate promises made by the police team dealing with the principal teenage girl witness. The investigation into the murder of Rachel Nickell on Wimbledon Common in 1992 was heavily criticised because the prosecution relied on a 'honey trap' to obtain evidence. An undercover female police officer struck up a relationship with the main suspect, a Mr Colin Stagg, in the hope that he would admit his crime. This was viewed as an unfair use of police power. This criticism may have been well founded as DNA evidence now appears to point to another individual already detained in secure psychiatric accommodation for other serious crimes.

Thirdly, the officer may be formally disciplined with consequences which range from formal warnings through to dismissal. This could be in addition to the consequences outlined above.

The final possible consequence is that the protection of the law may be removed from the officer. For example, if a person resists a search or arrest but either of these is in fact unlawful under **PACE** then the subject cannot be charged with assaulting a constable in the execution of his duty.

The **PACE Codes of Practice** we have mentioned have been described as being in practice like a 'Highway Code' in that breach is not in itself always a breach of the law. Any breach of the code however, would be taken into account when judging the legalities of the police actions in question or the admissability of gathered evidence. The codes were originally denoted A, B, C, D but after numerous revisions they now number eight, with E, F, G and H added by later legislation. They cover:

- A – Stop and search.

- B – Searching of premises and seizure of property.

- C – Detention, treatment and questioning of persons.

- D – Identification of persons by police.

- E – Tape recording of interviews with suspects by police.

- F – Video recording of interviews with suspects by police.

- G – Statutory power of arrest (**Section 110 SOCPA 2005**).

- H – Detention, treatment and questioning by police officers of persons under **section 41** of, and **Schedule 8** to, the **Terrorism Act 2000**.

ACTIVITY

Locate a copy of the codes at your station; you may well find it useful to purchase your own or download as necessary from the internet. Code G for example, is currently located at:

http://police.homeoffice.gov.uk/news-and-publications/publication/operational-policing/PACE_Chapter_G.pdf?view=Binary

Having looked through the codes and considered their major themes, prepare a debate with a fellow student officer, friend or family member. The hypothesis for each side is:

(a) PACE provides a 'thieves charter' and unacceptably hinders the investigation of crime.

(b) Despite PACE the police still have draconian powers which remain open to abuse with little safeguard.

Present your case for five minutes to an interested but uninformed audience and then allow your 'opponent' to do the same. Allow your audience a free vote on who has 'won' the debate.

If time is short (or volunteers in short supply), prepare the text of both arguments in note form. Much learning will be consolidated by that in itself.

Stop and search

This is one of the most controversial of police powers as it is a means of temporarily depriving the suspect of their liberty without being an arrest. Used carelessly it can also massively damage police/community relations. This point was made particularly in relation to the Brixton disorders in 1981.

The power to stop and search in a public place is distinct from any power which arises after an arrest has been made. The power is laid down in **Sections 1(1) and 1(2) of PACE. Section 1(2)** sets out the power to search:

Subject to subsection (3) to (5) below(#1), a constable-

(a) may search

    (i) any person or vehicle;

    (ii) anything which is in or on a vehicle, for stolen or prohibited articles, any article to which subsection (8A(#2)) below applies or any firework to which subsection (8B(#3)) below applies; and

(b) may detain a person or vehicle for the purpose of such a search

Notes

#1 These subsections refer to the restriction that a constable may not search a person or vehicle in the garden, yard or similar of a dwelling unless the officer has 'reasonable grounds for suspecting' the person does not reside there and is not there with permission (e.g. is a suspected intruder). The same principle applies to any vehicle found there (see 'The objective of the search' later).

#2 This refers to 'blades and points' under **s. 139 Criminal Justice Act 1988.**

#3 Inserted by **SOCPA 2005** (see 'The objective of the search' later).

It should be noted that in certain circumstances this power is conferred on PCSOs by the **Police Reform Act 2002** (see later and Chapter 4). Please also bear in mind that this provision does not authorise an officer to stop a vehicle. That power is covered in Chapter 19, 'Roads policing'.

Section 1 (1) delimits the places this power may be exercised:

A constable may exercise any power conferred by this section

(a) in any place to which at the time when he proposes to exercise the power the public or any section of the public has access, on payment or otherwise, as of right or by virtue of express or implied permission; or

(b) in any other place to which people have ready access at the time when he proposes to exercise the power but which is not a dwelling.

Section 1 (3) confers the all important requirement that the search must be on the basis of 'reasonable grounds for suspecting' a **Section 1(1)** search is necessary.

Reasonable grounds

'Reasonable grounds' are very difficult to explain and will differ as many times as there are real-life circumstances; in other words infinitely. It is easier to consider what will not be acceptable reasonable grounds and in doing so indicate what might be lawful grounds in the process.

The following list of circumstances which will not found reasonable grounds for a stop and search is not exhaustive:

- reasonable grounds for an arrest;

- race, colour, religion or ethnicity;

- previous convictions, generalisations and stereotyping;

- an unsubstantiated accusation/assertion by somebody else.

Guidance is provided in **Code A** at **paras. 2.2** to **2.7** especially. References to searches under **Section 60 Criminal Justice and Public Order Act 1994 (s. 60 search)** and the **Terrorism Act 2000** in this document should not be ignored but are dealt with elsewhere in this volume in more detail.

Reasonable grounds for an arrest

This is covered here to try to avoid confusion between the two. At first sight this might seem a strange inclusion in the above list. It may seem that suspicion at this level must cover suspicion to search as well. There is a power, discussed later, of search of an arrested person. What we are discussing here though is the situation where an officer detains a person in order to search them, finds nothing and remaining suspicious and in good faith, arrests them anyway. The following exchange in court could result:

Defence advocate: Officer, why did you not arrest my client when you first saw him?

Officer: Because I wanted to see if he had any stolen or prohibited articles on him first.

Defence advocate: Does that mean you had insufficient grounds to arrest him at that point?

Officer: Yes.

Defence advocate: Did you find anything?

Officer: No.

Defence advocate: Are you telling the court that you had insufficient grounds to arrest my client before the search, you found nothing during the search, therefore no new grounds were found, yet you still arrested him? Does that not mean that you arrested him without grounds to do so by your own admission?

41

The irony is that even if grounds to arrest had existed at the outset and the officer had stated that under cross-examination, this would still beg the question as to why the arrest was not made immediately. This could call the officer's competence into question. Given all of this discussion it is highly preferable to let the person go on their way if no new evidence is found. Observation can be maintained if possible and intelligence submitted if appropriate.

The fact that a search is voluntary does not remove it from the restrictions in these sections.

Race, colour, religion or ethnicity

The **Race Relations (Amendment) Act 2000** extends the provisions of the **Race Relations Act 1976** to police officers. The targeting of individuals for stop and search solely on the grounds above would transgress this legislation, not to mention possibly **Art. 5 Human Rights Act 1998 (HRA)**. More importantly though, it is morally indefensible.

In any event, given the discussion above about how **PACE** came to be deemed necessary at the beginning of this chapter it will be of little surprise to learn that these are not grounds on their own to stop and search an individual. **Code A** gives specific guidance which prohibits the use of race or appearance on their own as reasons for a stop and search. This is not to say that these could never be one of the factors going into the decision to stop and search someone. Clearly if a victim states they have just been robbed by a man of Chinese appearance, and on a sweep of the area such a person is seen to be walking down a nearby street then that person may be approached. It is worth stating here of course that he or she does not have to respond to questioning and in the case of **Rice v Connolly (1966)** a refusal to co-operate in these circumstances was held not to be a breach of the law. Only if further reasons for suspicion come to light on approach to this man would a search be justified. Such matters might be his running off on sight of the police or if he bore injuries which were consistent with the victim's account of any struggle. This man's vague, evasive or demonstrably untrue responses to the approaching officer's questions might be a further factor to be taken into account.

These are difficult points in practice, particularly in an era of global terrorism. Recently members of the public and media commentators alike have been expressing concern over the delays at ports and airports during security scares as every person is searched with equal vigour irrespective of their ethnic origin. Whilst these searches are almost always carried out under a different legal basis by security staff and not police officers, the principle remains the same. There is an argument circulating that suicide bombers and the like are currently more likely to be of Asian or Arab appearance and members of such ethnic groups might legitimately be targeted for searching. It is similarly argued that, for example, white airline pilots passing through the airport security cordon might be excused such a search. This argument rather falls down however, when one remembers that the infamous 'shoe bomber', Richard Reed, was of dual heritage and on first sight would definitely not fit the accepted profile of an Islamic fundamentalist terrorist.

Previous convictions, generalisations and stereotyping

These criteria are again specifically prohibited by **Code A** at **2.2**. The fact that previous convictions are excluded if used on their own may be surprising. There are two good reasons, however, for such an exclusion. Firstly, there is the belief which humanity as a whole still clings to, despite repeated assaults by the media, that everyone deserves a second chance. Repeatedly targeting someone for searching because of their previous convictions might in any event be a breach of **Art. 7 HRA** as this could be deemed punishment over and above that awarded by the court.

Secondly, in communities around the world members of ethnic minorities find themselves before the courts and in prisons in disproportionate numbers compared to the percentage of the population they represent. American prisons like Rikers Island hold huge numbers of black and Hispanic prisoners and British prisons house a disproportionate number of ethnic minorities similarly. This has more to do with social deprivation and economic disadvantage than any inherent tendency to criminality. Therefore to target people on the strength of their criminal history solely would arguably lead indirectly to a disproportionate number of stops and searches of ethnic minority people.

(?) *It is not uncommon for police trainers to set exercises, particularly role plays, where the 'suspect' has previous convictions or wears a 'hoodie' or in some other way conforms to a stereotype. In performing these exercises and in writing them up ensure that you recognise the limitations on your 'reasonable grounds' that exist here. If multiple factors appear on the briefing for the exercise combining many suspicious issues, that is of course a different matter.*

Stereotyping is of course different to 'profiling', which is a technique criminal psychologists use to narrow down the field of possible suspects to those which have a certain profile or set of characteristics. This is more common in the US criminal justice system and even there is not without its critics. It is not in huge favour in the UK since at least the Rachel Nickell murder case, described earlier, when the target of police activity was apparently wrongly selected at least partly by a psychologist's profile.

An unsubstantiated accusation/assertion by somebody else

This is of course likely to cause a problem because inevitably early in your service an officer, perhaps of senior rank or service, may say to you, 'I will search this one, you search him over there.' If this is a **Section 1** stop/search situation it is incumbent on you to be sure you have the grounds for a search. A couple of quick questions of your colleague as to the reasons, coupled perhaps with some enquiries of the suspect before you commence should satisfy you in this regard. If it does not, do not proceed. It will not be the other officer who is assaulting the suspect by performing an illegal search, it will be you.

The position described above is set out in case law. In **O'Hara v Chief Constable of the RUC (1997)** it was stated that the test was two-fold. The arresting officer must have formed a genuine suspicion in his own mind (one might call this a subjective test). Secondly though, it must be demonstrable that a reasonable man would also reach that same conclusion based on the available information (an objective test). Criminal law has a number of tests in it which are either 'subjective', 'objective' or both. Think of 'subjective' as representing what the accused thought and 'objective' what society (represented by the mythical 'reasonable man') would have thought.

The second objective limb described in **O'Hara** is unlikely to be satisfied where the search takes place because of a simple accusation.

Knowledge Check 1

PC Prajapati is on foot patrol when a call is received on his radio that a street robbery has taken place within the last five minutes two streets away. The victim fought with her attacker but he got away with a purse which contained cash and credit cards. The attacker is described as 5' 7" tall with stocky build, of Asian appearance and his breath smelt strongly of intoxicating liquor. Explain giving reasons, whether a Section 1 PACE stop and search is justified in the following situations.

(a) The officer sees a small group of Asian men standing together facing inwards looking at something and discussing it.

(b) The officer sees an Afro-Caribbean man of similar height and build to the description walking towards him who then throws something into the bushes.

(c) The officer sees a man of Asian appearance and of similar height and build to the description walking away from him, and he seems to quicken his pace when the officer approaches. It transpires after a talk with the man that he has previous convictions for fraud offences some ten years ago.

The answers are at the end of the chapter.

The objective of the search

Sections 6 to 9 set out the steps to be taken if an item is found and also what exactly is meant by a prohibited article:

> *(6) If in the course of such a search a constable discovers an article which he has reasonable grounds for suspecting to be a stolen or prohibited article, an article to which subsection (8A) below applies or a firework to which subsection (8B) below applies, he may seize it.*

The seizure power would form part and parcel of an arrest process of course. It should be noted though that, especially given the provisions of **SOCPA 2005,** it may be that the article is seized but the individual is proceeded against by way of a summons (see later in this chapter).

Sections 7 and 8A–C describe prohibited articles. These are what student officers will come to know as offensive weapons, 'blades and points' and articles that could be used to carry out a dishonesty offence like burglary or theft.

> *(7) An article is prohibited for the purposes of this Part of this Act if it is*
>
> > *(a) an offensive weapon; or*
> >
> > *(b) an article*
> >
> > > *(i) made or adapted for use in the course of or in connection with an offence to which this sub-paragraph applies; or*
> > >
> > > *(ii) intended by the person having it with him for such use by him or by some other person.*

(8) The offences to which subsection (7)(b)(i) above applies are

(a) burglary;

(b) theft;

(c) offences under section 12 of the Theft Act 1968 (taking motor vehicle or other conveyance without authority);

(d) offences under section 15 of that Act (obtaining property by deception); and

(e) offences under section 1 of the Criminal Damage Act 1971 (destroying or damaging property).

(8A) This subsection applies to any article in relation to which a person has committed, or is committing or is going to commit an offence under section 139 of the Criminal Justice Act 1988.

(8B) This subsection applies to any firework which a person possesses in contravention of a prohibition imposed by fireworks regulations.

(8C) In this section

(a) 'firework' shall be construed in accordance with the definition of 'fireworks' in section 1(1) of the Fireworks Act 2003; and

(b) 'fireworks regulations' has the same meaning as in that Act.

(9) In this Part of this Act 'offensive weapon' means any article

(a) made or adapted for use for causing injury to persons; or

(b) intended by the person having it with him for such use by him or by some other person.

Sections 8B and **C** were inserted by **SOCAP 2005** to address the apparent rise in anti-social use of fireworks in recent years. Prior to this the right to search for these, sometimes highly dangerous, explosives was not covered by this piece of legislation.

Crucially **Section 2(9)** stipulates that a search in public may not involve requiring the suspect to remove anything other than his or her outer coat, jacket or gloves. This may seem overly restrictive but it has to do with maintaining the dignity of the suspect in public. After all, would it really be justifiable to ask someone to remove their trousers in the street merely on suspicion of illegal activity? Extra powers are conferred by the **Terrorism Act 2000** (see later) in relation to clothing, however. **Section 2(9)** effectively excludes headgear however, which is a common site of concealment. The rationale is that some headgear has religious or cultural significance and given the history which led to **PACE** the drafters of the legislation were keen to reduce the possibilities for tension between the wearers of such headgear and the police. One only has to consider the civil strife in France (which in part flowed from the banning of the wearing of the *hijab* in state schools) in 2005 to see how passions can run high over religious garments.

It should be remembered that in order to carry out a more invasive search all that is required is that this is carried out in private. Most commonly this would mean conveyance to a police station. This is absolutely necessary if a search of the body orifices needs to be authorised.

Information given before the search

Section 2 further covers the fact that an officer does not have to carry out a search if he deems it unnecessary having carried out the stop. The section also sets out the requirements for information to be given to the suspect before the search can commence. Reasonable steps must be taken to impart this information. What will constitute reasonable steps will differ of course depending on circumstances; for instance, whether the stop is made on a sunny still day or in a hailstorm or whether the suspect is compliant or violently resists. In any event failure to take reasonable steps renders the search unlawful even if it is voluntary. Many police trainers reduce this information to be given to the following:

- grounds for the search;

- object of the search;

- warrant card (if in plain clothes or requested to be seen);

- identity of the officer;

- station base;

- entitlement to a copy of the search record;

- legal power exercised;

- 'you are detained for the purposes of a search'.

This produces the helpful mnemonic GOWISELY to help student officers remember this information.

These points were considered in some depth in **Osman v DPP (1999)**. There seemed some doubt as to whether the search in question was voluntary or not and indeed whether there would have been grounds for a **Section 1** search (this was a **Section 60** search – covered later). The case, however, turned on whether the officers provided enough information to Osman. Despite their shoulder numbers being clearly visible this did not satisfy the 'name and station' requirement of **Section 2**. Accordingly when Osman resisted he did not assault the officers in the execution of their duty as the search they were carrying out was unlawful. It should be noted that **Code A** sets out certain circumstances where the ID number and station of an officer will suffice, e.g. in terrorism situations.

Information given after the search

Section 2(6) and **2(7)** require that a notice be left in or on an unattended vehicle that has been searched and specifies what that notice must contain, namely the name and station of the officer, that the vehicle has been searched, that compensation for any damage may be applied for at the police station and that any written record of the search is an entitlement.

Section 3(6) covers the record required of the search itself:

The record of a search of a person or a vehicle

(a) shall state

  (i) the object of the search;

  (ii) the grounds for making it;

  (iii) the date and time when it was made;

  (iv) the place where it was made;

  (v) whether anything, and if so what, was found;

  (vi) whether any, and if so what, injury to a person or damage to property appears to the constable to have resulted from the search; and

 (b) shall identify the constable making it.

Sections 7–9 specify that the record must be made available to the person searched (or who had his vehicle searched) if requested within 12 months of the search.

In contrast to the information which must be given before the search, failure to make a record does not render the search unlawful.

Knowledge Check 2

PC Green has searched Edwina Smith. She formed reasonable grounds from Smith, fitting the description of a person seen fleeing the scene of a burglary a short time before and the time of night. Green asked Smith if a search could be performed. Smith did not say anything as the officer searched her and Green took this as compliance. Green is a member of a police force which requires the officer's name to be embroidered next to the number on the officer's epaulette. Smith is in fact not the offender but happens to resemble her. Nothing is found on her. Green forgot to make a record of the search afterwards.

1. Discuss what information must be provided to the suspect before the search may commence in these circumstances.

2. What would the effect be if the information were not provided?

3. How would your answer differ if it was definitely not a voluntary search?

4. What information should have been on the search record and how long should it have been available for?

5. What is the legal effect of the record having not been made?

The answers are at the end of the chapter.

Road checks

There is in fact a remaining common-law power to set up road checks in order to prevent an anticipated breach of the peace (see later in this volume). But we are concerned here with powers under **PACE**.

Section 4 of **PACE** empowers an officer of the rank of superintendent or above to authorise road checks in writing for up to seven days. In fact the power being exercised is that under **s. 163 Road Traffic Act 1988** which is a general power under which a constable in uniform can stop mechanically propelled vehicles or pedal cycles on a road. What **s. 4** does is allow a series of such stops to be made to ascertain whether a vehicle has in or on it certain persons. These would be persons who have committed, intend to commit or have witnessed an offence (other than a road traffic or vehicle excise (e.g. tax disc) offence) or who is unlawfully at large.

Entry onto premises

From time to time it will be necessary to enter, perhaps by force, premises to execute a warrant of arrest or commitment or in immediate pursuit of someone who is to be arrested or who is unlawfully at large.

For example, a person you have arrested but who breaks free and runs into the nearest dwelling would be unlawfully at large. If a victim stated they had just been seriously assaulted by a man who had gone into the house opposite, the officer would be empowered to enter that house to arrest the person if appropriate.

Section 17 PACE provides a power for entry in such circumstances:

> (1) *Subject to the following provisions of this section, and without, prejudice to any other enactment, a constable may enter and search any premises for the purpose*
>
> > (a) *of executing*
> >
> > > (i) *a warrant of arrest issued in connection with or arising out of criminal proceedings; or*
> > >
> > > (ii) *a warrant of commitment issued under section 76 of the Magistrates' Courts Act 1980;*

SOCPA has amended the following part of the provision such that the old concept of the 'arrestable' offence has been replaced with a requirement for the offence in question to be an 'indictable' one, i.e triable at Crown Court. At first sight this might suggest that the power would no longer exist for 'either way' offences. These are triable either summarily or at Crown Court and include theft and actual bodily harm. These would have been 'arrestable' under the old definition and a power of entry would have existed. It is likely though that the term 'indictable' is not going to be interpreted literally by the courts and therefore would include 'either way' offences because Parliament clearly intended that the powers be liberalised and not further restricted. **Section 17(1)** continues by stating that entry is lawful for the purpose:

> (b) *of arresting a person for an indictable offence;*
>
> (c) *of arresting a person for an offence under*

(i)   section 1 (prohibition of uniforms in connection with political objects) of the
       Public Order Act 1936;

(ii) any enactment contained in sections 6 to 8 or 10 of the Criminal Law Act 1977
       (offences relating to entering and remaining on property(#1));

(iii) section 4 of the Public Order Act 1986 (fear or provocation of violence);

Note

#1 A constable in uniform only (**s. 17(3)**).

 (?) *The new model of training police officers that you are undergoing envisages that
officers will not simply accept the law as it stands on the statute book. Rather that they
will be aware that it is as the courts have interpreted it in case law. It would add weight to
an assessed piece of work or a reflective entry to consider such as the above discussion
around the word 'indictable' as an example of how the meaning of words in statute may
change in practice.*

SOCPA inserts into the following part of this section a power to enter premises in pursuit
of someone who has failed to stop his or her motor vehicle or pedal cycle for a constable.
Alternatively the power would now exist when it is suspected that someone is guilty of
drink driving and has escaped into a dwelling, for instance. These were long-overdue
measures to address loopholes in the law. Under the old provision it was not possible to
chase someone into say, their home, in order to administer a breath test even if they had
driven erratically, abandoned the car on the drive and run into the house. Offenders who
were subsequently over the limit could always say they had a drink once inside to 'steady
their nerves'. This was in practice near impossible to disprove. **Section 17 (1)(c)** now
specifically states that entry is possible in pursuit of someone suspected of:

(iiia) section 4 (driving etc when under influence of drink or drugs) or 163 (failure to
        stop when required to do so by constable in uniform) of the Road Traffic Act 1988;

(iiib) section 27 of the Transport and Works Act 1992 (which relates to offences
        involving drink or drugs);

(iv) section 76 of the Criminal Justice and Public Order Act 1994 (failure to comply
        with interim possession order(#2));

(ca) of arresting, in pursuance of section 32(1A) of the Children and Young Persons Act
        1969, any child or young person who has been remanded or committed to local
        authority accommodation under section 23(1) of that Act;

Note

#2 A constable in uniform only (**s. 17(3)**).

SOCPA also inserted the following provision into the original **s 17 (1) PACE**. It is possible
to enter for the purpose:

(caa) *of arresting a person for an offence to which section 61 of the Animal Health Act
         1981 applies;*

The remaining part of this provision deals with entry to recapture a person or to save life or limb; **s. 17 (1)** again sets out further acceptable purposes of entry including the purpose:

> (cb) *of recapturing any person who is, or is deemed for any purpose to be, unlawfully at large while liable to be detained*
>
> > (i) *in a prison, remand centre, young offender institution or secure training centre, or*
> >
> > (ii) *in pursuance of section 92 of the Powers of Criminal Courts (Sentencing) Act 2000 (dealing with children and young persons guilty of grave crimes), in any other place;*
>
> (d) *of recapturing any person whatever who is unlawfully at large and whom he is pursuing; or*
>
> (e) *of saving life or limb or preventing serious damage to property.*

This last power is extended to PCSOs; see the discussion under **Police Reform Act 2002.**

With the exception of entry to save life or limb, the powers are only exercisable if the constable has reasonable grounds for believing that the person being sought is on the premises (**s. 17(2)**). Furthermore, under that subsection the search can be extended to common areas such as entrance stairwells. This is if the premises consist of multiple dwellings like a block of flats, for instance.

Finally, the entry and search may not be a 'fishing expedition'. It must be limited to the 'extent that is reasonably required for the purpose for which the power of entry is exercised' (**s. 17(4)**). Note that 'belief' is a stricter requirement than the 'suspicion' we have discussed thus far.

REVISION

✓ A constable can enter any premises in order to:
 – execute an arrest/commitment warrant;
 – arrest a person for
  • an indictable offence
  • other specific offences (both only if in 'hot pursuit');
 – recapture of persons;
 – to save life or limb.
✓ The entry must be on 'reasonable belief' the person is there.
✓ The extent of the entry and search is limited to the original purpose.

Searches after arrest

The fact that grounds exist for an arrest does not at all mean that grounds exist for a conviction. To a large extent the arrest of someone has become part of a sifting process. Some 400,000 arrests are made each year with only approximately one-quarter resulting in charges.

Evidence found after the arrest will help decide whether a charge is appropriate or not. There are two main search powers in this area. Immediately on arrest **s. 32 PACE** authorises a constable to search the person arrested and the premises (**Code B** covers premises) that he or she was at that time or immediately before being arrested. This power must be used more or less immediately on the person's arrest. If it is determined that there is a need to return to premises for a search, perhaps after questioning at a police station a **s. 18** power must be used (see later in this section). **Section 32 (1)** and **(2)** specifically state:

> *(1) A constable may search an arrested person, in any case where the person to be searched has been arrested at a place other than a police station, if the constable has reasonable grounds for believing that the arrested person may present a danger to himself or others.*

> *(2) Subject to subsections (3) to (5) below, a constable shall also have power in any such case*

>> *(a) to search the arrested person for anything*

>>> *(i) which he might use to assist him to escape from lawful custody; or*

>>> *(ii) which might be evidence relating to an offence; and*

Note that throughout these provisions **SOCPA** has amended this legislation to remove the old 'arrestable offence' term:

>> *(b) if the offence for which he has been arrested is an indictable offence, to enter and search any premises in which he was when arrested or immediately before he was arrested for evidence relating to the offence.*

Consequently this power would not exist if the arrest had been made for a summary offence such as a minor traffic matter. It will be seen though that arrests for these offences are to become even rarer when we consider the new arrest powers discussed later in this section. The qualifying matters mentioned in **s. 32(2)** above are from **s. 32 (3)** to **(5)**:

> *(3) The power to search conferred by subsection (2) above is only a power to search to the extent that is reasonably required for the purpose of discovering any such thing or any such evidence.*

> *(4) The powers conferred by this section to search a person are not to be construed as authorising a constable to require a person to remove any of his clothing in public other than an outer coat, jacket or gloves but they do authorise a search of a person's mouth.*

> *(5) A constable may not search a person in the exercise of the power conferred by subsection (2)(a) above unless he has reasonable grounds for believing that the person to be searched may have concealed on him anything for which a search is permitted under that paragraph.*

Student officers will recognise the requirement to have 'reasonable grounds' to believe the items may be found on the suspect. The term has been met in previous discussions. We have also already encountered restrictions on what may be searched in a public place. The section here specifically authorises an oral search, though.

The power to search premises is subject to the usual proviso that reasonable grounds must exist to believe evidence will be found there. It is also limited to where a person was on or just before arrest and any common areas such as, say, a lobby in the suspect's block of flats (**s. 32 (6)** and **(7)**). The constable may seize items found if there are reasonable grounds to believe they are evidence, may assist an escape or may injure, unless they are subject to legal privilege (**ss. (8)** and **(9)**). The power conferred by **s. 43 Terrorism Act 2000** (see later) is not affected by this provision.

Section 18 PACE is available to officers to allow premises to be searched which may not be within the ambit of **s. 32**. Consider the situation in which a suspect is apprehended at her place of work. There would be no power under **s. 32** to search her home address unless she lived in very close proximity and had just come from there. **Section 18** allows the constable to search a premises 'occupied or controlled' by the suspect. The section actually provides:

(1) *Subject to the following provisions of this section, a constable may enter and search any premises occupied or controlled by a person who is under arrest for an indictable offence, if he has reasonable grounds for suspecting that there is on the premises evidence, other than items subject to legal privilege, that relates*

(a) *to that offence; or*

(b) *to some other indictable offence which is connected with or similar to that offence.*

(2) *A constable may seize and retain anything for which he may search under subsection (1) above.*

(3) *The power to search conferred by subsection (1) above is only a power to search to the extent that is reasonably required for the purpose of discovering such evidence.*

Student officers will probably recognise the ethos here which is to provide a power of search but limits the possibilities for its abuse. What would be undesirable in a democratic society would be the situation were a constable could arrest for the most trivial of reasons and then conduct a full-scale search of the suspect's home, place of work and any other premises vaguely connected with him or her. This would be very easy to abuse to the point of virtually allowing random searches. What is also different in this power compared to **s. 32** is the need to obtain appropriate authorisation in writing or at least to inform retrospectively. There will also here be limited occasions where the identity of the officers need only be disclosed as their ID numbers and station (**Code B para. 2.9**). **Section 18** continues:

(4) *Subject to subsection (5) below, the powers conferred by this section may not be exercised unless an officer of the rank of inspector or above has authorised them in writing.*

(5) *A constable may conduct a search under subsection (1)*

(a) *before the person is taken to a police station or released on bail under section 30A, and*

(b) *without obtaining an authorisation under subsection (4), if the condition in subsection (5A) is satisfied.*

(5A) *The condition is that the presence of the person at a place (other than a police station) is necessary for the effective investigation of the offence.*

(6) If a constable conducts a search by virtue of subsection (5) above, he shall inform an officer of the rank of inspector or above that he has made the search as soon as practicable after he has made it.

The net result of these subsections is that an officer may carry out a **s. 18** search without prior written authorisation and before a person is taken to a police station if it is necessary to have the suspect present and to do the search immediately to prevent vital evidence being lost. This might be the case if it is necessary, say, to have the suspect guide the officers round a particularly expansive piece of ground he owns or to provide the means of access if parts of the building are inaccessible, say by a combination lock, etc.

Code B at **para. 2.3** referring to **s. 23 PACE** gives guidance as to what a premises actually is for the purposes of the forgoing sections, 'places, vehicles, vessels, aircraft, hovercraft, tents, moveable structures' as well as certain types of offshore structures are all included.

REVISION

✓ On arrest a constable can search the person and premises that the arrested person was at or just before arrest (s 32 PACE 1984).

✓ On arrest a constable can search the premises 'occupied or controlled' by the arrested person. Authorisation from an inspector must be obtained, preferably before the search (s 18 PACE 1984).

✓ Relevant material may be seized by the constable.

For the sake of completeness it should be noted that an oral search is non-intimate and can be conducted as part of the custody process under **s. 54** along with strip searches. **Section 55** requires authorisation before any intimate search is carried out. This means a search of any body orifice other than the mouth.

Additionally there is a wide power of seizure under **s. 19 PACE**.

ACTIVITY

Form a small discussion group with fellow student officers. Consider the following scenario.

Jeffery Evans is a stockbroker. There has been an accusation of a serious sexual offence at last night's office party corroborated by witnesses. Officers arrive at Evans' firm to arrest him mid-morning.

Discuss:

- who may be searched;

- to what extent they may be searched including any authorisations;

- where they may be searched and to what extent.

Ensure that relevant act and section are used in your discussion and, if appropriate, case law.

Please note that this exercise is not meant to be judged against criteria indicating right or wrong answers. It should be conducted 'open book' and is designed to facilitate the free flow of knowledge and ideas amongst peers.

Arrest by police constables

Colleagues with longer service will be more familiar with the older terminology of **PACE** such as 'arrestable offences' and 'general arrest conditions'. These terms have been fully super-seded. As from 1 January 2006 **SOCPA 2005** has introduced a completely new set of criteria for arrest. Popular fiction and TV programmes would give a different impression but in fact the presumption conventionally is that it is preferable to proceed by way of summons, with arrests being the resort if a summons is impractical or inappropriate. This has a logical base in arguments about civil liberties and practical issues like cost and police resources. A much greater burden is placed on these by arrest than by any other method of proceeding.

The majority of police powers of arrest were contained in **s. 24 PACE** and this continues to be the case. A new **s. 24** has been substituted by **s. 110 SOCPA** though. A constable now has powers to arrest for any criminal offence; there are, however, conditions. It is these conditions which render the change controversial in some quarters. Interpreted one way, the police now have draconian new powers to arrest offenders for offences large and small. Taking into consideration the conditions however, the effect may be to actually allow some offenders to be proceeded against by way of summons, who might hitherto have been arrested. According to the new **s. 24**:

> (1) A constable may arrest without a warrant
>
>   (a) anyone who is about to commit an offence;
>
>   (b) anyone who is in the act of committing an offence;
>
>   (c) anyone whom he has reasonable grounds for suspecting to be about to commit an offence;
>
>   (d) anyone whom he has reasonable grounds for suspecting to be committing an offence.

Put another way, police constables may arrest anyone actually breaking the criminal law or who is about to. He or she may also arrest anyone where there are reasonable grounds to suspect they are actually breaking the criminal law or are about to. This is if the PC knows an offence is being committed or is about to be.

An example of these situations might be where a police officer witnesses an assault per-sonally or sees a person walking up to a dwelling window with a crowbar late at night. **Section 24** goes on to state:

> (2) If a constable has reasonable grounds for suspecting that an offence has been committed, he may arrest without a warrant anyone whom he has reasonable grounds to suspect of being guilty of it.

Thereby a PC may arrest if he or she merely suspects that an offence has been committed with-out being sure of it. This criterion would be satisfied by a PC witnessing a man damaging a car. When questioned he says that it is his own but the PC knows he is having an ongoing dispute with his son over debts owed. The PC suspects the car belongs to the man's son whereupon criminal damage would have been committed. Further enquiries are obviously necessary but for now, subject to the forthcoming discussion, the man may be arrested.

Section 24(3) goes on to provide for who may be arrested:

If an offence has been committed, a constable may arrest without a warrant

(a) *anyone who is guilty of the offence;*

(b) *anyone whom he has reasonable grounds for suspecting to be guilty of it.*

There now follows the all important qualifications, the criteria which must be met before an arrest for an offence can be made. We must consider **s. 24(4)**:

But the power of summary arrest conferred by subsection (1), (2) or (3) is exercisable only if the constable has reasonable grounds for believing that for any of the reasons mentioned in subsection (5) it is necessary to arrest the person in question.

It is submitted that Parliament intended for police officers to have a power of arrest for any criminal matter but that was to be used only when absolutely necessary. The criteria which would make the arrest necessary are spelt out in **s. 24(5)**:

(a) *to enable the name of the person in question to be ascertained (in the case where the constable does not know, and cannot readily ascertain, the person's name, or has reasonable grounds for doubting whether a name given by the person as his name is his real name);*

(b) *correspondingly as regards the person's address;*

(c) *to prevent the person in question*

(i) *causing physical injury to himself or any other person;*

(ii) *suffering physical injury;*

(iii) *causing loss of or damage to property;*

(iv) *committing an offence against public decency (subject to subsection (6)(#1);* or

(v) *causing an unlawful obstruction of the highway;*

(d) *to protect a child or other vulnerable person from the person in question;*

(e) *to allow the prompt and effective investigation of the offence or of the conduct of the person in question;*

(f) *to prevent any prosecution for the offence from being hindered by the disappearance of the person in question.*

Note

#1 If members of the public cannot reasonably be expected to avoid the person.

Officers with some years service may recognise the old 'general arrest conditions' from the now repealed **s. 25** power within this subsection.

The conditions which render an arrest necessary then may be summarised as:

• Child or vulnerable person likely to be harmed.

• Obstruction of the highway likely.

- Physical injury or to the suspect or anyone else is likely.

- Public decency is likely to be offended against (assuming people cannot avoid passing near him or her).

- Loss or damage to property is likely.

- Address given is false or it's truthfulness suspect/not easily checked.

- Name given is false or it's truthfulness suspect/not easily checked.

- Effective investigation of the offence will be hindered otherwise.

- To prevent the person 'disappearing'.

The first letters of these criteria make the mnemonic COP PLANET, which may help you remember them This was based on a similar mnemonic in use for some years in police training schools to aid with learning of the old 'general arrest conditions'.

An additional code, **Code G,** has been written as guidance for these new arrest powers. **Para. 1.3** outlines the general ethos of the new powers:

> *The use of the power must be fully justified and officers exercising the power should consider if the necessary objectives can be met by other, less intrusive means. Arrest must never be used simply because it can be used. Absence of justification for exercising the powers of arrest may lead to challenges should the case proceed to court. When the power of arrest is exercised it is essential that it is exercised in a non-discriminatory and proportionate manner.*

Further, the code at **para. 2.8** outlines what the constable must take into account before making the decision to arrest.

> *In considering the individual circumstances, the constable must take into account the situation of the victim, the nature of the offence, the circumstances of the suspect and the needs of the investigative process.*

The kinds of criteria which will give rise to the need to arrest are also shown as examples in **Code G**. The list is not exhaustive but might include such matters as where there are reasonable grounds to believe that the person:

- has made false statements;

- has made statements which cannot be readily verified;

- has presented false evidence;

- may steal or destroy evidence;

- may make contact with co-suspects or conspirators;

- may intimidate or threaten or make contact with witnesses.

There may well be a need to arrest if it is necessary to gain evidence from questioning or a need to:

- enter and search any premises occupied or controlled by a person (see **s. 18** discussed earlier);

- search the person (see **s. 32** discussed earlier);

- prevent contact with others;

- take fingerprints, footwear impressions, samples or photographs of the suspect.

Code G also gives examples in relation to **s. 24(5)(f)** of a person who is likely to fail to attend court if not arrested and for whom street bail is likely to provide insufficient guarantee of their appearance at court. Such a person may be arrested.

Code G at **para. 3.1** goes on to reaffirm the information which must be given on arrest. An arrested person:

> *must be cautioned before any questions about an offence, or further questions if the answers provide the grounds for suspicion, are put to them if either the suspect's answers or silence, (i.e. failure or refusal to answer or answer satisfactorily) may be given in evidence to a court in a prosecution.*

This restates the need to caution a person if it is likely their answers to questioning could conceivably form evidence submitted to a court. This could equally be true about a minor traffic offence as it could about a murder.

A person need not be cautioned for all matters. For example, a caution would not be necessary merely to:

- establish their identity or ownership of any vehicle;

- obtain information in accordance with any relevant statutory requirement;

- further the proper and effective conduct of a search;

- seek verification of a written record.

(?) *It is inconceivable that student officers will not need to make a SOLAP or reflective entry on an arrest without warrant. Such an entry would be that much richer if it seeks to make some link with the arrest powers of old and comment on the development. Alternatively the thinking behind the liberalisation of these powers could be discussed briefly.*

REVISION

✓ A constable may arrest anyone without warrant under s. 24 PACE 1984 that:
- the officer knows is committing an offence or about to commit an offence;
- even if the constable only suspects but does not know the activity concerned is an offence;

✓ The arrest must be justifiable. Acceptable reasons are:
- child or vulnerable person likely to be harmed;
- obstruction of the highway likely;
- physical injury or to the suspect or anyone else is likely;
- public decency is likely to be offended against (assuming people cannot avoid passing near him or her);
- loss or damage to property is likely;
- address given is false or its truthfulness suspect/not easily checked;
- name given is false or its truthfulness suspect/not easily checked;
- effective investigation of the offence will be hindered otherwise;
- to prevent the person disappearing.

✓ Code G provides detailed guidance on these new arrest powers.

Section 26 PACE lists powers which are preserved from other acts of Parliament. This is where a power of arrest is given for use in a particular circumstance, usually within certain restrictions. Some preserved powers have been repealed. The list now comprises powers to arrest under the:

- **Air Force Act 1955 s. 186 and 190B** (deserters etc. from the RAF).

- **Army Act 1955 s. 186 and 190B** (deserters etc. from the Army).

- **Bail Act 1976 s. 7** (breach of bail).

- **Children and Young Persons Act 1969 s. 32** (absentees from local authority care).

- **Immigration Act 1971 s. 28A, Sch. 2 para.17, 24, and 33, Sch. 3 para. 7** (arrest of illegal immigrants by immigration officer or constable).

- **Mental Health Act 1983 s. 18, 35(10), 36(8), 38(7), 136(1) and 138** (arrest or recapture of those severely mentally ill).

- **Naval Discipline Act 1957 ss. 104 and 105** (deserters etc. from the Navy).

- **Prison Act 1952 s. 49** (abscondees from jail).

- **Repatriation of Prisoners Act 1984, s. 5(5)** (transferring prisoners in and out of the UK).

- **Representation of the People Act 1983, Schedule 1, para. 36** (impersonation of another person entitled to vote at a local or national election).

- **Visiting Forces Act 1952 s. 13** (deserters etc. from foreign military forces).

Arrests by other persons

Under **PACE** and indeed before ever the concept of the modern constable was born, there have been so called 'any person' powers. These form the basis of 'citizens' arrests' as they are often called in the popular media. Arrests by well-meaning members of the public are comparatively rare but do happen. Student officers should be aware of the extent of these arrest powers should they be called to such an incident. Unfortunately there are cases of members of the public sometimes unwittingly overstepping their powers and themselves being charged with assault, even kidnap. Some people's jobs involve making citizens' arrests on a semi-regular basis, such as store detectives and sometimes security guards and door supervisors.

Additionally there are now quite a number of government law enforcement agencies whose employees are not constables, such as the Asset Recovery Agency, Department of Work and Pensions (benefit fraud) and the planned uniformed border patrol force. In many incidences these people have arrest powers specifically designated to them for use within their job roles such as immigration and customs officers. Arrests made outside these specifically designated situations would be very rare but would have to happen as citizens' arrests.

The police themselves have a number of roles previously given only to constables which are now done by uniformed civilians. Perhaps the most prominent of those is the police community support officer (PCSO) brought into being by the **Police Reform Act 2002** (see later discussion). These officers have the power of a constable in certain limited circumstances, for instance to stop and search when in the company of a police constable. They also have special powers of detention for a limited time under the legislation where a chief officer designates. PCSOs also have 'any person' powers by virtue of being citizens and this cannot be removed from them. Force policy may dictate if, when and in what circumstances these powers may be used on duty however.

The new 'any person' powers are inserted by **s.110 SOCPA 2005** into PACE and set out in **s. 24A**:

(1) *A person other than a constable may arrest without a warrant*

    (a) *anyone who is in the act of committing an indictable offence;*

    (b) *anyone whom he has reasonable grounds for suspecting to be committing an indictable offence.*

(2) *Where an indictable offence has been committed, a person other than a constable may arrest without a warrant*

    (a) *anyone who is guilty of the offence;*

    (b) *anyone whom he has reasonable grounds for suspecting to be guilty of it.*

Thus far these powers seem to have a great deal in common with the constabulary powers. One of the significant limitations though is that the offence must be 'indictable'. As per a similar restriction in **s. 17 PACE** discussed earlier, it is arguable that this term must include 'either way' offences. Otherwise at a stroke Parliament would be depriving every store detective of the ability to apprehend shoplifters, theft being triable 'either way'.

The arrest can only happen if certain other criteria are true. These mirror the thinking in **s. 24**. Under **s. 24A(3)** the criteria are that:

    (a) *the person making the arrest has reasonable grounds for believing that for any of the reasons mentioned in subsection (4) it is necessary to arrest the person in question; and*

    (b) *it appears to the person making the arrest that it is not reasonably practicable for a constable to make it instead.*

(4) *The reasons are to prevent the person in question –*

    (a) *causing physical injury to himself or any other person;*

    (b) *suffering physical injury;*

    (c) *causing loss of or damage to property; or*

    (d) *making off before a constable can assume responsibility for him.*

The primary concern of Parliament here seems to have been to limit the situations where a citizen will feel morally obligated to make an arrest. He or she is never obligated by law of course in the way that a constable is. It is submitted here though that Parliament has placed a rather unreasonable burden on the citizen to know what is and what is not an indictable offence. By inference, additionally knowledge of what is meant by an 'either way' offence also is required of a member of the public, all without any legal training in most instances.

Knowledge Check 3

1. Dave Douglas has witnessed a man putting chocolate bars in his coat pocket without paying for them in Dave's shop.

   In what circumstances can he use his 'any person' powers to arrest the man?

2. PC Lenehan is called to the scene in (1).

   Explain the decision-making process that Lenehan will have to undertake to decide whether to arrest the man herself.

3. Lenehan's sergeant has advised her to arrest in as many circumstances as possible when dealing with shoplifting because sometimes the force legal staff or the CPS do not proceed with a shoplifting summons where the amounts are trivial. Is this a reason to justify arrest under **SOCAP 2005**?

The answers are at the end of the chapter.

There are of course many more sections to **PACE** and much more detail to the codes. The purpose of this section, however, is to provide a level of knowledge that the student officer will need for effective patrol duties. It is recommended that this knowledge is continually updated on these powers throughout your career. Force training departments will provide regular paper updates and training opportunities as legislation changes. Further updates can be obtained by regular visits to the Home Office website listed at the end of this chapter.

Other police powers arising from common law or other legislation are covered in the relevant chapter elsewhere in this volume.

Suggested research

There have been a number of high-profile murders where the victim has been black since Stephen Lawrence. Visit the Home Office website **http://police.homeoffice.gov.uk/community-policing/race-diversity/stephen-lawrence-inquiry** to view the legacy of the enquiry into Stephen Lawrence's murder. Research other more recent murders such as Damilola Taylor and Anthony Walker. Consider what lessons have been learnt and what work still has to be done with respect to the development of police powers and investigation in the light of those cases.

Further reading

It would be useful to read up on how the police have developed over time as an organisation. This provides a backdrop to how their powers have developed:

Crawford, A, Lister, S, Blackburn, S and Burnett, J (2005) *Plural policing – The mixed economy of visible patrols in England and Wales.* Bristol: The Policy Press.

Emsley C (1997) *Crime and policing in Europe since c. 1750.* Oxford: Oxford University Press.

Graef, R (1990) *Talking blues: The police in their own words.* London: Collins Harvill.

Specific detail of police powers outside the scope of this chapter can be found in:

English, J and Card, R (2005) *Police law* (9th edn). Oxford: Oxford University Press.

Sampson, F (2007) *Blackstone's police manual, Volume 4 – General police duties* (9th edn). Oxford: Oxford University Press.

Some useful discussion around the criminal justice system and crime and society can be found in:

Hale, C, Hayward, K, Wahidin, A and Wincup, E (2005) *Criminology.* Oxford: Oxford University Press.

McConville, M and Wilson, G (eds) (2002) *The criminal justice process,* Oxford: Oxford University Press.

Useful reports:

'Scarman':

The Brixton Disorders 10–12 April 1981, Report of an Inquiry by the Rt. Hon. The Lord Scarman, OBE (HMSO).

'MacPherson':

The Stephen Lawrence Inquiry, Report of an Inquiry by Sir William MacPherson of Cluny (Stationery Office).

Useful websites

The MacPherson Report:

www.archive.official-documents.co.uk/document/cm42/4262/4262.htm

The original 1981 BBC TV news item on the Scarman report including footage of the riots and interviews:

http://news.bbc.co.uk/onthisday/hi/dates/stories/november/25/newsid_2546000/2546233.stm

Home Office police practitioners' website:

http://police.homeoffice.gov.uk

Legislation:

www.opsi.gov.uk

Case-law and legislation databases:

www.westlaw.com* (a legal database)

www.lexis-nexis.com* (a legal database)

www.pnld.co.uk* (a police service specific database of case law and statute)

* Likely to be available through the virtual learning environment (VLE) which supports your course/training.

Answers

Knowledge Check 1

(a) PC Prajapati would be well advised to speak to the men before proceeding further. Even if the item they are discussing is a discarded purse they may have just picked it up. Without further enquiry or established facts there are arguably no grounds for a search. A name-check revealing recent previous relevant convictions or a smell of alcohol on the breath of one of the men or scratches/torn clothing, combined with the purse and description, would be grounds though.

(b) In this case the officer should consider if the appearance part of the description may be inaccurate. If the item thrown resembled a purse but cannot be found easily, this, coupled with the appearance may constitute reasonable grounds. A few questions to the man should be used to establish where he has walked from and to buy time to look him over for marks from a struggle and smell his breath. If these factors are found then this combination would almost definitely form grounds. If the item is found and is a purse then this plus his appearance alone would likely form grounds in the alternative. It should be borne in mind that under **Rice v Connolly (1966)** any refusal to answer questions would have no legal implications at this stage but might increase suspicion.

(c) It is arguable that the previous convictions would have no bearing here. The decision would rest on whether the apparent desire to put distance between himself and the officer was marked enough to form reasonable grounds when looked at in conjunction with appearance. For safety's sake again, if possible, some questions to establish any of the factors discussed in (a) or (b) would be wise before commencing the search.

Knowledge Check 2

1. Revisit the GOWISELY mnemonic. **Section 2 PACE 1984** specifies that an officer shall take reasonable steps to give the following information to the suspect before the search commences. Green must give the grounds for the search, object of the search, produce her warrant card (but only if requested here), state her identity and her station (the stitched name is unlikely to suffice as it is dark and anyway does not specify her station), entitlement to a record, the power exercised (i.e. **Section 1 PACE 1984**) and that 'you are detained for the purposes of a search'.

2. The failure to provide the information would render the search unlawful entitling the suspect to resist and possibly to compensation for assault and/or false imprisonment.

3. The answer would not differ if the search was not voluntary except in so far as if the search was violently resisted the information in (1) would not have to be given.

4. **Section 3 (6) PACE 1984** specifies that the record must contain the object of the search, the grounds for making it, the date and time when it was made, the place where it was made, whether anything, and if so what, was found, whether any, and if so what, injury to a person or damage to property appears to the constable to have resulted from the search; and must identify the constable making it.

5. There is no legal effect but it may leave the officer open to disciplinary proceedings.

Knowledge Check 3

1   Dave may have grounds for use of his citizen's powers. The man has committed an offence, theft, which can but not necessarily will be tried on indictment at Crown Court. Therefore arguably the power exists under **s. 24A PACE 1984**. The question mark will be over whether the conditions in **s. 24A(3)** are met. The most likely one is that the man would make off before police arrive. Clearly this would depend on circumstances. It would be far more true of a young man than it would be of an elderly wheelchair-bound man.

2.   PC Lenehan's powers emanate from **s. 24 PACE 1984**. Using her discretion and mindful of the guidance in **Code G** Lenehan must consider first if an offence has taken place, which, for our purposes here, it has. It matters not whether it is triable on indictment, 'either way' or summarily. Lenehan has reasonable grounds for suspecting that the man has committed it from the allegation made and the chocolate bars which she can search for under **s.1 PACE 1984** there and then. The more important problem is whether an arrest can be justi-fied. Considering the requirements in **s. 24(5)** this will depend on what is known about the suspected thief. If his identity and address are known from previous dealings and he has no history of absconding whilst on bail the likely way forward is by way of summons or even fixed penalty notice. If none of the other criteria in that subsection apply then there is no need to arrest him. Lenehan should caution the man before questioning him nevertheless.

3.   The sergeant's advice does not describe a valid reason for arresting under **s. 24(5)** and infringes on **Code G**. As the code says at **para. 1.3**. an arrest on this basis could lead to a legal challenge in court. It could also lead to disciplinary proceedings. It would be Lenehan who faced that challenge and those proceedings, not the sergeant.

4 Other police powers

(?) *Remember this symbol indicates that the material might be useful for your Student Officer Learning and Assessment Programme (SOLAP) portfolio or any attached reflective practice record you are required to make.*

Underpinning knowledge towards Patrol Officer NOS:

1A1, 1A4, 2A1, 2C1, 2C2, 2C3, 2C4, 2G2, 2G4, 2H2, 2I1, 2I2, 2J1, 2J2, 2K2

and PCSO NOS:

1A1, 1A4, 2A1, 2C1, 2C2, 2C3, 2C4, 2C5, 2J1, 2J2

For further information on these NOS, which are also Policing Level 3 and 4 NVQ unit titles, refer to Appendix 1 to this volume.

We have dealt with the main statutory powers that police have in the last chapter. The purpose here is to round up the remaining powers that exist under common law and statutes other than **PACE 1984** and **SOCPA 2005**.

We will be dealing with powers related to:

- terrorism;
- bail (including street bail);
- football;
- **Vagrancy Act 1824**;
- common law.

Non-SOCPA powers

By the end of this section you will be able to:

- describe the main counter-terrorism powers;
- describe powers under the Bail Act 1976, street bail, football and vagrancy powers;
- apply your knowledge to some multiple-choice questions.

Terrorism

This is obviously a vast area of existing and emerging legislation and case law. For our purposes the concentration will be on the stop-and-search powers and cordons.

Section 44 Terrorism Act 2000 allows an officer of the rank of Assistant Chief Constable or equivalent to designate an area such that stop and search of persons and vehicles may be carried out for the prevention or detection of terrorist acts. The designation if approved by the Home Secretary can last up to 28 days. This amounts to the power to do random stop and searches in a given area for that period. Accordingly it is used only in extreme cases.

Once the designation is in place, constables in uniform can carry out stop and searches. As for stop and search under **PACE 1984** described in the previous chapter though, they must be carried out in accordance with **PACE Code A**.

Should the preventative measures described above prove insufficient it may be necessary to exercise powers under the **Terrorism Act 2000** to aid the investigation of terrorism. Such an investigation is defined under **s. 32**:

In this Act 'terrorist investigation' means an investigation of –

(a) the commission, preparation or instigation of acts of terrorism;

(b) an act which appears to have been done for the purposes of terrorism;

(c) the resources of a proscribed organisation;

(d) the possibility of making an order [proscribing an organisation as terrorist], or

(e) the commission, preparation or instigation of an offence under this Act.

Under **s. 33** the police can set up cordons around the area where the investigation is to take place. Once the cordon is in place a constable in uniform may:

- order a person in a cordoned area to leave it immediately or to leave premises which are wholly or partly in or adjacent to a cordoned area;

- order the driver or person in charge of a vehicle in a cordoned area to move it from the area immediately or the constable may arrange for the removal of the vehicle;

- arrange for the movement of a vehicle within a cordoned area;

- prohibit or restrict access to a cordoned area by pedestrians or vehicles.

A person disobeying instructions from a constable commits an offence under this section.

For further detail of the offences that can be committed under this and other related legislation such as the **Explosive Substances Act 1883, Anti-Terrorism, Crime and Security Act 2001, Prevention of Terrorism Act 2005** and **Terrorism Act 2006,** see the further reading section at the end of the chapter.

Bail (including street bail)

The courts mostly deal with bail although a custody officer may release a person arrested on police bail pending further enquiries. The **Bail Act 1976** deals with bail, and there are often conditions attached by the courts. These can be for instance not to associate with certain persons or to sign at a police station at certain intervals. A person in breach of their bail conditions can be arrested and brought before the courts. A court can issue an arrest warrant, which is either backed for bail, or not. If it is not, the person arrested cannot be bailed but must be brought before the court. This often happens when people fail to appear at court, for example.

In contrast to the US system, in the UK bail rarely involves the exchange of any substantial sums of money. In practice it is a promise by the accused to return at a certain time or date to court effectively on pain of imprisonment. If bail is not considered suitable, such as for a murder case (except in exceptional circumstances), a person will be placed on remand to await their court date. Until that time they will be imprisoned but as an innocent person they will have certain privileges including not having to wear prison uniform or do work. They are often housed in prisons local to their home address as well.

Under the age-old presumption of innocence and now human rights considerations in general, bail will normally be granted. This is unless there are compelling reasons why a person should be remanded.

Street bail on the other hand is a relatively new innovation. The **Bail Act** does not apply here. Under the **Criminal Justice Act 2003 (Commencement No.2 and savings Provisions) Order 2004** the provisions of **s. 4 Criminal Justice Act 2003** were brought into force. This adds **s. 30A, 30B, 30C** and **30D** to **PACE 1984**. By this enactment a constable now has power to grant an arrested person immediate bail at the scene of arrest. This provision is designed to relieve pressures on custody suites and is obviously intended for cases were there is little expectation that the person will not answer bail.

By **s. 30A(1)** to **(3)**:

(1) A constable may release on bail a person who is arrested or taken into custody...

(2) A person may be released on bail under subsection (1) at any time before he arrives at a police station.

(3) A person released on bail under subsection (1) must be required to attend a police station.

A constable can impose conditions on street bail (other than to reside at a bail hostel). A constable may not take any security (i.e. money) or promise of money to secure the bail from the accused.

Section 30B sets out the written notice to be given to the accused and **s. 30D** empowers a constable to arrest for failure to appear at a police station.

This is as yet a relatively little used power as, perhaps understandably, police are reluctant to arrest and then release a suspect. Most PCs have been schooled in the early years of **PACE** in the importance of procedure and bringing every suspect to a designated police station once they had been arrested. This is a hard habit to break but only with consistent use will the desired result of reducing police man-hours spent in custody suites be achieved.

Football

We can afford to take a fairly broad-brush approach to this topic. As a student officer you would not normally be undertaking the policing of a football event except under the supervision of a senior rank. You will be briefed on the offences that you will need to be aware of. Essentially incidents such as the Hillsborough tragedy in 1989 and other football-related violence added weight to calls for specific legislation extending police powers to curb disorder in and around football matches. The key pieces of legislation are the:

- **Sporting Events (Control of Alcohol) Act 1985**

- **Football Spectators Act 1989**

- **Football (Offences) Act 1991**

Sporting Events (Control of Alcohol) Act 1985

(?) *It is a common misconception that hooliganism is a solely football-related phenomenon and a British one. University research has indicated that often the violence is a manifestation of a violent sub-culture where the offenders use violence routinely in all areas of their lives. Research in Italy indicates there may be loose political affiliations amongst the rival groups driving the violence. Another aspect of the research is that hooliganism is not class specific. Statistics tell us that it is an offence overwhelmingly committed by white males, however – all issues worth reflecting on.*

This legislation relates to designated football matches. The term 'regulated' is also used in the legislation. It will be apparent in your briefing before policing an event whether it is designated or not. **Section 1** states it is an offence to be in possession of or causing or permitting the presence of alcohol on a public service vehicle or railway passenger vehicle going to or from such an event. It is offence to be drunk on such a vehicle under this section also. **Section 1A** extends these offences to any motor vehicle in the same circumstances; the driver can commit the offence even if the passengers have the alcohol.

Section 2 prohibits the possession of alcohol when entering or trying to enter a designated sports ground, anywhere from which the match can be directly viewed or being drunk in the same circumstances. Fireworks, flares and similar objects are prohibited by **s. 2A.**

Football Spectators Act 1989

This legislation introduces a power of detention rather than arrest. Banning orders may be made by a court to prevent someone attending a football match if there are sufficient grounds. If in relation to a regulated/designated match a constable in uniform:

(a) *has reasonable grounds for suspecting that* [the person has at any time caused or contributed to any violence or disorder] *and;*

(b) *has reasonable grounds to believe that making a banning order in his case would help to prevent violence or disorder at or in connection with any regulated football matches.*

*(2) The constable may detain the person in his custody (whether there or elsewhere) until he has decided whether or not to issue a notice under **s. 21B** below, and shall give the person his reasons for detaining him in writing.*

The person could still be arrested if necessary. The power is limited to four hours (six with the authorisation of an inspector) and is for the purposes of serving a **s. 21B** notice as described below:

(1) ... if authorised to do so by an officer of at least the rank of inspector...

(2) The constable may give the person a notice in writing requiring him-

(a) to appear before a magistrates' court at a time, or between the times, specified in the notice,

(b) not to leave England and Wales before that time (or the later of those times), and

if necessary surrender his passport. The purpose of the appearance is to request the magistrates grant a banning order. If there is any doubt the person will appear at court, they may be arrested under this section.

Football (Offences) Act 1991

This legislation covers misbehaviour at a designated football match. The specific offences are:

- throwing missiles at the pitch, players or spectators (**s. 2**);
- indecent or racist chanting (**s. 3**);
- pitch invasion (**s. 4**).

Each creates a summary only offence.

ACTIVITY

Visit the Home Office site at: **http://police.homeoffice.gov.uk**. Search or follow the links for the press release dated 23 October 2006. Have football-related offences fallen or risen recently? To what are any changes in the figures attributed?

Clearly there are more football offences that we have not had time to cover here, such as those under the **Football Disorder (Amendment) Act 2002,** etc. Further reading is provided at the end of the chapter for those wishing to research further.

Vagrancy Act 1824

The Act contains a splendid example of the language of the time and is typically verbose and almost rambling. Most of the Act no longer applies but one important offence remains, that of being 'found on enclosed premises'. It is useful where there is evidence short of burglary but the person creates a great deal of suspicion as to why they are on private premises at all.

In summary, the offence is committed by every person found in or upon any dwelling house, warehouse, coach-house, stable or out-house, enclosed yard, garden or area for any unlawful purpose.

Clearly this latter point is likely to be the difficulty: the constable would need to show that an unlawful purpose was apparent. This arguably does leave the field open for a considerable amount of subjectivity by the officer.

It is worth considering how compatible this offence is with the presumption of innocence under **Art. 6 ECHR**.

Common law

Really the only power remaining under common law is arrest for breach of the peace. Not beloved of custody officers, it also does not carry with it any punishment in a real sense. It normally results in a bind-over or promise not to reoffend given to the magistrates. Nevertheless it may have its uses to remove a person from the scene of potential disorder where no actual offences are apparent but a breach of the peace is feared.

Breach of the peace is:

- where harm is actually done; or

- is likely to be done to a person;

- or harm is likely to be done or actually done in his presence to his property; or

- if a person is genuinely in fear of harm to himself or his property from assault (see Chapter 6), riot, affray (See Chapter 10) or unlawful assembly or other disturbance.

There are actually three situations where any person, not just a constable, may take action:

- where the breach is committed in their presence;

- to prevent a breach in the immediate future;

- where a breach has happened and it may happen again.

REVISION

✓ Cordons and stop and search for terrorism offences – Terrorism Act 2000.
✓ Bail – Bail Act 1976, Street bail – Criminal Justice Act 2003.
✓ Football offences – Sporting Events (Control of Alcohol) Act 1985, Football Spectators Act 1989 and Football (Offences) Act 1991.
✓ Found on enclosed premises – Vagrancy Act 1824.
✓ Breach of the Peace – Common Law.

Knowledge Check 1

1. Dave West has been found on a church roof, which has lead on it, with a large screw-driver and rope. Assuming there is not enough evidence for burglary, can he be arrested?

    (a) No there is no offence

    (b) Yes for **s. 5 Public Order Act 1986**

    (c) Yes for attempted theft

    (d) Yes for **s. 4 Vagrancy Act 1824.**

2. PC Mistry is stopping and searching people in a designated area under **s. 44 Terrorism Act 2000**. The searches are to be conducted under:

    (a) The **Terrorism Act 2006**

    (b) **PACE Code A**

    (c) **PACE Code B**

    (d) **PACE Code G.**

3. Mistry is later policing a football match. She notices that a car carrying would-be spectators to the match (which is designated) has cans of lager on the back parcel shelf. Mistry may take action under the:

    (a) **Sporting Events (Control of Alcohol) Act 1985**

    (b) **Football Spectators Act 1989**

    (c) **Football (Offences) Act 1991**

    (d) All of the above.

The answers are at the end of the chapter.

Suggested research

Leicester University has done some leading work on the study of football hooliganism. Visit their site at **www.le.ac.uk** and follow the links or search for information on this research. Look at what publications have been made and look them up in your local, college or university library.

Further reading

Specific detail of police powers outside the scope of this chapter can be found in:

English, J and Card, R (2005) *Police law* (9th edn) Oxford: Oxford University Press.

Sampson, F (2007) *Blackstone's police manual, Volume 4 – General police duties* (9th edn). Oxford: Oxford University Press.

Useful websites

Home Office police practitioners' website:

http://police.homeoffice.gov.uk

Legislation:

www.opsi.gov.uk

Case law and legislation databases:

www.westlaw.com* (a legal database)

www.lexis-nexis.com* (a legal database)

www.pnld.co.uk* (a police service specific database of case-law and statute)

* Likely to be available through the virtual learning environment (VLE) which supports your course/training.

Answers

Knowledge Check 1

1. Dave West has been found on a church roof, which has lead on it, with a large screwdriver and rope. Assuming there is not enough evidence for burglary can he be arrested?

   (d)   Yes for **s. 4 Vagrancy Act 1824**

2. PC Mistry is stopping and searching people in a designated area under **s. 44 Terrorism Act 2000** the searches are to be conducted under:

   (b)   **PACE Code A**

3. Mistry is later policing a football match. She notices that a car carrying would-be spectators to the match, which is designated, has cans of lager on the back parcel shelf. Mistry may take action under the:

   (a)   **Sporting Events (Control of Alcohol) Act 1985**

5 Police organisation

(?) *Remember this symbol indicates that the material might be useful for your Student Officer Learning and Assessment Programme (SOLAP) portfolio or any attached reflective practice record you are required to make.*

Underpinning knowledge towards Patrol Officer NOS:

1A2, 1B9, 2A1, 2C1, 2C2, 2C3, 2C4, 2I1, 2I2, 2K1, 4C1

and PCSO NOS:

1A1, 1B11, 2C1, 2C2, 2C3, 2C4, 2C5, 2K1, 4C1

For further information on these NOS, which are also Policing Level 3 and 4 NVQ unit titles refer to Appendix 1 to this volume.

The aim of this chapter is to look at the wider picture in terms of policing in this country. Predominantly we concentrate on the history and organisation of policing in England and Wales although some aspects are relevant to the rest of the United Kingdom.

Some student officers will not be new to the police service; they may for example be former detention officers, special constables or Police Community Support Officers (PCSOs). Even so, most police forces give only scant attention to the place that their police force occupies within the scheme of policing nationally and historically in the basic training that they offer 'non-attested' ranks. Consequently even those who have transferred internally to the role of student officer from other jobs in the police service will probably have only basic knowledge, if any, of what happens in other police forces and law enforcement agencies. This can lead to a very narrow view of how policing operates and most commentators agree that a professional needs a wider appreciation of how his or her profession operates no matter what geographical location it is situated in.

Recently there has been particular focus on the problems that occur if the systems and processes in policing become too localised. The Bichard Report (see Further reading at the end of the chapter) published in 2005 looked, amongst other things, at what problems arise when information gathering by law enforcement agencies does not cross county and other boundaries. The particular incident, which raised concerns leading to Bichard's inquiry, was the Soham murders and in particular the lack of information exchange between forces and other agencies about Ian Huntley, given he had previously come to police notice.

The term 'wider' or 'extended police family', containing as it does PCSOs, civilian investigators and other roles, is now accepted. Politicians and senior police officers often refer this as a new phenomenon. It would be worthwhile to look at just how new it really is and how much it is an extension of concepts that have always been around in a society which is based on 'policing by consent'.

(?) *Consider for a moment how much you really know about policing in the UK. Is the law the same in Scotland and Northern Ireland? How many police forces are there? Are they all county based? How much intelligence information about an individual could you obtain if they had just moved into your area? Continue to think about these issues as you read on.*

Policing today

By the end of this section you will be able to:

- describe the difference between a 'Home Office' force and other police forces;

- describe in outline the jurisdiction of the different police forces in the UK.

There are 43 police forces in England and Wales that are essentially county or region based. These are often referred to as 'Home Office forces' as the Home Office (as opposed to other government departments) administers them. There are, however, a variety of other police forces that have a remit to police a different type of community. The Ministry of Defence (MOD) Police, for example, police military sites, forces families who live on these sites and, to a certain extent, service personnel. This force is quite distinct from the Royal Military Police and RAF Police, for example, who police service personnel only. These latter two are outside the scope of this volume as they do not have as yet full constabulary powers and derive their authority from the various pieces of legislation governing service in the armed forces. There is even a police force dedicated to policing atomic energy sites. Since 2005 this has become known as the Civil Nuclear Constabulary. The various police forces of England and Wales are shown in Table 1.

We will shortly look at the historical development of the modern police force. Because of the rather piecemeal way that policing has developed there were considerably more police forces in operation than there are today; over 200 in fact. The relatively small number of forces that we see currently are the result of mergers and dissolution over nearly two centuries.

ACTIVITY

You may have noticed whilst on holiday in France or Spain for example or whilst watching US crime dramas or real crime shows on television that there are a variety of law enforcement agencies at work in each of these countries. Do some research on the internet. Some of these agencies such as the Federal Bureau of Investigation (FBI) in the USA and the French *Police Nationale* have national jurisdiction. Does the UK have a crime-fighting organisation with such jurisdiction? What are the advantages and disadvantages of separate local forces by comparison?

Table 1 – The police forces of England and Wales

Bedfordshire Police

Cambridgeshire Constabulary

Cheshire Constabulary

City of London Police

Cleveland Police

Cumbria Constabulary

Derbyshire Constabulary

Devon & Cornwall Constabulary

Dorset Police

Durham Constabulary

Dyfed Powys Police

Essex Police

Gloucestershire Constabulary

Greater Manchester Police

Gwent Police

Hampshire Constabulary

Hertfordshire Constabulary

Humberside Police

Kent Police

Lancashire Police

Leicestershire Constabulary

Lincolnshire Police

Merseyside Police

Metropolitan Police

Norfolk Constabulary

North Wales Police

North Yorkshire Police

Northamptonshire Police

Northumbria Police

Nottinghamshire Police

South Wales Police

South Yorkshire Police

Staffordshire Police

Suffolk Constabulary

Surrey Police

Sussex Police

Thames Valley Police

Warwickshire Police

West Mercia Constabulary

West Midlands Police

West Yorkshire Police

Wiltshire Constabulary

Non-geographic police forces

British Transport Police

Civil Nuclear Constabulary (formerly UKAEA Constabulary)

Ministry of Defence Police

Port of Dover Police

Port of Liverpool Police

NB: The Royal Parks Police were disbanded in 2005.

The development of policing over time

By the end of this section you will be able to:

- describe the development of policing since Norman times;

- analyse to what degree policing has been in the hands of 'the police';

- consider the factors which brought about the 'wider police family'.

The professional full-time police constable as we know him or her today was effectively created by the **Metropolitan Police Act 1829**. Police officers did exist before then, but not in the same form; the role had evolved over many centuries and was not particularly well organised or overseen.

It seems also that in the UK the development of the office of magistrate and that of constable were linked. At times through history they took over part of each other's role and then relinquished it by turns.

During the Anglo-Saxon period and later under the Normans in England there existed the system of the 'Frankpledge'. Groups of about ten households swore to keep order amongst themselves; if one member of this group committed a crime the remainder were duty bound to produce him to the authorities or be held accountable – an interesting concept when discussed in the context of today's rather more fractured communities. The idea of delegating law enforcement to an individual within the community was a step on from this.

Across Europe ideas about policing were developing at a similar pace over the next few centuries. In fact the word *policie* originated in France in the fifteenth century. The meaning has remained fairly constant in that it covered the day-to-day practical enforcement of the criminal law and maintenance of good order in a community and still does to this day. Originally policing was about enforcing the rule of those in positions of power but there was a gradual development, however, towards more liberal policing ideals.

To return to the developments in the UK, at least some of the reasons to reform or professionalise the police, firstly in London, came about because of the end of the Napoleonic Wars in 1815. The end of the war brought back to these shores 300,000 men brutalised by war and with thoroughly well-honed survival skills coupled with considerable courage and self-confidence born of their experience in the field. These skills transferred easily to various levels of street crime. Already high levels of unemployment and the lack of any real state welfare system fuelled this situation further.

Many historians also blame mobs and riots which were prevalent at the time. They claim this disorder gave rise to calls for a new, more professional police but this may not entirely have been the cause. It is true that there were crowds mobbing Parliament to demand social and political change from time to time. What really convinced the authorities that a professional, more centralised, uniform style of policing was needed was the rising number of property crimes perhaps generated by the mass unemployment mentioned above.

Another factor was a growing realisation that the military, even in the guise of local yeomanry, was too blunt a tool for keeping the peace. Squads of soldiers had been used for some centuries to affect an arrest if necessary pursuant to a warrant issued by a magistrate. As more recent events in Vietnam, Northern Ireland and Iraq have shown, soldiers are not trained, nor do they necessarily have the requisite skills or even want to be, police officers. As a last resort they can be a useful manifestation of armed state power but their use has often been dogged by controversy. Perhaps the best known example of this was the incident which came to be known as the 'Peterloo Massacre'. On 16 August 1819 the magistrates of Manchester sent the local Yeomanry (a forerunner of the modern Territorial Army) and a regular cavalry unit into a crowd of thousands to arrest the main speaker,

Mr Henry Hunt, a prominent reformer. There were 11 deaths and over 400 people were injured. This event might be described as the 'Tiananmen Square' of its day and crystallised thoughts about a new form of policing.

Before 1829 there were what might be described as early experiments in a more organised type of policing. There were such as the Bow Street Runners and Bow Street Horse Patrol. There was even a pretty well organised Thames River police paid for by the business community which stood to lose most from property crime in and around the docks and quays of the Thames. Nationally, most of the policing though, where there was any at all prior to the arrival of the 'New Police', was a mixture of parish constables (often elderly and infirm), night watchmen and private security. The County Record Office in Nottingham for example records that prior to 1835 the police establishment in the city was three permanent (parish) constables, up to 100 petty constables who worked part time in the day only, and a night watch of 40 to 50 private watchmen patrolling subscribers' streets. The petty constables were early versions of the special constable of today; arguably then the concept of the special pre-dates that of the regular constable. In Nottingham there was also a corporation watchman for The Shambles, a slum area just below the city's main prison of the time (now a museum of law enforcement).

In some instances these personnel, particularly the parish constables would call upon local people to give chase after a suspected thief or violent offender. This was known as a 'hue and cry' and was officially sanctioned. More frowned upon was the process of 'rough musicing' where local people would round on a suspected criminal and give them a beating without necessarily involving the authorities.

Some historians and commentators argue therefore that the mixture of public and private methods of policing shows that law enforcement has always been a variety of activities. These activities have long been the province of many different private and public agencies, for longer than the period of time that law enforcement has been perceived to be almost solely the remit of the professional police officer.

From 1815 to 1828 there was a widespread acceptance of the need for professional policing. It was considered that accountability and impartiality were more likely to be found in a professional, hierarchical and paid force. In 1829 Robert Peel famously introduced his Bill which ultimately led to the creation of the Metropolitan Police. Other enactments followed, such as the **Municipal Corporations Act 1835**, which provided for the creation of police forces outside London.

Almost immediately though, there was disquiet, both in terms of the constitutional powers of these new police officers and their cost. This latter point was particularly acutely felt because there were much fewer policemen than the 'watches' that preceded them. Given the more rigid hierarchical structure, uniforms and the strict discipline, it is perhaps unsurprising that the costs soared. According to a government report of the day the cost prior to the creation of the 'New Police' in London was £137,000 per year. The yearly expense of the Metropolitan Police between 1830 and 1832 was £207,000 despite the reduction in numbers of personnel.

Nottingham was typical of developments in policing in the provinces. Following the **Municipal Corporations Act 1835** the reformed corporation set up a watch committee and early in 1836 an embryo police force was in operation. In this city's case initially three entirely separate and unco-ordinated forces called the 'Day', 'Evening' and 'Night Police' respectively carried out this function. Unsurprisingly this was a failure and in 1841 there was an effective amalgamation of these into one force. This consisted of a nominal High Constable, an operational superintendent, five inspectors and 42 constables.

To give an idea of how localised the developments were, the county force for Nottinghamshire was created in a different way: the **County Police Act 1839** was a permissive measure which enabled Justices of the Peace to set up paid county police forces. In November 1839 it was proposed to inaugurate a Chief Constable, eight superintendents and 33 constables. The aim was to provide one county constable to every 5,000 persons in the county.

There was not universal praise for these new officers however; petitions were raised between 1842 and 1845, particularly against the increased costs but recurrent words in these documents are 'inefficient', 'obnoxious', 'expense', 'useless' and 'unconstitutional'. It may be that at least some of these sentiments are key references to a feeling that these officers were a step too far down the road that the French had taken with their centrally controlled national force. During the years after the French Revolution and Napoleon Bonaparte anything French was viewed with deep suspicion by the British political establishment. A common nickname for the 'New Police' officers, apart from 'Peelers' and the now familiar 'Bobbies' (both from Robert Peel, by then Home Secretary), was 'Jenny Derby' an unflattering corruption of the French word *gendarme.*

Suspicions deepened with the fact that the Metropolitan Police was not locally democratically governed but controlled by the Home Secretary. This is a unique situation which applies only to the Met and has existed, virtually without change, until the present day. By contrast all local forces have a police authority consisting of JPs, elected members and other prominent figures. The use of the word 'Commissioner' to describe the Metropolitan Police chief officer was also unfortunate as it sounded like the *commissaires de police* which existed in Paris at the time.

Despite these misgivings and complaints amongst the public, the 'New Police' became firmly established and continued to develop into the police forces of today. There were other legislative milestones: most recently the **Police Acts** of **1996** and **1997** and **Police Reform Act 2002.**

Difficulties and tensions have arisen however, particularly during the latter part of the twentieth century as the police have become more mechanised and more of a responsive, reactive force to cope with increasing and changing demands from the population they police. This has resulted in there being less of a preventative, community-focused role within the police constable's remit. To a degree this was the focus for the next major shift in policing and the advent of the 'wider police family' and the 'Neighbourhood Policing Model' of today, in particular the emergence of the Police Community Support Officer in 2003.

What happened to the 'beat bobby'?

By the end of this section you will be able to:

- describe how the role of the police constable changed;

- analyse the impact on community relations these changes had;

- consider any parallels which might be found with historical changes in policing.

The first duty of the new policeman was always, and still is, crime prevention; save only for saving life and limb, detection of crime comes third in the list. Even in the very early days there was an element of 'mission creep', a term borrowed from the military to describe being forced by circumstances to gradually take on a wider role than that originally envisaged. During the 1830s and 1840s constables of the Metropolitan Police invariably found themselves drafted in to deal with large-scale disorder. Tensions between roles within the police constable 'job description' are nothing new, it seems. In modern times however, these tensions are very marked. Chiefly the problem is between community policing, which is generally acknowledged to be the best format for preventing crime, and the need to be a rapid reaction force. Some commentators refer to modern crime-fighting as 'fire-brigade' policing in that the officers are forced by pressure of time to merely respond to emergency calls and are unable to go out and meet their community and interact with it. Officers themselves in studies have spoken of the 'tyranny of the radio', referring again to the fact that there is no time to deal with community issues before they are required to attend a further incident as directed through their radio.

Community policing and crime prevention have always been inextricably linked because the assumption has always been that by the presence of visible uniformed officers, offenders would be deterred. The beat model therefore developed, whereby officers would patrol a given area on foot for the majority of their shift, which in the early 1800s would have been 12 hours every day of the week with no rest days. It is very difficult to measure the effectiveness of the beat model but it does have two important issues associated with it. The first is that the visible presence of uniformed officers does have a significant reassuring effect on the public. The second is that according to studies, the work is potentially very boring and unpopular with officers.

(?) *According to politicians and the tabloid press there is widespread public dissatisfaction with the fact that there are less uniformed patrolling police constables on the streets compared to say, 50 years ago. To what extent do you consider this to be true? If it is true, what are the reasons for this reduction? Could it have been avoided?*

The debate about the problems of beat policing was paramount in the 1970s. The flash-point on the streets was the Brixton Disorders of 12–18 April 1981. The **Scarman Report** on the riots found the police were performing the community policing role (in areas of racial diversity at least) so badly that there was an 'appalling relationship between the police and the local community'. The report went on to blame the police in part for this breakdown. Scarman, a retired judge, felt that part of the problem was that the police, instead of being part of the community they serve, were becoming professionals with a highly specialised set of skills and behavioural codes of their own. This resulted in distancing them from the population that they serve.

ACTIVITY

Find out what you can about the 'neighbourhood policing model'. Where it is being properly and fully implemented? What effect do you think it will have on police–community relations?

In major research studies, the police themselves give varying views for why community policing is so unpopular. In one such study conducted by Roger Graef for his book *Talking blues* (see Further reading at the end of this chapter), interviewed serving officers. He found that some officers considered that anything to do with the community is not 'macho'. Talking to members of the community about what they may perceive the problems in the area to be does not sit easily for such officers with their desire to catch criminals and save life and limb, which is what they joined for.

The problem is arguably not just about a mismatch between expectations in officers brought up on a diet of cop shows and all-action heroes in the mass media and the reality of beat policing. For some at least the problem may lie in frustration with 'managerialism'. This is a word used to describe the ever-growing need to attach targets and performance indicators to all aspects of public-sector work in the way that has long been the case in the private sector. This may be done with the best of intentions but the very immeasurability of community policing makes it very difficult to apply targets to and even more difficult to meet the targets that are set. Put crudely, numbers of arrests can be measured, allayed fears and bridges built with disaffected groups cannot. The temptation then is to concentrate on work that can be quantified such as numbers of fixed penalty notices issued or pieces of intelligence submitted. Graef's interviewees similarly lament the fact that it is very difficult to get a tangible 'result' in community policing.

Scarman, however, felt that community policing was too important to be treated as just a slogan. He was nevertheless aware of what he called the 'soggy social work' nature of the perception of community policing by police officers themselves and recommended changes in training, accountability, police powers and complaints procedures amongst others.

The fracture between police and community was not healed, however, and further batterings to police/community relations were delivered by events such as the miners' strike and the aftermath of the MacPherson Report into the Stephen Lawrence murder, to name but two.

To summarise the position at the close of the twentieth century, the police constable's role was much less that of a foot patrol 'beat bobby'. He or she is more likely to be mechanised, specialised and mostly reactive and not proactive. This chapter is partly about discovering if there are any developments with the advent of the 'wider police family' (in particular the PCSO) or whether we have simply returned to the situation found prior to the advent of the modern PC. There are parallels with the pre-1829 notion of criminal law enforcement. In the 1820s the law enforcers were the parish constables, an assortment of private watchmen and the military if necessary. For many different reasons these were not deemed to be succeeding in their role. To an extent that process is similar to the evolution of the PCSO. The need to rejuvenate community policing is not unique to the UK. In the USA the 1994 Crime Act aimed to put 100,000 police officers on the beat to try to facilitate better interaction with the communities they serve.

When the New Police were brought onto the streets in 1829 there were many debates on their powers, their equipment (up to and including artillery pieces in the vision of one Chief Constable of the time), what uniform they should wear, whether they should look like the soldiers that had, in part, gone before them. It is debatable that the arguments raging in the nineteenth century concerning the early PCs being armed with rifles sound very like those which resound today around the arrest and protection equipment which should be carried by PCSOs.

In the next section we will consider how the new PCSO role was designed and what issues the early years of practice have highlighted.

The advent of the PCSO

By the end of this section you will be able to:

- describe in outline the different parts of the 'wider police family';

- make links with previous major changes in policing in this country;

- consider in more detail the role of a major component of the new scheme of policing, the Police Community Support Officer.

The wider or extended police family basically covers any civilian employed by the police force, or in some cases other organisations, to perform roles which might otherwise be carried out by attested (sworn) police officers. These diverse roles were historically (at least since 1829) mainly or wholly carried out by police constables and they are now part of the job profile of civilian police and other employees. Under the **Police Reform Act 2002 (Schedule 4)** the main branches of this family are:

- designated police employees;

- contracted-out employees;

- accredited employees.

Designated police employees are specifically:

- PCSOs;

- investigating officers;

- detention officers;

- escort officers.

A detailed discussion of all these roles is outside the scope of this volume but we will look in greater detail at the PCSO in a moment. Suffice it to say that civilian investigating officers have some powers of entry and search when in the company of a constable using reasonable force if necessary. Detention and escort officers may, for instance, use such reasonable force as is necessary to keep a person detained. The latter two designations can be given to employees of a private business who are contracted to provide escort and detention services (for example, a private security company transporting prisoners to and from police cells). These are the 'contracted-out' employees mentioned above.

Accredited employees, on the other hand, are not employed by the police force. They are employees of a local business or, more likely, a public-sector organisation like a local authority, to carry out a law enforcement or deterrence of antisocial behaviour function. Once certain arrangements have been made with the chief officer of police for a particular area, these staff may be recruited and have some powers as a result. The most common example of this type of arrangement is the local council's neighbourhood warden service. These uniformed officers have the powers of a constable to issue fixed penalty notices for such behaviour as littering and dog-fouling, and they can also require a name and address from an offender.

ACTIVITY

Neighbourhood wardens are usually based in police stations. Once you are posted to a station, seek out the wardens based there. Discuss with them their role and obtain their views on how their function interfaces with yours and that of a PCSO. Make contact with a warden from another local authority. Are their uniforms the same and do they have the same powers and role profile?

Special constables are also part of the wider or extended police family. Their forebears, the petty constables, actually pre-date the creation of the modern police constable as we saw in the previous section. We have looked at their powers in Chapter 3, 'Police powers'. They are essentially fully empowered police constables but only when on duty (typically four to six hours per week) and only in the county they are based and adjoining areas.

One way to represent the relationship between the warden, the special constable, the PCSO and the police constable is to look at the neighbourhood-policing model as a diagram. Modern beats are intended to be managed by a police constable, the 'beat manager', who co-ordinates a team, all with different roles, including the local neighbourhood watch. Note that the relationship is not really hierarchical but has all the different functions on an equal footing, except that constables are the only ones whose powers emanate from their office. The wardens and PCSOs draw their powers in a different way as we have discussed. In that respect alone the constables may direct the activities of the other team members always taking into account that the wardens have a different employer.

Neighbourhood policing model relationships

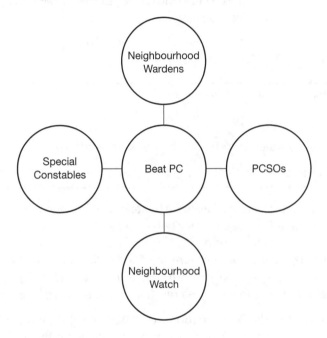

The Police Community Support Officer

Section 38 of the **Police Reform Act 2002** created the PCSO, and it is evident that the idea was to rejuvenate the relationship between police and policed. Perhaps it could be likened to the community policing function being 'contracted out' to the new PCSO with an acceptance that the modern police constable was not as suitable for this role as he or she once was. The legislators clearly felt that the act would set a framework in place which would mobilise the community itself. The neighbourhood watch would be enhanced by layers of uniformed civilians between it and police officers.

(?) *It would be worthwhile talking over some of the issues in this chapter with PCSOs based with you. Do they think of themselves as a new junior rank in the police service designed only to carry out the more mundane policing tasks? Alternatively do they see themselves as professionals in their own right with a distinct and specialised remit to build bridges with the community? If the former is true, you might want to reflect on what recruitment and training policies have brought that about.*

The role of PCSO is still very new, and the problem of how to define and delimit the role echoes the position in 1829 to a degree when the new PC's role was not well understood or accepted. Discipline and training problems in the PCSO ranks have been reported: a major newspaper sent one of its reporters undercover to train as a PCSO in 2005 and it was alleged that poor morale and lack of training were uncovered. Various other newspaper articles alleged poor discipline and high sickness levels. It is worth noting, to get this all into context, that of the approximately 2,500 'New Police' recruited in 1829, only some 500 of the original recruits remained in service three years later. The overwhelming majority had been fired for drunkenness on duty.

The powers of a PCSO

By the end of this section you will be able to:

• describe the powers of a PCSO;

• compare and contrast these powers with those of a police officer;

• apply your knowledge to some simple case study scenarios.

NB: Although the preceding sections have contained information vital to the study of modern policing, there have been no revision or knowledge check opportunities. This is because the material is background and unlikely to be assessed as part of IPLDP. The forthcoming material may well be of direct use to PCSOs in training, however, and therefore some revision and assessment material is provided. The material in this section does not have the academic rigour of that required for student police officers' training, however.

Part 1 of **Schedule 4** to the **Police Reform Act 2002** sets out what a PCSO is entitled to do, mostly in terms of equating him or her with a constable for the purposes of a given existing Act. **Paragraph 1(aa),** for example, states that a PCSO will have:

> *the power of a constable to give a penalty notice under s. 444A of the Education Act 1996.*

This is effectively an anti-truancy measure. It should be noted that many of the powers described are subject to their being designated as applicable by the chief officer of the force area concerned (**Police Reform Act 2002**). It will be necessary therefore for PCSOs to check local force instructions. Assume for the purposes of this volume that PCSOs have a designation which includes all powers. Unless stated otherwise all the powers are derived from the paragraphs of **Part 1** of **Schedule 4** to the **Police Reform Act 2002.**

ACTIVITY

It would be useful to know what powers the PCSOs in your local area have been designated with. Many forces issue an *aide-memoire* to their PCSOs listing their powers. When you are based in a station, ask to see the list of powers and perhaps talk it over with your PCSO colleagues.

Detention

The most controversial power is that of detention. This is because historically under the UK Constitution only a constable may arrest in circumstances where a citizen may not. These various powers are enshrined in **ss. 24** and **24A** of the **Police and Criminal Evidence Act 1984 (PACE)** (see Chapter 3). **Para. 2** of the Act therefore purports to convey a wholly new power on PCSOs to detain a person for up to 30 minutes pending the arrival of a police officer. What is not clear from the legislation is what happens if no police assistance is available within that 30-minute period, or whether a PCSO needs to caution a suspect who has been detained. This requirement is made of police constables when they arrest but not when they detain, for example, for the purposes of a search. Some police forces are training their PCSOs to caution in these circumstances as a matter of practicality. The problem will most likely surface where a case turns on a confession made during a period of detention where the PCSO involved has omitted to caution. The question will be whether that confession is admissible as evidence. It would not be if it were made by a PC in such circumstances.

There are several situations when a PCSO may exercise this power of detention, or if the person elects, to require them to accompany the officer to a police station (in practice a local one). There is also a power to use reasonable force to prevent a detained person making off:

- When an offence has been committed that the officer would issue an FPN but the offender has failed to provide a name and address or has provided one which the officer has reasonable grounds to believe is false or inaccurate.

- An offence under **s. 32(2)** of the **Anti-social Behaviour Act 2003** (failing to disperse, failing to leave the locality or returning to a locality in breach of a direction by a police officer). Note that this is not the same thing as a being in breach of an anti-social behaviour order (ASBO) awarded by a court.

- Offences against the **Parks Regulation Act 1872**.

- An offence under a local bye-law which warrants such detention.

- An offence under **s. 3** or **4 Vagrancy Act 1824**.

- An offence has been committed which appears to have caused injury, alarm or distress to any other person.

- An offence has been committed which appears to have caused loss of, or any damage to, any other person's property.

These last two powers are actually quite wide. A PC would have to specify an actual offence, but detention powers do not require the PCSO to demonstrate the reasonable grounds that a constable is obligated to show.

The controversy over the power to detain has led at least one force to withdraw the power from PCSOs having once granted it over fears for the officers' safety. Other forces have given their PCSOs authority to detain but not to touch the offender. Still other forces have dealt with the same issue by designating the power and equipping their PCSOs with stab vests, handcuffs and batons. The result is a wide variation across the country in powers and equipment given to PCSOs.

What cannot be withheld from a PCSO however is the common law 'any person' power of arrest (see Chapter 3). It is not in the power of anyone other than Parliament to restrict the ability of a citizen to make an arrest.

The remaining powers are split. There are powers which may be exercised when in the company and under the supervision of a PC. The rest are powers which are those of a constable but can be exercised by the PCSO independently. Failing to comply with a power is in itself an offence triable summarily.

Powers when in the company of a constable

These are chiefly powers to direct traffic, search, stop and search and also to seize material. The PCSO will have the powers of a constable to:

- direct traffic;

- direct traffic for the purposes of escorting a 'wide load';

- stop and search (and seize relevant material) in an area authorised under **ss. 44(1)(a), (b)**and **(2)(b)** and **s. 45(2)** of the **Terrorism Act 2000**;

- enter a premises under the power discussed below to seize vehicles used to cause alarm.

Powers of a PCSO when not necessarily in the company of a constable

A PCSO has powers derived directly from the **Police Reform Act 2002.** He or she has a power to issue fixed penalty notices (FPN) for :

- cycling on a footpath;

- dog fouling;

- graffiti and fly-posting;

- littering;

- truancy.

A PCSO also has power to issue FPNs for disorder for offences listed in **Criminal Justice and Police Act 2001**:

- Alcohol (under–18s)

  - Sale to person.

  - Purchase for a person.

  - Delivery to a person.

  - Consumption or allowing consumption.

  - Buying or attempting to buy for.

  - (Also there is a power to search for and confiscate.)

- Alcohol (any age)

  - Selling or attempting to sell to person who is drunk.

  - Drunk and disorderly behaviour.

  - Drunk in the highway.

  - Drinking in designated prohibited areas.

  - (There is also a power to confiscate in a designated place.)

  - (There is also a power of entry to licensed premises (limited – see **para. 8A**) and to enforce certain licensing offences (see **para. 2(6A)**.)

- Criminal Damage (under £500)

- Emergency services

  - Wasting police time.

  - Knowingly giving false report to person acting for fire and rescue authority.

- Fireworks (see **s.11 Fireworks Act 2003** etc.)

  - Breach of curfew.

  - Possession of Category 4 device.

  - Possession by an under-18 of an adult firework.

  - Supply of excessively loud devices.

  - Throwing.

- Harassment, alarm and distress, causing.

- Railways

  - Trespassing on the railway.

  - Throwing stones at a train.

- Using public electronic communications network for annoyance, inconvenience or needless anxiety.

The following are powers which PCSOs can be designated with:

- Anti-social behaviour

  - Require name and address of someone so acting.

  - (See also power to detain above.)

- Children and young people

  - Tobacco, power to search for and confiscate.

  - Disperse groups and remove under-16s to a place of residence.

  - Remove children in contravention of curfew to place of residence.

- Traffic

  - Escorting abnormal loads.

  - Other situations (if power to require name and address designated (**para. 3A**).

- Vehicles

  - Abandoned, power to remove.

  - Stop for a road check (**s. 4 PACE 1984**) and place traffic signs for the purpose.

  - Stop for testing (**s. 67 RTA 1988**).

  - Alarm, power to seize vehicle used to cause.

  - Pedal cycle, power to stop.

  - Require name and address for traffic offences.

  - Place traffic signs.

There are also miscellaneous powers to:

  - Control begging (see **Sched. 8** to **Serious Organised Crime and Police Act 2005**).

  - Enforcement of bye-laws.

  - Entry to save life or limb.

  - Seize drugs.

  - Require name and address for possession of drugs.

  - Photograph persons away from a police station.

  - Use reasonable force to transfer control of detained person for dangerous items/items to assist escape.

  - Give orders as a constable would be able to in a cordoned area (**s. 36 Terrorism Act 2000**)

  - Require name and address (see **para. 1(A)**).

Knowledge Check 1

1. PCSO Sprake is on routine foot patrol when she approaches Danielle Green (21 years) who is swaying and speaking in a slurred manner. She falls to the ground swearing profusely. The area is not designated alcohol-free under local bye-laws.

    Which one of the following is true? Sprake may:

    (a) Arrest Green for drunk and disorderly.

    (b) Issue Green an FPN for drunk and disorderly.

(c) Search Green for alcohol.

(d) Confiscate alcohol.

2. PCSO Sprake sees a youth running away from a shop with the owner running after them shouting 'come back you thieving b*****d.' The youth has an armful of what look like packets of cigarettes.

    If Sprake catches them she is best advised to (assuming personal safety issues have been taken into account):

    (a) Arrest the youth for theft.

    (b) Detain the youth for a maximum of 30 minutes.

    (c) Search the youth.

    (d) Issue the youth with an FPN for theft.

    (Select *one* answer)

3. PCSO Sprake next sees a dog owner walking his dog, the dog fouls the pavement and the man walks on. When challenged about the matter, the man tells Sprake to F**k off and do something useful instead. When asked to stop swearing the man replies 'B*****ks!'

    Sprake may (select *one* answer):

    (a) Issue the man with an FPN for dog fouling.

    (b) Issue the man with an FPN for behaviour likely to cause alarm harassment or distress.

    (c) Both of the above.

    (d) None of the above.

The answers are at the end of the chapter.

This concludes our discussion of the wider or extended police family, in particular the PCSO. As a final point it is worth remembering that this is a new role which will need many years to be fully developed, much as the PCs role did in 1829. It is a role which is likely to evolve continuously. It is a distinct role with arguably a unique opportunity to build bridges with the local community if it is allowed to develop its own distinct function; a function which is easily recognisable to the general public. This process may well be much more difficult if the role simply becomes a new junior rank under that of the PC, a kind of 'constable's assistant'. Any such moves would not be in keeping with the legislation which created the PCSO.

Suggested research

Go on the web and look up the White Paper *Building Communities: Beating Crime*. This is in effect a proposal for a new statute. Consider the proposals in it to integrate 'civilian' and police roles. These include making it easier for a civilian employee to become a constable and multiple points of entry to the force so that a person with the right skills could enter as a sergeant or inspector. Consider the advantages and disadvantages of these ideas.

Further reading

For a review of research specifically in the area of the wider police family and public reaction to it see:

Orr-Munro, T (2005) Blurred lines, *Police Review,* 25 March 2005, Jane's Publishing.

For the research itself see:

Crawford, A, Lister, S, Blackburn, S and Burnett, J (2005) *Plural policing – The mixed economy of visible patrols in England and Wales.* Bristol: The Policy Press.

The following works provide further insight into the history of the police constable and their forerunners:

Emsley, C (2006) *The English police, a political and social history,* (2nd edn). London: Longman.

Emsley C (1997) *Crime and policing in Europe since c. 1750.* Oxford: Oxford University Press.

Neocleous, M (2000) *The fabrication of social order – A critical theory of police power.* London: Pluto.

Palmer, S (1998) *Police and protest in England and Ireland 1780–1850.* Cambridge: Cambridge University Press.

Reynolds, E (1998) *Before the bobbies.* London: Macmillan.

These volumes add detail to the way that community policing has developed with more of a present day focus:

Graef, R (1990) *Talking blues: The police in their own words.* London: Collins Harvill.

Jason-Lloyd, L (2003) *Quasi-policing.* London: Cavendish.

Skogan, W (2004) *Community policing (can it work).* London: Thomson.

Zedner, L (2005) Policing before and after the police: The historical antecedents of contemporary crime control. *British Journal of Criminology.*

Reports:

The Brixton Disorders 10–12 April 1981, Report of an Inquiry by the Rt. Hon. The Lord Scarman, OBE (HMSO).

Bichard Report **http://www.homeoffice.gov.uk/pdf/bichard_report.pdf**

For more in-depth discussion and more case law on the topics in this chapter student officers might consider reading from:

English, J and Card, R (2006) *Police law* (9th edn). Oxford: Oxford University Press.

Sampson, F (2007) *Blackstone's police manual, Volume 4 – General police duties,* (9th edn) Oxford: Oxford University Press.

Useful websites

www.legislation.hmso.gov.uk (provides full text of statutes passed by Parliament as well as delegated legislation)

www.westlaw.com* (a legal database)

www.lexis-nexis.com* (a legal database)

www.pnld.co.uk* (a police service specific database of case law and statute)

* Likely to be available through the virtual learning environment (VLE) which supports your course/training.

Answers

Knowledge Check 1

1. PCSO Sprake is on routine foot patrol when she approaches Danielle Green who is swaying and speaking in a slurred manner. She falls to the ground swearing profusely. The area is not designated alcohol-free under local bye-laws.

   Sprake may:

   (b) Issue Green an FPN for drunk and disorderly.

2. PCSO Sprake sees a youth running away from a shop with the owner running after them shouting 'come back you thieving b*****d.' The youth has an armful of what look like packets of cigarettes.

   Sprake catches the youth and is best advised to:

   (a) Arrest the youth for theft.

3. PCSO Sprake next sees a dog owner walking his dog, the dog fouls the pavement and the man walks on. When challenged about the matter, the man tells Sprake to F**k off and do something useful instead. When asked to stop swearing the man replies 'B*****ks!'

   Sprake may:

   (c) Both of the above.

Note: In (2) the power of detention is available as well but the 'any person' power of arrest is not time limited.

6 Violence and intimidation

(?) *Remember this symbol indicates that the material might be useful for your Student Officer Learning and Assessment Programme (SOLAP) portfolio or any attached reflective practice record you are required to make.*

Underpinning knowledge towards Patrol Officer NOS:

1A1, 1B9, 2A1, 2C1, 2C2, 2C3, 2C4, 2G2, 2G4, 2H1, 2H2, 2J1, 2J2, 2K2, 4C1

and PCSO NOS:

1A1,1B11, 2A1, 2C1, 2C2, 2C3, 2C4, 2C5, 2J1, 2J2, 4C1

For further information on these NOS, which are also Policing Level 3 and 4 NVQ unit titles, refer to Appendix 1 to this volume.

Assaults

By the end of this section you will be able to:

- explain the difference between common law and statutory assaults;
- state the definitions of the assaults covered;
- apply relevant case law and statute to a range of hypothetical situations.

This chapter covers the law on the following assault offences:

- common assault;
- actual bodily harm;
- grievous bodily harm;
- wounding;
- racially aggravated or religiously aggravated assaults;
- assault on and obstruction of a police officer.

Indecent assault is dealt with in Chapter 7 as it is a specialist area of law. An understanding of assault gained from reading this chapter would aid study in the sexual offences area, however.

Common assault

This is the most minor of assaults and is in fact two separate offences; it is contended here that both are still common law. In police circles these types of assaults are often referred to as 'section 39 assaults'. This is because the penalties for these assaults are prescribed by **s. 39 Criminal Justice Act 1988**. The definitions of the offences themselves are not contained in any statute however, but are derived from case law. There was an attempt to codify the law on assaults into a single statute with simplified wording and some of the anomalies removed. This proposal was the Offences Against the Person Bill (an act is referred to as a 'Bill' while it is going through Parliament) which was circulated for consultation in 1998. This Bill never became law, however. This is regrettable when it is borne in mind that, for example, no less than five cases are cited in the process of defining what the *mens rea* for psychic assault is under the current law. The two offences are psychic (or technical) assault and battery. They are distinct offences from one another.

Despite the low level of severity it is important that these assaults are understood as they form the basis of other more serious offences such as actual bodily harm and indecent assault. Simple common assault is less often prosecuted unless the victim is particularly vulnerable, there is significant repetition of the offence or the victim is a member of a group which society is anxious to protect such as doctors or nurses.

ACTIVITY

It would be very useful at this point to know what the policies and procedures are nationally and locally in respect of common assault. Do some research in this area. Start by having a look at the CPS guidance and the 'charging standard' at: **www.cps.gov.uk/legal/section5/ chapter_c.html#02**. You could compare this with policies and procedures published by your home force. These will either be on the force intranet or circulated in paper form.

Psychic or technical assault

It may come as a surprise to discover that this type of assault can be committed without physically touching the victim at all. That is why it is referred to as 'psychic' assault as it could be viewed as an assault on the 'psyche', the term for the human mind. The definition is quite old and has been refined through many cases to stand currently as:

To intentionally or recklessly cause another to apprehend immediate unlawful force.

Minor deviations from this wording do not matter unduly but the key words and phrases are:

- intentionally;
- recklessly;

- cause;

- apprehend;

- immediate;

- unlawful force.

Commonly this is committed by threatening gestures. It has been held though that words alone can constitute an offence of this nature. This is logical, as otherwise a blind person could not be a victim of this offence.

Intentionally or recklessly

These constitute the *mens rea* of the offence. It might be useful at this point to revisit Chapter 1 to refresh your memory of basic legal concepts if you have not already done so.

Intention is best defined as a persons 'aim or purpose' (**R v Mohan 1976**). It can also extend to situations where a jury can 'feel sure that [prohibited consequence] was a virtual certainty … and the defendant appreciated that such was the case'. This latest definition of the concept of *oblique intention* was taken from the judgement in **R v Woollin (1998)** which in itself effectively confirmed the finding in the earlier court of appeal decision in **R v Nedrick (1985)**. In the Court of Appeal case of **R v Matthews and Alleyne (2003)** it was held however that foresight of virtual certainty is something does not equal intention but is something from which intention can be inferred. A fine distinction perhaps but essentially a jury can decide intention is present from such foresight but does not have to.

Although these cases concerned homicide it is generally accepted that this line of thinking would apply to a number of different types of prohibited acts. This means, in the current context, that a girl who, say, deliberately drops a brick from a motorway bridge on to a busy road below could be held to have intentionally assaulted drivers passing under her. This would be so even if she did not hit a vehicle and maintained that she never meant to. Proving intention would of course also depend on the jury agreeing that the girl appreciated it as virtually certain that the victims would expect further bricks to fall.

Alternatively, the prosecution can rely on proving recklessness. 'Cunningham recklessness' is required, that is the taking of a deliberate risk by the accused as per **R v Cunningham (1957)**. Consider the circumstances described above as slightly different and the girl was standing on a footbridge over a quiet but fairly well used country road. It would now be more difficult to show that causing motorists to expect to be hit by a brick was virtually certain. It might now be possible to show, usually by skilled questioning, that the girl knew of the risk and went ahead and threw the brick anyway. This discussion is illustrated diagrammatically below by means of a flowchart.

Intention and recklessness are concepts we have met before but, without a statute how is it determined that these are the correct *mens rea* for this offence? Again we turn to the case law. In the conjoined appeal cases of **R v Savage; DPP v Parmenter (1991)** the definitions of both battery and psychic assault were reaffirmed to contain the words 'intentionally' and 'recklessly'. This was later confirmed in **R v Ireland; R v Burstow (1998)** discussed in more detail later. In fact the *mens rea* for all the assaults studied here are the same with the exception of grievous bodily harm with intent (discussed later). It is also clear that no injury or harm of any kind need necessarily be sought by the accused for a conviction of psychic assault. It need only be proven that the accused intended (the jury may accept that he fore-saw the outcome as virtually certain instead) or was reckless as to the victim apprehending the force. We will consider what 'apprehend' means in a moment.

Diagram of relationship between intention, oblique intention and subjective reck-lessness (relates to psychic assault, battery, ABH, GBH)

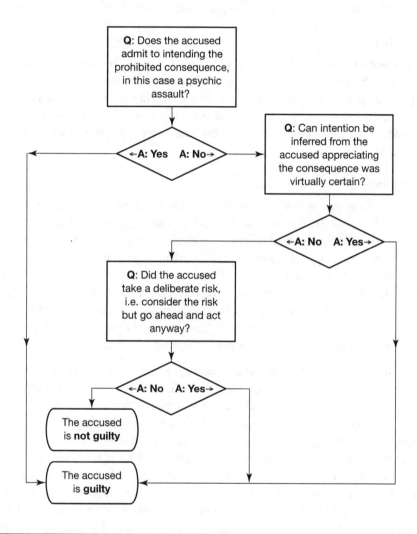

REVISION

The mens rea for psychic or technical assault is either:

✓ Intention (including oblique intention)
or
✓ Subjective recklessness.

Cause

Causation is a subject which we will keep returning to in different offences. For a general discussion of legal and factual causation you will need to revisit Chapter 1. Here though it will be necessary to show there was a causal link between the defendant's acts and the resultant apprehension in the victim of immediate unlawful force. This could be direct or indirect but more of that under battery and actual bodily harm.

Apprehend

To apprehend force is not the same as to fear it. There is no need for the victim to be in fear at all. Imagine a situation where a man of 5 feet in stature weighing no more than say 115 pounds, sees a heavyweight boxing champion in the street and approaches the prize fighter head on with fists clenched and teeth bared. The offence may well have been committed but it is highly unlikely that the boxer feels any fear. He merely expects force to be applied.

Immediate

Whether the threat of force is immediate or not is a particularly crucial part. It is not an area of the law which is completely clear either. Much depends on the realities of the situation, particularly in terms of whether words can negate (i.e. make ineffective) a psychic assault. In other words, if a youth raises his fist to a girl and says 'you are going to need an ambulance in a minute' a psychic assault may well have been committed. If however the words used are 'if I see you here again tomorrow you'll need an ambulance by the time I've done with you' then arguably a psychic assault has not occurred because there is no threat of immediate force. The level of threat and whether the words spoken can effectively remove that threat are central to the discussion, however.

The position is outlined in case law. Conveniently there is a pair of cases which illustrate where the line is drawn in these situations. In **Tuberville v Savage (1669)** two men were arguing in the street. It is necessary to understand the historical context. This was a time before policing as we would know it today. Rather like the 'Wild West' there was little organised law enforcement if the law enforcers were not in town. In **Tuberville** the protagonists were aware that the judges of the time, who travelled the country dispensing justice when they arrived at a particular location, were not currently sitting. The accused said 'if it were not assize time I would not take such language' and laid his hand on the hilt of his sword as he spoke. The courts in question were called 'assizes' at that time. The intimation that no threat existed because of the possibility of prosecution was enough for the charge of psychic assault to fail.

Despite its age the case remains highly relevant. If one substitutes the facts of two men outside a city-centre chip shop on a Friday night, one holding a knife and uttering the words 'if there weren't so many cops about tonight I'd stick you with this', a twenty-first-century policing situation is described.

R v Light (1857) however had a different outcome. Here a Constable George Cross of West Sussex Police attended a house after a report of a disturbance. Standing outside the house he saw Light standing over his wife holding a shovel above her head saying 'If it were not for that bloody policeman outside I would split your head open, for 'tis you who sent for the policeman.' Light was arrested and tried for this (effectively what we would now call psychic) assault and a later assault on Cross in the execution of his duty. Whether or not Cross was actually doing his duty turned on whether Light had committed an assault on his wife in the first place. The court felt that he had done so.

Taking these two cases together then, it would appear that one must weigh the threat posed by the would-be assailant against the words used. In **Tuberville** the words were arguably quite strong in their limiting effect in comparison with the relatively minor threat posed. In **Light** the reverse was perhaps true.

(?) *This was an early domestic violence case. In fact the term 'domestic' does nothing to indicate the true seriousness of these offences. When making a SOLAP or reflective entry on a domestic violence incidents you have attended make reference to the law on assault and also force policy and procedure in this area.*

There are also what are known as 'conditional threats'. This is a concept related to that discussed above. If a threat is made but the application of the force will be withheld as long as some condition is met, then this is a conditional threat. The traditional highwayman's 'your money or your life' would be an example. If the money is handed over there will be no force. It is not hard to think of modern-day street robbery situations which could be analysed in the same way. Despite the fact that there is a way to escape the immediacy of the threat, **Logdon v DPP (1976)** indicates that such situations will be dealt with as psychic assaults. The logic behind this is that the victim's freedom is unreasonably 'fettered' or limited by the accused.

The courts have had some novel situations to look at which might come under the general heading of stalking. After many of these cases legislation in the form of the **Protection from Harassment Act 1997** (discussed later in this chapter) has come in to deal with this kind of activity. Arguably though, this preventative measure does not adequately deal with situations where people suffer permanent or lasting damage to their mental health from the activities of stalkers. Consequently the law on assaults is still employed as well.

Firstly in **Smith v Chief Constable of Woking Police Station (1983)** the situation was that Smith was looking silently in through the window of the victim's home. No words or gestures occurred. Given the situation and the defendant's intention that the woman should be frightened, this was held to be a psychic assault. In practice much will depend on circumstances. A glance at you through your kitchen window from even a sworn enemy as he passes will obviously not constitute an assault. The same may not be true if this person stands for an hour staring at you through the same window from the pavement without moving.

The cases of **R v Ireland** and **R v Burstow** were heard as conjoined appeals (**R v Ireland; Burstow (1998)**). Ireland had subjected his victim to nuisance but silent telephone calls, and the court was quite happy to find that a silent telephone call could cause a victim to apprehend immediate force. There is an argument though that a caller cannot really be in sufficient proximity to the victim to cause such apprehension. This point can be countered by the assertion that there can now be the possibility that the caller is very close by with a mobile phone.

By contrast the accused in **R v Constanza (1997)** caused the apprehension of force by letter (the last of 800 or so abusive letters to the victim); the argument that the threat is immediate here is harder to sustain but the court accepted it. Costanza, Ireland and Burstow caused mental illness in their victims which was categorised as harm. These cases will be discussed later in the chapter when we look at statutory assaults. It will be seen there that psychic assault or battery is a key component of one type of statutory assault.

When writing up harassment incidents which border on assault, consider how tech-nology has affected the debate here. If letters and silent telephone calls can constitute a psychic assault then so can arguably, a text message. What about an email? Can you see a difference between the two?

Unlawful force

'Unlawful' and 'force' are two concepts common to battery. They will be discussed fully in that section.

REVISION

Psychic or technical assault can be committed by either:
✓ words (even written ones in extreme circumstances);
✓ words and gestures;
✓ silence (in fear-inducing circumstances).

Battery

The offence of battery is arguably more akin to what the layman might think an assault actually is. The accused must apply force to another here. The definition is again drawn from case law. The definition is:

>   *to intentionally or recklessly apply unlawful force to another.*

ACTIVITY

Revisit the CPS guidance and the 'charging standard' at:

www.cps.gov.uk/legal/section5/chapter_c.html#02, the subject of the last Activity. How does the CPS recommend that 'battery' is phrased in a charge?

The key words and phrases here are:

- intentionally or recklessly;

- apply force (to another);

- unlawful.

Intentionally or recklessly

These concepts are identical to those discussed under psychic assault above. The case law is equally relevant here and there is no need to repeat the discussion therefore.

Apply force

'Force' has quite a wide meaning and any touching at all will suffice. In fact in **R v Thomas (1985)** it was held that the touching of the clothes a person is wearing even when they are not aware of it is sufficient for this offence. You might wonder why this kind of activity might be criminalised but consider the situation where this behaviour has a sexual motive, for instance. There is one important exception, however, with particular relevance to police officers and PCSOs. It was decided in **R v Sherriff (1969)** that to pull away from a person's grip is not battery. This runs contrary to the principle discussed above in that clearly force is applied to the underside of the fingers as the arm or whatever is pulled away out of the grasp. Thus a person who struggles free during an arrest or detention is best dealt with under other headings (discussed later). There are a variety of remedies depending on the circumstances.

The force can be applied indirectly. Thus a prankster who places a trip wire across a doorway to a meeting hall just before people exit to delight in them all tumbling to the floor commits the offence. The force is applied as they impact the floor. One might say that the prankster in effect hits them with the floor. This concept was confirmed as correct in **R v Martin (1881)** where famously Martin blocked a theatre exit and shouted 'fire'. Injuries were caused in the ensuing panic. More recent cases have approved the point. In **DPP v K (1990)** a school student left a science lesson with a test-tube full of acid and went to the lavatory with it. On hearing someone approaching he panicked and poured it, inexplicably, into an electric hand dryer rather than a sink or toilet. Even more inexplicably the court accepted this version of events and that the boy intended to rectify the situation as soon as class was over. Before he could do so another child used the hand dryer and was permanently injured by having acid sprayed upon him. K (his juvenile status allows him to remain anonymous) was convicted of actual bodily harm with its battery component (see later) committed by indirect means.

In **Haystead v Chief Constable of Derbyshire (2000)** Haystead punched a woman, causing her to drop her baby to the floor. He was convicted of battery to the baby despite having not touched the child.

What is less clear is whether a battery can occur by omission. Student officers will recall the discussion in Chapter 1 around the 'Contemporaneity rule' and its application in **Fagan v MPC (1969)**. Commentators have argued that the complexity of the decision might have been avoided had the Divisional Court simply allowed that a battery may be committed by omission, thus when Fagan refused to move the car he committed the battery by doing so. There would have been no need to employ a legal fiction. Nevertheless the court was quite clear that battery by omission is not possible. The difficulty arises in that the Divisional Court in both **DPP v K (1990)** and **DPP v Santana-Bermudez (2004)** indicate that battery by omission is possible at least when a person makes a situation dangerous and then fails to rectify that (see the discussion around **R v Miller (1982)** under 'omissions' in Chapter 1). Santana-Bermudez had in fact not revealed the presence of a hypodermic needle in his pockets when a police officer asked him about the contents. The officer carried out a search (see Chapter 3) and injured herself on the needle. This was held to be actual bodily harm (through battery) by omission.

Unlawfully

There are many reasons why the application of force might be perfectly lawful; for instance, during arrest and detention in accordance with lawful procedures, self-defence and the prevention of crime and the 'moderate correction of a juvenile' by a parent or guardian. Note that this no longer extends to a teacher in either a state or public school. This whole issue is the subject of heated debate at the moment. It is generally accepted that smacking is still lawful unless it goes beyond what the law says a battery is and leaves marks or scars.

It could be said that CPS guidelines blur the distinction between battery and actual bodily harm. In law no visible injury is required. It will be seen that actual bodily harm requires some form of injury yet the CPS charging standard describes minor bruising and even a black eye as potentially only battery.

It may be that legislation will be forthcoming in the future which outlaws any kind of smacking but it seems inconceivable that restraint of a minor by force will ever be unlawful. This is even if restraint of an adult in the same circumstances would be a battery.

Knowledge Check 1

PC O'Dwyer attends an address in Groby Avenue, Lutonchester. There has been a report of banging and shouting from inside the house. Sgt. Bell arrives to assist O'Dwyer. The officers enter the house as the front door is partly open and they can hear shouting. The officers witness the following:

i)   A man they later discover to be Andy Gray is standing next to his partner Greg Evans. There is broken furniture and other items strewn about the room. Andy turns to see the officers and raises a smashed china figurine in the air. He says to Greg. 'You see what you've done, someone's called the f****** cops. That's lucky for you, I was about to smash your head in.'

ii) Greg grabs Andy's wrist and head-butts Andy; he succeeds only in making contact with the flowing folds of the bathrobe Andy is wearing.

iii) Andy pulls away from Greg who raises a fist as if to punch Andy. Andy is 6'4" tall. Greg is 5'2" in height. At this point the officers intervene.

Outline the offences committed by each party, if any, at each of i), ii) and iii).

The answers are at the end of the chapter.

The issue of consent is important. The approach of English law to this issue is complex and not that consistent. For this reason and the fact that the consent discussion applies to all assaults there is a separate section fully exploring that topic. It is mentioned here because it is best understood with some assault law already discussed.

Consent in assaults generally

The presence or absence of consent can make the difference between an act being a totally lawful activity and it being an assault, perhaps a serious one. The easy answer would be to treat all applications of force as legitimate as long as the victim consented. That seems a logical approach in an era of civil liberties as it gives primacy to the wishes of the individual in respect of their own bodies. We know that the law does not allow all consents to be valid. A 15-year-old cannot lawfully consent to sexual intercourse for example. Similarly no one currently can consent lawfully to being killed as an act of euthanasia. Any such consent in fact would have no bearing on any conviction for murder.

It is quite difficult to draw a distinct line between what will and will not be an act for which consent will be valid. Much depends on what we will call here the 'social utility' of that act. In other words, it depends on how useful or worthwhile the act is to society as a whole. It is worth pointing out that most of the decisions in this area are of a legal rather than factual nature and therefore made by judges not juries. For reasons outside the scope of this volume, the vast majority of judges are still white, male, middle-aged, of the professional classes and of a public school and/or Oxbridge (Oxford or Cambridge University) background. It is argued by some that the social attitudes persisting in some of this group of people are visible in many of the decisions made in the following case law. Also, as a result of this, law is made in this area according to what has 'social utility' to this rather select stratum of society rather than what the man in the street might view as acceptable.

The best way forward is to look at areas where 'assaults' routinely take place and consent is given. These areas arguably contain grey areas in the law.

Sport

Here much will depend on the rules of the game. Obviously a certain level of injury is explicitly accepted in boxing and the martial arts. It is also impliedly accepted in sports like football and rugby (**R v Barnes 2004**). The tape placed around some rugby players' head and ears is there to stop the ears getting caught and partially torn from the surrounding scalp during a scrum. Such an injury would draw an instant police response in most other circumstances but the injury, provided it is non-deliberate, is consented to by the player as an accepted risk. See the case of **R v Billinghurst (1978)** where the defence of consent was allowed in a game of rugby.

There is a limit though: no one impliedly consents to death during a game. There has been at least one Australian manslaughter case from an essentially bad (i.e. illegal in the game rules sense) tackle. Although death or serious injury is a possibility in a boxing match, provided there has been no impropriety there will be no prosecution.

Other sporting activities are best approached with common sense and that issue of 'social utility' in the back of one's mind. Clearly a greater level of risk is consented to in a hockey match than a table tennis tournament and so on. Further, if a contact sport is being played, if an injury results from a properly organised and refereed bout that is one thing. If the protagonists have been 'slugging it out' in a garage or basement in some kind of unofficial bare-knuckle contest, that is quite another. Consent may not be valid here.

Sexual activity

Public attitudes to sex during history have not been as stable as one might assume. The Greeks and Romans took quite a liberal view of practices that were not tolerated in late Western society until the latter quarter of the twentieth century. Similarly, the particularly rural dwelling, pre-Victorian nineteenth century folk were much more relaxed about sex before official marriage than any society existing later until that of the 1960s.

This ebb and flow of public morality is followed, albeit falteringly and slowly, by the legal system. If we begin our discussion around the mid twentieth-century for practical purposes, it can be seen from **R v Donovan (1934)** that what might be termed 'spanking' (in legal terms a battery) for sexual reasons could not be validly consented to in law. In **Boyea (1990)** it was accepted that 'the level of vigour in sexual congress' was likely now to be greater than when **Donovan** was decided. Boyea's conviction for indecent assault was upheld despite the victim's consent, however. This was due to the fact that the injury he caused to her vagina was always likely in the particular circumstances of the case and the victim could not be held to have consented to that.

The manslaughter case of **Slingsby (1992)** is interesting, however. Here the man had caused internal injuries to the victim which he neither intended nor foresaw. Despite her death from septicaemia, the victim's actual consent to his extremely vigorous love-making practices was seen as valid in law.

The present law is as laid down in **R v Brown (1993)**. This was an extremely-high profile case, not least because of the salacious detail it provided for the tabloids. The case concerned a group of male homosexuals who met in private to engage in sado-masochistic practices. The injuries they inflicted on each other where all consensual. Activities included sandpapering and nailing through genitalia, branding with hot wires and so forth. Any lasting injuries they treated themselves rather than going to a medical practitioner. The acts concerned only came to light when the police found video evidence whilst investigating another matter.

Arguments raged about whether the police should be involved in prosecuting such 'self-regarding' activities (J.S. Mill applied this term to behaviour that he argued the state has no right to interfere with). Set against this was the general feeling that these activities were so unwholesome that society had a duty to discourage others from acting in the same way. The court eventually upheld the convictions against the defendants ranging all the way up to GBH. The court considered the consent given to be invalid in the circumstances.

In giving judgment the Law Lords ranged across a number of areas where assault might be committed with consent, such as religion, before giving judgment. This was that effectively no more than battery could be committed lawfully for the purposes of sexual gratification. Anything greater would be prosecutable on the grounds that any consent given would not be recognised in law.

R v Wilson (1996) provides an interesting loophole in this ruling and is discussed under 'Body art' below.

Religion

There are a number of practices carried out on religious grounds which would otherwise be assaults. The law here is not consistent though and much will depend on how well recognised the practice is in Western society and what the perceived benefits versus the actual benefits are. In **R v Brown (1993)** a hypothetical situation of a father confessor whipping a genuinely remorseful religious devotee at his request was given as an example of what would be lawful. Similarly male circumcision is perfectly lawful even though consent has to be given by someone else in the case of say, a three-day-old baby. We know from the **Female Genital Mutilation Act 2003** that circumcision of a female is not lawful, however. The argument raised in support of this is the contention that male circumcision is for religious and physical cleanliness. The equivalent procedure performed on a female is to prevent her enjoying sex, however, thus reinforcing the dominance of her male partner, it is argued.

An illustration of where the line is drawn here is provided by **R v Adesanya (1983)** in which the defendant cut the cheeks of her 14-year-old sons in accordance with West African custom. This initiated the children into 'manhood'. Adesanya was convicted of actual bodily harm.

At first sight it may be difficult to discern why the law supports the mutilation of the genitalia of one sex but not another and supports mutilation when it is done in pursuit of one cultural custom but not others. The answer lies in the cultural and historical context. It may be that the whole area is nevertheless due for review.

(?) *Consider the handling of, and the writing up of, any incident where an injury was inflicted for cultural reasons. This would have to be handled extremely sensitively. The bottom line is that the law of the land precludes certain activities. The subjects of your enquiries and their communities may not understand or accept this restriction easily, though. It is a sobering thought that in a recent poll of 500 British Asians of varying religions, 1 in 10 felt that violence and even 'honour killings' were acceptable to avenge a slight to family honour.*

Whilst considering this part of the syllabus it would be useful to look at the situation where consent to sex has been procured by a fraud. Only though, if the consent was obtained based on falsehood regarding the identity of the accused or the nature of the act will consent be invalid. Say for example Dr A examined a female patient internally on the pretext that it was necessary but actually it was for sexual gratification (such as in the initial scenes of the film *'The hand that rocks the cradle'*), any consent would be invalid. In just the same way consent would be invalid if the man was in fact not Dr A but a sexual deviant wearing a stolen white coat. Again the law here is undergoing development through time. In **R v Clarence (1888)** it was held that a husband who did not tell his wife he had a venereal disease did not assault her when they had consensual sex. This is even though her consent would not have been forthcoming had she known. Unsurprisingly this approach has not survived the era of HIV/AIDS. In **R v Dica (2004)** when the accused knowingly failed to inform his sexual partner of his infection before intercourse it was held that the consent extended to the sexual act but not the risk of infection. Accordingly Dica was convicted of GBH.

Medical practice

It is interesting to note that many of us have consented to what would otherwise be GBH, probably more than once in our lives. We may not all have had a surgical procedure but many of us have had a tooth extraction by a qualified dentist. The reason this is so painful is because the tooth is joined to the bone in which it is seated and when it is extracted it is snapped away from that, causing minor damage to the jawbone. A description like that of a non-consensual injury would leave the reader in no doubt a serious assault had taken place. We of course consent to this and other medical procedures quite lawfully.

The consent can be rendered unlawful, however. In **R v Tabassum (2000)** 'research subjects' allowed themselves to receive a breast examination by Tabassum who said he was doing research to help him create a software package for the medical profession. This was untrue and he was convicted of assault as the victim's consent was invalid.

It was determined that this way of thinking would not extend to the validity of consent to treatment carried out by a dentist who was practising whilst suspended. In **R v Richardson (1998)**, perhaps a rather odd decision, it was held consent was valid notwithstanding the patient's lack of knowledge of the disciplinary proceedings against the dentist.

Body art

There are various practices carried out by people on themselves and others for the purposes of enhancing bodily appearance. These range from traditional tattooing to piercing and even the 'scarring' of patterns into the skin using surgical instruments. All of these would of course involve assaults if the consent of the subjects were not given. In terms of tattooing the law is clear in that a person under the age of 18 cannot give valid consent to a tattoo under the **Tattooing of Minors Act 1969**. No such specific statute applies to body piercing however, and it is perfectly lawful to have a young child's ears pierced as some parents do. There is some doubt however, as to the position if unqualified people carry out the procedure, perhaps in less than sterile situations. Consent is less likely to be valid then.

The law in this area is even less straightforward when the reason for inflicting the 'injury' is in doubt. In **R v Wilson (1996)** a doctor noticed that the buttocks of one of his female patients had initials burned into them. These permanent scarring marks had been applied by Wilson at the lady's request with a hot knife apparently during sexual activity. Wilson was no doubt aware that, following **R v Brown (1993)**, the lady could not consent in law to this for sexual gratification which would mean that an assault had occurred. Wilson therefore contended that the marks were a 'desirable piece of physical adornment', in other words had been put there because they looked nice. Any argument that they did not in fact look pleasant at all was of course futile because the same could be said of any body art. To put these injuries into a category where consent would not be valid would potentially at a stroke render all tattoos and body piercing unlawful. The maxim 'beauty is in the eye of the beholder' held sway and Wilson was accordingly found not guilty.

'Rough and tumble'

It is possible to consent to what is known in judicial circles as 'rough and undisciplined horseplay', in other words 'goofing around on the park with your mates'. If this results in injury in the absence of any coercion this is unlikely to result in any prosecution.

REVISION

Battery requires:

✓ intentional or reckless;
✓ application of unlawful force to another;
✓ consent can render force lawful, the validity of consent depends on:
  • how useful or worthwhile the activity is
  • accepted 'norms' of public morality
  • the severity of the injury.

We can now return to the discussion of assaults and the true statutory offences. These all derive from an old piece of legislation that is arguably long overdue for an overhaul (see the discussion in the previous sections about the 1998 Offences Against the Person Bill which did not make any real headway). This legislation is the **Offences Against the Person Act 1861**. This statute, sometimes even referred to as a 'rag-bag of offences', contains many different crimes. These range from illegal abortions to poisoning and bigamy. We are concerned with the main assaults here however, starting with actual bodily harm (ABH).

Actual bodily harm

The definition of this offence is found in **s. 47 Offences Against the Person Act 1861.** The wording is as follows:

> *Whosoever shall be convicted upon an indictment of any assault occasioning actual bodily harm shall be liable...to imprisonment for not more than five years...*

This is not the most helpfully worded statutory provision. It is also relatively unusual for a statute to specify the jail term, even in terms of a maximum, in such a way. Furthermore, there is no real guidance in the section as to what an assault is or what actual bodily harm might look like. The case law that has developed since, however, does provide some example. The definition provided above can be broken down thus:

- assault;

- occasioning (causing);

- ABH.

REVISION

Actual bodily harm is covered by s. 47 Offences Against the Person Act 1861. In summary the definition can be broken down into:

✓ assault (i.e a common assault);
✓ causing (i.e. in legal terms);
✓ actual bodily harm.

In this context the type of assault referred to is common assault of either the psychic or battery variety discussed in the preceding sections. This offence is committed when that assault leads to an identifiable injury. The CPS guidelines muddy the waters somewhat here because they list types of injury which will still be treated as just a battery. In law however, the line between battery and ABH is crossed when an identifiable injury is caused.

The *mens rea* of this offence is therefore the same as that required for the battery or the psychic assault, that is, intention or subjective recklessness (**R v Savage; Parmenter (1991)**). This of course does not tell us what the accused has to intend or be reckless to before he or she can be guilty of the offence. In other words, would the accused have to intend merely the original battery, etc., or the subsequent injury? In fact only intention or recklessness to the original battery or psychic assault is required. If, by some bad luck, say, the person trips and bangs their head as a result of the battery, that will still be treated as ABH.

Occasions

The assault must cause the ABH. The word 'occasions' is just obsolete English for 'cause'. It is useful to look at how direct and indirect causation has been treated by the courts. Clearly if a punch is thrown, that blow connects with its target and there is an identifiable injury (see next section) then there is no causation issue. There may be a need for a discussion if, as a result of the accused's actions, the victim injures themselves. This situation was considered in **R v Roberts (1971)**. The accused was driving a car in which the victim was a front-seat passenger. Roberts made lewd suggestions to the victim and tried to remove her coat. In response the victim leapt from the moving vehicle and suffered actual bodily harm, effectively by her own hand. Roberts contended that he was not responsible for these injuries even if he was responsible for the initial battery as her reaction to his advances was an extreme one. The court upheld his conviction because they felt that the lady's reaction was a reasonable one in the circumstances. This is viewed as indirect causation but causation nevertheless.

It should be noted that following such as **R v Ireland**; **Burstow (1998)**, discussed already under psychic assault, the harm can be caused by such means as stalking, silent telephone calls and hate-mail. It could potentially include text messages and email as well. If it is psychiatric harm though a general feeling of stress, anxiety or unhappiness will not suffice; the condition must be diagnosable. This point was most recently reaffirmed in **R v D (2006)**.

Actual bodily harm

Clearly the legislators intended that the harm would be greater than that in the assault category. The generally accepted definition of the *phrase* actual bodily harm (as opposed to the *offence*) is provided by **R v Miller (1954)**. In this case the term was felt to encompass any 'hurt or injury likely to interfere with the health or comfort of the victim'. Thus significant bruising, a burn, cut (short of wounding – see next section), concussion or say a broken and displaced nose would all come within this definition. As we have seen, this is also true of mild psychiatric disorders such as panic attacks or depression.

The harm must be more than 'transient or trifling' as was said in **R v Donovan (1934)**. This was supported by the ruling in **R v Chan Fook (1994)**.

When dealing with an assault, even of a relatively minor nature as discussed here, your points of reference are case law, statute, CPS policy or guidelines and local force policy. When you write up such an incident in your SOLAP or reflective diary be sure to make links with each of these to ensure your entry receives maximum credit.

Grievous bodily harm

The definition of this offence is found in **s. 20 Offences Against the Person Act 1861**. The wording is:

> *unlawfully and maliciously wound or inflict any grievous bodily harm upon any other person, either with or without any weapon or instrument.*

This is not the most transparent of legislative provisions and is not the same as the more serious grievous bodily harm with intent discussed in the next section. In fact, defying logic, it bears only the same maximum sentence as that for ABH, being five years in prison. This definition may be broken down as follows:

- unlawfully;

- maliciously;

- wound or inflict grievous bodily harm.

Unlawfully

We have discussed at length what might render an assault lawful. Such issues as self-defence and consent could do so. The force used in self-defence would have to be reasonable and proportionate to the threat posed by the assailant.

ACTIVITY

The Tony Martin case (a Norfolk farmer who shot and killed a burglar, wounding another) provoked great controversy over what could and could not be lawfully done to another in the defence of oneself, other people and one's property. Politicians have proposed greater or lesser degrees of force as 'reasonable'. The CPS moved to produce guidance on this issue in January 2005. You can see the updated version of this guidance at:

www.cps.gov.uk/legal/section5/chapter_d.html#04

Read it and consider this: some politicians have argued that the force used could be disproportionate as long as it is not grossly so. What arguments can you think of for and against this proposition?

Maliciously

The *mens rea* of the offence is contained in the word 'maliciously', a term not used as much as it once was and like 'occasions' (encountered under ABH) requires an up-to-date meaning. **R v Savage; Parmenter (1991)** again provides this meaning, holding it to be synonymous with intention or subjective recklessness (i.e. the same as in common assault and battery). The accused need not have intended or be reckless as to the exact nature or level of injury that is actually caused. He will still be guilty, however. **R v Mowatt (1968)** held that *mens rea* as to 'some harm' is all that is required for a conviction. In practice this means that if an accused throws, say, a brick at a victim intending to only bruise her, a conviction for GBH can follow if what actually transpires is a broken jaw.

There are limits to this way of thinking, however. In **R v Sullivan (1981)** the accused drove his car at his victims intending only to frighten them; in the event he lost control of the vehicle and struck them. His conviction for GBH was quashed and it was held that an intention merely to frighten the victims would not suffice.

Wound or inflict grievous bodily harm

There are in fact two separate offences here; a wound is not necessarily GBH and vice versa. Wounding requires a breach of both upper and lower layers of skin, i.e. both the dermis and epidermis. A knife wound which penetrates to the bone or internal organs would clearly constitute the *actus reus* of the offence whereas a long but more shallow slash with a 'box-cutter' knife would not despite its equally debilitating effect. The alternative charge of GBH would still be available however in these latter circumstances.

What is essential though is that the correct charge is selected at the outset. The arrest can in good faith be for wounding, say in the 'box-cutter' situation above, as there are reasonable grounds to suspect a wounding has taken place (see Chapter 3 for relevant arrest powers). The charge was incorrect, for example in **JJC v Eisenhower (1983)**. Eisenhower had shot his victim with an air rifle, the pellet had pierced the eyeball causing blood vessels in the eye to rupture and bleed. It has to be remembered that not all of the body is covered by epidermis. For example, the tongue and gums can be exposed to the outside world and so can the eyes but these (excluding for the moment the eyelids) are covered by other than epidermis, in the case of the eyes, a membrane. Accordingly as Eisenhower had not pierced his victim's dermis or epidermis, he could not be guilty of wounding.

ACTIVITY

These biological terms may be unfamiliar to you. A basic description of the epidermis and dermis with diagrams can be found at such as: **http://en.wikipedia.org/wiki/Dermis**

Inflicting GBH used to give a different meaning to the word 'cause' found in the other statutory definitions. Since cases such as **R v Ireland; Burstow (1998)**, it is fairly clear that if one can inflict harm by means of stalking then there is no need for a direct assault as the old definitions held.

What GBH actually means was the subject of a number of cases culminating in **R v Saunders (1985)**. The injuries that fell to be considered here included a broken nose and the court considered that GBH meant 'serious harm' to the victim. Generally speaking GBH will mean something which has resulted in significant disablement of the victim, even if only temporarily.

GBH with intent

This is the most serious assault and is second only to attempted murder. Many cases turn on whether the offence can be deemed a 'section 18' or an attempt to take life. For this reason the sentence is discretionary life. This means that it is in the judge's discretion whether to award the maximum penalty or something lesser. In the case of a mandatory life sentence (see murder in the next section) the judge has no choice but to award life if the jury convict. There is much talk of 'life not meaning life' in the popular press. It is quite possible for a 'lifer' to serve less than his or her natural life behind bars. It should be remembered though that someone on a life sentence is only ever released on licence and is subject to recall to prison at the discretion of the prison authorities. It would not necessarily need a further criminal offence to trigger this.

Many of the words in this offence are the same as those already encountered and do not require further discussion. The section should be read in conjunction with the rest of this chapter on assaults, however. The definition is found in **s. 18 Offences Against the Person Act 1861**:

Whosoever shall unlawfully and maliciously by any means whatsoever wound or cause any grievous bodily harm to any person, with intent to do some grievous bodily harm to any person, or with intent to resist or prevent the lawful apprehension or detainer of any person, shall be guilty of an offence...

The statement is unnecessarily long and there are some superfluous words and phrases in it. The key elements are:

- unlawfully;
- wound or cause GBH;
- with intent/with intent to resist arrest.

Unlawfully (and maliciously?)

You will note the absence of the word 'maliciously' from the breakdown provided above. It is generally accepted via case law that the word adds nothing to this particular definition and, in contrast to **s. 20**, may be ignored. 'Unlawfully' has the same meaning as within **s. 20**. Readers should also revisit the section on consent in this chapter.

Wound or cause GBH

Wound and GBH have the same meaning as within **s. 20**. Cause has the same meaning as in **s. 47**. The discussion around direct and indirect causation in previous sections applies here. It is evident from discussion such as **R v Ireland; Burstow (1998)** that GBH could potentially be caused by something as difficult to measure as nuisance telephone calls and other harassment if sustained enough.

With intent/with intent to resist arrest

This constitutes the *mens rea* of the offence and is restricted to intention alone. The diagram for this offence which differs from the previous one on page 95 covering common assault to **s. 20**, is overleaf.

There are in fact four quite distinct offences here. These are:

- wounding with intent;
- GBH with intent;
- wounding with intent to resist arrest;
- GBH with intent to resist arrest.

The latter two require the individual to seriously injure another in the process of escaping from lawful detention. This is actually much wider in scope than merely arrest. Prison or youth detention, local authority secure care, detention under **s. 1 PACE 1984** for a stop and search, an arrest by a such as a store detective or detention for 30 minutes by a PCSO would all be examples of 'lawful detainer'. Escape from any such detention using this level of violence could lead to a conviction for a **s. 18** offence.

Diagram of relationship between intention and oblique intention (s.18 GBH)

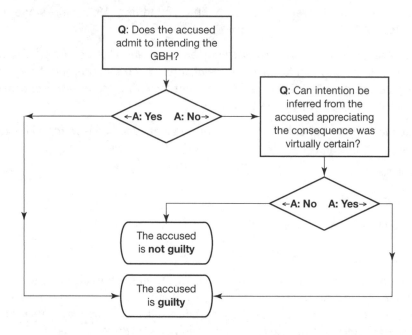

REVISION

✓ GBH and wounding are separate offences
  ● GBH is 'serious harm'
  ● Wounding requires a cut through both layers of skin.

✓ GBH and wounding are found in:
  ● s. 20 Offences Against the Person Act 1861 (GBH)
  ● s. 18 Offences Against the Person Act 1861 (GBH with intent).

✓ The *mens rea* differs:
  ● s. 20 requires either intention or subjective recklessness
  ● s. 18 requires intention to GBH/wound or resist arrest.

Knowledge Check 2

Bob Green arrives at Charles St Police Station, Lutonchester, and gives himself up to police. His subsequent statement is an account of a fight caught on CCTV outside a city-centre pub the previous evening. It contains the following passages:

(a) *I saw Ali getting punched by a man several times so I ran over to him and hit him a number of times on the head and shoulders with an iron bar. He lay on the floor moaning a bit until the paramedics came.*

(b) *A woman who was with the man I hit pulled a knife out of her handbag and was waving it at me and screaming. I got the knife off her but in the struggle it must have caught her arm because it started to bleed heavily. It was dripping off her fingers.*

(c) *Two people tried to hold me back. I got free from one and head-butted the other in the face. By the time I was arrested a few minutes later I could see that his left eye was starting to close up.*

Assuming no deaths occur and ignoring for now attempted murder, what offences appear to have been disclosed that Bob Green may have committed?

The answers are at the end of the chapter.

Racially aggravated or religiously aggravated assaults

These are not distinct offences really. Instead more recent statutes refer back to the **Offences Against the Person Act 1861**. They increase the severity of the punishment if racial hatred (from **Crime and Disorder Act 1998**) or religious hatred (from **Anti-terrorism, Crime and Security Act 2001**) motivate the attack.

In effect **s. 29 Crime and Disorder Act 1998** extends the maximum sentence for a **s. 47** or **s. 20 Offences Against the Person Act 1861** offence to seven years if the attack is 'racially or religiously aggravated'.

Section 28 (1) Crime and Disorder Act 1998 goes on to differentiate between offences where the offender demonstrates toward the victim 'hostility based on the victim's membership (or presumed membership of) a racial or religious group…' and those where the 'offence is motivated…by [a general] hostility towards members of a racial or religious group…'. Both are equally serious.

One should be careful about what the law treats as an identifiable group for the purposes of this statute. It is demonstrable that 'African' is not a literal term as it does not include Arabs or whites (from e.g. Zimbabwe or South Africa). Also followers of Islam and Rastafarians are religious groups but would not qualify as racial groups. This may be at odds with the way that the groups see themselves. A fuller discussion of this point is outside the scope of this volume but see Card, Cross and Jones, *Criminal law* (full reference at the end of the chapter) where the topic is amply discussed.

You are likely to come across assaults in your career which are motivated by prejudice against a certain group. Unfortunately the law tends to adopt a piecemeal approach with different offences for racists, religious zealots and perhaps none at all where hatred exists but has not yet been legislated against yet, such as homophobia. You may wish to comment on this in your SOLAP or reflective entry. You could perhaps do this by linking to our earlier SOLAP hints around 'what is a community'.

Assault on and obstruction of a police officer

These are in fact two offences, assaulting a constable in the execution of his duty and obstructing or resisting a constable in the execution of his duty. Both are offences under the **Police Act 1996** are therefore statutory rather than common law. **Section 89(1)** covers the assault and **s. 89(2)** the obstruction, which must be wilful and includes the obstruction or resisting of a person assisting the constable, which would now of course include a PCSO acting in such a capacity.

The assault referred to is a common assault and therefore could be a battery or a psychic assault. The accused need not know that the person is a constable, say if he or she is in plain clothes, to commit the offence. However, if the constable is not acting in the course of his or her duties, perhaps through malice, or more likely over-zealousness or a misinterpretation of the law, the situation is different. If the assault is a reasonable reaction such that would satisfy the test discussed earlier for self-defence/prevention of crime, then these offences are not committed.

Harassment

Protection from Harassment Act 1997

By the end of this section you will be able to:

- evaluate the development of legislation in this area;

- explain the difference between an assault and harassment;

- explain the various criminal and civil remedies under the legislation.

We have already discovered that the over 165-year-old laws on assault are not ideally suited to counter the 'stalker' of today. The assault laws have been adapted to apply to the most serious manifestations of this behaviour where they result in identifiable psychiatric damage. A person's life may be made a misery without the assailant's conduct causing such a diagnosable condition. This conduct can be dealt with through the civil law but requires the victim to pursue a civil injunction with the help of a solicitor. This is not without its technical legal pitfalls and carries a potential cost to all but the most needy who may possibly claim state assistance.

The **Protection from Harassment Act 1997** goes some way towards addressing this gap in the law. This act provides both civil and criminal remedies. These allow the police to become involved in preventing low-level obsessive and intrusive conduct. Alternatively or additionally they allow the victim to pursue the matter in the civil courts on a firmer footing than was provided by the previous common law. The civil injunction also carries a criminal penalty for its breach which would again require police involvement. This is nothing new: traditional domestic violence injunctions can carry a power of arrest despite being a civil measure.

Essentially the civil and criminal remedies would require proof of any one of two prohibited behaviours. **Section 1(1)** prohibits 'a course of conduct which amounts to harassment of another and...which he knows or ought to know amounts to harassment...'. **Section 1(1A)** was inserted by **s. 125** of the **Serious Organised Crime and Police Act 2005** and contains the second prohibition, specifically: '...a course of conduct which involves harassment of two or more persons, and which he knows or ought to know [is harassment]...by which he intends to persuade any person...not to do something that he is entitled or required to do, or... to do something that he is not under any obligation to do'. **Section 2(1)** of the Act makes it an offence to breach the prohibitions described above.

Finally **s. 4(1)** of the Act provides for a more serious offence. Under this provision causing another to fear, on at least two occasions, that violence will be used against him is a crime. The distinction between this and psychic assault discussed in the first part of this chapter is that there is no requirement that the violence should be immediate.

Section 32(1) of the **Crime and Disorder Act 1998** creates a racially or religiously aggravated version of the offences in **s. 2** and **4** of the **Protection from Harassment Act 1997**. The ethos of this provision is rather like that for similarly aggravated assaults in that it merely allows for stiffer penalties in these circumstances.

Malicious communications

> **REVISION**
> ✓ The act prohibits a course of conduct that amounts to harassment of another.
> ✓ If committed against two or more persons with the intention of persuading them to do or not do something, a further offence is committed.
> ✓ Causing another to fear, on at least two occasions, that violence will be used against him is a further offence, as is racially/religiously aggravated harassment.

By the end of this section you will be able to:

• explain the different malicious communications the law prohibits;

• describe the limits to the legislation in this area;

• explain the remedies under the legislation.

It is possible to send 'hate mail' or other disturbing and frightening text or images in a variety of ways nowadays. If these communications fall short of an assault or harassment they may still constitute an offence.

The **Malicious Communications Act 1988** covers both mail and electronic communications or an 'article of any description', for example a voodoo doll or other effigy with malicious overtones. In order to constitute an offence, by **s. 1** these must convey in whole or in part:

- an indecent or grossly offensive message;

- a threat (of an unwarranted nature, so not including legal debt-recovery procedures);

- information known or believed to be false by the sender.

In addition, any other article or electronic communication which is indecent or grossly offensive in nature is covered.

Any telecommunications system is covered by the act so this could extend to internal emails, for example.

The **Telecommunications Act 1984, s. 3** covers messages or other matter which is 'grossly offensive or of an indecent, obscene or menacing character'. It also covers sending '…for the purpose of causing annoyance, inconvenience or needless anxiety to another, a message that he knows to be false or persistently makes use for that purpose of a public telecommunications systems'.

Note that this offence is limited to public telecommunication systems so would not apply to internal telephone calls or emails within a business unless they were routed through a public system.

REVISION

✓ Sending offensive, threatening, obscene or false material by mail or any electronic means:
  - s. 1 Malicious Communications Act 1988.
✓ Sending offensive, threatening, obscene or false material by public telecommunications system:
  - s. 3 Telecommunications Act 1984.

Homicide

By the end of this section you will be able to:

- evaluate and define the major case law on murder;

- explain the difference between voluntary and involuntary manslaughter;

- answer questions on topics in this area.

Student officers will not normally investigate a homicide but may well be involved on the periphery of a, say, murder investigation. This could range from being first officer on scene at a fatal stabbing or in making house-to-house enquiries as part of a major operation. It is important therefore that officers are aware, even early in their careers, of what different types of homicide there are. This is vital to understand the importance of pieces of evidence they discover or testimony given to them by witnesses, etc. There is a limit, however, of how deeply such a topic can be covered in a volume of this nature. It is proposed to limit the discussion to murder, the partial defences which give rise to a potential finding of voluntary manslaughter and involuntary manslaughter.

Sadly, some domestic violence (DV) cases end up as murder investigations. In those DV cases you deal with and write up for the purposes of your SOLAP, consider how easy it is for the level of violence to escalate in relationships in crisis like this. Make reference to homicide cases as appropriate, that contain a history of DV from your studies. This demonstrates you do not underestimate the seriousness of DV incidents. This underestimation is unfortunately something officers and forces have been accused many times of being guilty of in the past.

Road traffic offences involving fatalities are dealt with at Chapter 19, 'Roads policing'. Infanticide and suicide pacts for example, are substantially excluded for reasons of space but further reading sources can be found at the end of this chapter.

The relationship of murder to voluntary and involuntary manslaughter

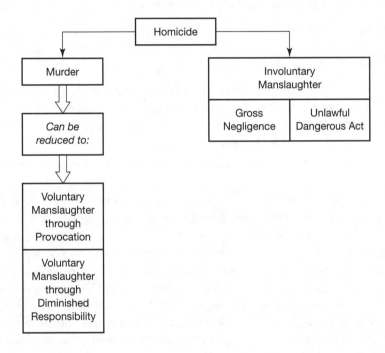

Murder

The definition for this most heinous of crimes is very old and is not contained in any statute. The 'modern' definition is attributed to Coke, writing in the seventeenth century. The language is archaic and our needs are best served by simply illustrating the main components of the offence. In essence a person is guilty of murder if he:

- unlawfully kills

- a Human being

- under the Queen's peace

- with malice aforethought

- death occurring within a year and a day (now amended to three years).

Unlawful killing

This has much in common with the discussion around lawfulness in assault cases. Particularly relevant is the issue of self-defence or prevention of crime. Killing will normally only be lawful if it is a proportionate and reasonable response to the perceived threat posed by the person ultimately killed.

ACTIVITY

Revisit the CPS guidance on assault from the activity on page 93. The guidance was in part stimulated by the Tony Martin case (a Norfolk farmer who shot and killed a burglar, wounding another):

www.cps.gov.uk/legal/section5/chapter_d.html#04

Consider also the Stockwell shooting where, in the aftermath of the so-called 7/7 bombings of 7 July 2005 in London, an innocent Brazilian, Jean Charles De Menezes, was mistaken for a suicide bomber and shot dead by police.

Form an informal discussion group with your colleagues and consider these two incidents. The same test is set for 'civilians' as for those in the uniformed services who carry lethal weapons to determine whether either acted in self defence/prevention of crime. Should the tests differ or is this a fair state of affairs?

There have been a number of cases where the crucial issue has been one of self-defence. For example, in **R v Clegg (1995)** the defendant was a soldier engaged in policing a road block in Northern Ireland. Private Clegg and his colleagues were confronted with a car speeding towards them. Fearing it was an IRA attack the soldiers opened fire. The car went through the road block and Clegg fired at the rear of the retreating vehicle. His shot killed a rear-seat passenger. The car was in fact being driven by joy-riding teenagers and not terrorists. It was determined that Clegg had shot at the car when it should have been clear that it was no longer a threat – a fine distinction in such tense circumstances perhaps but one soldiers and police in these situations are often asked to make. Controversially, Clegg was convicted of murder, as the killing was not proportionate to the threat the teenagers posed.

Human being

There is rarely any doubt that the victim is a human being. There has been some debate in the case law about the situation prior to birth, however. The law only deems a foetus to be a human being when it 'crowns' or begins to leave its mother at the moment of birth. Prior to that it is protected as a foetus under the **Abortion Act 1967** or **Offences Against the Person Act 1861**. Alternatively it is protected as part of the mother and attacks on it are normally viewed as GBH on the woman. The position is somewhat complicated when the attack causes the woman to go into premature labour causing harm to the child, however. For a discussion on this point see **A-G's Reference (No 3 of 1994)**. There have been cases where the status of a person on a life-support machine as a human being have been in question as well but these are outside the scope of this volume.

Under the Queen's peace

This is just a rather quaint way of saying 'where the British monarch has jurisdiction'. Obviously that would be the geographical limits of the United Kingdom although for our purposes we should limit our discussion to England and Wales. It would also extend to, for instance, a number of dependent territories, British forces bases and embassies abroad which are deemed UK territory while the land is so used. British ships would also be included.

With malice aforethought

'Malice aforethought' refers to the *mens rea*. This has been held to be intention to kill or commit GBH. The discussion in Chapter 1 about the relationship between intention and the concept of 'foresight of virtual certainty of a prohibited consequence' is highly relevant to murder. This is not least because the majority of cases on this point such as **R v Mohan (1976)** and **R v Woollin (1998)** are murder cases. You should revisit that chapter to familiarise yourself with the points raised. In summary, it is possible to be found guilty of murder if, although you did not possess intention, you did foresee death or GBH as virtually certain; this concept is known as 'oblique intention'.

What is particularly interesting is that the *mens rea* includes the intention to commit another offence altogether, grievous bodily harm. This is perhaps because intentional GBH is a very serious matter and if you set out to do this level of damage to another person you cannot 'weigh to a nicety' the amount of force you are using. If death happens to result you should not therefore be able to escape liability for the death on grounds of public policy.

Death occurring within a year and a day (now amended to three years)

The classic definition limited prosecutions for murder to situations where the victim had died before one year and one day had elapsed. With advances in medical science it became perfectly possible to injure someone severely and for the medical profession to be able to keep them alive for a very long time with the aid of machinery. A change in the law came about in the mid-1990s. The **Law Reform (Year and a Day Rule) Act 1996** abolished the rule and by **s. 2** substituted a requirement that the Attorney General's consent is needed before a prosecution may take place for a fatal offence if the death occurs more than three years after the incident. It is at least arguable perhaps that any prosecution in this sort of situation may breach the 'double jeopardy' rule, however. This is because by definition anyone who has caused this level of injury will almost certainly have been successfully prosecuted for GBH. If the victim subsequently dies and the convicted person is then also tried for murder there will be a second trial arising out of exactly the same facts.

REVISION

The definition of murder is:
- ✓ unlawfully killing;
- ✓ of a human being;
- ✓ within the jurisdiction of UK law;
- ✓ with intention or oblique intention to kill or commit GBH;
- ✓ death occurring within three years (prosecutions may still occur after this, with A-G's permission).

Involuntary Manslaughter

This type of manslaughter is not one that an accused will be charged with. It arises when there is a charge of murder but there are certain mitigating circumstances which the defendant can use to mount a partial defence to the charge. If this tactic is successful the defendant's conviction is not one of murder but voluntary manslaughter on the grounds of:

- provocation;

- diminished responsibility;

- suicide pact.

This latter category arises when two or more people enter into an agreement to mutually end their lives, e.g. by a 'lovers leap' type of suicide from a high place together. Any survivor can be charged with murder and raise this defence.

The death penalty for murder was removed in 1965. There had been a limitation on how many types of murder could be counted as deserving the death penalty before that in 1957. The only way to appease the supporters of the death penalty of the time was to assure them that murder would carry a mandatory life sentence in future. There was however, an acknowledgement that some intentional killings were not deserving of a life sentence, even were the *actus reus* and *mens rea* of murder were present. These would include killing in the grip of a mental illness (falling short of the legal definition of insanity) and killing under severe provocation.

The following sections are a summary of what is an extremely complex and highly inconsistent area of case law. It is worth noting that almost all of it would be completely redundant if judges were simply given discretion in sentencing for murder as they are in all other offences. This is of course arguably a politically dangerous thing to do in the current climate of tabloid attacks on perceived 'soft' sentencing by judges.

Provocation

This partial defence is a statutory one. **Section 3 Homicide Act 1957** contains quite a lengthy definition. The key elements of it as interpreted by subsequent case law (see brackets) are:

- The accused must have been charged with murder.

- The jury can then consider whether the accused was provoked to (*suddenly*) lose control by 'things said or things done'.

- If so they can consider whether a 'reasonable man' (*with certain of the accused's characteristics*) would also have lost control.

This gives rise to a twofold test. Firstly the defendant must be held to have actually lost control. The element of suddenness was added by **R v Duffy (1949)**. This then is the subjective test as it is based on what the defendant was actually thinking.

Problems arise in cases where the central issue is how sudden the loss of control actually was. There is a need to allow for extreme stress which would have made almost anyone react in a similar manner. It would be unfortunate though if this provided a 'cloak' for premeditated murder. It would be very difficult to provide a time limit, whether measured in seconds, minutes, hours or days, beyond which the defence would fail. Instead each case is judged individually. This problem is particularly worrying to those who campaign on the issue of domestic violence. Many of them feel the law is too harsh on battered women and does not take into account specific female characteristics. There have been some domestic violence situations were the abuser has been killed by the victim of her, or much more commonly his, abuse.

Particularly some of those who campaign on behalf of battered women argue that a woman is 'socialised' or conditioned by society to react to violence in a very different way to men. They also argue that differences in physical size and strength make it difficult for women to react 'suddenly' to violence in situations were they are clearly outmatched by their opponent. Taken together this means that women are argued to have a 'slow-burning fuse' whereby they are more likely to react some time after the provocative conduct and should not be judged against the same criteria as men. This argument is not reflected in the current law on the subjective test however, although some leeway has been created in the objective test and in diminished responsibility (see later).

In **R v Thornton (1992)** and **R v Ahluwalia (1992)** the central issue was that the defendant in each case equipped herself with the murder weapon and in each case attacked her abusive husband after a period of time when he no longer posed a direct threat. Thornton by her own admission calmed down and 'sharpened the knife'. Ahluwalia poured petrol over her sleeping husband and set him alight. Both had their defences of provocation rejected and were convicted of murder. It is true to say that both were retried and a manslaughter conviction substituted but not on the grounds we are discussing here.

(?) *Not all domestic violence (DV) incidents you will attend will be between heterosexual couples. In murder cases arising from DV consider what complications would arise if the 'slow-burning fuse' argument were adopted. It could lead to different standards being applied to analyse the legal consequences of a delay between the provocative conduct and the killing. A woman could rely on this latitude in the law, a homosexual man could not. Comment on this if it is appropriate, in your reflective entries. This could be perhaps on diversity issues and the law generally or in relation to a particular incident you have attended.*

The 'things said or things done' element of the definition covers virtually any course of conduct. Thus if the provocative conduct is directed at other than the accused or alternatively is emanating from someone other than the victim, the defence may still be raised. This is also true even if the provocative conduct is itself generated by, say, threats or abuse from the killer. Case law has further determined that all conduct however petty must be left to the jury to determine its relevance as provocation.

The second test is an objective one. The statute itself refers to the idea of the 'reasonable man' and what this hypothetical person would have done in the circumstances. The problem is the answer to this question is never that he would have killed as the reasonable man would never do that. What is needed is some allowance for the particular characteristics of the accused. No such allowance was made in earlier decisions such as **Bedder v DPP (1954)**. Here the fact of a man's impotence could not be taken into account when he was severely taunted about this very fact by a prostitute he ultimately killed. He was convicted of murder.

A more relaxed approach was taken in **DPP v Camplin (1977)**. In this case a 15-year-old boy retaliated violently against a much older man who had just committed a serious sexual offence against him. Camplin killed him with a chapatti pan in response to the assault and the man's taunts. The court accepted that a boy of Camplin's age would react differently to a man and proposed some other characteristics which might be taken into account by future courts. Over the years that followed, the courts wrestled with the problem of how much allowance was to be made for a person's characteristics. Too little allowance was thought unfair but too much risked the test not being objective at all. In a series of cases there was an attempt to differentiate between characteristics which might affect:

- the gravity or seriousness of the provocation in the eyes of the killer;

- the ability of the killer to control their actions.

Only the former, such as taunting a short person about their height or a fat person about their weight, was considered an acceptable characteristic to give to the reasonable man. By contrast, characteristics in the latter category would appear to be such as brain damage as a child or developmental problems. It was whether this type of characteristic could be considered by the jury that produced differing judgments over time.

The law has been clarified to a degree by the cases of **A-G for Jersey v Holley (2005)** and **R v James; Karimi (2006)**. These cases indicate that the only characteristics which can be taken into account by the jury are the defendant's age and sex when applying the objective test.

REVISION

Provocation is a statutory partial defence and requires:
- ✓ The defendant was actually provoked to suddenly lose their self-control.
- ✓ A reasonable man would also have lost self-control.
- ✓ The reasonable man may be given the age and sex of the defendant in order to make a fairer comparison.

Diminished responsibility

This is again a ground for the substitution of a manslaughter conviction and thence a lower sentence than murder would attract. The definition is found in **s. 2 Homicide Act 1957** and again there must have been a charge of murder. The key points are as follows, there must be:

- an abnormality of mind;

- from specified causes;

- resulting in substantial impairment of responsibility.

Abnormality of mind

The state of mind described here is different to that in insanity, which is a full defence. A discussion of insanity is outside the scope of this volume but further reading suggestions can be found at the end of this chapter.

The abnormality of mind needs to be, according to the finding in **R v Byrne (1960)**, a state of mind so different from that of an ordinary person that the reasonable man would term it abnormal. This covers quite a range of mental infirmities in practice. Byrne himself was a sexual psychopath who mutilated the body of his victim. Peter Sutcliffe, the 'Yorkshire Ripper' who heard voices from God telling him to rid the world of prostitutes and killed 14 women in the early 1980s, would also probably have met the definition for diminished responsibility had he decided to plead it.

There are also however, cases which are arguably more touching. Diminished responsibility is the defence sometimes pleaded when a so-called 'mercy killing' takes place, euthanasia not being lawful. Certainly if the offender is suffering from something like depression from the anguish of living with a terminally ill loved one a conviction for voluntary manslaughter on the grounds of diminished responsibility can follow, often without a custodial sentence. In **R v Price (1971)** a father found the stress of looking after his severely disabled son unbearable and put him in a river, watching him float away to his death from drowning. There was evidence Price was in a 'dissociative state' at the time of the killing and he was not convicted of murder but of voluntary manslaughter as a result.

Specified causes

There are essentially three categories of specified cause allowable under the **Homicide Act s. 2**:

- disease or injury;

- inherent cause;

- condition of arrested or retarded development.

Disease or injury could cause a person to have a mental illness, for example brain damage could result from either of these.

Inherent causes could be from a very wide range of factors, usually innately present in the defendant, although not necessarily from birth. In **R v Ahluwalia (1992)**, also discussed under provocation above, an innate depressive illness founded the alternative defence of diminished responsibility. 'Battered women's syndrome', a condition recognised by the medical profession, could also fall into this category and has been allowed in voluntary manslaughter cases.

A 'condition of arrested or retarded development' is a rather outmoded phrase, today we might refer to a person having severe learning difficulties instead. A mental age of, say, 11 in a 21-year-old would be good evidence for this part of the defence.

Recent cases have indicated that the consumption of excessive alcohol does not mean that the defence automatically cannot succeed which was hitherto the case. Much will depend on whether there is a condition underlying the drinking which is a crucial factor in the killing.

Substantial impairment of responsibility

The key to this part of the definition is that the specified cause must have had a great deal to do with the fact that the accused is claiming not to have full responsibility for the killing. The defence will not succeed therefore if the cause is only a minor factor.

REVISION

Diminished responsibility is a statutory partial defence and requires:

✓ abnormality of mind;

✓ from specified causes;

✓ leading to a substantial impairment of responsibility for the killing.

Involuntary manslaughter

As the diagram in the 'Homicide' section on page 115 depicts, this is a totally different proposition to voluntary manslaughter. In this situation, the *actus reus* of murder is present but the *mens rea* is not. There is a state of mind, which is morally blameworthy however, and, if proven the charge of involuntary manslaughter will succeed.

Gross negligence manslaughter

Cases in this category often centre on professionals, like doctors for example, who have fallen far below an acceptable level of professional competence and killed someone. It need not be a professional, however, and anyone who breaches a duty of care they have to another so badly that death results could be liable.

The definitions in this area are all case law. In **R v Adomako (1994)** the law fundamentally changed from the idea of 'reckless manslaughter' which went before it. Adomako was an anaesthetist working in an operating theatre during an operation where the patient died. There was a catalogue of blunders that caused the death and which were attributed to Adomako. Specifically he failed to notice that the patient had stopped breathing and had signs of cyanosis (blueness of the skin caused when a patient's blood is not oxygenating properly), nor that the oxygen mask was not connected to anything. He also failed to notice that the alarm on the machine monitoring breathing was switched off. Adomako was tried for manslaughter and the following definition was derived. Gross negligence manslaughter is:

- breach of a duty of care [where the]

- breach causes death [and the]

- breach is grossly negligent.

This definition is derived from the civil counterpart found in the law of torts (see Chapter 20 for an overview of tort as it pertains to police officers), although there the similarity ends. It is evident from **R v Wacker (2003)**, a case where 58 Chinese illegal immigrants died from suffocation in a lorry due to the lorry driver's actions, that important principles of civil negligence do not necessarily apply to gross negligence.

Unfortunately the definition is also somewhat circular, as it does not really discern for us what gross negligence actually is. A useful starting point though could be the case of **R v Bateman (1925)** where gross negligence was differentiated from civil negligence by stating that the former was 'more than a mere matter of compensation between subjects' and therefore a criminal act. In other words, if the payment of damages will not sufficiently deal with the matter as it is too serious a wrong, it passes out of the realm of the civil law into the criminal domain.

Other cases illustrate the type of act which will be an example of gross negligence. In **R v Holloway (1993)** an electrician connected the live wire in a central heating system to the outlet water pipe in error. Thus the metal sink taps were capable of delivering an electric shock to anyone who used them. Minor instances were reported to Holloway who returned but failed to spot the mistake he had made. Ultimately the victim received a fatal shock from the taps. Similarly in **R v Prentice and Sulman (1993)**, an appeal heard at the same time as **R v Holloway (1993)**, two junior doctors attempted to carry out a spinal injection; neither was particularly competent at this task and neither noticed that the syringe, which had been prepared by a nurse, contained a drug which was fatal if spinally injected. They administered the drug and the patient died. All three defendants in these two cases were ultimately cleared on appeal but on a separate point. The facts still illustrate what might be found to be gross negligence.

REVISION

Gross negligence manslaughter:
- ✓ Breach of a duty of care.
- ✓ Breach causes death.
- ✓ Breach is grossly negligent.

Unlawful dangerous act manslaughter

This is also known as 'constructive manslaughter' and is not well loved in legal and judicial circles. It still survives but the Law Commission has recommended its abolition. This offence requires that the defendant commits a criminal act (but not a homicidal act) which leads to the death of another. The act could be a simple burglary of an elderly and infirm victim who dies from the shock of witnessing the intruder but the thief continues to ransack the house. It could be a criminal damage, as we shall see.

The definition was laid down in **DPP v Newbury and Jones (1976)**. These two defendants dropped a concrete block from a bridge onto a train. This would have been criminal damage and that was all they set out to do. Unfortunately though, the block fell through the roof of the train and killed the train guard. In the case the following requirements for unlawful dangerous act manslaughter were set out. There must be:

- an intentional unlawful act

- which is dangerous

- and causes death.

Intentional unlawful act

This is not to say that intention to kill is there – that would lead to a murder conviction. Rather the act (not omission – **R v Lowe (1973)**), which from **R v Franklin (1883)** must be a criminal one, cannot be an accident or a reckless course of conduct. Examples range from criminal damage to burglary and armed robbery. Some recent cases have caused difficulty concerned with persons taking illegal drugs together where one of them dies. In **R v Kennedy (No. 1) (1999)**, a conviction for constructive manslaughter centring on Kennedy supplying a made-up syringe of heroin to the victim who self-injected, failed. This was because the victim broke the chain of causation by administering the drug himself. In **R v Kennedy (No. 2) (2005)** this type of factual situation was dealt with by treating all involved as joint participants in the offence of 'administering an obnoxious substance' which then formed the basis of a successful constructive manslaughter conviction.

Dangerous

The question arose in **R v Church (1965)**: 'dangerous to who?' In other words, is it a subjective or objective view that is taken by the court? Church took his girlfriend to a secluded country spot in his car. The sexual act that followed left something to be desired as far as the victim was concerned and she slapped Church. In turn, Church then punched the woman, knocking her unconscious. Thinking she was dead he threw her 'body' into the nearby river where she died from drowning. It was held that by the standards of 'reasonable sober' men (meaning sensible and no reference was intended to drunkenness) this was a dangerous act. It mattered not whether the accused realised it was dangerous. Accordingly this is an objective test.

Causes death

The principles governing death are those already well rehearsed in this chapter and in Chapter 1. You should revisit the relevant sections if you are unsure of the principles of causation.

REVISION

Unlawful dangerous act manslaughter requires:

- ✓ intentional unlawful act (not omission);
- ✓ which would be dangerous to the 'reasonable sober man';
- ✓ which causes death.

Knowledge Check 3

Given that a detailed knowledge of homicide law is not required for IPLDP, this chapter has given it a relatively 'light touch'. A selection of short-answer questions is offered here to check the elements covered.

1. Thinking of the *mens rea* and *actus reus*, which is common to all types of homicide?

2. Explain the type of manslaughter that can you be charged with.

3. What is the effect of pleading diminished responsibility successfully as a defendant?

4. Which type of involuntary manslaughter does the Law Commission favour?

5. The accused burgles a factory but is challenged by a security guard. Before a struggle can take place, however, the guard falls to the floor clutching his chest. The accused takes the opportunity to spend another 30 minutes searching the premises for valuables. He leaves and the security guard dies of a heart attack.

In brief, what type of homicide is potentially committed here?

The answers are at the end of the chapter.

Suggested research

Mention has been made in this chapter of attempts to create a draft criminal code and separately of the Law Commission's views on homicide. Many textbooks such as Heaton and Card, Cross and Jones mentioned below consider these issues in greater depth. Read up on the progress made towards a criminal code in this country. Alternatively you could visit **www.lawcom.gov.uk/murder.htm** and consider the proposals put forward to change the law on murder and manslaughter.

Further reading

Further detailed discussion of all the topics in this chapter can be found by reading:

Card, R, Cross, R and Jones, P (2005) *Criminal law*. London: Butterworths.

Elliott, C and Quinn, F (2006) *Criminal law* (6th edn). Harlow: Pearson.

English, J and Card, R (2005) *Police law* (9th edn). Oxford: Oxford University Press

Heaton, R (2001) *Criminal law* (3rd edn). London: Butterworths.

Useful websites

The Law Commission:

www.lawcom.gov.uk

The Crown Prosecution Service:

http://cps.gov.uk

Legislation:

www.opsi.gov.uk

Case law and legislation databases:

www.westlaw.com* (an educational case law and statute database)

www.lexis-nexis.com* (an educational case law and statute database)

www.pnld.co.uk* (a police service specific database of case law and statute)

* Likely to be available through the virtual learning environment (VLE) which supports your course/training.

Answers

Knowledge Check 1

i)   Andy has not struck Greg, therefore of the offences studied so far the only possibility is assault, i.e. psychic assault. This and battery are often referred to as **s. 39** assault but they are in reality common law offences. The definition of a psychic or technical assault is 'to intentionally or recklessly cause another to apprehend immediate unlawful force'. At this stage it may well be possible to prove all the components of this offence with exception of the immediacy element. It is possible to infer from the facts that Andy has refrained from striking only because of the presence of the officers. In **Tuberville v Savage (1669)** it was held that words in the same vein as those used here could 'negate' the assault. In **R v Light (1857)** however, it was felt that the words may not have that effect if the threat was particularly significant. The facts do bear a passing resemblance to those in **Light** and it could be argued this situation is a psychic assault being committed. The officers could arrest subject to the provisions of **s. 24 PACE 1984**.

ii) Greg may have committed a battery; the definition is to 'intentionally or recklessly apply unlawful force to another'. Force is certainly applied as he grabs the wrist. Arguably though, Greg is not applying unlawful force as he may argue he is acting in self-defence initially. The head-butt may be beyond what is self-defence however, especially as the officers are on the scene by now. It matters not that contact is only with the clothing (**R v Thomas (1985)**). Again the officers could arrest subject to the provisions of **s. 24 PACE 1984**.

iii) On the face of it Andy applies force to Greg as he pulls away. We know from case law though that this is not considered a battery (**R v Sherriff (1969)**). Greg is now committing a psychic assault however, according to the definition cited in (i). The relative difference in size of the protagonists makes no difference as it is unecessary that the victim feels fear, only that he apprehends the force is coming. Once again the officers could arrest subject to the provisions of **s. 24 PACE 1984**.

Knowledge Check 2

(a) The victim appears to have been disabled, albeit possibly temporarily by Bob's actions. The starting point should be GBH, which is described in **R v Saunders (1985)** as 'serious harm'. The possible offences then are **s. 18** and **20 OAPA 1861**. Only some of each statutory definition is still relevant today. The most serious offence is **s. 18**, with a potential life sentence. The key points are:

- unlawfully

- wound or cause GBH

- with intent/with intent to resist arrest.

It is most unlikely that the attack was a lawful one, the only possible lawful excuse would be prevention of crime (akin to self-defence). This would require the attack to be proportionate and reasonable to the perceived threat posed to Ali. This does not seem to be the case. Wounding is not relevant here and we have already said that GBH appears to have been caused. The question is, was it Bob's 'aim or purpose' (**R v Mohan (1976)**) to do 'some harm' or at least did he appreciate that 'some harm' was virtually certain (**R v Woollin (1998), R v Matthews and Alleyene (2003)**)? Note that the requirement that 'some harm' is all that need be in the mind of the accused is from **R v Mowatt (1968)**. If the answer is 'yes' to either question then Bob is not guilty of a **s. 18** offence. If Bob took a deliberate risk that 'some harm' would be caused then he may be guilty of subjective or '**Cunningham** recklessness'. This is part of the requisite *mens rea* of a **s. 20** offence according to **R v Savage; Parmenter (1991)**.

(b) The injury to the woman could be a wound, providing it has pierced both the dermis and epidermis at some point along its length. It seems unlikely that Bob intended the injury to the woman but could be reckless. The most likely offence then would be **s. 20**. The key points for this are:

- unlawfully

- maliciously

- wound or inflict grievous bodily harm.

There is a debatable point around whether the attack is in self-defence, initially struggling with the woman would probably be justified as reasonable and proportionate. The cutting of her arm is a more difficult point to separate on the facts we are given. Bob's aggressive conduct in (a) and (c) will not help his case, however.

The word 'maliciously' means to intend or be subjectively reckless, from **R v Savage; Parmenter (1991)**. The wound may not have been Bob's aim or purpose (**R v Mohan (1976)**) but he may have taken a deliberate risk that would satisfy the requirements for **Cunningham** recklessness. From **R v Mowatt (1968)** only 'some harm' need be contemplated by the accused for a conviction. It remains only to query whether the injury, if not a wound, is GBH. The cut would be temporarily disabling and would probably satisfy the **R v Saunders (1985)** definition of GBH as serious harm.

(c) This looks like ABH. This is defined in **s. 47 OAPA 1861**:

- assault

- occasioning

- ABH.

There has clearly been a battery in that intentional 'unlawful force' has been applied to another. Following **R v Sherriff (1969)** the charge would have to rely on the head-butt, not the pulling away. There has therefore been an assault that has directly caused the injury, there is no evidence at this stage of another cause for the swelling. **R v Miller (1954)** stipulates that ABH is 'interference with the health or comfort of the victim'. Given that the swelling is likely to pass in time it is arguably more likely that this charge will be preferred over GBH.

Knowledge Check 3

1. The *actus reus* is the common factor, the actions must always cause death. The *mens rea* is quite different in each offence, however.

2. Involuntary manslaughter would be the correct answer. Alternatively unlawful dangerous act or gross negligence manslaughter is also correct. By contrast, voluntary manslaughter only arises when a partial defence is raised.

3. The defendant would be acquitted of murder but convicted of voluntary manslaughter. The judge is not bound to give a life sentence in this eventuality.

4. The Law Commission has recommended the abolition of unlawful dangerous act or 'constructive' manslaughter. It therefore favours gross negligence manslaughter.

5. The appropriate offence would be unlawful dangerous act manslaughter based on the burglary causing death. That is not to say that a case for gross negligence could not be made out on these facts if constructive manslaughter were to be abolished.

7 Sexual offences

(?) *Remember this symbol indicates that the material might be useful for your Student Officer Learning and Assessment Programme (SOLAP) portfolio or any attached reflective practice record you are required to make.*

Underpinning knowledge towards Patrol Officer NOS:

1A1, 1A4,1B9, 2C1, 2C3, 2H1, 2H2, 2J1, 2K2, 4C1

and PCSO NOS:

1A1, 1A4, 1B11, 2C1, 2C3, 2C5, 2J1, 2K1, 4C1

For further information on these NOS, which are also Policing Level 3 and 4 NVQ unit titles, refer to Appendix 1 to this volume.

This is a highly specialised area but a student officer can find themselves involved with sexual offences as first officer on scene or on the periphery of any investigation. Specialist officers and units and even other agencies like the NSPCC (see also generally Chapter 15 'Children, young persons and the mentally ill') would normally handle most sexual offences. It is not necessary therefore to do more than outline the major sexual offences here, although we do spend a little time on those committed on the streets such as exposure and prostitution, etc. This may seem inconsistent as homicide and other serious violent offences are similarly not within the likely remit of the student officer but are dealt with in depth in this volume. The difference is that many of the general concepts such as intention and causation are shown in context in murder, etc., warranting a fuller discussion as found at Chapter 6.

ACTIVITY

Many sexual offences revolve around the issue of consent, particularly those who cannot consent in law such as those under 16 years of age. Despite the fact that in the UK this age was raised from 13 to 16 as long ago as Victorian times, the teenage pregnancy rate (generally accepted as a term for people under 16 who are pregnant) in the UK is one of the worst in Europe. Use the internet and other sources to find out what the age of consent is

▶

---

in Iran, Dubai, the Netherlands, Germany and a sample of US states. You will see examples of stricter and more lenient approaches compared to the UK. The results might surprise you, though. Recently there has been discussion around lowering the age to 14 in the UK. Will this help or hinder the problem in your view?

The law in this area is largely governed by the **Sexual Offences Act 2003**. The changes made since the **Sexual Offences Act 1956** have made the law in some senses more strict and in some respects less so. For instance, some predatory activity is now outlawed that simply was not covered before. Sexual activity with a child under 16 is, however, no longer a strict liability offence so that a genuine error as to a person's age (within reason) will afford a defence. Also in (some would say) a headlong rush to outlaw some of the most unpleasant paedophile activities, the net effect of some of the provisions was arguably to subject passionate 'teenage fumbling' to a potential five-year sentence. This despite Crown Prosecution Service assertions that they would be unlikely to prosecute two 15-year-olds and under for such activity.

(?) *Suppose the mother of a 14-year-old girl calls you. She complains that the girl and her boyfriend of 15 are having a sexual relationship and she 'wants something done about him'. Under the old law the implicit emphasis was on the male as the wrongdoer. Under the* **Sexual Offences Act 2003** *however, there is no real differentiation; both parties commit the offence. Reflect on the sensitivity you will need when you tell her that in all probability if you proceed against the boy you will need to consider proceeding against the 14-year-old girl as well. How will you explain this to the mother effectively?*

We have selected the following offences to deal with in this chapter:

- rape;

- sexual assault;

- under-age sexual activity;

- indecent photographs of children;

- prostitution;

- indecent exposure.

Rape

By the end of this section you will be able to:

- define rape;

- evaluate the necessity of a distinction between 'date rape' and other forms of rape.

(?) *Only a tiny fraction of rape allegations are prosecuted successfully. Reflect on and consider the many reasons why a person, either male or female, might not want to report a rape or why they may want to withdraw an allegation. Reflect also on why so many juries acquit potential rapists. Can a woman ever be 'asking for it'?*

Rape is defined by reference to **s.1(1) Sexual offences Act 2003:**

A person (A) commits an offence if–

(a) he intentionally penetrates the vagina, anus or mouth of another person (B) with his penis,

(b) B does not consent to the penetration, and

(c) A does not reasonably believe that B consents.

The wording of this provision sweeps away for good any anomalies under old laws about insertion into other body orifices and the assumption (at least until changes in 1994) that rape could only be committed against a woman. It is worth noting that a woman can be an accomplice to rape (see generally Chapter 16).

Section 1(2) goes on to say:

Whether a belief is reasonable is to be determined having regard to all the circumstances, including any steps A has taken to ascertain whether B consents.

As recent media campaigns have reiterated, this clearly covers a situation whereby a woman is too drunk to give adequate consent. Such circumstances could well lead to a rape charge despite being termed by the unhelpful label 'date-rape'. Administering a drug such as GHB to attempt to ensure the woman consents would also fall within this offence as it could not be shown that the accused 'reasonably believed' that the victim consented.

Section 74 Sexual Offences Act 2003 further illustrates the point by defining consent:

… a person consents if he agrees by choice, and has the freedom and capacity to make that choice.

Clearly a drugged or intoxicated person could not have that capacity, neither could a seriously mentally impaired person.

ACTIVITY

In what is now an infamous judgement given in the early 1980s a judge directed a jury with words to the effect that:

… no does not always mean no, if she does not want it she only has to shut her legs and she will not get it without force…

The judge was arguably almost dismissing the concept of 'date rape' altogether. Initiate a discussion between family, friends or work colleagues. Do such attitudes still pervade today amongst the police, the wider criminal justice system and even society in general?

Rape of a child is separate offence and remains strict liability in part at least. No *mens rea* need be shown with respect to consent if the child concerned is under 13 per **s. 5(1):**

A person commits an offence if

(a) he intentionally penetrates the vagina, anus or mouth of another person with his penis, and

(b) the other person is under 13.

131

Nor indeed will it be any defence under the statute to say that the accused thought the victim older than that age.

Sexual assault

By the end of this section you will be able to:

- define sexual assault by penetration;

- define sexual assault;

- apply your knowledge to some multiple-choice questions.

It is quite possible to penetrate a victim's body orifices for sexual gratification with other than a penis. This is catered for by the offence of assault by penetration. **Section 2(1) Sexual offences Act 2003**:

A person (A) commits an offence if–

(a) he intentionally penetrates the vagina or anus of another person (B) with a part of his body or anything else,

(b) the penetration is sexual,

(c) B does not consent to the penetration, and

(d) A does not reasonably believe that B consents.

There is a corresponding offence in relation to a child under 13 which again deliberately leaves out any consideration of the consent of the child or reasonable belief in relation to age. **Section 6(1)** provides:

A person commits an offence if-

(a) he intentionally penetrates the vagina or anus of another person with a part of his body or anything else,

(b) the penetration is sexual, and

(c) the other person is under 13.

It is a fact not always recognised that many rapes and other serious sexual offences are not about having sexual intercourse as much as about asserting power and dominance over the victim. Thus the insertion of other implements such as bottles or knives is sometimes done as a way of humiliating the victim. This activity is covered by these sections provided it is done in the pursuit of sexual gratification.

Sexual assault may occur without the insertion of anything, of course. Many a victim has been left traumatised by being caressed or fondled against their will, for example. **Section 3(1)** covers the basic offence of sexual assault:

A person (A) commits an offence if

(a) he intentionally touches another person (B),

(b) the touching is sexual,

(c) B does not consent to the touching, and

(d) A does not reasonably believe that B consents.

As with all the offences so far, reasonable belief will be judged having regard to all the circumstances. It is an objective standard which means that in effect a jury or panel of magistrates will be asked to judge whether any such belief was reasonable no matter how honest it might have been. This sweeps away, in relation to sexual offences at least, the rather unsatisfactory state of the law on honest and reasonable mistakes that came from **R v Morgan (1972)**.

As a general note the offence of incest (sex with a close family member) remains under the 2003 act as does bestiality – sex with a living animal.

Under-age sexual activity

By the end of this section you will be able to:

- define the age of consent in the UK;
- explain what differences are introduced where the accused is potentially abusing a position of trust;
- apply what you know to some multi-choice questions.

The age that a young person may validly consent in law to sexual activity is 16 years. In Holland it is 12 (unless there is a big age gap between the parties), in Iran it is 12, recently raised from 9. In Germany and some US states it is 14. Interestingly it is a federal offence in the USA to take a young person across a state line to take advantage of a lower age of consent in a neighbouring state. In Dubai it is unlawful at any age unless the parties are married. In the UK the relevant age was 13 until just over 100 years ago. It follows then that the age of consent may not always remain the same and tends to follow the traditions and social norms of the society which sets it. The law can respond to changes in attitudes. Certainly the age of consent for homosexual activity fell from 21 to 16 over a very short time after heated debate in the House of Lords in the late 1990s.

For enforcement purposes the crucial issue is the age of consent now and the law says that sexual activity with someone under 16 is unlawful; **s. 9(1)** stipulates:

A person aged 18 or over (A) commits an offence if–

(a) he intentionally touches another person (B),

(b) the touching is sexual, and

(c) either

(i) B is under 16 and A does not reasonably believe that B is 16 or over, or

(ii) B is under 13.

The touching can be any of a sexual nature but the following are viewed most seriously:

- penetration of B's anus or vagina with a part of A's body or anything else;

- penetration of B's mouth with A's penis;

- penetration of A's anus or vagina with a part of B's body;

- penetration of A's mouth with B's penis.

An offence is committed by an under 18-year-old in the same circumstances but is charged under **s. 13** and involves a maximum five-year penalty as opposed to 14 years under **s. 9.**

Crucially if the adult is in a position of trust such as a secondary school teacher or warder in a young offenders institution, the relevant age for consent is raised to 18. Thus, in this situation, the consent of a 16- or 17-year-old victim would be irrelevant.

REVISION

✓ Rape – s. 1 Sexual Offences Act 2003 (child – s. 5)
✓ Assault by penetration – s. 2 Sexual offences Act 2003 (child – s. 6)
✓ Sexual assault – s. 9/13.

There are further offences such as causing or inciting an under-age person to engage in sexual activity. There are also the offences of engaging in sexual activity in the presence of a child or causing a child to watch a sexual act in addition.

Indecent photographs of children

By the end of this section you will be able to:

✓ describe the legislation prohibiting the offences;

✓ explain the major offences in relation to indecent photographs of children;

✓ apply what you know to some multi-choice questions.

The lower age limit of the subject in relation to photographs of an indecent nature, which may be lawfully possessed or distributed, is 18. Even 'hard core' pornography where the subjects are over 18 is legal but subject to a licence, so-called 'soft' pornography is not restricted.

Section 1(1) Protection of Children Act 1978 prohibits a person:

(a) to take, or permit to be taken or to make, any indecent photograph or pseudo-photograph of a child; or

(b) to distribute or show such indecent photographs or pseudo-photographs; or

(c) to have in his possession such indecent photographs or pseudo-photographs, with a view to their being distributed or shown by himself or others; or

(d) to publish or cause to be published any advertisement likely to be understood as conveying that the advertiser distributes or shows such indecent photographs or pseudo-photographs, or intends to do so.

ACTIVITY

A raid by the FBI on a business running so called 'kiddi-porn' sites in the US yielded the credit card details of some 75,000 people worldwide. 7,000 of these people were British including a judge, a senior prosecutor, a number of police officers and at least one celebrity. To date less than 3,000 of these UK cases have been investigated. Contact the section in your force responsible for investigating these offences and find out why there is such a backlog.

This offence relates to those who make or publish the material. It is more likely that people who view or possess this type of material, such as on their computer hard drives, will come to police notice. This offence is dealt with under **s.160(1) Criminal Justice Act 1988** where it:

… is an offence for a person to have any indecent photograph or pseudo-photograph of a child in his possession.

There are defences in the statute, however:

- that he had a legitimate reason for having the material; or

- that he had not himself seen the material and did not know, nor had any cause to suspect, it to be indecent; or

- that the material was sent to him without any prior request made by him or on his behalf and that he did not keep it for an unreasonable time.

Prostitution

By the end of this section you will be able to:

- identify which prostitution offences remain illegal;

- reflect on the particular plight of child prostitutes.

Being a prostitute or paying for sexual activity is not illegal and have not been so since the 1960s. It remains illegal to live off the earnings of a prostitute, keep a brothel, or procure a woman to be a prostitute or to solicit or importune persistently for an immoral purpose, however. This latter offence could be committed by men loitering in public toilets or even woods hoping to engage in sexual activity there (i.e. in a public place). **Section 71 Sexual Offences Act 2003** renders illegal sexual activity in a public lavatory.

The main offences we are concerned with here are soliciting and 'kerb crawling'. It is an offence under **s.1 Street Offences Act 1959** for a prostitute to solicit or loiter in a street or public place. Per **Smith v Hughes 1960** this would extend to attracting the attention of clients from their own front window, etc. Historically all prostitutes were potentially prosecuted for this offence. Since 2000 though there has been a general recognition that children under 16 offering themselves in these circumstances, whilst technically committing the offence, should be treated as victims of child sexual abuse. Such is the policy of criminal justice agencies nowadays.

The offence of 'kerb crawling' is provided by **s.1 Sexual Offences Act 1985** which prohibits the solicitation of prostitutes from a motor vehicle in a public place. Such men are often diverted into a voluntary treatment programme on a first-time offence by many police forces.

Indecent exposure

By the end of this section you will be able to:

- identify the legislation relevant to this offence.

The stereotypical 'dirty old man' in a raincoat is not necessarily typical of the offenders in this category. It is just as likely to be a young man 'mooning' at passers by or revealing himself generally as a result of drinking excessively. It is however only the genitalia of either sex being exposed which founds the offence per **s. 66(1)**:

(a) he intentionally exposes his genitals, and

(b) he intends that someone will see them and be caused alarm or distress.

Other parts of the body exposed could found the offence of outraging public decency under common law or **s. 5 Public Order Act 1986**. Thus a woman flashing her breasts at passing motorists would not normally be dealt with under **s. 66**.

REVISION

✓ Indecent photographs of children – Protection of Children Act 1978/Criminal Justice Act 1988.
✓ Prostitution/kerb crawling – Street Offences Act 1959/Sexual Offences Act 1985.
✓ Indecent exposure – s. 66 Sexual Offences Act 2003.

Knowledge Check 1

1. A person who inserts a pencil into the anus of an adult victim without their consent for sexual purposes is guilty of:

   (a) rape

   (b) sexual assault

   (c) assault by penetration

   (d) none of the above

2. S. 66 Sexual Offences Act 2003 creates the offence of:

    (a) rape

    (b) indecent exposure

    (c) assault by penetration

    (d) sexual assault

3. Which of the following are offences:

    (a) Being a prostitute?

    (b) Being a male prostitute?

    (c) Being a prostitute in a private dwelling?

    (d) None of the above?

4. S.1 Protection of Children Act 1978 prohibits:

    (a) the taking of photographs, etc., of children

    (b) possessing photographs, etc., of children

    (c) causing a child to witness a sexual act

    (d) sexual activity between those 15 and under.

The answers are at the end of the chapter.

Suggested research

The member of the Association of Chief Police Officers (ACPO) with special responsibility for children recently made a controversial statement. He recommended that not all paedophiles should be jailed. He was referring especially to those at the very beginning of offending and viewing child pornography rather than abusing children directly. Use the web to find out what you can about this news item. Look at the websites of concerned groups such as the NSPCC and Barnardos to try to discern what their reaction to this policy suggestion is.

Further reading

For a general overview of rape within the legal system:

Temkin, J (2002) *Rape and the legal process* (2nd edn) Oxford: Oxford University Press.

More detailed coverage of the criminal offences in this chapter can be obtained by reading:

Card, R (2003) *Sexual offences: The new law*. Bristol: Jordans.

Card, R, Cross, R and Jones, P (2005) *Criminal law*. London: Butterworths.

English, J and Card, R (2005) *Police law* (9th edn). Oxford: Oxford University Press

Heaton, R (2001) *Criminal law* (3rd edn). London: Butterworths.

Sampson, F (2007) *Blackstone's police manual, Volume 1 – Crime*. Oxford: Oxford University Press.

Useful websites

Crown Prosecution Service:

www.cps.org.uk

Legislation:

www.opsi.gov.uk

Case law and legislation databases:

www.westlaw.com* (an educational case law and statute database)

www.lexis-nexis.com* (an educational case law and statute database)

www.pnld.co.uk* (a police service specific database of case law and statute)

* Likely to be available through the virtual learning environment (VLE) which supports your course/training.

Answers

Knowledge Check 1

1. A person who inserts a pencil into the anus of an adult victim without their consent for sexual purposes is guilty of:

    (c) Assault by penetration.

2. **S. 66 Sexual Offences Act 2003** creates the offence of:

    (b) Indecent exposure.

3. Which of the following are offences?

    (d) None of the above.

4. **S. 1 Protection of Children Act 1978** prohibits:

    (a) The taking of photographs etc. of children.

8 Drugs and solvents

(?) *Remember this symbol indicates that the material might be useful for your Student Officer Learning and Assessment Programme (SOLAP) portfolio or any attached reflective practice record you are required to make.*

Underpinning knowledge towards Patrol Officer NOS:

1A1, 1B9, 2A1, 2C1, 2C2, 2C3, 2G2, 2G4, 2H1, 2H2, 2I1, 2I2, 2J1, 2J2, 2K2, 4C1

and PCSO NOS:

1A1, 1B11, 2A1, 2C1, 2C2, 2C3, 2C5, 2J1,2J2, 4C1

For further information on these NOS, which are also Policing Level 3 and 4 NVQ unit titles, refer to Appendix 1 to this volume.

This topic is potentially very large and it is something that later in your career you can choose to specialise in. The information provided here is the basic outline that is required for you as a student police officer. You will have access to specialist drugs teams in your force should you require practical advice and assistance with a drugs matter.

Solvents have been included here, as there are a number of household items like glue and butane gas cylinders ('camping gas') that can be misused in the same way that controlled drugs can. These items present problems for police and retailers alike. They cannot be restricted in the same way as drugs yet their availability to potential misusers needs to be limited in some way. What little relevant law there is in the area is set out at the end of the chapter.

As the title suggests, the matters to be dealt with here are:

- drugs;
- solvents, glue, etc.

Drugs

By the end of this section you will be able to:

- describe the legislation governing the misuse of drugs;

- outline police powers in respect of the misuse of drugs, solvents, glue, etc;

- apply what you know to some multiple-choice questions.

Drugs have not always been controlled in this country as they are today; some may have been more or less socially acceptable at certain times and in certain cultures. Even opium, whilst frowned upon, could be purchased and smoked in Victorian London without fear of the kind of penalties which would be handed out today. Cannabis was not rendered illegal until the 1930s. There is considerable debate about whether the control of drugs should be tightened still further or whether that simply fuels drug-related crime.

⑦ *We ask you here to reflect on similar themes to those in the chapter on alcohol. A great deal of property-related crime and violent crime has drugs as its root cause. Shoplifting and robbery can be carried out to fuel a drug habit. People high on drugs can carry out violent attacks they would never have contemplated when sober. Is the answer to increase police powers in relation to drugs and stiffen sentences or has that so far proved ineffective? Alternatively, would the removal of some of the drugs from being outside the law decrease their value and therefore the related crime? Would that simply create more addicts?*

Nevertheless, the legislation which must be enforced currently is the **Misuse of Drugs Act 1971**. The Act, together with attendant secondary legislation classifies drugs in order of their serious effects on the people that misuse them and also therefore that correlates to the level of penalty. Class A drugs are perceived as the most harmful and therefore would attract the stiffest penalty on conviction. Readers may well be aware that cannabis was recently downgraded to the point that, although it remains illegal to grow, possess or supply the drug, as a matter of policy possession of small amounts will normally only attract a warning or at most formal caution. Some drugs, such as the equine tranquilliser 'ketamine', have moved onto the classification system as their harmful effects and popularity have come to the attention of police, courts and legislators. This type of adjustment to the law is possible without going back to Parliament for new drugs legislation because the **Misuse of Drugs Act 1971** allows this to be done through subordinate legislation.

According to current Home Office information the classifications are, in outline as follows:

- **Class A** – Amphetamines (prepared for injection), crack cocaine, ecstasy, LSD, heroin, magic mushrooms.

- **Class B** – Amphetamines, ritalin, pholcodine.

- **Class C** – Cannabis, gamma hydroxybutyrate (GHB – one so called 'date rape drug'), ketamine, painkillers (some), tranquillisers.

ACTIVITY

Prepare a short briefing for your class or shift. Visit the Home Office website at **www.home-office.gov.uk** and follow the links or search for 'drugs' and 'Class A, B,C'. You will find information there on the penalties for dealing and for possession. Prepare a flipchart or a set of electronic presentation slides to deliver the information. Practise with friends, family or colleagues first making sure your voice is audible, you make eye contact with everyone in the room at some point and that you know your material.

(?) *Alcohol and tobacco are said to be more addictive and damaging than many soft drugs. Why are these drugs not controlled in the same way as heroin and cocaine? Are we moving in that direction with tobacco at least? Is this a good thing or simply likely to strengthen the black market?*

In relation to these controlled drugs, the Act sets out, amongst other things the requirements for the offences of:

- unlawful supply;

- unlawful possession;

- premises for drug taking;

- defences;

- police powers.

Unlawful supply

In practice, supplying may require the production of the drug. This is also looked at here. **Section 4(1) Misuse of Drugs Act 1971** states:

> *Subject to any regulations [the Home Secretary might make to the contrary] it shall not be lawful for a person*
>
> *(a) to produce a controlled drug; or*
>
> *(b) to supply or offer to supply a controlled drug to another.*

The regulations referred to in this section are, apart from anything else, lists of people who are permitted to lawfully possess the drug concerned. A doctor might possess Valium for example, or a vet, Ketamine.

'Produce' means manufacture or grow, etc. It would appear from **R v Maginnis (1987)** that 'supply' would include giving back something that the accused merely had for safe-keeping. An associate of Maginnis feared a police raid and gave the drugs to Maginnis to keep in his car. Maginnis was arrested as he handed the drugs back.

Section 4(2) extends the offence to merely being concerned in the production:

> *Subject to [the statutory defence in **Section 28**] of this Act, it is an offence for a person*

(a) to produce a controlled drug in contravention of subsection (1) above; or

(b) to be concerned in the production of such a drug in contravention of that subsection by another.

Likewise under **s. 4(3)** merely offering or being concerned in the offer is sufficient for a conviction, this even if there is no intention to carry out the offer or there is some mistake about the nature of the substance being offered, i.e. it is harmless powder, for example:

*Subject to [the statutory defence in **Section 28**] of this Act, it is an offence for a person*

(a) to supply or offer to supply a controlled drug to another in contravention of subsection (1) above; or

(b) to be concerned in the supplying of such a drug to another in contravention of that subsection; or

(c) to be concerned in the making to another in contravention of that subsection of an offer to supply such a drug.

The statutory defence mentioned in the sections above will be considered in more detail later. Offences involving all classes would be arrestable subject to the amended **s. 24 PACE 1984** (see Chapter 3).

Unlawful possession

Clearly possession of a drug for personal use is not viewed as dimly by the courts compared to supplying it to others, especially for profit. Nevertheless the possession of any amount of any drug in any class under the Act is an offence. How it is proceeded with differs greatly dependent on the class as we have intimated in the introductory paragraphs of this chapter.

S. 5(1) Misuse of Drugs Act 1971:

Subject to any regulations [the Home Secretary might make to the contrary] it shall not be lawful for a person to have a controlled drug in his possession.

S. 5(2): *Subject to [the statutory defence in **Section 28**] of this Act and to subsection (4) below, it is an offence for a person to have a controlled drug in his possession in contravention of subsection (1) above.*

S. 5(3): *Subject to [the statutory defence in **Section 28**] it is an offence for a person to have a controlled drug in his possession, whether lawfully or not, with intent to supply it to another…*

Again the regulations referred to in this section are in part exceptions for people to be able to possess lawfully in certain circumstances. A person prescribed Mogadon by a medical practitioner would not be guilty of possessing a Class C drug unlawfully, for example. Despite urban myths to the contrary, it is not yet lawful to possess raw cannabis for its pain-relieving qualities in conditions like multiple sclerosis. Medically prepared cannabis in tablet form may be prescribed, however.

Note that under **s. 5(3)** possession with intent to supply is a separate offence which would come into play if a suspect had more drugs on them or in their property than would suffice for personal use. A conviction would be possible without evidence of actual dealing.

Physical possession is unnecessary: 'control' of it would be a better term. If A and B are in London and A buys a consignment of drugs currently in the hold of a boat in Felixstowe harbour from B by giving him a suitcase full of cash, A possesses the drugs as soon as ownership passes. It is immaterial that he never has nor never will, personally visit Felixstowe.

Premises for drug taking

You may remember the case of **Sweet v Parsley (1970)** which we met in Chapter 1. This concerned the forerunner of this drugs statute and the offence of being concerned in the management of premises used for taking drugs. You may remember that in the case that it was highlighted that the previous statute did not call for any *mens rea,* a simple omission by Parliament. This mistake was subsequently rectified in **s. 8 Misuse of Drugs Act 1971** which effectively added the word 'knowingly':

A person commits an offence if, being the occupier or concerned in the management of any premises, he knowingly permits or suffers any of the following activities to take place on those premises, that is to say

(a) producing or attempting to produce a controlled drug...

(b) supplying or attempting to supply a controlled drug to another..., or offering to supply a controlled drug to another.....

(c) preparing opium for smoking;

(d) smoking cannabis, cannabis resin or prepared opium.

Defences

There are two specific defences in the Act concerned with knowledge and apparent lawful purpose:

- **s. 28 Misuse of Drugs Act 1971;**
- **s. 5(4) Misuse of Drugs Act 1971.**

S. 28 Misuse of Drugs Act 1971
By **s. 28(2):**

... in any proceedings for an offence to which this section applies it shall be a defence for the accused to prove that he neither knew of nor suspected nor had reason to suspect the existence of some fact alleged by the prosecution which it is necessary for the prosecution to prove if he is to be convicted of the offence charged.

A further qualification is added, basically placing the burden of proof on the accused to prove that he or she did not know the substance was a controlled drug. The problem is that this is rather a strong assault on the concept of the presumption of innocence, the so called 'Woolmington principle' found also in **Article 6 European Convention on Human Rights** (See Chapter 2 'Human rights' and Chapter 14, 'Introduction to evidence'. In **R v Lambert (2001)** it was held the reverse burden of proof in **s. 28** and by inference **s. 5(4)** (see below) would no longer apply as it was incompatible with **Art. 6**. This means that the prosecution will have to disprove the accused's assertion that he or she did not have the requisite knowledge, etc., a subtle but important difference.

S. 5(4) Misuse of Drugs Act 1971

This provision is designed to protect those who are attempting to thwart the misuse of drugs through their own actions or deliver them to the authorities.

> **S. 5(4)**: *In any proceedings for an offence under subsection (2) above in which it is proved that the accused had a controlled drug in his possession, it shall be a defence for him to prove*
>
> *(a) that, knowing or suspecting it to be a controlled drug, he took possession of it for the purpose of preventing another from committing or continuing to commit an offence in connection with that drug and that as soon as possible after taking possession of it he took all such steps as were reasonably open to him to destroy the drug or to deliver it into the custody of a person lawfully entitled to take custody of it...*

You will note from the words in **s. 5(4)(a)**above and **s. 5(4)(b)** immediately below that the exemption is limited in so far as there must be fairly immediate steps taken to dispose of the drugs or deliver them to, most likely, the police:

> *(b) that, knowing or suspecting it to be a controlled drug, he took possession of it for the purpose of delivering it into the custody of a person lawfully entitled to take custody of it and that as soon as possible after taking possession of it he took all such steps as were reasonably open to him to deliver it into the custody of such a person.*

What exactly were 'all such steps as were reasonably open to him' will be a matter of fact in each case.

Police powers

In addition to the search powers you have already encountered in Chapter 3 under **PACE 1984** there are specific powers under the **Misuse of Drugs Act 1971**, a warrant can be applied for but in any event by **s. 23(2)**:

> *If a constable has reasonable grounds to suspect that any person is in possession of a controlled drug in contravention of this Act or of any regulations made thereunder, the constable may*
>
> *(a) search that person, and detain him for the purpose of searching him;*
>
> *(b) search any vehicle or vessel in which the constable suspects that the drug may be found, and for that purpose require the person in control of the vehicle or vessel to stop it;*

Note the term 'vessel' is added as well as vehicle and certainly includes waterborne craft. This is useful in that it is not unknown for inland waterways such as canals and navigable rivers to be used to transport drugs inland having brought them across the Channel or North Sea. The sleepy image of canal boating can be misleading.

Once a search has been successful a power of seizure will be needed; one such is provided by **s. 23(2)(c)**, a constable may:

> seize and detain, for the purposes of proceedings under this Act, anything found in the course of the search which appears to the constable to be evidence of an offence under this Act.

Additional powers are provided by **s. 50 Criminal Justice and Police Act 2001**. The wording is almost impenetrable but the provision is in part designed to allow seizure of material that is part of something else, which is not seizable. In other words, if drugs were found which were embedded in something which the police had no power to seize prior to this Act, presumably in order to hide the drugs more effectively, this Act gives them the power to seize the whole item.

REVISION

✓ Unlawful production and supply of a controlled drug – s. 4 Misuse of Drugs Act 1971.
✓ Unlawful possession of a controlled drug – s. 5 Misuse of Drugs Act 1971.
✓ Stop, search and seizure – s. 23 Misuse of Drugs Act 1971 and s. 50 Criminal Justice and Police Act 1971

Solvents, glue, etc.

The issue of glue and other household substances obtained to be inhaled, as we mentioned at the very beginning of this chapter, is a difficult one. It is difficult for Parliament to legislate to ban substances which have a legitimate everyday and commonplace use just because they are misused by a minority of people. Exactly the same conundrum is faced in relation to kitchen knives and box cutters when considering weapons preventative law (see Chapter 17 generally). There has been some legislative intervention in relation to the supply of the substance in the first place. The **Intoxicating Substances (Supply) Act 1985** introduces a summary offence in **s. 1(1)** to:

> ...supply or offer to supply a substance other than a controlled drug
>
> (a) to a person under the age of eighteen whom he knows, or has reasonable cause to believe, to be under that age; or
>
> (b) to a person
>
> (i) who is acting on behalf of a person under that age; and
>
> (ii) whom he knows, or has reasonable cause to believe, to be so acting,

Critically a state of knowledge is required as *mens rea* in relation to the age of the customer and what he or she intends to do with the material:

> if he knows or has reasonable cause to believe that the substance is, or its fumes are, likely to be inhaled by the person under the age of eighteen for the purpose of causing intoxication.

Section 1(2) provides a statutory defence if the supplier is a minor and the transaction was not for profit:

> *In proceedings against any person for an offence under subsection (1) above it is a defence for him to show that at the time he made the supply or offer he was under the age of eighteen and was acting otherwise than in the course or furtherance of a business.*

Of course in many instances police will encounter glue-sniffers or those inhaling solvents or who have already done so with no realistic hope of catching the supplier. The person will simply be acting in an intoxicated manner. If it is not clear whether the person is drunk, on drugs or glue, etc., it may be possible to proceed as for drunk or drunk and disorderly (see Chapter 18). Care should be taken though: the constable must be acting genuinely under the reasonable suspicion that the person is drunk on intoxicating liquor even if it later it transpires that the substance was not alcohol. If this provision is used merely as a 'ways and means' knowing that the substance was, say camping gas because of the number of gas canisters lying about the vicinity, there is a risk of action for unlawful arrest at least.

Another course of action is present but it may depend on the person's actions. If they are acting in a disorderly manner to the extent that they are a real and imminent danger to themselves then they could be taken into custody under the general duty to prevent loss of life or limb. Finally, public order legislation could be considered if the behaviour contravenes, for example **ss. 5, 4** or **4A Public Order Act 1986** (see Chapter 10).

REVISION

✓ Supply of glue, etc, – s.1(1) Intoxicating Substances (Supply) Act 1985.
✓ Intoxicated people – if unsure proceed as drunk /drunk and disorderly otherwise under Public Order Act or to prevent injury or death.

Knowledge Check 1

1. PC Mason is on mobile patrol on the ring road of Grooby, Lechonshire when he notices a female apparently intoxicated. On approach there is no smell of intoxicating liquor. The female is throwing stones at passing cars and refuses to stop. She has failed to hit any vehicles and there is a plastic bag containing clear liquid in her hand. Mason may:

   (a) Not act as there has not yet been any offence.

   (b) Arrest the female for being drunk and disorderly.

   (c) Issue an FPN for being found drunk.

   (d) Arrest for a public order offence.

2. Later Mason notices a youth pass a foil-wrapped object similar to a stock cube to another in exchange for what appeared to be a quantity of notes. On approach Mason may:

(a) Search the youths under **s. 1 PACE 1984**.

(b) Search the youths under **s. 23(2) Miuse of Drugs Act 1971**.

(c) Arrest the youths for possession under **s. 5 Misuse of Drugs Act 1971**.

(d) Arrest one of the youths for supplying under **s. 4 Misuse of Drugs Act 1971**.

3. Mason receives information from one of the youths that cannabis is being grown at an address in the next street. Mason may:

(a) Obtain a warrant, search the premises and seize the plants.

(b) Arrest the occupier under **s. 4(1) Misuse of Drugs Act 1971**.

(c) Consider **s. 8 Misuse of Drugs Act 1971**.

(d) Do all of the above.

The answers are at the end of the chapter.

Suggested research

It might be useful in terms of background reading to look at some of the initiatives that exist, both officially and unofficially to try to persuade (particularly) young people from starting to take drugs in the first place. Explore **www.laurenslink.org.uk** for information on a charity set up by the mother of a heroin overdose victim and the government sponsored website **www.talktofrank.com**

Further reading

More detailed coverage of the topics found in this chapter can be obtained by reading:

Card, R, Cross, R and Jones, P (2005) *Criminal law*. London: Butterworths.

English, J and Card, R (2005) *Police law*. (9th edn). Oxford: Oxford University Press.

Heaton, R (2001) *Criminal law* (3rd edn). London Butterworths.

Sampson, F (2007) *Blackstone's police manual, Volume 4 – General police duties* (9th edn). Oxford: Oxford University Press.

Useful websites

Crown Prosecution Service:

www.cps.org.uk

Home Office:

www.homeoffice.org.uk

Legislation:

www.opsi.gov.uk

Case law and legislation databases:

www.westlaw.com* (an educational case law and statute database)

www.lexis-nexis.com* (an educational case law and statute database)

www.pnld.co.uk* (a police service specific database of case law and statute)

* Likely to be available through the virtual learning environment (VLE) which supports your course/training.

Answers

Knowledge Check 1

1.   (d)   Arrest for a public order offence.

   NB She is obviously not drunk on intoxicating liquor, act on other offences disclosed.

2.   (b)   Search the youths under **s. 23(2) Misuse of Drugs Act 1971**.

   NB An arrest without a search might be premature, depending on the circumstances.

3.   (d)   Do all of the above.

9 Property offences

(?) *Remember this symbol indicates that the material might be useful for your Student Officer Learning and Assessment Programme (SOLAP) portfolio or any attached reflective practice record you are required to make.*

Underpinning knowledge towards Patrol Officer NOS:

1A1, 1B9, 2A1, 2C1, 2C2, 2C3, 2C4, 2G2, 2H1, 2H2, 2J1, 2J2, 2K2, 4C1

and PCSO NOS:

1A1,1B11, 2A1, 2C1, 2C2, 2C3, 2C5, 2J1, 2J2, 4C1

For further information on these NOS, which are also Policing Level 3 and 4 NVQ unit titles, refer to Appendix 1 to this volume.

This chapter covers the law on the following property offences:

- theft;
- burglary;
- going equipped;
- robbery;
- handling;
- TWOC and vehicle interference;
- making off without payment;
- criminal damage;
- deception and fraud offences.

Theft

By the end of this section you will be able to:

✓ define theft;

✓ evaluate problems in the application of the definition;

✓ apply relevant case law and statute to a range of hypothetical situations.

Theft is probably one of the most common offences that a student officer will come across. It is also a major component of offences such as burglary and robbery, which are both theft with some other aggravating feature. In addition this chapter will enable you to use the correct terminology for each offence, you will often hear a member of the public refer to their house having been 'robbed' when they mean burgled, for instance. Such terms as 'mugging' and even 'fraud' or 'arson' are a little imprecise on their own. The specific offences are best discussed for professional purposes in terms of the statutory provision which relates to them.

Much of the law in this area is statutory. This should make for clarity but unfortunately some of the provisions are not well worded and recourse has to be made to case law for interpretation, especially if the act is rather dated. Sometimes the acts pre-date by some years the technology which makes some 'thefts' possible, such as the internet. This can throw doubt on whether the definition has actually been met in certain cases where no physical property changes hands such as in a mortgage transaction. In some cases these kinds of anomalies have been addressed by later legislation, but not in all.

The theft definition is contained within **s. 1 Theft Act 1968 (TA '68)**. It is:

> *A person is guilty of theft if he dishonestly appropriates property belonging to another with the intention of depriving the other of it and 'thief' and 'steal' shall be construed accordingly.*

The key components then are:

- dishonestly (**s. 2 TA '68**);

- appropriates (**s. 3 TA '68**);

- property (**s. 4 TA '68**);

- belonging to another (**s. 5 TA '68**);

- intention to permanently deprive (**s. 6 TA '68**).

As can be seen **s. 2** to **6 Theft Act 1968** elaborate on the key points in **s. 1**. Knowing **s. 1** very well has the added benefit therefore of being an *aide mémoire* as to what **s. 2** to **6** cover.

REVISION

Theft is defined in s. 1 Theft Act 1968:
- ✓ dishonestly
- ✓ appropriates
- ✓ property
- ✓ belonging to another
- ✓ intention to permanently deprive

Dishonesty

This forms part of the *mens rea* of the offence together with intention discussed later. A meaningful definition of the word 'dishonesty' is sadly lacking in the Act. Rather the relevant subsection merely concentrates on what will not be construed as dishonesty. **Section 2 (1)** cites the three such situations:

- if the accused believed he had the right in law to deprive the other of the property (**s. 2(1)(a)**);

- if the accused believed he would have the other's consent in the circumstances had he known of the appropriation (**s. 2(1)(b)**);

- if the accused believed that the true owner of the property could not be found by taking reasonable steps (**s. 2(1)(c)**). This would not apply if the accused was a trustee or personal representative, e.g. if an executor kept all the deceased's goods without passing it on under the will.

In each of these situations the accused will not be guilty of theft, as they would lack the component of dishonesty. Raising these specific defences successfully would of course depend on the accused being able to convince the jury that he or she genuinely believed these things to be true.

An example of a defence based on a belief in a right in law would be if a debt-recovery agent took goods from the house of a debtor genuinely believing because of poor training that he was empowered to do that. In fact usually only a certificated bailiff can do so under a court order and within significant restrictions.

An employee might believe he or she had the employer's consent to take some stationery items and computer consumables home to use when they are working on work projects on their home computer in the evening. Whether this was a believable defence would probably rest on the amount of material taken home in proportion to the work done there.

Finally, property found on the street is a good example of the latter defence listed above. If ten pounds are found on the pavement but not handed in to the police as lost property, this is technically **s.1** theft (by finding). A person who finds this in the form of ten pound coins would potentially have the defence that an owner could not be identified by taking reasonable steps as the coins are not individually identifiable. A person who finds a ten-pound note would not technically be able to avail themselves of the defence, however, as the note is uniquely numbered. It would be possible therefore to at least attempt to trace the owner by tracking down the bank which issued it and possibly to whom. This might be ultimately fruitless and many police forces may not routinely do it because of cost but the attempt (the 'reasonable steps') has been made by handing it in. The property often reverts to the finder in practice in any case if unclaimed after 30 days.

In cases of other types of property, what 'reasonable steps' are will depend on the circumstances .

It has been left to case law to establish a test for dishonesty. In **R v Ghosh (1982)** a surgeon had been using NHS facilities to carry out private operations. These facilities would have to have been paid for had Ghosh told the hospital management what he was doing. The case revolved around whether not telling them could properly be described as dishonest. The court laid down a two-stage test; the jury had to consider:

- firstly whether the accused acted honestly by the ordinary standards of 'reasonable and honest people'. Only if the answer is no then –

- did the accused realise he was being dishonest when compared to those standards?

A practical approach to deciding whether an accused is to be charged with theft where dishonesty is the issue in question would be to consider the statutory 'defences' first. If these defences are not relevant then turn to the **Ghosh** test and apply that.

REVISION

Dishonesty, (s. 2 TA '68) did the:
✓ accused believed that he had a right in law, or
✓ accused believed he would have had the others consent, or
✓ accused is not in a position of trust and took reasonable steps to find the owner, then still:
✓ Would a reasonable honest person think he was dishonest, if yes
✓ Did the accused think he was being dishonest by those standards? (R v Ghosh 1982)

Appropriate

This is part of the *actus reus* of the crime in that you actually have to take control, even sometimes partial control, of the property away from its rightful owner to be guilty of the offence. It may not mean that the accused ever takes hold of anything. For example, a thief may bid on an internet auction site, win the item and induce the unwary seller to post the item to the thief's mother as her birthday present. He may subsequently pay using a cheque which he has known all along will be dishonoured, assuming he is charged with theft and not deception (see later), he will never have laid eyes on the property much less physically taken it. A conviction for theft is likely to stand in these circumstances, however.

In **R v Morris (1983)** the judges interpreted the words 'any assumption of the rights of an owner' in **s. 3 Theft Act 1968** quite widely to include any of the rights of the owner. This has not been disturbed by later case law. Morris was peeling the labels off goods in a shop and swapping them around. In doing so he placed labels showing incorrect lower values on items in order to obtain them without paying the full price when he went through the checkout. The case revolved around: at what point did he appropriate any property? Much of the case is not now considered good law but this definition of what appropriation means survives.

The question may arise as to when is appropriation going to amount to a criminal act. We all routinely appropriate goods well before we pay for them and treat them as our own, when a delivery from a home shopping catalogue arrives for instance or, for a short period of time, when we place fuel in the tank of a car. Appropriation itself is not the central issue therefore on its own; it is the dishonest appropriation which matters. The problem then is, what happens if the goods were taken by permission even if that permission would not have been given if the full facts had been known? In **Lawrence v MPC (1971)** an unscrupulous taxi driver helped himself to 12 times the amount of the legal fare when a non-English-speaking tourist proffered his open wallet. Lawrence was convicted of theft having appropriated the extra money notwithstanding the passenger's implied permission given at the time.

The leading case in this area is now **R v Gomez (1993)**. This case involved collusion between a thief and Gomez. Gomez worked in a shop stocking electrical items and persuaded the management to accept his accomplice's cheques for goods to the value of some £17,000. These cheques were stolen and both men knew this. The management did not find out the cheques would not be honoured until the goods had passed, with their consent, to the thief. The defence sought to argue that no appropriation had taken place because **R v Morris (1983)** had seemed to suggest that the assumption of rights under **s. 3 Theft Act 1968** had to be in some way 'adverse', i.e. something that the owner did not give permission for. **Morris** was the leading case at the time. In **Gomez** the court took the opportunity to clarify the point and said that consent makes no difference, appropriation takes place in these situations too. Therefore if dishonesty is present, an offence of theft is made out.

R v Williams (Roy) (2000) was a case involving a builder who pressurised elderly people he had persuaded to trust him into paying exorbitant bills for work he had done. Since this case it would appear the **Gomez** approach applies to other situations where property is handed over in a manner which is consensual. Gifts are another example but there would of course only ever be a case if there were real doubt about the validity of the 'gift'. The court affirmed in **R v Hinks (2000)** that there could still be appropriation if a valid gift has been made. This would be a theft situation if the component of dishonesty were added. Good evidence of this would be, as here, if a victim of low intelligence were persuaded to hand over large sums of money to the accused for dubious reasons.

REVISION

'Appropriates' means (s. 3 TA '68):
- ✓ To assume any of the rights of the owner (R v Morris 1983).
- ✓ Even with their consent.
- ✓ Gifts and other voluntarily handed over property can be appropriated (R v Gomez 1993, R v Hinks 2000, R v Williams 2000).

Property

This is covered by **s. 4 Theft Act 1968**. For the purposes of theft not everything one might commonly think of as property is deemed so in law. The section specifies that the following are property in this context:

- real property (houses and land etc. but see limitations below);

- personal property including;

- money;

- 'things in action' (a right to acquire something of value, cheques are a good example);

- other intangible property (intangible here means you cannot touch it but it has value, such as a funeral plan or a debt).

It is probably most helpful to discuss what would not be property and where the law is unclear on this point. Despite its specific mention in the section, land and buildings are not normally considered property, nor are crops, etc., unless:

- The land is in the appropriated by someone who was looking after it under a position of trust. This would occur for example if an executor of a will sells land left in it cheaply to a dummy company he has secretly set up.

- The land is not in the possession of the defendant and he appropriates items that he severs (detaches), causes to be severed or after they have been severed, from the land. Good examples would be a neighbour sawing down overhanging branches belonging to a tree in the next garden without permission. He is only entitled to do that if he returns the wood and any fruit. Similarly, stripping copper pipe out of an empty house without permission would be covered.

- The land is the subject of a tenancy and the tenant removes a fixture or fitting from the property. Taking down a fitted wardrobe when leaving a rented property and taking it with you would be an example of this even if you fitted it. This is because fixtures the tenant puts up become the landlord's property under civil law.

Section 4 goes on to say that in addition wild plants are not property unless they are picked by the accused for commercial purposes. Wild animals will not be property either unless they are appropriated whilst being 'reduced into the possession of' someone else. An example might be if a hunt saboteur took any part of the body of a fox killed by hounds before the members of the hunt got a chance to retrieve it. It is still possible to hunt foxes with dogs legally even after the anti-fox hunting legislation if certain restrictions are adhered to.

As a related point, human body parts will not be property unless they are altered for medical or scientific examination and therefore acquire value (**R v Kelly and Lindsay (1998)**). An arm severed in a road accident retrieved by a ghoulish passer by and kept would therefore not be treated as stolen but the same arm in formaldehyde in a laboratory jar would be if appropriated dishonestly.

Turning now to cheques, if such are stolen, it is not the paper which is important, despite some decided cases indicating that it is. The right to draw money out of an account (termed a 'thing' or occasionally (from the French) 'chose' in action) is what matters. The piece of paper is virtually worthless but the words written on it, together with the signature, can be worth thousands or even more. A problem arises though if a cheque is stolen which relates to an account which is empty or over its overdraft limit. In such a case an arrest would be perfectly lawful as reasonable grounds exist and the state of the account the cheques are drawn on cannot be known to the officer dealing. A charge might ultimately fail though as no actual right to draw money exists here whatever words and numbers are written on the face of the cheque. The courts have not yet been able to come up with a workable solution to this problem although attempted theft might succeed in these circumstances.

It is clear from **Oxford v Moss (1979)** where a student stole an exam paper, that information cannot be property. The theft could only be of the paper itself therefore. Obtaining and distributing information illegally would be dealt with under a range of other statutes such as the **Computer Misuse Act 1990**, the **Data Protection Act 1998**, and under copyright and patents law, for example, which are not normally enforced by the police.

Old mortgage fraud cases tried to treat the 'money' which travels along wires from bank to bank or bank to solicitor when a house is bought or sold as property. **R v Preddy (1996)** indicated this was stretching the definition too far and a new offence was created to deal specifically with the situation where people obtain mortgages by lying (see later in this chapter).

REVISION

The following are not property (s. 4 TA '68):
- ✓ Anything forming part of land and buildings unless it is 'severed' (dug up, broken down), removed unlawfully by a tenant or the accused is in a position of trust.
- ✓ Wild plants unless taken commercially, wild animals unless in the process of being captured or killed or human body parts unless altered for scientific purposes.
- ✓ Information (Oxford v Moss 1979) or electronic transfers of money (R v Preddy 1996).

Belonging to another

The definition is much wider than simply ownership. **Section 5** covers property that has been merely borrowed by the victim or that he or she merely has a 'proprietary right or interest' in. The victim may merely have the property on loan or for safekeeping. Thus theft could even occur if the accused took back his own property that was under someone else's control in certain circumstances. This is precisely what happened in **R v Turner (1971)**. The accused decided to use a spare key to retrieve his car that had gone into a garage for repair work, thus avoiding paying the bill. In law businesses often retain an interest in work they have done until it is paid for. A solicitor would have such a right over your file of papers as the client, a builder's merchant over loose materials delivered and a garage over a car they have worked on. Turner was accordingly convicted of theft.

Under **s. 5**, property can still belong to you even after you have handed it over to a third party. Suppose money is paid weekly by customers to a small toyshop that advertises it will provide a 'Christmas Club' facility. No toys are provided by the shop as the money is used instead to pay the shop owner's mounting debts. The shop closes without fulfilling a single order. Consider two alternative situations:

(a) The small print customers receive on joining the club states the money they will pay represents instalments on a credit arrangement they have with the shop owner. The owner buys the goods when the club is joined irrespective of how much has been paid by the customer into the plan and releases the goods to them when the arrangement is paid up.

(b) The small print states the money will be used to pass on to suppliers less a small cut for the shop. The suppliers will despatch the goods when the amount is paid up.

In fact only in (b) would the money be considered to have been appropriated by the shop owner and be belonging to another. The existence of an obligation under civil law to treat the money in a certain way must be known to the accused under **R v Wills (1990)**. A situation albeit with very different facts but analogous to (a) above developed in **R v Breaks and Huggan (1998)**. The defendants were acquitted.

(?) *Supposing you are called to a theft of a homeless shelter charity box from a shop counter, and the thief has been apprehended. In framing the charge it is going to be quite important to ascertain who the property belongs to and why under law. Your options are i) the shop, ii) the charity, iii) the homeless, iv) the public who donated. The answer is ii): reflect on why if the opportunity arises in any reflective entry you make relevant to this point.*

> **REVISION**
>
> Belonging to another can include:
>
> Items that do not belong to the victim (s. 5 TA '68):
> ✓ Items borrowed by, loaned or hired out to the victim.
> ✓ The accused's own property if another party has a right to it (R v Turner 1971).
>
> Money paid may still belong to the payer:
> ✓ Deposits and other instalments if there is a specific purpose that they should be put to and are not (R v Breaks and Huggan 1998).

Intention to permanently deprive

This is the rest of the *mens rea* for the offence. Intention as a concept has been encountered before and the discussions around **R v Mohan (1976)**, **R v Woollin (1998)** and R v **Matthews and Alleyne (2003)** whilst being murder cases are arguably just as applicable here. See Chapters 1 and 6 for a fuller discussion but in summary, in law a person's intention is their 'aim or purpose'. That being said it is quite possible for a jury to infer that intention was there if the accused foresaw that the (in this case) permanent deprivation was virtually certain. Consider the situation of an accused taking a car and dumping it below the tide-line on a deserted beach. It could be shown he appreciated that the car's owner was virtually certain to be deprived of it. The same would not be so easily shown if he dumped it in the same place if the beach had plenty of holidaymakers on it.

Difficulty in showing that an owner of a motor vehicle was permanently deprived of it where it remained roadworthy and in substantially one piece after its theft led to the creation of a separate offence. The argument was that the owner could always go and get the vehicle once its whereabouts were known. Taking without owner's consent is dealt with under a separate section. There will be no such argument of course where the vehicle has been sold, shipped overseas, scrapped or wrecked. The **s. 6** requirements will be met.

Where difficulties may lie is when property is borrowed, damaged and returned, after all, taking the above discussion into account a car is rarely in immaculate condition when discovered. Further, what of the situation where the victim is unable to use the vehicle because psychologically they see it as having been 'defiled' or 'sullied' and cannot bring themselves to sit in it. Has the vehicle, or indeed whatever the property might be, been permanently deprived then? The key is in the degree of 'goodness' that has gone out of the property. In **R v Lloyd (1985)** cinema films were taken, copied and returned undamaged to their original place. The judges in the case stated that an item was only permanently deprived if it could truly be said that all 'its goodness or virtue is gone'. Unfortunately this would be unlikely to be true of the vehicle which the owner felt was too 'defiled' to be used again. If it is physically only lightly damaged it will be considered to not have been permanently deprived.

Other property, such as clothing, could be considered permanently deprived in this situation. Thus if a shop worker takes an expensive designer dress from her shop without permission, intending to wear it once at an event and then return it the next day may still be liable for theft given the reduction in value this may cause. Much then depends on circumstances as **Clinton v Cahill (1998)** demonstrates. Hot water from a communal source was piped through a payment meter in the defendant's residence. The meter was tampered with and hot water was obtained without payment. A conviction could not be sustained however, as the water returned to its source slightly depleted of heat but otherwise perfectly reusable for heating.

As a final point related to that above it is worth noting that returning identical property may not assist the accused. Consider if the shop worker mentioned above was to take notes from the till on Saturday (without permission) on closing at 5pm to spend on the town that night. She then returned the same amount on Monday morning having borrowed it from another source. Theft would still have taken place (**R v Velumyl (1989)**). This is because the bank notes would not be the same ones as those taken.

Knowledge Check 1

PC Gregory attends the Saver-Save Supermarket just outside of town having received information about a shoplifter. Decide if theft occurred in the following:

(i) A man came to the information desk with four items of clothing still with labels attached and asked for a cash refund, he has a receipt for £98.96. A store detective is suspicious and stops him at the exit after he has received his refund, the receipt looks to him like a photocopy cut down to size. A store colleague confirms the man took the items from the shelf and has not been through a checkout.

(ii) A checkout operator has been found to have been taking food home that is past its sell by date and was destined for the skip at the back of the shop as waste.

(iii) A local animal rights campaigner has been caught putting slips of paper inside the cellophane wrapping of battery chicken carcasses with the words 'meat contaminated with the cruelty of man' written on the paper.

Outline the offences committed by each party, if any, at each of (i), (ii) and (iii).

Burglary

By the end of this section you will be able to:

- define burglary;

- explain the difference between burglary, burglary with intent and aggravated burglary;

- apply relevant case law and statute to a range of hypothetical situations.

Burglary is essentially 'theft with trespass'. But what is less well known is that the trespass can be linked with other offences for a conviction for burglary as well. The definition is contained in **s. 9 Theft Act 1968**. It is split into two parts.

Section 9(1)(a) stipulates a person is guilty of burglary if *'he enters any building or part of a building as a trespasser and with intent to commit [theft, GBH or criminal damage]'*. The key phrase is 'intent' in other words none of these offences need actually be committed for the full offence to be chargeable, the offence is committed on entry. This is known as burglary with intent.

Section 9(1)(b) however caters for the situation where a person *'having entered any building or part of a building as a trespasser he steals or attempts to steal anything in the building...or inflicts or attempts to inflict on any person therein grievous bodily harm'*. This is burglary. Both crimes carry the same maximum sentence; the only differential is that the sentence is 14 years for dwellings and 10 for non-dwellings.

In some situations it may not be clear when entry has occurred, however. Similarly, what if only a part of the accused, not the whole of him or her is found to have entered? What if the accused used an implement or a child under ten to make the entry? We will consider these points in the light of some hypothetical scenarios.

a) Bob Green is 18 and his brother Geoff, 20 has been invited to a twenty-first birthday party. Bob tags along and they are both admitted to the party, which is in a private house. Geoff is mixing with his friends while unknown to him Bob has nipped upstairs to go to the toilet having assumed it is acceptable to do this. He notices coats and handbags on the spare room bed and goes in to take a look. Bob rifles through the garments, finds a wallet containing £38 in cash and keeps it. Bob also urinates on the bedclothes.

It is best to consider these kinds of problems on a timeline. As Bob enters the building he is not a trespasser, he has at least implied permission from the occupier (it is arguably incumbent on him in these circumstances to refuse entry to anyone he does not wish to be present). As Bob goes upstairs he is probably, on the face of it, still doing that which he has implied permission to do, i.e. use washroom facilities at a party. This permission will be invalid in law at the point when Bob forms the intent to steal. If Bob went to the premises with that intention he will be a trespasser from the start. If he forms the intent on the stairs or landing, that is when he is a trespasser and will have entered part of a building as a trespasser with intent to steal contrary to **s. 9(1)(a) Theft Act 1968**. A similar factual situation was encountered in **R v Walkington (1979)** where a man entered a department store but became a trespasser as soon as he entered a part of a building he should not have been in to steal. Arguably people who enter shops with the avowed intent to steal are always burglars as their implied permission to be there would be revoked if the shop owner was aware of their intent. In **R v Jones and Smith (1976)** even the implied permission extended to a son by his parents to be in the family home was held revoked by his act of entering it to steal a television set. It is most likely the difficulty in proving when the intent was formed that prevents more shoplifters being charged with burglary. When Bob goes into the spare room he almost certainly breaches **s. 9(1)(a)** by the same token.

When Bob takes the wallet he is in breach of **s. 9(1)(b)** as it would seem hard to dispute that he is a trespasser now. He commits criminal damage to the bedclothes as well but would not be caught by **s. 9(1)(b)** for this as this section does not cover unlawful damage. He would only be caught by **s. 9(1)(a)** if he intended to do this when he went into the room. A stand-alone criminal damage charge might be a safer alternative.

b) Bob leaves the party and goes to No. 40 where he knows Albert Goldstein lives. Albert is 86, very short-sighted and almost completely deaf. Bob knows he looks a lot like Albert's son. Bob knocks on the half-open door and Albert looks up from the kitchen table and motions him in. Bob grabs some money on the side and runs out, at which point Albert realises his mistake about the identity of his visitor.

It is a requirement for both **s. 9(1)(a)** and **9(1)(b)** that the accused is a trespasser as he or she enters the building or part of a building in question. On the face of it Bob is not a trespasser as he has been invited into the premises albeit under a misapprehension. A similar situation was encountered in the remarkable case of **R v Collins (1972)**. Until the **Sexual Offences Act 2003** came into force **s. 9(1)(a)** could be committed by someone who intended to rape. Collins set out after a night's drinking intent on finding a sexual partner and not necessarily a consensual one. He climbed a ladder to an 18-year-old girl's window wearing just his socks. Incredibly the girl saw him perched on her windowsill and welcomed him in thinking he was her boyfriend paying her a visit. They had sexual intercourse at which point the girl realised her mistake. Collins was charged with burglary. Rape was clearly not an option as the sex was consensual. He climbed up to the window with the intent to rape but as he entered the building through the window he was invited in by the girl and therefore could not be a trespasser. The judges felt that merely standing on a windowsill did not constitute 'substantial and effective entry'.

The difference with Bob is that he is possibly aware of the potential for a mistake to be made. In contrast to Collins it could be said that it was a mistake he has done nothing to create but on the other hand he has done nothing to counter it either. The key though is that substantial and effective entry must be made while still a trespasser for these offences to be made out. The charge of theft is of course available for the taking of the money.

c) Bob next goes to a mobile home park nearby where he knows several of the homes are empty during the week. It is a seaside town with many more residents in these mobile homes at weekends. Bob is unable to force entry to any of the mobile homes but succeeds in finding one with a small open window. Bob puts his arm in but can get no further, he next uses a nearby clothesline prop to try to reach in to hook small items from inside the caravan. Failing again he finds his younger brother Dave who is $8\frac{1}{2}$ years old. Dave climbs in the open window for Bob and passes the items out to him.

The key here is what constitutes a building under **s. 9 (4) Theft Act 1968**. Reference is made to an 'inhabited vehicle or vessel' and this would normally stretch to any permanent or semi-permanent structure, including one with wheels or which floats which is inhabited. The only question here perhaps is whether these caravans are deemed inhabited or if they are in fact empty. The argument that structures do not have to be permanent to be buildings was upheld in **B and S v Leathley (1979)** although this is only a Crown Court case. In this case a walk-in freezer container connected to mains electricity and in place for three years was held to be a building. It is possible to consider further points about entry here as well. In **R v Brown (1985)** and **R v Ryan (1996)** the insertion of the top half of the body and even head and arm alone have been held to constitute an entry for these purposes. Certainly the old law on burglary which pre-dates the **Theft Act 1968** allowed the use of an instrument such as a fishing rod or other hooking implement to retrieve property to be treated as if the defendant had themselves entered the building. The use of a child under the age of criminal responsibility as an 'innocent agent' would be treated in the same way as if an inanimate implement had been used. Liability falls squarely on Bob therefore for **ss. 9(1)(a) and 9(1)(b)**.

Aggravated burglary is defined in **s. 10 Theft Act 1968**. Specifically *'a person is guilty of aggravated burglary if he commits any burglary and at the time has with him any firearm or imitation firearm, any weapon of offence* [including something 'made or adapted' for such use], *or any explosive'*. Note that if persons are present in the building at the time and aware of what the intruder has with him this could very easily constitute robbery, which we will discuss later. Assuming the building is unoccupied, it seems that the defendant would need to know that he had the weapon on him (**R v Russell (1984)**) and would have a defence if he had forgotten it was there. **R v Klass (1998)** would seem to indicate that it must indeed be on or about his person and not merely in the vicinity especially if it were not that accessible, say a cosh in his van up the street. The penalty for this offence is potentially life.

REVISION

Burglary with intent (ss. 9(1)(a)TA '68):
✓ Enter building/part as a trespasser with intent to:
- Steal
- Injure
- Damage.

Burglary (s. 9(1)(b) TA '68):
✓ Having entered building/part:
- Steal
- GBH
- Attempts either.

Aggravated burglary (s. 10 TA '68):
✓ Commit any burglary having with him:
- Firearm/imitation
- Weapon of offence (made or adapted)
- Explosive.

Going equipped

By the end of this section you will be able to:

- explain the different offences an offender can 'go equipped for';

- explain where the offence may take place;

- apply relevant case law and statute to a range of hypothetical situations.

This offence is designed to give the police powers to prevent burglaries and other dishonesty offences before they even take place. The items mentioned are part of the list of those which a police officer may search under **s.1 PACE 1984** during a stop and search (see Chapter 3).

The definition is in **s. 25 Theft Act 1968**: ' *Any person when not at his place of abode has with him any article for use in the course of or in connection with any burglary, theft or cheat'* shall be guilty of an offence.

'Cheat' refers to deception but not fraud offences under **Fraud Act 2006** which, from the date of it's commencement deletes the word 'cheat' from the going equipped definition. We shall cover this later. **Section 25** can be committed in public as well as private, in fact the only place the offence cannot be committed is when the accused is in his own home. Whether the articles found on a person breach this provision will depend on each case taken individually. Some articles could be readily explained away. To use a crude example, leather gloves and a jemmy could be seen as burglary implements but if being carried by someone whose genuine occupation involved working with wooden packing cases they could be legitimate. Similarly being found with a credit card in someone else's name could be explained by saying that it had just been found and was about to be handed in. Being found with three or four such cards would likely be grounds for arrest for this offence however.

Robbery

By the end of this section you will be able to:

- differentiate between robbery and burglary;

- explain how literally the courts interpret certain elements of the definition;

- apply relevant case law and statute to a range of hypothetical situations.

Robbery is best explained as theft with force. This can be quite minor, a bag snatch for example. The street robbery or 'mugging' is much more common than the bank heist.

ACTIVITY

Look up the case ***Attorney-General's Reference (Nos 4 & 7 of 2002)* [2002] Cr App R (S) 77**. This could be done on an online database like Westlaw or LexisNexis, both likely to be available through the educational institution providing your academic input: **www. westlaw.com** or **www.lexis-nexis.com** Alternatively you could use the law library of a university or college law school. This case involves fairly minor street robberies: why do you think the sentences were increased in this case?

The definition of the offence is found in **s. 8 Theft Act 1968.** Specifically, *'a person is guilty of robbery if he steals, and immediately before or at the time of doing so and in order to do so, he uses force on any person or puts or seeks to put any person in fear of being then and there subjected to force'.*

The simple addition of the two components of force and theft together will not suffice. Thus if two women fight outside a pub and a mobile 'phone falls out of the handbag of one of them, there will be no robbery if the woman's adversary opportunistically makes off with the 'phone. This will be a case of simple theft.

According to the statute the timing of the force is also crucial. It would appear that force applied too far in advance of the theft or indeed after it, would negate the act being a robbery at all. In fact the courts take a fairly liberal view of this provision, keen as they are to dissuade people from committing this most unsettling of crimes. In **R v Hale (1979)** two defendants committed what would otherwise have been a burglary. The householder was at home however, and was restrained by being tied up. It was quite possible that the items stolen were taken at the same time as the force or even that the thefts took place before the restraint was applied. The Court of Appeal had no difficulty in applying the principle that the *actus reus* was a continuing act similar to that encountered in **R v Thabo Meli (1954)** (see Chapter 1). In so doing the sequence of events in **R v Hale (1979)** made little difference and the defendants' appeals were dismissed. A similar approach was applied in **R v Lockley (1995)**. In a more commonplace scenario two defendants left an off-licence having appropriated some liquor. They used force to exit the premises. Despite the theft being complete before the force was used they were convicted.

A crucial part of this offence is that a theft actually takes place. If the defendant can take advantage of one of the defences to theft in **s. 2 Theft Act 1968** or perhaps does not meet the definition for dishonesty in **R v Ghosh (1982)** there can be no robbery whatever force is used. The former situation occurred in **R v Robinson (1977)** where the accused believed he had a right to the money in question. There was still no robbery even though the accused knew he had no right to use force as emphasised in **R v Skeavington (1968)**. Thus overzealous debt collectors may not be seen as robbers even if the violence they use may amount to an assault or harassment as it will almost certainly be unlawful (see Chapter 6).

> **REVISION**
>
> Going equipped (s. 25 TA '68):
>
> When not at his place of abode has with him:
>
> ✓ Any 'article for use in the course of or in connection with any burglary, theft or cheat (omitted for offences post Fraud Act 2006)'.
>
> Robbery (s. 8 TA '68):
>
> Steals and 'immediately before or at the time' and in order to steal:
>
> ✓ Uses or threatens force.
> ✓ Courts are flexible about what constitutes 'immediately before or at the time' (R v Hale 1979).

Knowledge Check 2

PC Keenan is on foot patrol at 2 am on Grosvenor Road, in response to a rapid increase in burglaries in the area reported recently. He greets two youths who are walking in the opposite direction as they pass him. Having walked another 5 metres he notes two screwdrivers on the ground just under a hedge, one of which is still rolling around. He catches up with the youths who give evasive answers to his questions and he searches them. Keenan discovers another screwdriver and a pair of pliers slipped into the back of the belt of one of the youths. On attempting to arrest the youths they attack him and knock him to the floor, Keenan's helmet falls to the ground as well and one of the youths makes off with it laughing.

Other than any assaults, which you may briefly mention, consider the liability of the two youths.

Handling

By the end of this section you will be able to:

- explain the definition of handling stolen goods;

- describe factual situations, which could give rise to a charge of 'handling';

- apply relevant case law and statute to a range of hypothetical situations.

This offence is described variously as 'handling', 'receiving' and 'fencing'. At one end of the scale is buying, say, 600 cigarettes in a pub from a stranger for £5. This is something which members of the public do not always perceive as criminal, especially as some perceive that 'everybody does it' and anyway they were not stolen, they 'fell off the back of a lorry'. This is a phrase which in itself student officers will now realise potentially describes theft by finding. At the other end of the scale, organised garage operations repair stolen cars and fit them with a new identity to order before shipping them overseas with an order fulfilment system that would be the envy of many legitimate businesses.

In the laudable desire to deny thieves a market for their booty, Parliament placed the maximum sentence above that for the theft itself. It was hoped to create a deterrent by setting a 14-year term.

(?) *You might want to reflect on the discussion above. Given the apparent gap between public perception and the law in this area, is there likely to be any deterrent value in the sentences handed out? What kind of media campaigns, even at local level, might prove useful do you think?*

The law on 'receiving' comes from **s. 22 Theft Act 1968**:

> *A person handles goods if (otherwise than in the course of stealing) knowing or believing them to be stolen goods he dishonestly receives the goods, or dishonestly undertakes or assists in their retention, removal, disposal or realisation by or for the benefit of another person or if he arranges to do so.*

Student officers may well by now be able to identify the *mens rea* of this offence. The key words are:

- knowing; or

- believing;

- dishonestly.

R v Brook (1993) indicates that some *mens rea* is necessary at the time the goods are 'received'. According to **R v Hall (1985)** knowing is a state of certain knowledge whereas believing falls short of that. Believing is more than just suspicion though and was described in this last case as a situation where no other reasonable conclusion as to the origin of the goods could be reached on the facts known to the accused. Thus if an accused has been offered a car without documents and with obvious damage to the steering column and door lock but at a 'knock-down' price there may be little else he can deduce other than that it is stolen. Add to that the fact say that the seller has brought the car to the accused's house rather than inviting him to his own abode then the evidence is mounting that this is not a legitimate bargain.

Dishonesty is not defined in the Act and the exceptions in **s. 2 Theft Act 1968** discussed in the section on theft apply only to **s. 1** offences. Any doubt over an accused's dishonesty would have to be resolved using the test in **R v Ghosh (1982)**. In other words, the question would have to be asked of the jury, was the defendant dishonest according to the standards of reasonable honest people? If yes, did the accused realise he was being dishonest by those standards?

In terms of the *actus reus* the accused commits the offence by:

- receiving; or
- undertaking or assisting in:
  - retention
  - removal
  - disposal
  - realisation
  - or arranging to do these with
- stolen goods.

The goods must be actually stolen and continue to be stolen (i.e. not have been returned to their owner) when the handling takes place. If they are not stolen but the accused believes they are, he or she may still be guilty of an attempt as you can attempt the impossible in law. 'Stolen' encompasses other criminal forms of obtaining property, specifically deception and fraud, blackmail or in making use of a wrongful credit.

Receiving means being in possession of the goods according to **R v Smythe (1980)**. Possession would mean being in exclusive control of the goods and someone else would have to have passed them on. It would not be handling to stumble upon stolen goods and keep them. This might well be **s.1** theft by finding however unless they were handed in during a reasonable time.

Retention, removal or disposal warrant little discussion here arguably. Realisation means the turning of the goods into monetary value, for example selling them to make money.

REVISION

Handling (s. 22 TA '68), the accused must have:
- ✓ Knowing/believing them to be stolen dishonestly,
- ✓ received.
- ✓ or undertook or assisted in:
  - retention
  - removal
  - disposal
  - realisation
  - or arranged to do so with.
- ✓ goods.

TWOC and vehicle interference

By the end of this section you will be able to:

- explain the relationship between TWOC and s.1 theft;

- explain the relationship between TWOC and vehicle interference;

- apply relevant case law and statute to a range of hypothetical situations.

Taking without owner's consent (TWOC), also known in some forces as 'taking and driving away' (TDA), is a **Theft Act** offence. TDA is a misnomer, as we shall see, in that you do not have to be driving, nor does the vehicle have to be under its own power. Vehicle interference is not a **Theft Act** offence however, as vehicle interference may simply be an incomplete TWOC or an attempt which has been thwarted in some way it seems logical to deal with it in the same place in this volume. It should also be noted that there is no such thing as attempted TWOC.

A separate offence where vehicles are taken was created because of the difficulty in proving **s. 6** of the **Theft Act 1968** – intention to permanently deprive when an accused is charged with **s. 1** theft. This is of course in situations where the vehicle has not been destroyed or sold on. There are two offences: **s. 12 Theft Act 1968** covers the basic offence and **s. 12A Theft Act 1968** concerns the aggravated version. **Section 12(1)** states:

> *a person shall be guilty of an offence if, without having the consent of the owner or other lawful authority, he takes any conveyance for his own or another's use*

Secton 12(1) goes on to bring passengers potentially under the ambit of the offence:

> *…knowing that any conveyance has been taken without such authority, drives it or allows himself to be carried in or on it.*

The offence may be committed by so-called 'joyriders' that take the vehicle and dump it after they have driven it around. It may also be committed when a vehicle is taken with authority but that authority is then exceeded. This is usually when the permission to use fleet vehicles is abused by an employee. Finally this offence could be committed 'technically' in the sense that there has been an offence but there may be some public interest or other consideration why a prosecution is not proceeded with. For example, a teenager whose parents are away on holiday who is stopped by police driving his parents' car. If it transpires on their return to the country that this driving was despite express instructions not to do so, an offence under **s. 12 Theft Act 1968** at least has been committed. It is likely though that only in exceptional circumstances would a prosecution go ahead.

According to **s. 12(7)(a)** a conveyance is *'any conveyance constructed or adapted for the carriage of a person or persons whether by land, water or air…'*. Thus a park pedalo, mini-moto, invalid carriage and ride on motor mower would all be covered as well as cars, motorbikes and the like. Bicycles are not covered however, and are dealt with separately under a similar offence created by **s. 12(5)**. The words used are 'constructed or adapted' so no beast of burden would be covered, but a cart pulled by a horse would. Similarly, no vehicle controlled by a pedestrian or controlled remotely would be covered, as there would be no 'carriage of a person'.

From case law we can deduce that the car need not be driven under its own power for the offence to take place. According to **R v Marchant (1985)** it can be merely pushed a few feet. It is clear from **R v Bogacki (1973)** that some movement must take place. A technical transfer of possession or control would be insufficient, say when someone finds car keys and forms intent to take the vehicle they fit but has not done so when apprehended.

The aggravated version of the offence is contained in **s. 12A Theft Act 1968** inserted by legislation enacted in 1992. This provision was brought about in response to increased concern caused by joyriders who drove exceptionally dangerously when they committed the basic **s. 12** offence. This provision relates only to mechanically propelled vehicles, in practical effect only cars and motorcycles. The inserted **s. 12A(1)** states that to be guilty of the aggravated offence the person must commit a **s. 12(1)** offence first and:

> *…it is proved that, at any time after the vehicle was unlawfully taken…and before it was recovered, the vehicle was driven, or injury or damage was caused, in* [circumstances such that]…

- the vehicle was driven dangerously (on road/in public place); or

- owing to the driving of the vehicle, a personal injury accident was caused or damage to other property was caused; or

- damage was caused to the vehicle.

Note that there is a complete absence of a need to prove a causal link between the defendant's manner of driving and any of the consequences above such as injury or damage. The consequence merely has to happen while the vehicle is in the possession of the taker. The driving could be very good but damage results from say the conduct of another driver. The liability is the same as if it was the fault of the accused according to **R v Marsh (1997)**.

The defendant will have a defence if the prosecution cannot disprove that the consequence occurred before the basic TWOC did. Alternatively, that the accused was nowhere near the vehicle when the damage, etc., happened. Such a situation could arise if the original 'twoccer' abandons the car but it is taken for a further, more dangerous drive by a second person without authority.

Vehicle interference

This offence was created because there was no offence of attempted TWOC. The definition is in **s. 9 Criminal Attempts Act 1981**. The coverage is broader than the types of vehicles in **s. 12 Theft Act 1968** in that trailers, even those not designed to convey people, such as horseboxes, are protected.

The definition in **s. 9(1)** specifically prohibits interfering:

> *...with a motor vehicle or trailer or with anything carried in or on* [them] *with the intention that...*

- theft of the vehicle/trailer; or

- theft of anything in or on them; or

- TWOC (**s. 12 Theft Act 1968**);

will be committed.

It is difficult to say what would constitute interference. Clearly very little activity would be required if pushing a vehicle only a few feet would constitute the full offence of TWOC under **s. 12 Theft Act 1968**. The CPS publishes guidance on this and refers to the fact that 'The mere placing of a hand on a door may not be an act of interference. Putting pressure on a vehicle's door handle is an act of interference' however (see **www.cps.gov.uk/legal/ section9/chapter_b.html#52**).

The guidance goes on to cite situations where a charge might be appropriate instead of attempted theft:

- *when the act of the accused fall short of what is required for attempted theft of the vehicle/trailer or content, for example, because they are acts merely preparatory to theft;*

- *when the accused attempts to take a motor vehicle without the owner's consent but does not succeed;*

- *when the accused's fingerprint or DNA is found on the interior of a vehicle that he did not have authority to enter or use.*

This may be the only charge available if there is insufficient evidence for anything more serious. The offence is triable summarily only, though.

REVISION

TWOC (s. 12 TA '68), the accused must have:

✓ Taken a conveyance without the owner's consent and
✓ not necessarily have deprived them of it permanently.
✓ Alternatively he could have knowingly allowed himself to be carried in or on a vehicle or driven a vehicle someone else had 'twocced'.

Aggravated TWOC (s. 12A TA '68), the accused must have committed a s. 12 TA '68 offence and before the vehicle is recovered it has

✓ been driven dangerously or;
✓ been involved in an accident where someone is injured or property damaged or;
✓ sustained damage.

Vehicle interference (ss. 9(1) Criminal Attempts Act 1981) occurs when the accused interferes with a motor vehicle or trailer or with anything carried in or on them with the intention that there will be a:

✓ theft of the vehicle/trailer; or
✓ theft of anything in or on them; or
✓ TWOC (s. 12 Theft Act 1968).

Making off without payment

By the end of this section you will be able to:

- explain the relationship between making off without payment and other offences such as s.1 theft or deception/fraud offences;

- explain when making off without payment may be the most appropriate offence to charge;

- analyse the offence in terms of *mens rea* and *actus reus*.

This offence is most commonly committed in the form of people driving off from petrol station forecourts without paying. These are often referred to as 'drive-offs' or 'bilking'. Other instances commonly encountered by the patrol officer are people making off from eating establishments without having paid for the food and running off having not paid a taxi fare.

The offence has existed at common law for many years but was superceded by a statutory version in the **Theft Act 1978**, a statute we have not yet encountered. **Section 3(1)** lays out the elements required to commit the offence:

> *Subject to subsection (3) below, a person who, knowing that payment on the spot for any goods supplied or service done is required or expected from him, dishonestly makes off without having paid as required or expected and with intent to avoid payment of the amount due…*

There always was a remedy at common law for the proprietor to be able to give chase and use reasonable force to subdue the offender in these situations. It is submitted here though, that this is now best viewed in the light of **s. 24A PACE 1984** (see Chapter 3).

The *mens rea* of this offence requires knowledge (a state of certain knowledge) and dishonesty. There is no statutory guidance as to the meaning of this latter word in this **Theft Act**. The appropriate test would be that in case law as developed in **R v Ghosh (1982)**. See under **s. 2 Theft Act 1968** for a description of the relevant considerations in deciding if a person is dishonest or not. Finally intent not to pay must be proved, in other words it was the accused's 'aim or purpose' **(R v Mohan 1976)** not to pay or possibly that he or she must have foreseen it was virtually certain they would not be going to pay (oblique intention). This might occur when a person runs from a taxi and leaps aboard an inter-city train about to depart. His motive might have been to catch the train but it could also be open to a jury to infer he had no intent to pay the taxi driver either.

Turning to the *actus reus*, there are two main issues:

- payment 'on the spot' is actually required;

- the accused has 'made off'.

Payment 'on the spot' would not be required if the accused had in effect negotiated credit but then failed to make the payment. **R v Vincent 2001** considers this very point. It is arguable for example, that a car driver who announces he has forgotten his wallet to a petrol forecourt cashier and then leaves what turns out to be a false name and address has not committed the offence. There might be an alternative offence, however (see under deception/fraud later).

'On the spot' generally means the premises (or vehicle) as a whole. It would probably not avail the accused to try to differentiate between, say, the till area of a restaurant and the rest of the square footage of the premises as the point from which he or she 'made off'. There are conflicting authorities on this point though. To err on the side of safety it may be better to charge with an attempt rather than have someone acquitted simply because they were apprehended before they could go through an exit door as in **R v Brooks and Brooks (1983)**. What is fairly clear though is that a nonchalant stroll out of a restaurant, etc, commits the offence just as a sprint would.

(?) *One of the difficulties in being a police officer is how to know when something has become a civil matter and therefore outside your jurisdiction. In making off cases it is important to consider whether the service, etc., has been carried out as per the contract. A refusal to pay for a substandard meal or a taxi fare when the journey is incomplete (see* **Troughton v MPC (1987)** *for an interesting example) would not automatically be a 'making off'. Comment on the sometimes thin dividing line between civil and criminal law as appropriate in reflective entries that you make.*

REVISION

'Making off' (s. 3 TA '78), the accused must have:
✓ Known that payment is expected on the spot.
✓ Dishonestly made off (not necessarily run) with intent to avoid payment.
✓ Payment must in actual fact have been required on the spot and not later through dispute or credit arrangement.

Criminal damage

By the end of this section you will be able to

- explain the definitions of a range of criminal damage offences;

- analyse developments in the *mens rea* of this offence;

- consider relevant case law and legislation in short-answer questions.

The guiding legislation in this area is still the **Criminal Damage Act 1971** and differs from the other property offences considered so far in that there is no need for dishonesty to commit this offence. Indeed it is aimed at discouraging wanton destruction and vandalism rather than property acquisition.

The term 'criminal damage' actually describes four different offences in three separate

---

ACTIVITY

Go back to **www.crimestatistics.org.uk** featured on page 150. You can compare police-recorded statistics with those compiled under the BCS, which is a victimisation survey. Which offences are first and second in terms of prevalence in both sets of figures?

---

subsections of the act. These are:

- intentional criminal damage;

- reckless criminal damage;

- the commission of either of these offences with intent or recklessness in respect of endangering life;

- the commission of either of these offences by fire (arson).

The first two of these are found in **s. 1(1) Criminal Damage Act 1971**:

> *A person who without lawful excuse destroys or damages any property belonging to another intending to destroy or damage any such property or being reckless as to whether any such property would be destroyed or damaged shall be guilty of an offence.*

The *actus reus* requires that property belonging to another is destroyed or damaged. That presents a problem to patrol officers called to deal with domestic violence incidents. It is common to find that one or other of the partnership is accusing the other of damaging their property. In many cases property in a matrimonial home or that of a cohabiting couple will be deemed to be jointly owned unless there are specific records, such as receipts, that indicate the contrary. In such cases, unless life is endangered, there is no offence under this statute as a person is merely damaging their own property.

Having a 'lawful excuse' can exonerate the accused completely. Obviously when called upon to effect entry to a premises with a sledgehammer to carry out a lawful search a police officer is not committing criminal damage. In the same way the fire brigade are expected to smash their way in to a premises adjoining that on fire if it is necessary to help them fight the fire. The presence of a lawful excuse is a defence and this issue is dealt with in **ss. 5(2)(a)** (consent of the owner) and **(b)** (necessity of protecting other property). **Section 5(3)** is particularly important as well in that it specifically states that an honest belief that the action is necessary even if it subsequently turns out to be unjustified.

Contested cases may arise when individuals believe they have a defence from their firmly held, but not universally recognised, convictions. In **Blake v DPP (1993)** a vicar who wrote graffiti during an anti-war rally in 1991 did so believing that God had consented to his actions; his appeal was dismissed. In **R v Hill and Hall (1988)** protestors cut through the perimeter fence of an airbase to protest against nuclear weapons and therefore protect the local residents' property. The protestors believed the residents and their property would be wiped out by a nuclear blast should such a weapon fall on the base in the event of war. This defence was unsuccessful but in **R v Wang (2005)** it was held a defence of this nature should at least be left to the jury to decide.

The damage must be more than merely trivial, although the authorities appear to be confusing and contradictory on this point. For instance in **A (a juvenile) v R (1978)** saliva spat onto a policeman's coat did damage it temporarily as it was rendered unusable. It was considered too easily cleaned off however, to warrant a criminal damage conviction. However, in **Hardman v Chief Constable of Avon and Somerset Constabulary (1986)** water-soluble paints used on paving slabs by a street artist were considered to be criminal damage. This was despite the fact that the elements would have worn the picture away very quickly. In fact the local authority chose to wash the paint away. It was also held in **Roe v Kingerlee (1986)** that words smeared across a surface in mud could be considered damage despite the relative ease with which it could be removed. The chief difference appears to be the relative cost of each cleaning operation rather than any principle.

The definition of property in this Act is very similar to that in the **Theft Act** with the main exception being that land can be damaged. Property belongs to another if another has *'custody or control of it…any proprietary right or interest…or…a charge on it'*.

The *mens rea* has been the subject of many judicial debates since 1971 when it was enacted. For many years there was earnest discussion in the cases about the recklessness element. The word 'intention' was not an issue as its meaning was consistent with that already discussed (see for example Chapter 1) in relation to other offences. The two possibilities for recklessness were:

- Recklessness as the 'reasonable man' would see it. So-called objective or **Caldwell** recklessness.

- Recklessness even in the opinion of the accused. Often termed subjective or **Cunningham** recklessness.

Under the definition of recklessness in **MPC v Caldwell (1982)** a failure to even give thought to a risk could lead to liability as well as knowing there was a risk and doing the act anyway. In **R v Cunningham (1957)** (see Chapter 1) the type of recklessness described was that of 'deliberate risk taking'.

In **R v G and Another (2003)** children were prosecuted for over £1m worth of damage by fire to a shop. They had been camping one night with their parents' permission. They had been playing with newspaper by lighting it in the backyard of a shop. They threw the lighted papers under a wheelie bin where they thought the papers would extinguish. They did not do so and the fire spread to the shop itself and adjoining premises through the roof space. It was held that young children could not appreciate the risk they were taking in the same way as adults. To criminalise them for not giving thought to a risk was thought wholly unfair therefore and not what Parliament intended. It is abundantly clear from this case that henceforth the *mens rea* for reckless criminal damage is to be **Cunningham** recklessness.

Criminal damage with intent to endanger life is found in **s. 1(2) Criminal Damage Act 1971**, if the property concerned is damaged by the accused who is:

a) *intending to destroy or damage any property or being reckless as to whether any property would be destroyed or damaged; and*

b) *intending by the destruction or damage to endanger the life of another or being reckless whether the life of another would be thereby endangered,*

he or she will commit an offence which potentially carries a life sentence.

Note that although this is commonly known as criminal damage with intent to endanger life, it can be committed by recklessness. Further even if merely recklessness as to the endangerment of life exists the offence is complete. Both would be **Cunningham** recklessness given the discussion in **R v G and Another (2003)** (above).

Section 1(3) states further that if either **1(1)** or **1(2)** is committed by fire the charge will be one of arson contrary to the relevant one of these subsections.

REVISION

Criminal damage:
- ✓ The *mens rea* is intention or Cunningham recklessness.
- ✓ The *actus reus* is destroying or damaging another's property (s. 1(1)) or even your own if endangering life is the ulterior aim (s. 1(2)).
- ✓ Any of the above are charged as arson if fire is used (s. 1(3)).

Knowledge Check 3

1. A man I hardly know offers me a case of wine in a pub. It should retail at £40. He is offering it to me for £10, 'no questions asked'. What offence may I commit if I accept and do you think I will have the *mens rea*?

2. A couple orders and eats a meal in a restaurant. They are presented with a bill for £57.10. They refuse to pay because the coffee was cold which ruined the whole dining experience for them. They walk out without paying but are stopped up the street by restaurant staff. Has any offence been committed?

3. In what circumstances, if any, can a passenger in a car be charged with TWOC?

4. If I set fire to a house knowing that there is a family of four inside asleep and that there are no functioning smoke alarms fitted, what Act and Section should I be charged under?

We have already encountered the offence of 'going equipped' under the **Theft Act 1968**. There is similar legislative provision in the **Criminal Damage Act 1971**. The relevant section is **s. 3** which makes it an offence to, without lawful excuse, have *'anything in his custody or in his control intending ... to use it...'* to commit criminal damage under the sections we have discussed. This would include causing or permitting another to use the item. It appears to cover storing material at home to use in this connection. In this respect it is therefore wider in scope than the **Theft Act** preventative measures which are only operative when the accused is not at their place of abode.

For the sake of completeness we should mention that an offence is also committed under **s. 2 Criminal Damage Act 1971** if a person makes threats without lawful excuse to commit **s. 1** criminal damage. This is providing that the accused intended the victim to fear the threats would be carried out.

Fraud and deception offences

By the end of this section you will be able to:

- explain the definitions of a range of older deception offences and why they remain relevant;

- explain the main provisions of the Fraud Act 2006;

- apply the law to a range of hypothetical scenarios.

The law in this area was mostly contained in the **Theft Act 1968, Theft Act 1978** and the **Theft (Amendment) Act 1996**. This law remains relevant because many serious frauds lie undetected for sometimes years. The **Fraud Act 2006** did not receive Royal Assent until November 2006. The initial deceit in many future fraud cases may have occurred when the old law was still in place so at least an outline knowledge of this legislation will be necessary for some years to come. We will deal with that before looking at the main provisions of the new legislation.

The main offences under the old legislation are:

- obtaining property by deception;

- obtaining services by deception;

- obtaining a pecuniary advantage by deception;

- obtaining a money transfer by deception;

- evasion of liability by deception.

Obtaining property by deception

This offence covers very similar ground to that of theft. All obtaining property by deception situations will also fit the definition of theft. However, not all thefts will fit the deception definition because some thefts will not involve deceit, such as pick pocketing.

The definition of this offence is found in **s. 15 Theft Act 1968**:

> *a person who by any deception dishonestly obtains property belonging to another with the intention of permanently depriving the other of it...*

commits the offence. 'Obtaining' in practice means much the same as appropriating under **s. 3 Theft Act 1968**. If the items obtained would satisfy **s. 4 Theft Act 1968** then they will be property for the purposes of this offence as well, additionally though land, wild animals and plants can be obtained by deception.

Section 5 Theft Act 1968 would also apply here in that it delimits what 'belonging to another' means. There have been some problems in mortgage fraud cases however, where the property in question arguably never exists in a tangible form. Value passes along a wire in these automated computer transactions from the lender to the vendor, in many cases briefly passing through the account of the buyer's solicitor. In an important case it was decided these electronic 'funds' could not amount to property. The specific offence of obtaining a money transfer by deception was created by Parliament as a direct response to this case (see later).

Deception is a harder word to define: **s. 15(4) Theft Act 1968** unhelpfully refers to a 'deception' being any *'...deception (whether deliberate or* [**Cunningham**] *reckless) by words or conduct as to fact or as to law...'* This does not really get us very far, as it is a somewhat circular discussion. We can discern however, that an accused can deceive by what is said or what is done. If a woman goes into a shop with a stolen credit card she may simply offer it and her purchases to the cashier without uttering a word. By her conduct though, she is holding herself out as authorised to use the card. Consider further the situation where a man stands in the street wearing a forged identity card and holding out a collecting tin bearing the logo of a non-existent charity. When he says 'please give to the needy', he also deceives by words. Both situations would fall under **s. 15 Theft Act 1968**.

In order to satisfy the *mens rea* however, the accused must know that they are representing something which is not true. In **R v Lambie (1981)** the accused had a credit card which she was instructed not to use by the card issuer because she was over the limit. She continued to do so to make purchases, something which would not be so easy to do in these days of 'chip and PIN' except online or by telephone. She was guilty of a **s. 15(4) Theft Act 1968** offence. In **MPC v Charles (1977)** the accused found himself in a similar situation when he wrote out a series of cheques he knew would not be honoured.

It remains to say in relation to the *mens rea* that dishonesty would be shown using the test in **R v Ghosh (1982)**. The exceptions in **s. 2 Theft Act 1968** would not apply here.

Obtaining services by deception

This offence was created to deal with situations where no goods are obtained. This would happen for instance if cinema tickets were purchased using a stolen credit card. Similarly it would be possible to obtain both goods and services at the same time. Consider the situation of booking a car in for an MOT. If it fails it will require repairs, most likely involving spare parts. If this is paid for using a cheque in a false name, both goods and the services of the garage to fit them, have been obtained.

The relevant section is **s. 1 Theft Act 1978** (note *not* the 1968 Act), specifically, the offence is to ' [obtaining by deception] ...*services where the other is induced to confer a benefit by doing some act, or causing or permitting some act to be done, on the understanding that the benefit has been or will be paid for'*. There is no additional meaning to the words 'deception' or 'obtaining' over and above that in **s. 15 TA '68**. It is important that students absorb the wording of this section accurately as the words 'has been or will be paid for' preclude this offence being committed by someone who obtains a free service by pretending to be someone else, say.

At first sight it might appear that this is a suitable offence to charge with in mortgage fraud cases. There have been particular problems in this area including the electronic transfer of money not being considered property. What is of concern here is that there is case law which states that the obtaining of a mortgage may not be construed as obtaining a service either. The safest option with mortgage fraud is to charge with obtaining a money transfer by deception (see later in this chapter, but see comments earlier about the **Fraud Act 2006** and the date of the offence).

Obtaining a pecuniary advantage by deception

The language used in this section is not always helpful; a pecuniary advantage is basically a financial one. The offence is contained in **s. 16 TA '78**. **Section 16(2)(b)** and **(c)** specifically set out what a 'pecuniary advantage' is limited to, for example:

- an overdraft facility is obtained;

- insurance is obtained;

- an annuity contract (basically a pension) is taken out;

- terms on any of the above are improved (e.g. by gaining reduced insurance premiums);

- a bet is won;

- or a job (or piece of work if self-employed) or promotion (with a higher wage) is obtained.

If any of these occurs and there has been an operative deception to achieve this end then a **s. 16** offence has occurred.

(?) *You might want to reflect on how discretion and other variable factors would operate here. If a person puts more GCSE passes on their CV than they actually possess would that be treated the same in all cases? Compare, say, the case of a pizza delivery driver who* did this. Would it have the same weight as if, say a deep-sea diver falsified his GCSEs bearing in mind that specialist training and experience may well be more crucial factors? How do insurance companies tend to deal with problems like this when customers 'forget' for instance to declare that they had an accident two years ago?

It should be noted also that, although there is little direct case law on the point, the type of borrowing covered by the Act is unlikely to be anything other than a bank overdraft facility. Analogous arrangements like credit cards accounts and loans would not, it seems be covered. **Section 15** obtaining property by deception may well be more appropriate though.

ACTIVITY

There have been some quite high-profile cases in the media of this type of offence. Consider for example the case against Mr Neil Taylor in 2005. He was the Chief Executive of a hospital trust on £115,000 per year; see: **http://society.guardian.co.uk/print/ 0,,5264637-105965,00.html** What untruths had led to him being charged?

Obtaining a money transfer by deception

This offence arrived on the statute books in something of a rush in 1996. The case of **R v Preddy (1996)** amongst other things exposed a huge loophole in the then theft and deception laws in relation to mortgage fraud. The House of Lords maintained that the reduction in the bank balance of a mortgage lender such as a building society and the corresponding increase in the bank balance of the seller was not the same thing as obtaining property. Even if this electronic transfer of funds had been obtained by means of a blatant lie by the purchaser, such as fraudulent details of his income, no deception offence had been committed.

The answer was to create a specific offence of obtaining a money transfer by deception. **Section 1 Theft (Amendment) Act 1996 (T(A)A '96)** does this by inserting a new **s. 15A** into the **TA '68.** It should be noted however, that some deception of a human being must occur. Any purely automated process would not be covered. See however, offences under the new **Fraud Act 2006.**

Evasion of liability by deception

Not paying a debt as it falls due is very much the province of the civil law. Police officers do not get involved in this kind of civil dispute except when called upon to assist bailiffs and the like to prevent a breach of the peace. This offence however, does not relate to simple debt recovery but is invoked if an individual uses an untruth to escape liability for some or all of the debt. There are three offences covered by the **TA '78.** They are to dishonestly and by deception:

- secure remission of a liability (**s. 2(1)(a)**);

- make someone wait or forgo payment (**s. 2(1)(b)**);

- obtain an exemption or abatement from a liability (**s. 2(1)(c)**).

Again the wording is unnecessarily confusing and the meaning of the words arguably makes the sections overlap in terms of the illegal activity they cover. As we have found before, the best way to describe these offences would be to use examples.

a) Simon owes £45 on one credit card, £46 on the second and £27 on a third, totalling £118. Simon knows it is not cost-effective for credit card companies to pursue debts of less than £50. Simon writes to all three telling them he has a terminal disease, which he does not. They each exercise their discretion and write off the debt. Simon obtains remission of the debt and is guilty of a **s. 2(1)(a)** offence.

b) Jatinderpal owes £750 council tax. He is just about to start moving out of his flat to live abroad for a year when the council debt collector calls. Jatinderpal tells the debt collector he paid a collector that called last week. The debt collector calls his office to check on his mobile but is unable to get through. Jatinderpal arranges for the collector to call the day after when he has completed his checks at the office. The collector calls the following day to find the flat empty. Jatinderpal has persuaded the council to wait and ultimately to forgo payment and commits a **s. 2(1)(b)** offence.

c) Janet has £10 per week deducted from her salary by her company to park her car at the firm's premises in a city-centre location on an annually renewed arrangement. Janet knows the company does not charge disabled blue badge holders on its staff. Prior to renewing the arrangement for another year Janet colour photocopies a friend's blue badge, alters it to show her details and photocopies it again, submitting it with her application for a parking permit. Janet has obtained an exemption from a future debt which therefore falls under **s. 2(1)(c)** rather than **s. 2(1)(a)** or **s. 2(1)(b)** where the debt must be in existence at the time of the deception.

REVISION

Deception (pre Fraud Act 2006), in summary the offences are:
- ✓ s. 15 TA '68 Obtaining property by deception, (services – s.1 TA '78).
- ✓ s. 16 TA '78 obtaining a pecuniary advantage by deception (e.g lying on a job application).
- ✓ s. 1 T(A)A '96 Obtaining a money transfer by deception (e.g. fraudulent mortgage applications).
- ✓ s. 2 TA '78 Evasion of liability (debt) by deception.

Fraud Act 2006 offences

The Fraud Act 2006 has now received Royal Assent and will apply to all offences where the commencement of offending is after the commencement date of the new act. The Fraud Act 2006 repeals the following offences dealt with above:

- **s. 15 TA '68** – obtaining property by deception.

- **s. 15A TA '68** – obtaining a money transfer by deception.

- **s. 16 TA '78** – obtaining a pecuniary advantage by deception.

- **s. 1 TA '78** – obtaining services by deception.

- **s. 2 TA '78** – evasion of a liability by deception.

It is vitally important to remember that the old offences will still apply if the fraud begins to take place before the commencement of the new act.

The new **Fraud Act 2006** offences that concern us here are:

- **s. 2** – Fraud by false representation.
- **s. 3** – Fraud by failing to disclose information.
- **s. 4** – Fraud by abuse of position.
- **s. 6** – Possession or control of articles for use in frauds.
- **s. 7** – Making or supplying articles for use in frauds.
- **s. 11** – Obtaining services dishonestly.

As student police officers you are unlikely to be dealing with large or complex frauds. These would normally be the province of the CID or even SOCA. Rather like your local doctor however, it is important that you can recognise problems so that you can pass them on to the appropriate specialist. Furthermore, until the new Act has been in use some time we can do little more here than present the definitions and make passing comment as to comparisons with the old offences. We can address any emerging case law in later editions. **Section 1** of the Act merely stipulates that a person is guilty of fraud if he is in breach of **ss. 2, 3** or **4**. The words 'gain' and 'loss' should be read to mean in terms of money or property and to include keeping as well as getting. Conversely, loss might include not getting what could have been received.

Fraud by false representation

Section 2 covers the offence we are discussing here. **Section 2(1)** stipulates that *'a person is in breach of this section if he...dishonestly makes a false representation, and...intends by making the representation...to make a gain for himself or another, or...to cause loss to another or to expose another to a risk of loss'*.

Section 2(2) goes on to describe a representation as being *'as to fact or as to law'* and *'false'* as being *'untrue or misleading and...the person making it knows that it is, or might be, untrue or misleading'*.

A representation may be express or implied and, crucially the offence is committed even if the representation is made to any form of automated system. Student officers may remember that under the old provisions it was not considered possible to deceive a machine – a very important development in the era of 'chip and PIN'.

Dishonesty is not defined and may be considered to be as held in **R v Ghosh (1982)** with the subjective and objective limbs already discussed under **s. 1 Theft Act 1968** above. It is also worthy of note that, in contrast to the old acts, no successful deception is necessary, only a knowledge or **Cunningham** recklessness as to the falsehood on the part of the accused is required.

Fraud by failing to disclose information

Under **s. 3 Fraud Act 2006** a person is in breach of this section if he *'dishonestly fails to disclose to another person information which he is under a legal duty to disclose* *and...intends, by failing to disclose the information...to make a gain for himself or another, or...to cause loss to another or to expose another to a risk of loss'.*

The offence requires that a legal duty to disclose the information be present. Obviously a person who is in a special relationship of utmost trust (often called a fiduciary relationship), such as a solicitor or accountant, could fall foul of this provision as there are specific statutory duties on them to give information. The offence could arise from failing to give information as required by the terms of a contract. This could then apply to not disclosing previous motoring misdemeanours to an insurance company to obtain cheaper cover, for example.

Fraud by abuse of position

Under **s. 4(1)** *'a person is in breach of this section if he...occupies a position in which he is expected to safeguard, or not act against, the financial interests of another person...dishonestly abuses that position, and...intends, by means of the abuse of that position...to make a gain for himself or another, or...to cause loss to another or to expose another to a risk of loss'.*

This provision is intended to prevent dishonesty by such as solicitors, company directors or the executors of wills. Even under the **TA '68** there were special measures to make this kind of activity harder to evade liability for such as in the exceptions to dishonesty under **s. 2(1)(c)**.

On a practical note, bear in mind that where there has been a confidence trick and money, etc., has been obtained by gaining the trust of say, an elderly person and then abusing it, **s. 1 TA '68** theft may be the more appropriate charge still. See the discussion around **R v Williams (Roy) 2000** and **R v Hinks (2000)** above.

Possession or control/making or supplying articles for use in frauds

These offences deal with similar ground to that which was formerly covered by 'going equipped' and certain provisions of the **Forgery and Counterfeiting Act 1981,** which we do not cover in this volume.

In relation to possession or control of the articles, **s. 6 (1)** specifies that *'a person is guilty of an offence if he has in his possession or under his control any article for use in the course of or in connection with any fraud'.* It is useful to find that an article would include a computer program or data, fraud being perpetrated via computer technology so much more today.

In terms of making or supplying the articles in the first place, **s. 7(1)** delimits the extent: *'a person is guilty of an offence if he makes, adapts, supplies or offers to supply any article...knowing that it is designed or adapted for use in the course of or in connection with fraud, or...intending it to be used to commit, or assist in the commission of, fraud'.* Again this offence would cater for possession of, say, the devices placed on the outside of ATMs to copy bank card details.

Obtaining services dishonestly

This offence has much in common with the **s. 1 TA '78** offence which we have met previously and which will not apply after the date the **Fraud Act 2006** is in force. The new provision contained in **s. 11** reads: *'a person is guilty of an offence under this section if he obtains services for himself or another...by a dishonest act, and...*[the services] *are made* *available on the basis that payment has been, is being or will be made...he obtains them without any payment having been made...and when he obtains them he knows...that they are being made available* [on the basis that payment has been, is being or will be made or that they might be] *but intends that payment or* [payment in full] *will not be made'.*

Again this provision is wider than the old legislation in that no deception is required, merely knowledge of the falsity.

REVISION

Fraud Act 2006 (outline knowledge required only):
- ✓ s. 2 – Fraud by false representation.
- ✓ s. 3 – Fraud by failing to disclose information.
- ✓ s. 4 – Fraud by abuse of position.
- ✓ s. 6 – Possession or control of articles for use in frauds.
- ✓ s. 7 – Making or supplying articles for use in frauds.
- ✓ s.11 – Obtaining services dishonestly.

Knowledge Check 4

1. On 21 January 2005 Jitesh hires a car using a false name and documents. He may well have committed theft but can you make out a case for deception? Consider the circumstances if he returns the car and makes full payment.

2. Consider the same scenario if he does not return the car at all.

3. Consider the same two scenarios above, in outline only, where the offence takes place on 21 January 2008.

Suggested research

A draft Criminal Code has been in existence for some years now. Find out what it is and what it covers by looking at references such as Card, Cross and Jones or Heaton (both below) on the subject. Consider also the changes the Fraud Act 2006 has made to the law in this area. Do you think a Criminal Code is still necessary?

Further reading

Further detailed discussion of all the topics in this chapter can be found by reading:

Card, R, Cross, R and Jones, P (2005) *Criminal law*. London: Butterworths.

Elliott, C and Quinn, F (2006) *Criminal law* (6th edn). Harlow: Pearson.

English, J and Card, R (2005) *Police law* (9th edn). Oxford: Oxford University Press.

Heaton, R (2001) *Criminal law* (3rd edn). London: Butterworths.

Useful websites

Home Office strategies to target the market in stolen goods:

www.crimereduction.gov.uk/burglary/burglaryminisite07.htm

The Law Commission:

www.lawcom.gov.uk

The Crown Prosecution Service:

http://cps.gov.uk

Legislation:

www.opsi.gov.uk

Case law and legislation databases:

www.westlaw.com* (an educational case law and statute database)

www.lexis-nexis.com* (an educational case law and statute database)

www.pnld.co.uk* (a police service specific database of case law and statute)

* Likely to be available through the virtual learning environment (VLE) which supports your course/training.

Answers

Knowledge Check 1

(i)   The first stage is to set out the key elements of the **s. 1 Theft Act 1968** definition: dishonestly, appropriate, property, belonging to another, intention to permanently deprive. Assuming the receipt is a forgery and ignoring any non-theft offences for now, there appears to be little doubt in relation to the elements of dishonesty, property belonging to another and intention to permanently deprive. Turning to appropriation, this is covered by **s. 3 Theft Act 1968** and is satisfied by an assumption of the rights of the owner, any right according to **R v Morris (1983)**. Appropriation would still take place even if it was with the consent of the owner per **R v Gomez (1993)**. Thus when the cashier at the information desk freely handed over the £98.96 the man appropriated it. In fact arguably the man appropriated the clothes when he took hold of them from the shelf. Taking hold of any item in a shop is usurping one of the rights of the owner. He did not of course intend to permanently deprive the clothes however. It may also be that obtaining property by deception is an appropriate offence as an alternative (see later).

(ii)   Considering again the **s. 1 Theft Act 1968** definition, there is little doubt around the issues of appropriating, property, belonging to another or intention to permanently deprive. The central issue is whether this is a dishonest act. The first stage is to consider **s. 2 Theft Act 1968.** The cashier would have either believed that he had a right in law, or believed he had the store's consent in the circumstances, the issue about finding the owner taking reasonable steps is obviously not relevant. There might be some mileage in the accused arguing they believed he had consent unless there is some policy document or instruction which he was aware of which states the opposite.

If none of these apply then the test from **R v Ghosh (1982)** would apply. Firstly, would a reasonable honest person think he was dishonest? If the answer is yes, did the accused think he was being dishonest by those standards? Again, whatever his instructions were on the subject will be crucial to securing a conviction, it could be argued.

(iii) Considering the definition of theft, appropriation has taken place as discussed in answer to (i) above when he touched the chickens. In terms of the *mens rea* was it his aim or purpose or did he foresee it as virtually certain that (**R v Mohan 1976, R v Woollin 1998, R v Matthews and Alleyne 2003**) the store would be permanently deprived of the meat? It is arguable that he must have known no one would buy such meat because of the hygiene issue; therefore it could be at least inferred that he intended the loss, a jury would have regard to his beliefs in deciding this. Further from **R v Lloyd (1985)** it can be argued that 'all [the meat's] goodness or virtue is gone' even if it remains in the possession of the shop and it has therefore been permanently deprived. We shall see that criminal damage may be an alternative here as well.

Knowledge Check 2

Keenan would need to form reasonable grounds for a stop and search under **s. 1 PACE 1984**. The combination of the time of day, the prevalence of burglaries in the neighbourhood during these hours coupled with the appearance of the tools and the suspects' demeanour may well be enough grounds. It is worth pointing out that it may have been unwise to search without assistance from a colleague but the attack probably constitutes a common assault (battery) and therefore assault on a constable in the execution of his duty as he is acting lawfully under **PACE**. If any injuries are very severe GBH with intent could be considered.

The youths may be 'going equipped': **s. 25 Theft Act 1968** states 'any person when not at his place of abode has with him any article for use in the course of or in connection with any burglary, theft or cheat' commits an offence. The presence of all these tools and their being hidden in various ways will take some explaining if it is alleged they are not for burglary or some other theft, it may well be the offence has been committed.

To deal with the taking of the helmet, there seems little doubt that this would constitute theft under **s. 1 Theft Act 1968** however robbery may be stretching a point. To consider **s. 8 Theft Act**, the force and the theft appear to happen in the right order (this of course might not matter anyway after **R v Hale (1979)** and **R v Lockley (1995)**). The problem though is that it does not appear that the force was executed in order to commit the theft. The theft appears to be an afterthought with the force being used to effect an escape from lawful apprehension.

Knowledge Check 3

1. Receiving stolen goods contrary to **s. 22 Theft Act 1968**. The *mens rea* would probably be satisfied by the fact that I heard the words 'no questions asked' but still purchased the case. It could be shown I believed the item was stolen at least.

2. The only option is that of making off without payment contrary to **s. 3(1) Theft Act 1978**. The problem is that arguably the contract has not been completed satisfactorily by the restaurant rather like **Troughton v MPC (1987)** although for very different reasons. There is probably therefore no offence here. As a matter of good practice advice should be given that this is a civil dispute, once addresses have been exchanged there is no need for further police action.

3. A passenger can commit TWOC contrary to **s. 12 Theft Act 1968** if he or she knows the conveyance is being driven without authority and allows him or herself to be carried in it.

4. A charge of arson contrary to **s. 1(2) Criminal Damage Act 1971** should be preferred as arguably there must at least have been recklessness as to the endangerment of life.

Knowledge Check 4

1. The offence is one of deception; given the date of commission, the offences prior to **Fraud Act 2006** should be considered. On hiring the car Jitesh has obtained a service but not property at this stage. The offence would therefore potentially be obtaining a service by deception contrary to **s. 1 TA '78**. The definition of a service is 'where the other is induced to confer a benefit by doing some act, or causing or permitting some act to be done, on the understanding that the benefit has been or will be paid for'. This would appear to cover a car hire contract.

   Let us turn to the issue of the dishonesty and deception. Dishonesty would need to be proved under the test in **R v Ghosh (1982)**. It may be that Jitesh has acted dishonestly under both limbs of the test. He has also deceived by his words and conduct per the meaning of the word in **s. 15 TA '68**. It may well be true that the car would not have been hired to Jitesh if the company had known he was presenting a false identity. It can be argued therefore that the fact that the car hire has been paid for does not preclude an offence under this section.

2. If Jitesh does not return the car at all then he may well have obtained property by deception contrary to **s. 15 TA '68**. The above comments on dishonesty and deception would equally apply here. There is little doubt that real property has been obtained in these circumstances.

3. Under the **Fraud Act 2006**, the hire would be considered under **s. 11**. On the wording of this section though, it seems possible that no offence has been committed if payment is made notwithstanding the obvious dishonesty. It remains to be seen if the courts interpret this wording as limiting the scope of the section compared to **s. 1 TA '78**. This does not seem likely, however. The non-return of the car would seem to generate a potential charge under **s.2 Fraud Act 2006,** fraud by false representation.

10 Public order

(?) *Remember this symbol indicates that the material might be useful for your Student Officer Learning and Assessment Programme (SOLAP) portfolio or any attached reflective practice record you are required to make.*

Underpinning knowledge towards Patrol Officer NOS:

1A1, 1B9, 2C1, 2C3, 2C4, 2J1, 2J2, 2K2, 4C1

and PCSO NOS:

1A1, 1B11, 2C1, 2C2, 2C3, 2C4, 2C5, 2J1, 4C1

For further information on these NOS, which are also Policing Level 3 and 4 NVQ unit titles, refer to Appendix 1 to this volume.

The primary focus here will be on the **Public Order Act 1986** with the main concern being the most likely offences which a student officer will encounter on general patrol duties. Thus although riot will be mentioned, it will not be covered in as much detail as the remaining offences. In addition Anti-Social Behaviour Order (ASBO) law is covered here despite it being a civil remedy. This is because they are commonplace, to do with public disorder and breach can lead to arrest. Some of the terminology is common to criminal law as well. The **Public Order Act 1936** is also touched upon.

(?) *What is public order? There is inevitably an element of subjectivity in determining what is meant by the term. Bear in mind diversity issues as some cultures and sectors of society consider a great deal more noise and lively behaviour as acceptable compared to others. As one judge put it in a civil case, 'what will be a nuisance in Belgrave Square will not necessarily be so in Bermondsey'. (Belgravia being a much wealthier area of London compared to Bermondsey). Nevertheless the law must be applied. All that a police officer can hope to do is maintain the level of order that is generally acceptable in a given location, without fear or favour.*

We will tackle the topics in this order:

- **Public Order Act 1986;**

- **Public Order Act 1936;**

- **ASBOs.**

Public Order Act 1986

By the end of this section you will be able to:

- evaluate the major public order offences;

- evaluate some of the legislative changes made more recently;

- apply your knowledge to some multi-choice questions.

The **Public Order Act 1986** was prompted in part by the failure of the previous legislation and common law to deal adequately with the civil disturbances arising out of the Miners' Strike in 1984.

ACTIVITY

Visit the BBC news archive 'On this day' for 12 March 1984. Go to **http://news.bbc.co.uk/ onthisday** and search or follow the links to the 'Miners strike over threatened pit closures' item. The page includes video footage and interviews with striking miners and police officers involved. The strike had a huge political and social impact with families set against each other, pitched battles with police reminiscent of medieval warfare and large numbers of police bused around the country to deal with disorder. Roger Graef's book (see further reading at the end of the chapter) includes some interesting insights into the time from a police perspective.

The important offences are:

- riot;

- violent disorder;

- affray;

- **Section 4 Public Order Act 1984;**

- **Section 4A Public Order Act 1984;**

- **Section 5 Public Order Act 1984;**

- stirring up religious hatred;

- stirring up racial hatred;

- racially or religiously aggravated public order offences.

Some police officer trainers and lawyers refer to some of these offences with such phrases as 'causing alarm, harassment and distress' and 'disorderly conduct', etc. The problem is that some of these words exist in more than one of the relevant statutory provisions and therefore confusion is possible. It has been decided here to simply refer to the section numbers for clarity.

Riot

You may have heard the phrase of being 'read the riot act' when you have been accused of doing wrong. This refers to the telling off that you might receive from a parent or draconian employer. This phrase has its roots in law. Under the old Riot Act, the police could not proceed to disperse a rioting mob until a magistrate had read the salient parts of the Act to them and they had failed to disperse. Placing Justices of the Peace in the front line like this was clearly not popular with the magistracy and the practice was eventually dropped.

The modern offence is found in **s. 1(1) Public Order Act 1986** and requires a surprisingly small number of people to commit it:

Where 12 or more persons who are present together use or threaten unlawful violence for a common purpose and the conduct of them (taken together) is such as would cause a person of reasonable firmness present at the scene to fear for his personal safety, each of the persons using unlawful violence for the common purpose is guilty of riot.

A prosecution can only be initiated with the consent of the Director of Public Prosecutions, however. Visit the CPS guidance at **www.cps.org.uk** to learn more about the circumstances which will make a prosecution for riot likely. Once this decision has been made, certain other issues come to the fore. The key is that all must act for a common purpose but the 12 need not act entirely in concert; see for example **s. 1(2)**:

It is immaterial whether or not the 12 or more use or threaten unlawful violence simultaneously.

Furthermore under **s. 1**:

- the common purpose may be inferred from conduct;

- no person of reasonable firmness need actually be, or be likely to be, present at the scene;

- riot may be committed in private as well as in public places.

The *mens rea* for this offence is intending to use violence or being aware that the conduct may be violent. This is the first time we have come across 'awareness' as a *mens rea* concept in this volume.

Given the special nature of this offence and the fact that you are unlikely to attend an incident involving riot unsupervised, we can safely move on to more common offences.

Violent disorder

This might be described as a miniature version of riot. It has some similarity in that a person acting on his or her own cannot commit it. **Section 2(1)** provides:

Where three or more persons who are present together use or threaten unlawful violence and the conduct of them (taken together) is such as would cause a person of reasonable firmness present at the scene to fear for his personal safety, each of the persons using or threatening unlawful violence is guilty of violent disorder.

Section 2 adds similar provisos to those found under **s. 1**:

- it is immaterial whether or not the three or more use or threaten unlawful violence simultaneously;

- no person of reasonable firmness need actually be, or be likely to be, present at the scene;

- violent disorder may be committed in private as well as in public places.

This offence creates quite a broad concept of people acting as a group, albeit potentially quite a small one, to intimidate a victim. In **R v Brodie (2000)** it was held that even following someone as a group for a distance with the requisite intent created sufficient menace to found the offence.

The *mens rea* is set out in **s. 6(2)**:

> ....*if he intends to use or threaten violence or is aware that his conduct may be violent or threaten violence.*

Again there is considerable similarity with riot in the sense of this statement.

Affray

We now encounter the first public order offence that a person can commit alone. It is quite a serious 'either way' offence with a maximum penalty of three years. The definition is in **s. 3(1)**:

> *A person is guilty of affray if he uses or threatens unlawful violence **towards another** and his conduct is such as would cause a person of reasonable firmness present at the scene to fear for his personal safety.*

The author's emphasis is added here as this adds a fundamental difference that the violence must be directed at another person in contrast to **s. 1** and **2**.

Section 3 goes on to add that:

- where two or more persons use or threaten the unlawful violence, it is the conduct of them taken together that must be considered;

- no person of reasonable firmness need actually be, or be likely to be, present at the scene;

- affray may be committed in private as well as in public places;

- a threat cannot be made by the use of words alone.

This latter provision was presumably added to avoid the debate that surrounds this issue in such as common assault (see Chapter 6). In addition the courts have held in **I v DPP (2002)** that the threat must be directed at persons actually present. This does not conflict with the provision (listed first above) that no person of reasonable firmness need be present. This point is just to illustrate that the test is an objective one. In other words, 'what would a person of reasonable firmness have thought?' This is irrespective of the fact that a person of considerable fortitude actually received the threat and was not troubled by it.

As with violent disorder the *mens rea* is intention to use or threaten violence or an awareness that the conduct may be violent or threaten violence.

ACTIVITY

Visit the BBC news archive at **http://news.bbc.co.uk/onthisday** and search or follow the links to the 'Violence flares in poll tax demonstration' link. On 31 March 1990, 340 people were arrested in rioting over the unpopular 'Community Charge'. View the video footage and listen to the audio on the site and see if you can identify individual instances of **s.1, 2 or 3 POA 1986** offences taking place.

Section 4 Public Order Act 1984

Section 4 offences and some examples that follow are more commonly found around towns and cities. This is particularly at night-time and sometimes connected with alcohol (see Chapter 18 for a general discussion around the changes in licensing hours and the effect if any on public order).

This was the original offence to deal with this level of disorder as enacted in 1986. **Section 4A** was brought in later to deal with perceived shortcomings in **s. 4** and is dealt with in the next part of the chapter.

The offence in **s. 4** is as follows:

A person is guilty of an offence if he

(a) *uses towards another person threatening, abusive or insulting words or behaviour, or*

(b) *distributes or displays to another person any writing, sign or other visible representation which is threatening, abusive or insulting,*

An offence under this section may be committed in a public or a private place, except that no offence is committed where the words, behaviour or images/effigies/signs are in a dwelling and the victim is outside.

What differentiates this from **s. 4A** (see next section) is the *mens rea*. In **s. 4** it is to act:

- with intent to cause that person to believe that immediate unlawful violence will be used against him or another by any person; or

- to provoke the immediate use of unlawful violence by that person or another; or

- whereby that person is likely to believe that such violence will be used or it is likely that such violence will be provoked.

Brutus v Cozens (1973), a case which survives from the law before the 1986 Act, illustrates that the litmus test is whether an ordinary member of the public would consider the conduct threatening, abusive or insulting. Running onto the centre court at Wimbledon and distributing leaflets was held not to be so in this particular case.

R v Oakwell (1978) further points out that words are not necessary, as fighting can itself be threatening. **Atkin v DPP (1989)** however, is authority for the fact that the words must be used in the presence of and directed at the victim.

Section 4A Public Order Act 1984

This offence was introduced to deal with behaviour similar to that in **s. 4** which is done with the intent of causing a person harassment, alarm or distress. **Section 4A(1)** specifically provides that:

A person is guilty of an offence if, with intent to cause a person harassment, alarm or distress, he

(a) uses threatening, abusive or insulting words or behaviour, or disorderly behaviour, or

(b) displays any writing, sign or other visible representation which is threatening, abusive or insulting,

thereby causing that or another person harassment, alarm or distress.

The provisos in relation to words or conduct emanating from a dwelling found in **s. 4** hold for this offence as well. There is also a statutory defence with a reverse burden of proof, either:

- that the offender was inside a dwelling and had no reason to believe that the words or behaviour used, or the writing, sign or other visible representation displayed, would be heard or seen by a person outside that or any other dwelling; or

- that the conduct was reasonable.

Section 5 Public Order Act 1984

Offences under **s. 5** are the most minor and now most likely to be dealt with by fixed penalty notice. PCSOs can be designated with the power to award these FPNs under **Police Reform Act 2002** (see Chapter 5). The wording of the offence under **s. 5(1)** is:

A person is guilty of an offence if he

(a) uses threatening, abusive or insulting words or behaviour, or disorderly behaviour, or

(b) displays any writing, sign or other visible representation which is threatening, abusive or insulting, within the hearing or, sight of a person likely to be caused harassment, alarm or distress thereby.

The same provisos regarding being in a dwelling and the victim outside, having no reason to believe the words or behaviour, etc., could be heard/seen outside and reasonable conduct are present here as well. The interesting point is that the courts have held that if behaviour is 'threatening, abusive and insulting' then it cannot be reasonable. This rather negates the point of the defence, it could be argued.

It is also clear that only a constable (or PCSO) in uniform can proceed against this offence and that a warning to stop must be given. The conduct after the warning need not be the same as that before as long as it is still threatening, abusive or insulting.

The *mens rea* is intention or awareness that the conduct etc. is threatening, abusive or insulting.

REVISION

✓ S. 4 POA 1986 – threatening, abusive or insulting words/behaviour/displays.
✓ S. 4A POA 1986 – with intent to cause a person harassment, alarm or distress uses threatening, abusive or insulting words/behaviour/displays.
✓ S. 5 POA 1986 – uses threatening, abusive or insulting words/behaviour/displays within the hearing or sight of a person likely to be caused harassment, alarm or distress.

Stirring up racial hatred

Sections 17 to **23 Public Order Act 1986** outline the offences referring to stirring up racial hatred. In many of these offences the provisos mentioned in **s. 4, 4A** and **5** about being in a dwelling, etc., are present.

Section 17 defines racial hatred as against 'a group of persons...defined by reference to colour, race, nationality (including citizenship) or ethnic or national origins'.

By **s. 18(1)** it is an offence to use:

> *...threatening, abusive or insulting words or behaviour, or displays any written material which is threatening, abusive or insulting, is guilty of an offence if*
>
> *(a) he intends thereby to stir up racial hatred, or*
>
> *(b) having regard to all the circumstances racial hatred is likely to be stirred up thereby.*

Section 19(1) extends this offence to '...a person who publishes or distributes written material which is threatening, abusive or insulting...' in similar circumstances.

Sections 20 to **22** extend the prohibition to plays, visual or sound recordings and broadcast programmes which are intended to stir up racial hatred.

Section 23 prohibits possession of racially inflammatory material. There are also powers of search, seizure and forfeiture provided for as well in other sections.

Stirring up religious hatred

The new law has been introduced by the **Racial and Religious Hatred Act 2006** which was introduced to deal with some of the more inflammatory religious teachings of some clerics which hitherto had caused much distress but had been difficult to deter or prosecute. The offences are created and inserted into the **Public Order Act 1986**. We can only list these here as they have little or no case law on their provisions given how recently they were enacted.

Section 29A provides the meaning of religious hatred:

...hatred against a group of persons defined by reference to religious belief or lack of religious belief.

The amendments in the new **s. 29B-29H** make similar but not identical provision to the offences in relation to racial hatred but obviously substituting the requirement that the offence will be on religious grounds:

s. 29B Use of words or behaviour or display of written material;

s. 29C Publishing or distributing written material;

s. 29D Public performance of play;

s. 29E Distributing, showing or playing a recording;

s. 29F Broadcasting or including programme in programme service;

s. 29G Possession of inflammatory material;

s. 29H Powers of entry and search.

Racially or religiously aggravated public order offences

In addition to the offences described above, the **Crime and Disorder Act 1998** as amended brings in racially aggravated versions of **ss. 4, 4A** and **5 Public Order Act 1986**. In essence the basic offence is committed but aggravated under one of two heads. Hostility could be directed at a person based on the person's actual or presumed membership or association with members of a racial or religious group. Alternatively, the hostility is even partly motivated by general hostility towards such groups.

Public Order Act 1936

By the end of this section you will be able to:

• identify the remaining important offences under the Public Order Act 1936;

• analyse their relative importance compared to other legislation.

The only remnants of this act that are important are those relating to political uniforms and unofficial or quasi-military organisations. The act dates from a time when neo-nazi political organisations like Oswald Mosley's 'Black Shirts' were prominent. The prohibitions are twofold. **Section 1(1)** deals with political uniforms:

Subject as hereinafter provided, any person who in any public place or at any public meeting wears uniform signifying his association with any political organisation or with the promotion of any political object shall be guilty of an offence...

Clearly the Salvation Army or Boy Scouts would not be committing this offence as their uniform signifies nothing political. The term 'uniform' is not defined. It is an entirely academic point but a political candidate's rosette could be termed a uniform although it is not suggested here that officers should arrest such people under this Act.

The Chief Officer of Police can authorise uniforms when they are worn for ceremonial reasons.

Section 2(1) is concerned with prohibited organisations:

If the members or adherents of any association of persons, whether incorporated or not, are

(a) organised or trained or equipped for the purposes of enabling them to be employed in usurping the functions of the police or of the armed forces of the Crown; or

(b) organised and trained or organised and equipped either for the purpose of enabling them to be employed for the use or display of physical force in promoting any political object, or in such manner as to arouse reasonable apprehension that they are organised and either trained or equipped for that purpose.

The key phrase here is usurping the functions of the police, etc., which implies some kind of unlawful taking over. 'Accredited persons' such as wardens, etc., could not therefore be guilty of this offence as they are allowed to act with some police powers in effect by the Chief Officer of Police under the **Police Reform Act 2002**.

The likelihood of offences under this statute is much reduced. The prohibition on membership of terrorist and other proscribed organisations are much more important and dealt with elsewhere in this volume.

ASBOs

By the end of this section you will be able to:

- identify the important legislation relevant to Anti-social Behaviour Orders;
- define anti-social behaviour under the legislation.

Anti-social behaviour orders were brought in as a preventative measure to deal with nuisance behaviour and the like; specifically behaviour which is not yet at the level of being criminal but nevertheless blights some neighbourhoods. The orders were brought in by the **Crime and Disorder Act 1998** but many of the provisions were amended by such as the **Police Reform Act 2002**. Dealing with anti-social behaviour is also very much within the role profile of a Police Community Support Officer (PCSO). The enforcement powers are outlined in Chapter 5, 'Police organisation' and the material in this section should be read in conjunction.

As we have said at the head of this chapter, ASBOs are civil orders. **Section 1(1) Crime and Disorder Act 1998** provides that a relevant authority may bring an application for an order with respect to anyone over ten years of age:

(a) *that the person has acted, since the commencement date, in an anti-social manner, that is to say, in a manner that caused or was likely to cause harassment, alarm or distress to one or more persons not of the same household as himself; and*

(b) *that such an order is necessary to protect relevant persons from further anti-social acts by him.*

The term 'anti-social behaviour' can cover a great many acts. It has been criticised as meaning that an order, which must last two years, can be granted on little more than an allegation. The term has been used to apply to anything from rowdy young people to soliciting on the street by prostitutes and even the keeping of large numbers of animals or birds. It was probably outside the contemplation of those who framed the Act but in some parts of the country these orders have been applied to cantankerous elderly residents as well as the young and unruly.

Section 1A defines who may bring an action for an order. A relevant authority is:

(a) *the council for a local government area;*

(aa) *in relation to England, a county council;*

(b) *the chief officer of police of any police force maintained for a police area;*

(c) *the chief constable of the British Transport Police Force;*

(d) *any person registered under* **s. 1 Housing Act 1996** *as a social landlord who provides or manages any houses or hostel in a local government area; or*

(e) *a housing action trust established by order in pursuance of* **s. 62 Housing Act 1988.**

In essence this means a local authority, housing associations and other social landlords and chief constables can apply for such an order.

Conversely, the relevant person or victim of the behaviour according to **s. 1B** (referring to **S. 1A** above) can be:

(a) *....persons within the local government area of that council;*

(aa) *in relation to a relevant authority falling within paragraph (aa) of subsection (1A), persons within the county of the county council;*

(b) *in relation to a relevant authority falling within paragraph (b) of that subsection, persons within the police area;*

(c) *in relation to a relevant authority falling within paragraph (c) of that subsection*

(i) *persons who are within or likely to be within a place specified in* **s. 31(1)(a)** *to* **(b)** *of the Railways and Transport Safety Act 2003 in a local government area; or*

(ii) *persons who are within or likely to be within such a place;*

(d) *in relation to a relevant authority falling within paragraph (d) or (e) of that subsection*

    (i) *persons who are residing in or who are otherwise on or likely to be on premises provided or managed by that authority; or*

    (ii) *persons who are in the vicinity of or likely to be in the vicinity of such premises.*

An application is made to the magistrates' court.

The criminal offence is committed if the order is breached according to **s1(10)**:

If without reasonable excuse a person does anything which he is prohibited from doing by an anti-social behaviour order, is guilty of an offence and liable

(a) on summary conviction, to imprisonment for a term not exceeding six months or to a fine not exceeding the statutory maximum, or to both; or

(b) on conviction on indictment, to imprisonment for a term not exceeding five years or to a fine, or to both.

Only local councils can bring proceedings for a breach, however. Special provisions are in place to comply with such as **Children and Young Persons Act 1933** (see Chapter 15 generally) where the order relates to a person under 18.

? *ASBOs are controversial and attacked from both sides of the political spectrum as being either too draconian or being little more than a badge of honour for 'hoodies'. It would be worth reflecting, after discussions with colleagues, whether these orders have been effective in the area you police.*

Knowledge Check 1

1. Riot can be committed by:

    (a) 12 or more persons.

    (b) 3 or more persons.

    (c) 100 or more persons.

    (d) None of the above.

2. S. 5 Public Order Act 1986 offences:

    (a) Can only be dealt with by FPN.

    (b) Can be dealt with by arrest in all cases.

    (c) Can be dealt with by arrest when a warning has been given and relevant conduct has continued.

    (d) Can be dealt with by arrest by a constable in uniform when a warning has been given and relevant conduct has continued.

3. Affray is found in:

   (a) S. 2 Public Order Act 1936.

   (b) S. 1 Public Order Act 1986.

   (c) S. 3 Public Order Act 1986.

   (d) S. 1 Crime and Disorder Act 1998.

4. An ASBO can be applied for by, amongst other organisations:

   (a) A private individual.

   (b) A social landlord.

   (c) A chief superintendent.

   (d) A Member of Parliament.

The answers are at the end of the chapter.

Suggested research

Look through your local press for cases involving anti-social behaviour. Do some informal primary research amongst local inhabitants, family and friends. Ask questions around whether ASBOs are perceived to be effective and how they might be improved. Consider perhaps whether it is right that they should they be applied to those under ten.

Further reading

Background reading of the police experience of policing disorder can be obtained by reading:

Graef, R (1990) *Talking blues: The police in their own words*. London: Collins Harvill.

More detailed coverage of the criminal offences in this chapter can be obtained by reading:

Card, R, Cross, R and Jones, P (2005) *Criminal law*. London: Butterworths.

English, J and Card, R (2005) *Police law* (9th edn). Oxford: Oxford University Press.

Heaton, R (2001) *Criminal law* (3rd edn). London: Butterworths.

Sampson, F (2007) *Blackstone's Police Manual, Volume 1 – Crime*. Oxford: Oxford University Press.

Some discussion of the background issues of ASBOs can be found in:

Hughes, G, Mclaughlin, E and Muncie, J (2002) *Crime prevention and community safety: New directions*, London: Sage.

Useful websites

Crown Prosecution service:

www.cps.org.uk

Legislation:

www.opsi.gov.uk

Case law and legislation databases:

www.westlaw.com* (an educational case law and statute database)

www.lexis-nexis.com* (an educational case law and statute database)

www.pnld.co.uk* (a police service specific database of case law and statute)

* Likely to be available through the virtual learning environment (VLE) which supports your course/training.

Answers

Knowledge Check 1

1. (a) 12 or more persons.

2. (d) Can be dealt with by arrest by a constable in uniform when a warning has been given and relevant conduct has continued.

3. (c) **S. 3 Public Order Act 1986.**

4. (b) A social landlord.

11 Crime prevention

(?) *Remember this symbol indicates that the material might be useful for your Student Officer Learning and Assessment Programme (SOLAP) portfolio or any attached reflective practice record you are required to make.*

Underpinning knowledge towards Patrol Officer NOS:

1A2, 1B9, 2A1, 4C1

and PCSO NOS:

1B11, 2A1, SLP6, 4C1, 4C2

For further information on these NOS, which are also Policing Level 3 and 4 NVQ unit titles, refer to Appendix 1 to this volume.

Crime prevention is in fact the second of the three core functions of a police officer as stated in the **Metropolitan Police Act 1829**. A police officer's duties are to:

- save life and limb;

- prevent crime;

- detect crime.

It is perhaps surprising then that crime prevention receives so little prominence in the media and indeed in police culture generally. The reason may be that there is little glamorous about giving advice on window locks compared with say foiling a bank robbery in progress. This of course reflects the perception of crime prevention more than the reality. Crime prevention is much more complex than fitting better door locks and burglar alarms. There is a part of the study of criminology devoted to it and a whole industry geared up to sell products related to it.

Most of your colleagues with longer service than you will be able to give examples of crime prevention, such as avoiding unlit areas to walk home at night or to park your car. We are all familiar with Home Office sponsored advertisements extolling us to keep valuables in our vehicles out of sight and so on. What this chapter hopes to do is put all of this information in a wider context: to also show that crime prevention is much more about building collaborative working practices across organisations and good communication links than carrying a rape alarm. Personal safety of course plays a part in this whole arena.

The topic is potentially so vast that we can only cover the parts of it that relate to being a patrol officer. We have limited this to three main areas therefore:

- situational crime prevention;
- social crime prevention;
- multi-agency partnerships.

Due to the nature of this subject there will not be formal assessment exercises provided. Opportunities to consolidate knowledge will be given through suggested activities. There is some criminological theory in this chapter but only at a very basic level. This is provided to give a context to the legislation and practice in this area.

Situational crime prevention

By the end of this section you will be able to:

- define the term 'situational crime prevention';
- evaluate routine activity theory (RAT);
- begin to engage with the crime-prevention issues in your local area.

ACTIVITY

Go to **www.crimereduction.gov.uk** to study the Home Office Crime Reduction Unit promoting crime reduction initiatives. The work of this department is highly relevant to this chapter. There is much useful information on the website to assist your studies. Familiarise yourself with what is available before reading further.

The Home Office Crime Reduction Unit refers to situational crime prevention (SCP) in the following manner. It emphasises:

- the importance of opportunity for crime to occur, reduce the occurrence of these and crime will reduce;
- the settings (locations, sets of circumstances and coincidence of events) that allow crime to occur;
- prevention rather than cure, i.e. there is less interest in detection and punishment, rather a concentration on stopping crime from happening in the first place.

Sometimes this can happen as a by-product of legislation. For instance, when it became mandatory to wear a motorcycle crash helmet the opportunist theft of motorcycles decreased dramatically. The reason was that it became almost impossible to steal an unattended motorcycle on the spur of the moment without being obvious or always carrying a helmet just in case.

The theoretical base for this discussion is routine activities theory (RAT) introduced by researchers Cohen and Felson in 1979 and further developed by Felson in 1998 (see further reading below). The essence of this is that the maximum risk of crime is present when there is a coincidence of a:

• motivated offender;

• suitable target; and

• absence of a capable guardian.

This can just as easily be applied to a business without a good quality alarm system in a high-crime area as to a child walking alone in the hours of darkness visibly carrying a £100 mobile phone and an £80 MP3 player. These are everyday occurrences but illustrate the theory in a contemporary way. Clearly both hypothetical scenarios require a motivated offender but assuming these are present then the real issue may be the lack of a suitable guardian, be that electronic or parental. In recent years robberies of mobile phones and MP3 players from under-16s have increased dramatically against a backdrop of generally falling crime figures, further illustrating the point.

This brings us to the issue of the traditional police crime prevention officer's advice about window and door locks and the theory of crime prevention. One way to reduce the risk of crime according to RAT is to make the target less suitable, for example by removing it altogether, say by not allowing young children out in the hours of darkness unsupervised. Alternatively by 'target hardening' targets that cannot be removed or hidden. This is a phrase borrowed from the military to describe making a target such as an aircraft hanger or bunker almost completely bomb-proof. Applied to crime prevention and a residential home it could mean installing the best-quality alarm, fitting the highest-specification window locks and door security fittings. Internally beaded double glazing and exterior lighting could also be added to the list. This of course requires money and it is no surprise that some of the worst-hit areas for burglary are the poorer neighbourhoods, not necessarily the leafy suburbs.

(?) *Think about the area you patrol. Are there any properties that seem to get burgled many times whilst others remain untouched? If so, is it something about the building itself? Is it something to do with the attitude of the occupier or their socioeconomic status? Is there anything you can do or advice you can give to help prevent this repeat victimisation? Visit* **www.crimestatistics.org.uk** *and follow the links on domestic burglary. The British Crime Survey information there could help you reflect on this issue.*

Critics of the SCP approach will say that because there can never be a uniform approach across all areas to this type of crime prevention, some areas will always be better at reducing opportunities for crime than others. It is argued that all SCP can do is displace crime to another area. This obviously benefits those areas with an organised approach to SCP but does not achieve much in terms of national crime reduction. In support of this, studies of prison inmates in Holland have discovered that virtually all the offenders interviewed said that they moved onto other targets or other forms of crime when SCP techniques made their chosen offending difficult. This rather supports arguments for more social crime prevention, discussed later. In reality a mix of approaches probably provides the best solutions.

Social crime prevention

By the end of this section you will be able to:

- define the term 'social crime prevention';

- evaluate some key theorising in this area;

- begin to engage with the crime-prevention issues in your local area.

The main theme within social crime prevention is the emphasis on social policies at both local and national level that alleviate the need to commit crime. The government has for instance used the catch phrase 'tough on crime, tough on the causes of crime' to describe its law-and-order policies. The second part of this phrase means tackling poverty and social exclusion, so that people can achieve material wealth and a happy meaningful life by legitimate means. Thus removing the temptation to commit crime. The idea that social policies can have an effect on crime is underpinned by a number of theories, too many to cover here. We offer three as examples.

- the 'Chicago school';

- 'broken windows' theory;

- strain theory.

The Chicago school

This does not refer to an educational institution but rather to a 'school of thought' based on studies of the city of Chicago in the USA. Criminologists like Park and Burgess in 1925 postulated that cities have a lot in common with natural ecologies: they evolve and invade other, e.g. rural, territories, colonising as they go. Under this theory a diagram of a modern city might look like this:

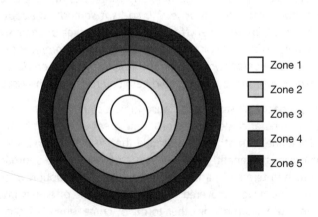

Diagram of Chicago school city zones

The zones numbered are:

- Zone 1 – central business district;

- Zone 2 – 'zone of transition';

- Zone 3 – working-class zone;

- Zone 4 – residential zone (more middle-class family homes);

- Zone 5 – commuter zone (affluent 'leafy' suburbs).

This theory was of course developed at a time when traditional distinctions between working class and middle class were perhaps more marked than they are today. You may recognise these basic demarcations in a city that you know. The key is the 'zone of transition'. This is an area where people do not perhaps stay very long. Immigrant families may settle here initially before moving on, student dwellings are often sited here and the area generally is not well kept nor is there any real community. People do not stay long enough to form bonds with each other. This area of low income and general depravation is a breeding ground for crime and there is no community spirit to resist it. One approach is for government and charities to bring in funding to encourage jobs and economic development in Zone 2 and to target community-building initiatives at the area. This has been done with varying degrees of success in several major British cities.

Broken windows theory

Allied to these notions is 'broken windows' theory. Wilson in 1985 identified that when an area is not well kept, further damage and degradation of the area both physically and in terms of criminality occurs. If the window of a house is left unrepaired, others will become smashed – such is human nature. Put in wider terms, if small crimes are ignored the malaise will spread and greater crimes will result. This is the essence of 'zero-tolerance' policing said to have been so successful in New York in the 1990s. The policy is to deal with every minor crime from littering to parking offences, vagrancy to anti-social behaviour without much use of discretion. This spreads the message that no crime will be tolerated, thus raising the character of the neighbourhood. This approach has its critics however, who say that it targets the poor in say the 'zone of transition' which can inflame tensions, sometimes racial ones given the likely high immigrant population in this zone, with the police.

Strain theory

Robert Merton in 1938 articulated that there is a 'strain' between what the media in a consumer society leads the population to believe they can and should attain and what they can actually obtain in terms of material success. We are all presented with idealised lifestyles with cars, nice houses and state-of-the-art electrical goods all appearing to be the norm. The theory takes account of the fact that a delivery driver earning the minimum wage will aspire to own these goods in exactly the same way as a hospital consultant earning £75,000 per year. The delivery driver may have no hope of attaining those goods legitimately, no expectation of significant advancement because further training is too expensive or too difficult for him and yet consumer society will only judge his or her success in material goods. Strain theory indicates that it is inevitable that some people will succumb to the temptation of crime to achieve material wealth. We have used an extreme example above but the same theory might explain just as well why a person in a management position falsifies her expense claims. There are always people who possess more material goods than you and these are recognised as a mainstream measure of success in modern society.

There are several ways to tackle this but investing government money into creating affordable ways to retrain is one and legislating to create minimum standards of pay is another. Both are current government policy.

ACTIVITY

Engage friends, family members or work colleagues in conversation. Is poverty ever a reason (not an excuse) for crime? What is poverty? Is it a base level of income below which people are poor or is poverty relative to the wealth of the affluent? This is the absolute versus relative poverty debate. With relative poverty you could be considered poor if you have some luxury goods but far less than most people. Whereas under the absolute approach it could be argued that you could only be poor if you are starving or homeless for instance. Finally canvass opinion about what can be done about poverty. Is government funding ever capable of making a difference to poverty and/or crime?

Multi-agency partnerships

By the end of this section you will be able to:

- explain why multi-agency partnerships have come increasingly to the fore in crime prevention;

- describe the legislation underpinning some of these themes;

- describe the function of a crime reduction partnership and a MAPPP.

There is not scope here to touch on all of the multi-agency work nor to examine the selected samples in any depth. It is intended here to concentrate on Crime Reduction Partnerships and MAPPPs or multi-agency public protection panels.

The reasons why multi-agency working is so essential to crime prevention and is now mandatory have become clear in the preceding sections. It is less likely as society develops that the police can hope to have sole responsibility for crime prevention. Some would argue that the police never had this monopoly in truth, nor should they want it.

Take SCP for example; this is partly about preventing the settings for crime to occur. Sometimes crime possibilities can be designed out of buildings and therefore some dialogue with architects and town planners is appropriate. Further, if RAT is considered, the presence of motivated offenders in a location may be down to prison parole boards and local mental health facilities. Clearly the police can have little direct influence over the poverty or otherwise of a neighbourhood but by interacting with schools they may develop programmes which steer children away from crime and towards legitimate employment opportunities. Partnerships already exist between major motor manufacturers and young offender institutions toward that end.

Crime-reduction partnerships

There is a general requirement in **s. 17 Crime and Disorder Act (CDA) 1998** that local authorities will take into account the crime consequences of any policy decision within their remit, **s. 17(1)**:

> *Without prejudice to any other obligation imposed on it, it shall be the duty of each authority to which this section applies to exercise its various functions with due regard to the likely effect of the exercise of those functions on, and the need to do all that it reasonably can to prevent, crime and disorder in its area.*

Section 17(2) explains that an authority extends to a local authority, a fire and rescue authority, a police authority, a national park authority and the Broads Authority.

This might be a decision on any reduction on waste collection (which might encourage fly-tipping) to say provision of education opportunities for excluded children (which might cut down on anti-social behaviour by these children). The partnerships mentioned were in existence in some areas on an *ad hoc* basis for many years. They were given a statutory footing and made mandatory by **s. 5 Crime and Disorder Act 1998**. This provision requires local authorities, health authorities, probation committees and the police to work together towards reducing crime and disorder locally. **Section 6 CDA 1998** requires partnerships to perform a 'crime audit' and publish a strategy for reducing these problems.

ACTIVITY

Visit your local council and ask to see their crime audit figures and crime-reduction strategy. Alternatively go to your local council's website and follow the links to crime reduction partnership. An example from a suburb of Nottingham is provided here to demonstrate the format: visit **www.broxtowe.gov.org**, follow the links to Community and Safer Communities or search for 'Crime and Disorder Reduction Strategy'.

A crime audit might highlight a need to tackle hate crime or abandoned vehicles as priorities, for instance. These both need a co-ordinated approach. There is perhaps more that the local authority can do in relation to the vehicles than the police and some perhaps that the education authority can do to educate children about racism, sexism and homophobia before ideas become entrenched in later life.

Multi-agency public protection panels (MAPPPs)

MAPPPs exist to work in conjunction with the Sex Offender's Register. This is a civil measure introduced by the **Sex Offenders Act 1997**. This requires anyone convicted of any of a specified number of sexual offences after the date the Act came into force to notify the police of their address within three days of any change. This means several thousand sex offenders are not registered as they were convicted prior to 1997. The stipulation to register could be for life or a specified number of years at the discretion of the original sentencing judge. Breach of this condition could result in imprisonment.

Again there were *ad hoc* local arrangements in place to monitor the register from 1997 but **ss. 67**and **68** of the **Criminal Justice and Court Services Act 2000** put these on a statutory footing. MAPPPs consist of police, social services, housing, probation and health care provider representatives typically but others could be involved. MAPPPs also have a remit to monitor violent and other sex offenders not on the register imprisoned for more than 12 months and any other offenders considered likely to pose a risk to the community.

It was a concern raised by a MAPPP about the potential recruitment of a teacher with a minor sexual offence record that prompted a media furore in 2006. There was a media driven 'panic' about sex offenders on the Education Department's so called 'List 99' being allowed to work in schools albeit with restrictions.

Methods to consistently monitor unregistered sex offenders remain a problem but various pieces of legislation have come in to strengthen this area such as under the **Sexual Offences Act 2003**.

As we have said, crime prevention is a vast area of study to which we cannot fully do justice here. There are opportunities for further reading and research at the end of the chapter.

Suggested research

Another area of multi-agency working is the Youth Offending Team or YOT. Visit the website of your local county council or unitary authority and follow the links to 'Youth Offending Team'. Discover who the team consists of, what work they do and how they interact with the courts and police.

Further reading

Further detailed discussion of the Chicago School of Criminology can be found by reading:

Burgess, EW (1925) The growth of the city, in Park, RE, Burgess, EW and Mckenzie, RD (eds) *The city*. Chicago: University of Chicago Press.

And on SCP:

Clarke, RV (ed.) (1997) *Situational crime prevention: Successful case studies* (2nd edn). New York: Harrow and Heston.

Clarke, RV and Eck, J (2003) *Become a problem-solving crime analyst: In 55 small steps.* London: Jill Dando Institute of Crime Science, University College London
www.jdi.ucl.ac.uk/publications/manual/crime_manual_content.php

On RAT:

Cohen, L and Felson, M (1979) Social change and crime rate trends: A routine activity approach. *American Sociological Review*, 44 (4): 588–608.

Felson, M (1998) *Crime and everyday life: Insights and implications for society* (2nd edn). Thousand Oaks, CA: Pine Forge Press.

A general read on the various social theories on criminology and crime prevention:

Hale, C, Hayward, K, Wahidin, A and Wincup, E (2005) *Criminology*, Oxford: Oxford University Press. There is a companion website at **http://www.oup.com/uk/booksites/content/0199270368/student**

For a discussion of crime prevention as a discipline:

Hughes, G, Mclaughlin, E and Muncie J (2002) *Crime prevention and community safety: New directions*, London: Sage.

On 'broken windows' theory:

Wilson, JQ and Kelling, G (1982) Broken windows, *Atlantic Monthly*, 29–38.

Useful websites

Home Office Crime Reduction Unit: **www.crimereduction.gov.uk**

Legislation:

www.opsi.gov.uk

Case law and legislation databases:

www.westlaw.com* (an educational case law and statute database)

www.lexis-nexis.com* (an educational case law and statute database)

www.pnld.co.uk* (a police service specific database of case law and statute)

* Likely to be available through the virtual learning environment (VLE) which supports your course/training.

12 Animals

Remember this symbol indicates that the material might be useful for your Student Officer Learning and Assessment Programme (SOLAP) portfolio or any attached reflective practice record you are required to make.

Underpinning knowledge towards Patrol Officer NOS:

1A1, 2A1, 2C2, 2C3, 2G2, 2I1, 2I2, 2J1, 2J2, 4C1, 4G2

and PCSO NOS:

1A1, 2A1, 2C1, 2C2, 2C3, 2C5, 2J1, 2J2, 4C1, 4G2

For further information on these NOS, which are also Policing Level 3 and 4 NVQ unit titles, refer to Appendix 1 to this volume.

Even if your beat is not a rural one you may be called to deal with incidents involving animals on a regular basis. Incidents involving dogs and increasingly exotic animals such as snakes and reptiles are not unheard of in urban areas by any means. You may well have seen reality TV footage of motorway police trying to remove horses, cattle, even swans from the carriageway. It is vitally important that the relevant law is studied to enable these incidents to be dealt with adequately.

We are going to concentrate on the groups of animals and in some cases, specific breeds that are most likely to cause an issue that you as a student patrol officer could be called to deal with. There is not scope here to cover the law on game, nor can we look at the finer points of law in relation to rarer species such as deer and poaching, etc. Ideas for further reading, which would cover these aspects of animal law, are at the end of the chapter.

We will be endeavouring to cover the most important aspects of law relating to:

- domestic dogs;
- wild animals;
- cruelty, neglect, injuries and disease.

Domestic dogs

By the end of this section you will be able to:

- define a 'dangerous dog' under legislation;

- describe the law relating to guard dogs, hunting with dogs and dog fouling;

- apply what you know to some multiple-choice questions.

Within this section it is intended to consider the following:

- **Dangerous Dogs Act 1991**;

- guard dogs;

- hunting with dogs;

- dog fouling.

Dangerous dogs

ACTIVITY

Search the BBC 'On This Day' for 5 August 1991 at **http://news.bbc.co.uk/onthisday** 'Toddler "poorly" after dog attack'. This and linked stories were the type of news coverage which arguably inadirectly led to the Dangerous Dogs Act 1991. The legislation has not been universally well received and is said to be a flawed piece of legislation. Visit the detail of the act itself at **www.opsi.gov.uk/acts/acts1991/Ukpga_19910065_en_1.htm** Can you work out roughly how quickly it was written and became law? What conclusions can you draw from this?

Prior to 1991 there had been legislation on pet animals and particularly dogs. Much of it though created civil rather than criminal liability. With the advent of the **Dangerous Dogs Act 1991** controls are placed on the possession of certain types of dogs. The deliberate use of the word 'type' as opposed to 'breed' allows for certain cross-breeds to be covered by the Act provided they have the characteristics of the type.

The dogs prohibited are the:

- dogo Argentino;

- fila Brazileiro;

- Japanese tosa;

- pit bull terriers.

There are inevitably going to be disputes about the exact breed or type of dog, especially as this may be a key to successful prosecution and destruction of the dog concerned. **Section 5(5)** of the **Dangerous Dogs Act 1991** provides for the resolution of these disputes and actually places the burden of proof on the accused to refute that the dog is a prohibited type once the allegation has been made.

Unless in the process of seizing it or destroying it lawfully, it will be an offence under **s. 1(3) Dangerous Dogs Act 1991** to have one of these dogs in custody or possession. Further, under **s. 1(2)** it will be an offence to:

- abandon;

- advertise, sell or give away;

- allow unmuzzled and unleashed in a public place (in effect a temporary provision while the Act came fully into force);

- breed;

one of the dog types in the list above.

These are strict liability offences in that they do not require *mens rea* (see Chapter 1, 'legal concepts'). There is a specific defence to the charge of advertising however, if the advertiser is wholly unaware of the nature of the dog and he or she did not create the advert themselves. This would prevent third parties, even free-ad newspapers falling foul of this provision.

Section 5(1) allows a constable or authorised officer (normally a council dog warden) to seize the dog if it is in a public place, even if it merely 'appears' to be a prohibited type. If the dog is not a prohibited type but yet appears to be dangerously out of control (see below), seizure is lawful under this section also. Seizure of a dog from other than a public place would require a warrant to enter and search, which a magistrate could issue.

Seizure of a stray dog is also possible under other legislation but is almost always going to be carried out by such as the RSPCA or council dog warden service in practice.

(?) *It is worth taking a moment to reflect on how you might deal with a situation where you encounter a prohibited dog. It may be that, however naively, the owner is unaware of the true nature of the dog. Furthermore one or more of the family, perhaps young children, may be very attached to the creature. Set against this the dog probably presents a danger to the very people who love it. Consider how you might use powers of persuasion, tact and diplomacy when dealing with this whilst ever mindful of serious safety implications – a very difficult balance to strike.*

The harsher effects of the 1991 Act have been mitigated in part by the creation of a list of 'exempted dogs' which the Act does not apply to, mostly specific animals determined not to be a threat to the public. Also the **Dangerous Dogs (Amendment) Act 1997** removes the mandatory requirement for the destruction of dogs which fall under the Act.

Cases under this act are triable summarily only and it is the magistrates courts that will impose sentence.

Control of dogs

In certain circumstances the **Dangerous Dogs Act 1991** also applies to all breeds and types of dogs. **Section 3(1)** creates an 'either way' offence. This would be committed in its basic form if an owner or person for the time being in charge of a dog (if under 16 this will include the 'head of the household') allows it to be 'dangerously out of control' in a public place. This would occur if there were grounds for 'reasonable apprehension' that the dog might attack and injure someone. Under **s. 10(3)** there are 'grounds for reasonable apprehension' that it will injure someone even if it does not actually do so. Indeed if it does injure someone, an aggravated offence is committed. **Section 3(3)** effectively extends both offences to circumstances where the animal is allowed into private premises without the occupiers permission and it behaves in like manner.

Again these are strict liability offences but there is a statutory defence. Under **s. 3(2)** an owner can avoid liability if he or she can state that the dog had been at the material time transferred to the charge of a person who was 'reasonably believed' to be fit and proper to take charge of it. This would mean the owner might not be liable if the incident happened whilst the animal was in the charge of a paid dog-walking or grooming service, for example.

In addition, **s. 27 Road Traffic Act 1988** creates an offence for any person to 'cause or permit' a dog to be on any road designated by the local authority without being held on a lead. Exceptions apply for working sheep dogs, etc.

A landowner, farmer or his or her farmhands, etc., can kill a dog which is 'worrying' livestock on land they are responsible for. There will be exemption from liability for the death under certain circumstances from **s. 9 Animals Act 1971**. In addition, the owner or person for the time being in charge of the dog commits an offence under **s. 1(1) Dogs (Protection of Livestock) Act 1953**. There are however, exempted dogs such as police dogs and statutory defences such as that the livestock were trespassing. A police officer may seize such a dog which is worrying livestock under **s. 2**.

Guard dogs

The **Guard Dogs Act 1971** applies to such as security guards with dogs. Under the Act three things are required for a legal use of a guard dog:

- the dog must be under the direct control of a handler capable of controlling the dog;

- alternatively the dog must be secured so that it cannot roam freely about the premises;

- there must be a warning sign as to the presence of dogs clearly displayed at all entrances to the property.

The **Guard Dogs Act 1971** does not apply to family pets or farm dogs.

Hunting with dogs

This is a controversial area and it is very unlikely that you as a student officer will have to deal unassisted with a hunt, which is likely to contravene **s. 1 Hunting Act 2004**:

a person commits an offence if he hunts a wild mammal with a dog…

There is a limit to how much of this complex area can be explored in a volume of this nature. If an allegation of illegal hunting is made, the best approach is to take full details and seek advice from a supervisor. The offence will *prima facie* be made out if the activity described above takes place. Hasty action would be ill advised however, unless the nature and extent of all the exemptions is researched first to see if any apply.

Dog fouling

The primary legislation for this is the **Dogs (Fouling of Land) Act 1996**. Under that Act a local authority can designate certain land for the Act to apply to. This secondary legislation or so called 'poopa-scoop council bye-laws' will be normally be referred to on signs around these designated areas. It should be remembered that:

- only dog faeces are covered by the Act;

- the person in charge of the dog commits the offence;

- the offence is failing to remove the faeces forthwith.

The offence is one of strict liability and neither failing to notice the dog defecating nor failing to have a suitable means to remove the faeces such as a bag or shovel is any defence.

It should be remembered that these offences can be dealt with by fixed penalty notice which, under the **Police Reform Act 2002** an 'accredited' person such as a neighbourhood warden is most likely to award in the place of a constable.

> **REVISION**
> ✓ Dangerous Dogs Act 1991 applies to:
> - dogo Argentino/fila Brazileiro
> - Japanese tosa/pit bull terriers
> - any dog 'dangerously out of control'.
> ✓ Guard dogs must be under control of a handler or secured.
> ✓ Failing to clear up dog faeces is an offence under Dogs (Fouling of Land) Act 1996.

Knowledge Check 1

1. PC O'Donovan attends an address in The Willows, Lutonchester.

   i) Whilst on the street outside she sees a man apparently watch his dog attack another smaller dog then bound around that dog's owner barking and growling. The man does not intervene. Which is the relevant Act and section?

      (a) s. 1(1) Dogs (Protection of Livestock) Act 1953

      (b) s. 1(3) Dangerous Dogs Act 1991

      (c) s. 3(1) Dangerous Dogs Act 1991

      (d) s. 1 Hunting Act 2004.

   ii) Further along the street she finds a dog which she thinks might be a Japanese tosa. The dog is ill at ease and there are small children in the vicinity, The owner is compliant. O'Donovan may:

      (a) Not act as the dog's type cannot be determined.

      (b) Seize the dog and take it into custody.

      (c) Warn the dog's owner about the danger and report for summons under s. 1(3) Dangerous Dogs Act 1991.

      (d) Arrest the owner.

2. John Choi owns a business in an industrial unit. He allows a rottweiler dog to roam the premises freely at night. It cannot escape from the premises but is very likely to attack an intruder. Which of the following is true?

   (a) John commits no offence.

   (b) John commits an offence under the Guard Dogs Act 1975.

   (c) John commits an offence under the Guard Dogs Act 1975 unless he has a warning sign displayed at the entrances.

   (d) John commits an offence under the Dangerous Dogs (Amendment) Act 1997.

The answers are at the end of the chapter.

Wild animals

By the end of this section you will be able to:

- explain how to define a dangerous wild animal for these purposes;

- describe some of the most important legislative provisions relating to wild animals.

It would be very difficult here to cover all other areas of animal law. In-depth training would normally be available should you specialise later in your career.

The main topic headings in this section are:

- keeping wild animals;

- treatment of wild animals.

Keeping wild animals

Under **s. 1 Dangerous Wild Animals Act 1976** it is necessary to obtain a licence from the local authority before keeping any animal listed in the Act. It is not possible to provide a full list here as it is extremely long. The most up-to-date list is provided by the **Dangerous Wild Animals Act (Modification Order) 1984**. This statutory instrument can be obtained by visiting **www.defra.org.uk** and following the links. Keeping animals on the list without a licence is an offence.

Treatment of wild animals

There is much here which overlaps with the following section on cruelty, etc. The relevant statutory provisions are contained in the following:

- **Protection of Badgers Act 1992;**

- **Wild Mammals (Protection) Act 1996;**

- **Wildlife and Countryside Act 1981.**

Protection of Badgers Act 1992

This act specifically protects the species of badger. It is an offence if a person 'wilfully kills, injures or takes, or attempts to kill, injure or take, a badger'. Selling or offering for sale a live badger is also prohibited. Stop, search and seizure are empowered under **s. 11** (persons and vehicles).

Wild Mammals (Protection) Act 1996

Section 1 of this Act specifically prohibits a considerable list of activities such as kicking and beating but crucially 'with intent to inflict unnecessary suffering'. **Section 4** adds a specific power to stop and search persons and vehicles in relation to this offence including seizure of relevant material.

Wildlife and Countryside Act 1981

This Act prohibits the killing injuring or taking of any wild bird, eggs, wild animals or young either absolutely in the case of rarer species or during the close season of, for instance, game birds. Certain species classed as vermin such as pigeons, rabbits and the like may be killed as long as it is done without unnecessary suffering.

Picking or uprooting wild plants is also prohibited.

Cruelty, neglect, injuries and disease

By the end of this section you will be able to:

* explain police powers in relation to dealing with cruelty and neglect of animals;

* explain police powers in relation to dealing with injured and diseased animals;

* apply that knowledge to some multiple-choice questions.

Obviously there are a myriad ways in which a person might mistreat an animal. The RSPCA prosecute in many cruelty cases but it may be that you come across an offence as a student officer and you must know how to deal with it. The ill treatment dealt with in this volume is limited to:

* cruelty;

* fighting;

* injuries and disease.

Obviously this latter category may occur through no fault of the owner of an animal. In many cases though neglect may cause or exacerbate the illness or injury.

Cruelty

Much of the legislation relevant to this topic is found in the **Protection of Animals Act 1911** as amended. The Act prohibits a vast range of ill treatments which are to be regarded as cruel. In practice the state of the animal will have given rise for concern for you to be considering action. If the matter is an emergency the RSPCA can be summoned and may wish to pursue the matter themselves in any event. If there is time to do so and any doubt as to whether the Act has been breached, the full text of **s. 1(1)(a)** to **(f)** should be consulted either online or in a suitable law text (some useful titles are listed at the end of the chapter).

The Act provides a power of seizure in relation to the animals concerned and any vehicle stopped in connection with a suspected offence. This might occur for example if a vehicle were found in a remote woodland area with equipment on board which might be used for animal baiting of some kind.

Fighting

The deliberate setting of animals against each other to fight is a criminal offence. Various different pieces of legislation could be involved, however. If the offence is one of badger baiting then, depending on how the fight is arranged and how many dogs are involved, either the **Hunting Act 2004** or **Protection of Badgers Act 1992** might be most appropriate. The keeping of places for the fighting of animals is prohibited under the **Metropolitan Police Act 1839** and the **Town Police Clauses Act 1847.**

The fighting of dogs or other animals would almost certainly would be an offence of cruelty under **s. 1 Protection of Animals Act 1911**. In addition, **s. 5B** and **s. 5A** of the Act prohibit promotion of the fight and attendance at it as a spectator respectively.

Cockfighting is dealt with under the **Cockfighting Act 1952**. This could lead to a conviction at magistrates court.

Injuries and disease

Offences in relation to the transportation, etc., of diseased animals have been designed to address the potential or actual threat of such as rabies and foot and mouth. The **Animal Health Act 1981** creates an arrestable offence in relation to the importation of animals with rabies. The **Animal Health Act 2002** extends powers, such as stop and search, to situations involving other diseases such as foot and mouth.

We have not provided much detail in the preceding sections, rather indicated where you might do further research should you need to. This is because, as a student officer, apart from the receipt of intelligence, your involvement with animal baiting or an outbreak of animal disease will be most likely part of a planned police operation during which you should be fully briefed by those with specialist knowledge.

With respect to an injured animal, the provisions of **s. 11 Animals Act 1911** relates to horses, mules, asses, bulls, sheep, goats and pigs only. A constable may summon a vet and ask him to destroy the animal if in the constable's opinion the beast is in such a poor condition that it cannot be removed without cruelty: this is even if the owner cannot be found or refuses consent. It is quite lawful for the constable to perform the act of destruction but of course in practice this should only be done by a vet.

REVISION

The legislation relevant to animals for student officer purposes is:

✓ Animal Health Act 2002 – communicable diseases
✓ Cockfighting Act 1952 - cockfighting
✓ Dangerous Wild Animals Act (Modification Order) 1984 – restrictions on exotic pets
✓ Metropolitan Police Act 1839/Town Police Clauses Act 1847 – keeping of places for baiting
✓ Protection of Animals Act 1911 – cruelty to animals
✓ Protection of Badgers Act 1992 – killing/taking badgers
✓ Wild Mammals(Protection) Act 1996 – cruelty to wild mammals
✓ Wildlife and Countryside Act 1981 – disturbing/taking wild birds, animals and plants.

Knowledge Check 2

1. PC O'Donovan is now based in a rural area.

   i) She receives a report of egg stealing at a local nature reserve. The likely relevant legislation will be:

   (a) Dogs (Protection of Livestock) Act 1953

   (b) Hunting Act 2004

   (c) Wildlife and Countryside Act 1981

   (d) Animal Health Act 2002.

   ii) When called to an abandoned smallholding O'Donovan finds a sheep in a pen. The animal is malnourished, diseased and near death. O'Donovan may:

   (a) After consultation with a vet, kill the animal herself with her baton.

   (b) Seize the sheep and take it into custody.

   (c) Have to find and warn the animal's owner about the condition of the sheep before acting further.

   (d) Take action under the Wildlife and Countryside Act 1981.

2. Joe Kalinski keeps a three-toed sloth in a cage in his garden. In order to check whether he needs a licence for this animal O'Donovan must consult:

   (a) The Guard Dogs Act 1975

   (b) A supervising officer

   (c) Dangerous Wild Animals Act (Modification Order) 1984

   (d) The Dangerous Wild Animals Act 1976.

The answers are at the end of the chapter.

Suggested research

This area of law cannot receive a full treatment in a volume such as this. Given the area that you will be serving in, research the relevant legislation mentioned above in more depth. For instance, if your location suffers from spates of illegal badger baiting, research the **Protection of Badgers Act 1992**. Conversely, if your area is urban but you here that certain local criminals are known to have exotic pets such as large snakes, you may wish to know more about the **Dangerous Wild Animals Act (Modification Order) 1984**. Tailor your research to your likely need.

Further reading

More detailed coverage of the topics found in this chapter can be obtained by reading:

English, J and Card, R (2005) *Police law*. (9th edn). Oxford: Oxford University Press.

Sampson, F (2007) *Blackstone's police manual, Volume 4 – General police duties* (9th edn). Oxford: Oxford University Press.

Useful websites

Department of Environment, Farming and Rural affairs: **www.defra.org.uk**

Legislation:

www.opsi.gov.uk

Case law and legislation databases:

www.westlaw.com* (an educational case law and statute database)

www.lexis-nexis.com* (an educational case law and statute database)

www.pnld.co.uk* (a police service specific database of case law and statute)

* Likely to be available through the virtual learning environment (VLE) which supports your course/training.

Answers

Knowledge Check 1

1. PC O'Donovan attends an address in The Willows, Lutonchester.

    i)   (c) **s. 3(1) Dangerous Dogs Act 1991**

    ii) (b) Seize the dog and take it into custody.

    NB It is only necessary that the animal appears to be a Tosa.

2. (b) John commits an offence under the **Guard Dogs Act 1975.**

    NB The animal is not secured and there is no handler present.

Knowledge Check 2

1. i) (c) **Wildlife and Countryside Act 1981**

    ii) (a) After consultation with a vet, kill the animal herself with her baton.

    NB Technically correct but the vet would do it for her.

2. (c) **Dangerous Wild Animals Act (Modification Order) 1984**

    NB As this contains a more up-to-date list than the Act itself.

13 Sentencing issues

Remember this symbol indicates that the material might be useful for your Student Officer Learning and Assessment Programme (SOLAP) portfolio or any attached reflective practice record you are required to make.

Underpinning knowledge towards Patrol Officer NOS:

1B9, 4C1

and PCSO NOS:

1B11, 4C1

For further information on these NOS, which are also Policing Level 3 and 4 NVQ unit titles, refer to Appendix 1 to this volume.

Introduction to sentencing

By the end of this section you will be able to:

- describe the place of sentencing in a police officer's training;
- describe different types of sentence from prison to community sentences;
- consider the depth of study of sentencing possible at this level.

The subject matter of this chapter should always form part of a student officer's training. This knowledge is required to allow an officer to know the full consequences of his or her actions, part of the new ethos of police training. In addition it will enable the police officer of tomorrow to give a fuller measure of support to victims and witnesses. No formal assessment activities will be presented to check learning in this chapter as the emphasis will be on reflection.

It will be rare to find someone who does not have an opinion about sentencing of offenders. Many argue for tougher sentencing, including politicians and the news media. Other, quieter voices are concerned that modern criminal justice policy of a harsher nature actually makes crime more likely. As you read through this chapter it would be useful to reflect on your own views; are they yours or those of your family and friends or of the popular press?

This chapter does not attempt to spell out the various statutory provisions and decided cases that exist on sentencing; this is a vast legal field and one that is rapidly changing. The purpose here is rather to look at the theories, issues and practical difficulties that surround the sentencing of offenders.

Howwver, it is worth pointing out that all the sentences are at the judge's discretion save one: the sentence for murder is mandatory life. The 'tariff' or time of that sentence spent in a prison as opposed to out on licence remains at the judge's discretion, however. Contrary to popular perception, life does in fact mean life. A 'lifer' is always subject to recall to prison at the discretion of the prison authorities even when out on licence at the end of the sentence; no further offences need be committed.

There are a small number of prisoners, about a dozen, who will remain behind bars for the whole of their lives: they are on a 'whole life tariff'. Members of this exclusive group included Myra Hindley who was one of the 'Moors murderers'; Harold Shipman, a doctor and Britain's worst serial killer and still includes Rosemary West.

We encountered the debate about whether the life sentence was actually just in all cases, including mercy killings and killings by abused spouses under the Homicide section of Chapter 6, 'Violence and Intimidation'. You might like to revisit that topic at this time.

Moving away from murder for a moment, most people associate sentencing generally with prison. There are of course a great many other types of punishment and a variety of community sentences are discussed below:

- Community Punishment Order: previously known as community service, 40–240 hours of unpaid community work.

- Community Rehabilitation Order: the new name for probation, where an offender is supervised from six months to three years by a probation officer employed by the National Offender Management Service. The Punishment Order and Rehabilitation Order can be combined in a Combination Order.

- Compensation Order should not to be confused with claiming compensation through the civil courts or the Criminal Injuries Compensation Scheme which are entirely separate. A Compensation Order is made in a criminal court, usually involving a nominal sum, to force the offender to make at least token financial recompense to the victim.

- Curfew Order: an offender wears a tag and must be at home at certain times. The monitoring of this is carried out by private companies.

- Drug Treatment and Testing Order: the offender has to agree to regular reviews at court, treatment for drug addiction and testing for drug abuse. This is not currently available for alcohol dependency.

- Discharge: this is where there has been a finding of guilt and therefore a recordable criminal conviction but no sentence is given, usually when the offender is ordinarily of exemplary character. A Conditional Discharge would require good behaviour for a period of time, an Absolute Discharge would not.

- Fines: magistrates may hand out a maximum of £5,000 and Crown Courts have no limit on the fine they can impose. In practice though, high figures are rarely reached.

In the same spirit as the conditional discharge, prison sentences can be handed out but suspended for up to two years provided no further offences are committed.

Who sentences and when?

By the end of this section you will be able to:

- explain who has the power to sentence an offender;

- describe the point in proceedings when sentencing occurs.

This depends on the court that the case is heard in. In the magistrates' court the magistrates decide on the issue of guilt or innocence and, if the verdict is one of guilt, the sentence. In fact magistrates spend a great deal of their time deciding on sentence as a large proportion of the cases they hear are guilty pleas. Bearing in mind they are not legally trained they rely heavily on their legal adviser (formerly known as a court clerk) to ensure they apply the appropriate sentence.

In a Crown Court the judge has the job of deciding which law to apply once the jury has decided on what is factually true or not. Therefore the jury will decide on guilt or innocence but will play no part in the sentencing process. The judge will apply a sentence according to the limits set by Parliament in statute as interpreted in relevant case law. In contrast to the impression that many tabloid newspapers give, the judge is not at liberty to 'make it up as he or she goes along'.

Sentencing occurs once a trial is over and the jury have a pronounced a guilty verdict. Sentencing will also occur, perhaps at a separate hearing for the purpose, if the defendant pleads guilty. There will be no need for a trial in this eventuality. On some occasions the judge will adjourn the case for reports (such as psychiatric) to be prepared; this is so that the sentencing is the most appropriate. Clearly it would be inappropriate to give someone a community sentence knowing that they are a danger to themselves and others from, say, a psychiatric condition.

ACTIVITY

'Populist punitivism' is a term applied to sentencing policy which is overly harsh in the face of scientific evidence that severe sentencing can actually make crime more likely. The measures are nevertheless 'popular' and are often espoused by the tabloid press. Examples of this would include the campaign by the *News of the World* to promote the idea of 'Sarah's law' where the names and addresses of paedophiles are publicly known.

This is not strictly speaking a sentencing issue, it is more on the closely related issue of the monitoring of offenders. It is a good example of the types of issues raised in sentencing discussions nonetheless. Have a look at **www.forsarah.com** and consider the arguments proposed. Go to the site for childrens' charity Barnardos at **www.barnardos.org.uk** and follow the links to find out why they are opposed to the idea of a 'Sarah's law'. Who do you think has the stronger argument?

(?) *Politicians are sometimes accused of following the tabloid press when formulating sentencing policy. It is argued that the press provides a guide as to the public mood on these matters. Reflect on whether you think the press tells its readers what to think or whether the newspapers print what readers already agree with in order to ensure they keep their readership and sales.*

Sentencing theories

By the end of this section you will be able to:

- explain the main theories behind sentencing;
- explain which theories centre on the welfare of the offender;
- contrast theories which centre on the issue of justice with the above.

Sentencing is a field of study all of its own, called penology. Sentences are not designed on a whim in the creation of a statute or handed down by a judge arbitrarily. There are solid theories behind sentencing. Different sentences owe more or less to each of these theories dependent on what they are intended to do. For example, consider the case of a normally law-abiding person who kills another during a bout of dangerous driving, perhaps whilst sending a text message to a girlfriend and losing concentration momentarily. Such a person is unlikely to commit such a crime again so does not need to be deterred from driving in such a manner again as a priority. The shock of the incident and attendant legal proceedings and publicity is probably enough for that. The rest of the driving public, however, needs to be deterred from dangerous driving and the victim's relatives will perhaps want revenge. Such an offender could receive a prison sentence of the order of say, two to five years. The theories behind this sentence would be ones of general rather than individual deterrence and retribution.

By contrast, a sociopath serial killer will probably need to be imprisoned indefinitely if only to protect the public. The theory here would be one of incapacitation. We will consider each of the leading theories now in turn.

Deterrence

Deterrence is sometimes referred to under a general heading of 'reductivism' in that it is aimed at reducing crime by preventing it from happening. There are two forms:

- general deterrence;
- individual deterrence.

A sentence underpinned by a theory of general deterrence would be one which was quite harsh in relation to the crime but was designed to 'set an example' and dissuade others from committing the same crime. The sentencer would have less concern about the welfare of the offender and more about justice being seen to be done. Many people when asked about sentencing will say that the courts are too soft and that they ought to set an example more often with lengthy prison sentences. Unfortunately the statistics do not support this, with very high reoffending rates both here and in the USA for those released from prison.

There is also a fundamental issue to take into consideration: the vast majority of people who commit crime do so in the belief that they will not get caught. There has to be a question mark over the value of deterrent sentencing therefore with this borne in mind.

ACTIVITY

Have a look at **www.hmprisonservice.gov.uk** and follow the links to reoffending rates. At time of writing they are around 55 per cent but see how they stand at the time you are researching. Reoffending rates in the USA, where imprisonment is used more than here, can be as high as 75 per cent. Consider possible reasons why it seems quite likely that a prisoner will reoffend. Engage family, friends or colleagues in a conversation about this issue and weigh up their views.

Consider the last time you broke the law if (you have allowed yourself to break the speed limit, jump a red traffic light or drop litter then you have committed a crime!) You know that there is a potential penalty for these offences. Reflect on whether you would have done the same acts in the presence of a traffic camera, police officer or neighbourhood warden, etc. If you would not, clearly you acted on the assumption that your crime, be it ever so minor, would remain undetected. Is there a limit therefore on the deterrent value of a fixed penalty notice (a form of sentencing)?

Consider the issue of the death penalty in the USA. This is primarily carried out for deterrent reasons, it is argued. There is no conclusive evidence however, that offending rates are any lower in states that have the death penalty compared with those that do not. It would be difficult to sustain an argument to 'bring back hanging' on this basis.

Deterrent sentencing can be controversial even where the death penalty is not an issue. There was some disquiet, believe it or not, amongst the public and press about the length of sentences handed out to the 'great train robbers' in the 1960s. Public attitudes have hardened however, especially since incidents such as the Jamie Bulger murder case in 1993. Still some do question the justice of severe sentences handed out to 'send a message' to potential offenders. One such was the five-year term given to Garry Hart for the dangerous driving which lead to the Selby train crash in 1995. He fell asleep at the wheel and his vehicle careered down a railway embankment causing two train crashes, multiple deaths and millions of pounds' worth of damage. It is argued that a huge amount of ill-luck coincided with his failure to take proper care when driving. A harsh sentence like this might be justified on the basis of retribution (discussed later) of course.

Individual deterrence on the other hand, is concerned with attempting to dissuade the offender from reoffending. The statistics on reoffending mentioned already tend to indicate that sentences may not have the desired effect. May be individuals assume that they have a fair chance of not being caught. It may also be that life after prison may contain few possibilities of 'survival' using legitimate means. This leaves ex-offenders with few options but to resume a criminal lifestyle. Even with non-custodial sentences this can be demonstrated. If a magistrate fines a street prostitute, there are an extremely limited number of ways that the money can be raised by such a person to pay the fine. It is also interesting to note that reoffending rates amongst convicted soldiers after military prison are very low. The key difference is that, in the main, they go straight back into their army job on release.

Neither type of deterrence factor would have much bearing on impulse crimes, such as matrimonial violence or crimes committed whilst intoxicated or mentally ill.

Retribution

This theory focuses on the sentence as being a form of punishment as payment to society by the offender. It is not concerned with the welfare of the offender. It is one of the harsher theories and as society has become less forgiving over a period of time may be partly responsible for the rise in the prison population over the last few years. The following figures are taken from the Prison Population and Accommodation Briefing for 20 April 2007 published by the Home Office:

Male	75,728
Female	4,302
No. of prisoners held in police cells under Operation Safeguard	138
TOTAL	**80,168**

Because of prison overcrowding a number of prisoners are being held in police cells at this time. This strategy is called 'Operation Safeguard'.

The thinking is not at all centred on reducing crime or reforming the offender, but is concerned with making the punishment fit the crime. This is a popular approach to sentencing at the moment both with the general public and some sections of the media. Proponents of it link crimes to degrees of 'moral blameworthiness'. The roots of this theory are to an extent religious; the Christian Old Testament refers to the concept of 'an eye for an eye' and some other faiths justify retributive, vengeful punishments in the same way. Looking at punishment from a moral standpoint is of course very much suited to the way that the press covers stories. Tabloid headlines like 'Face of a monster' and 'Evil rapist' are not uncommon. This may be something of a simplistic view however: a homicide may be characterised as a mercy killing for example, where a spouse kills their terminally ill partner at their request. This would mean a murder charge and a life sentence if proved – there is no euthanasia provision in English law. It is not a straightforward matter to categorise this act as evil, however.

Furthermore, there is a great deal of crime which has drug or alcohol dependency or serious mental illness as its root cause. A great many prisoners are drug dependent or mentally ill. It is more difficult to look at offences as the product of an inherently evil mind in these cases.

Rehabilitation

This theory has the reform of the offender as its goal. It is concerned with the welfare of the offender in this context. A Community Rehabilitation Order for instance requires the offender to meet with his or her probation officer at regular intervals and look for work, usually with the assistance of the probation officer. Drug Treatment and Testing Orders basically require the offender to give up drug abuse.

Even prison can have rehabilitative aspects to it. Anger management courses and sex offender programmes, prison education and training schemes all aim to improve the offender and send them on their way less likely to offend again. This way of thinking was popular particularly during the 1970s. It has since fallen a little out of favour as disillusionment and the notion that 'nothing works' in the treatment of offenders came to the fore. Consequently with limited financial resources available it is no great surprise that prison education programmes and the like are one of the first to be cut back. It costs in excess of £30,000 per year per prisoner to imprison someone. This figure of money is a great deal to spend to only achieve a reoffending rate of a little under 60 per cent. Without well-funded rehabilitation programmes in prisons it could be argued that it is hard to see how ex-offenders can change the pattern of their lives on release.

(?) *A great many people seem to see rehabilitation as a 'soft option'. Take a moment to reflect on whether the harshness or otherwise of prison life is really the main issue. What do residents in the community you police really want? Is it a reduction in levels of crime or to feel that people in prison are suffering appropriately? There are often calls to build more prisons without really looking at what goes on inside them and whether it is working. If a hospital only cured 40 per cent of its patients, reflect on whether it would be prudent to build another one that functioned in exactly the same way.*

Reparation and restorative justice

In Western society we have long perceived a benefit of making the offender repair the damage they have done to society. The 'chain gang' has been used in the United States for many years working on roads and agricultural land, for example. In the UK the nearest equivalent is the Community Punishment Order, formerly known as community service, where the offender is made to do beneficial work to the community such as clearing hedgerows and picking litter. This type of sentencing has had mixed reviews. Some feel it is not a harsh enough punishment and others that it is a good idea in principle but is not sufficiently well funded to be effective. The lack of funding usually leads to poor supervision and hence to perceived underemployment of those on the scheme.

Compensation Orders also allow society to feel that some compensation has been paid by the offender towards the victim. The true level of damage is rarely addressed however, there being little point in awarding compensation the offender cannot pay and the significance is largely symbolic.

The Criminal Injuries Compensation Scheme is entirely separate from the courts and is administered by the government. In essence a figure of compensation is paid to the victim if certain criteria are met. Chief amongst these is that someone has to be successfully prosecuted for the offence. Larger levels of compensation can, however, be obtained by the victim taking action in a civil court directly against the offender; the process here is outside the scope of this volume. Litigation of this nature is seldom advisable however, unless the offender is wealthy or an insurance policy such as his or her employer's liability cover would pay out. A solicitor's advice should always be sought.

Restorative justice attempts to make 'repairs' in a more subtle way. It can be traced back to ancient Moari tribal custom. The essence is that both offender and victim can potentially have an input into sentencing. It is a radical departure in that it looks both at the needs of the offender and those of the victim, it is both a 'welfare' and a 'justice' approach to sentencing. In modern UK criminal justice this is most evident in the youth courts. Here an order referring the young offender can be made to a Youth Justice Panel. There professionals hold a conference to determine the best way for the offender to be dealt with. The young offender can have an input and so can the victim. In these circumstances there can be an opportunity for the victim to obtain some 'closure' from meeting the offender. Conversely, the offender can be forced to confront the consequences of their actions by hearing first hand about the effect on the victim of the offending behaviour. Despite initial scepticism this approach was quite successful in pilot schemes, particularly in the Thames Valley Police area. Restorative justice schemes now operate across the country.

(?) *Involving victim and offender in the process like this may be surprising. It may seem impossible that an offender would not know the effect on the victim when they steal. Reflect for a moment on this. If you were a young person brought up in care and then benefits-dependent because you were unable to find a job, you may never have owned anything significant, in terms of material goods, at all in your life. It would be necessary for a process like this for you to understand what the loss of hard-earned material goods feels like. This is of course an extreme example but one which demonstrates that life experience can differ vastly between socioeconomic groups.*

Incapacitation

This theory pays no heed to the welfare of the offender at all but simply seeks to put the person convicted in a situation where they cannot commit this crime again. The most obvious example of this is the death penalty where that exists. In the UK a lengthy prison sentence might have this as an aim. This of course does not prevent a violent offender from attacking prisoners and prison warders nor does it stop a drug smuggler from peddling the same wares inside prison, for example. It merely makes it impossible for these crimes to be committed in the wider community by these people.

Incapacitation underlies some community sentences as well. In fact a fine is partly designed to prevent the offender from having the spare cash and time to commit crime if all his or her efforts are directed at working to pay the fine. Curfew orders are also designed similarly to have a limiting effect on the opportunity to commit crime.

Some remaining issues, FPNs and appeals against sentence

By the end of this section you will be able to:

- explain the rationale for fixed penalty notices (FPNs);
- describe in brief the notion of appeal against sentence.

Fixed penalty notices – the move to summary justice

Now more than ever before there is the possibility of being punished for an offence without ever going to a court. The rise of those offences which can be dealt with by a fixed penalty notice, from dog-fouling to minor theft, from littering to a public order offence, is considerable. Leaving civil liberties and natural justice arguments aside it is important to remember that a fixed penalty notice commences a legal process. A person served with such a notice can contest it. In that respect it is a court summons, they may choose to defend the matter in court and could be found not guilty. The payment of the penalty is, however, an admission of guilt and circumvents the need for a court hearing. The fact remains that the award of the penalty is in effect a sentence of a fine.

Appeals against sentence

It will be no surprise that it is possible, in limited circumstances, to appeal against conviction. Unfortunately the mechanism for this is outside the scope of this volume. It is also possible for both defence and, in a more limited set of circumstances, for the prosecution to appeal against sentence. The defence may use stated cases to try to establish that the sentence was unduly harsh. Conversely, in a growing number of cases the Attorney General is submitting a case that a particular sentence is unduly lenient.

That concludes our discussion of the issue of sentencing. We have looked into this area in as much detail as we can in a volume of this nature. As always, further reading and research ideas are available at the end of the chapter.

Suggested research

Research the following statutes in a criminology, penology or even a general English Legal System textbook:

- Children and Young Persons Act 1933 and 1969

- Criminal Justice Act 1991

- Crime (Sentences) Act 1997

- Crime and Disorder Act 1998.

Not all are entirely in force today but essentially you should look at whether the thrust of each these was 'welfarist', 'punitive' (or 'justice') orientated.

Further reading

For general discussions of sentencing in the broad context of criminological thought you could read:

Downes, D and Rock, P (2003) *Understanding deviance* (4th edn). Oxford: Oxford University Press.

Hale, C, Hayward, K, Wahidin, A and Wincup, E (2005) *Criminology*, Oxford: Oxford University Press. There is a companion website at **www.oup.com/uk/booksites/content/0199270368/student**

Jones, S (2005) *Criminology* (3rd edn). Oxford: Oxford University Press.

Maguire, M, Morgan, R and Reiner, R (2002) *The Oxford handbook of criminology*, (3rd edn). Oxford: Oxford University Press.

Williams, KS (2004) *A textbook on criminology* (5th edn). Oxford: Oxford University Press.

To look further into the thinking behind punishment through the centuries in a more philosophical way:

Foucault, M (1975) *Discipline and punish: The birth of the prison*. London: Penguin.

To consider further the emergence of summary justice and the place of the fixed penalty notice within that:

Hillyard P and Gordon D (1999) *Arresting statistics: The drift to informal justice in England and Wales*. 26 JLS 502.

Home Office (2000) *Reducing public disorder: The role of fixed penalty notices*. London: Home Office.

Useful websites

www.barnardos.org.uk (a children's charity with policies on the sentencing of juveniles and paedophiles)

www.hmprisonservice.gov.uk (information on the state and private-sector custody sector)

www.howardleague.org (a charity and lobby group dedicated to prison reform)

www.legislation.hmso.gov.uk (provides full text of statutes passed by Parliament as well as delegated legislation)

www.westlaw.com* (a legal database)

www.lexis-nexis.com* (a legal database)

www.pnld.co.uk* (a police service specific database of case law and statute)

* Likely to be available through the virtual learning environment (VLE) which supports your course/training.

14 Introduction to evidence

My thanks to Professor Michael Hirst for his help in compiling this chapter.

(?) *Remember this symbol indicates that the material might be useful for your Student Officer Learning and Assessment Programme (SOLAP) portfolio or any attached reflective practice record you are required to make.*

Underpinning knowledge towards Patrol Officer NOS:

2A1, 2C2, 2C3, 2G2, 2G4, 2H1, 2H2, 2I1, 2I2, 2J1, 2J2, 4C1

and PCSO NOS:

2A1, 2C2, 2C3, 2J1, 2J2, 4C1

For further information on these NOS, which are also Policing Level 3 and 4 NVQ unit titles, refer to Appendix 1 to this volume.

The trial process

By the end of this section you will be able to:

- describe the main courts of first instance in the UK;
- analyse the processes that happen within the trial;
- identify differences with trials in foreign jurisdictions.

In the UK there are 'first instance' courts and appeal courts. First instance simply means the court that the initial trial will be held in. The appeal courts would, as the term suggests, hear any appeals. Thus most trials take place in the magistrates' courts as a court of first instance; in fact about 97 per cent of all cases are heard here. The remainder of cases are heard in the Crown Court after an initial brief appearance at the magistrates' courts as an administrative step. As offences are created by statute it is determined whether they are to be tried at Crown Court, magistrates' or 'either way'. For instance, rape is triable at Crown Court only and for indecent exposure, summary-only trial is possible. A trial before magistrates is called a 'summary trial' and one before the Crown Court is called a trial 'on indictment' (indictment charge sheet). This will involve a judge and if the plea is not guilty, a jury.

ACTIVITY

You may have been surprised to learn that so many cases come before magistrates. This is perhaps all the more surprising when you consider how magistrates are selected and trained. Have a look for magistrate recruitment adverts in the local and national press, go on the web or even pay a visit to your local magistrates' court. Find out how magistrates are selected and what prior legal knowledge they are required to have. The answer may not be what you expect. Find out what training and time commitment magistrates are expected to undertake in addition.

The appeal courts are basically the Court of Appeal and House of Lords. The House of Lords which is there to make law as one of the Houses of Parliament, has a small number of Lords, called the Law Lords, to hear appeals. Their decisions are generally binding and create new law for other judges to follow in similar cases. In some cases a Crown Court and also the High Court can hear appeals over minor issues (for this purpose the High Court is known as the Queen's Bench Division). The relationship is shown below in simplified diagrammatic form.

Court Hierarchy in England and Wales (simplified)

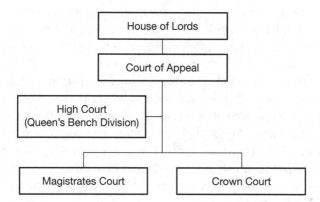

Trials

Assuming that the defendant has pleaded not guilty there will be a hearing to decide guilt or innocence. If the defendant pleads guilty there need only be a hearing to decide sentence. This is irrespective of which court of first instance the matter is heard in.

Trials in England and Wales follow what is known as the 'adversarial' model. On the continent they use a method known as 'inquisitorial'. The adversarial method of dispute resolution has the judge performing the role of a neutral umpire ruling on whether a particular piece of evidence or line of questioning is fair or not. This is not dissimilar to a Wimbledon tennis umpire ruling that a ball is 'out' or a foot fault has occurred. The inquisitorial method however, places the judge as questioner and investigator of the matter before him or her. In fact in France there is a whole branch of the judiciary who lead investigations into serious crimes out in the field, something unheard of in the UK.

The adversarial method originates from knights in armour when in dispute with each other would battle it out for real in front of the monarch. The swords have been replaced by the spoken word and the armour by wigs and gowns but the principle remains essentially the same. The winner is the one who persuades the magistrates or jury of the truth of their case.

REVISION

✓ The criminal courts of first instance are the magistrates and Crown Courts.

✓ The Court of Appeal, House of Lords and occasionally the High Court (Queen's Bench Division) hear appeals.

✓ The UK courts use the 'adversarial' model in trials.

Evidence

By the end of this section you will be able to:

- describe what evidence is;

- evaluate who has the 'burden of proof';

- analyse what is meant by 'standard of proof'.

Evidence is information which helps to prove or disprove an allegation. This may be an eye-witness account, an alibi, a piece of evidence such as a fibre or single human hair. Scientific evidence such as this is often called 'forensic' evidence. As well as the law in terms of what is and is not forbidden, there are further laws on what evidence may be given in court and which may not. You have already encountered the issue of the caution in Chapter 3, 'Police powers'. If it is not given, any confession or other oral evidence given by the accused may not be presented in court as evidence. The judge would not be able to allow it. This is an example of evidence law but there are many others. What can be done if a witness is extremely young or terrified to give evidence for fear of reprisals, for instance? Can a witness ever give evidence derived from other than what his or her own five senses detected? In other words, is second-hand evidence, such as hearsay, to be allowed in some circumstances?

(?) *Many police officers express frustration when evidence against an accused is ruled inadmissible and a person they believe to be guilty walks free. It is worth reflecting on the fact that the state has enormous power, resources, money and time to put into the preparation and conduct of its case. The accused is almost always an individual, sometimes an imprisoned individual with limited financial state aid to conduct his case and a small team of lawyers. Considering all this, it cannot be right to allow the state to use unfair tactics just to win its case, especially if a dubious evidence-gathering practice is tolerated in one case, it must be tolerated in later cases because a legal precedent will have been set.*

It is also necessary to consider the issue of proof: how much proof is required and who has to provide the proof?

The burden of proof

A jury is often asked if they are sure of a person's guilt. This is not the same thing as being 100 per cent certain. There has to be a bar or threshold therefore that the prosecution can reach, which will be sufficient in law to allow a verdict but is less than certainty. This is because no jury can know what happened without being there themselves, but they still must perform their function.

The fact that an accused is presumed innocent until proven guilty is a fundamental aspect of the English legal system. It was reaffirmed in a leading case **Woolmington v DPP (1935)** and has become known as the 'Woolmington principle'. There is a saying that, 'it is better that a hundred guilty people go free than that one innocent person is found guilty'. You would certainly be glad the law takes that approach if you were ever falsely accused of, say, assault in the process of arresting someone. The 'presumption of innocence' as it is known is not common to all legal systems. More than one jurisdiction abroad takes the view that if the state levels an accusation at you, it is for you to disprove it.

ACTIVITY

Article 6(2) of the European Convention of Human rights (ECHR) provides that

Everyone charged with a criminal offence shall be presumed innocent until proved guilty according to law.

Look up **Bates v UK** (EHR Commission) and **R v Lambert** [2001] 3 All ER 577 in a law library or an electronic source such as Westlaw (see end of chapter). What measures have the judges applied to bring UK law into line with the above provision? How is it, do you think, that, despite this principle, it is still perfectly lawful for the prosecution to force you to incriminate yourself in a speeding or traffic-light violation case where the evidence is entirely photographic?

Generally the prosecution has to prove guilt. There are exceptions to this rule, such as if the statute specifically says something like 'it will be a defence for the accused to prove X, Y or Z'. Statutory exceptions are:

- **Dangerous Dogs Act 1991, s. 5**;

- **Homicide Act 1957, s. 2(2)** – diminished responsibility;

- **Prevention of Corruption Act 1916**, s. 2;

- **Prevention of Crime Act 1953** – carrying offensive weapons (excuses for).

The situation can arise that the defence has an implied burden of proof. Most commonly this is where the defendant is relying on an exemption, such as a medical certificate to exempt them from wearing a seat belt. The defendant must of course present that document. This principle is found in **s. 101 Magistrates' Courts Act 1980**, in respect of summary trials and in **R v Hunt (1987)** in relation to Crown Court matters.

Where the burden of proof falls on the prosecution, if it does not satisfy that burden the jury must find the defendant not guilty or 'acquit' him or her. We therefore say that the legal burden of proof falls on the prosecution in most situations. In fact if the prosecution fail to come up with enough evidence to support their case they do not even meet what is separately called their evidential burden and the judge must direct the jury that the defendant has 'no case to answer'. In the first Damilola Taylor trial this is exactly what happened when a key prosecution witness, a teenage girl (referred to as 'Bromley' to maintain her anonymity) was held to have been tainted by police inducements to testify. Without this evidence there was little evidence against the accused at all and the judge ruled there was no case to answer. In **R v Galbraith (1981)** in fact two situations were laid down in which a jury 'could not properly return a guilty verdict':

- when there has been no evidence to prove an essential element in the alleged offence;

- when the evidence adduced by the prosecution has been so discredited by cross-examination or is so manifestly unreliable that no reasonable tribunal could safely convict on it.

If either is held to be true the trial must be stopped.

The standard of proof

You will have heard of the phrase 'beyond reasonable doubt' even in crime dramas, but what does this phrase actually mean? Judges tend to use the phrase 'sure' now when they are directing a jury as to what level of certainty they should have before convicting. This implies something slightly less than certainty but a good deal more than 'probably'. This applies when the jury or magistrates are assessing the prosecution case. If it is for the defence to prove something, such as that the accused was suffering from diminished responsibility at the time of a killing, the jury need only be satisfied that this is more likely to be true than not. We call this being proved 'on the balance of probabilities' and is in fact the standard of proof required in all civil trials. You will therefore sometimes hear it referred to as the 'civil standard' of proof. This standard is much easier to reach but there is good reason: remember that the defence has minuscule resources compared to the vast amounts of money and time the state can call upon. It is really a question of trying to level the playing field between the parties.

ACTIVITY

Judges have to keep up to date with their training as do other professions. A body called the Judicial Studies Board carries out this function. Visit **www.jsboard.co.uk** to find out more. In particular have a look at what guidance is given to judges on the issue of 'reasonable doubt'.

In fact judges do not get into long discussions about what 'sure' or 'reasonable doubt' actually mean with jurors as a rule, even if they ask. This would probably not help them. In **R v Stephens (2002)** an appeal partly on the basis that the judge allegedly misdirected the jury when entering into such a discussion was turned down. The judgment however, criticised the judge for trying to draw a distinction between the words 'certain' and 'sure'.

Probably the best piece of guidance for case law is from **Miller v Minister of Pensions (1947)** where it was said that 'proof beyond a reasonable doubt does not mean proof beyond the shadow of a doubt'. The judge went on to say that case is proved if possibilities other than guilt 'can be dismissed with the sentence "of course it is possible but not in the least probable"'.

REVISION

✓ Evidence is information, which helps to prove or disprove an allegation.

✓ The burden of proof almost always falls on the prosecution, they have to prove guilt. Occasionally there may be issues only the defence can prove.

✓ The criminal standard of proof which must be reached by the prosecution is 'beyond reasonable doubt' or 'sure' in other words.

Is all evidence admissible in court?

By the end of this section you will be able to:

- explain the meaning of the term 'admissible';

- evaluate which types of evidence are not normally admissible;

- analyse exceptions to these rules.

Evidence is inadmissible if the court may not hear it. There are rules whereby some evidence would never be allowed in open court, such as if it were proved that a confession was beaten from a suspect while in police custody. There are still further rules that require a judge to exercise his or her discretion in deciding whether the jury may hear a particular piece of evidence. In summary, evidence will not be admissible if it is:

- irrelevant;

- hearsay;

- opinion;

- evidence of previous bad character;

- illegally or unfairly obtained evidence.

There are exceptions to some of these principles, which we can now examine.

Hearsay

This is essentially anything other than what the witness personally perceived through their own five senses. It may be nothing to do with anything heard or said at all therefore, but something derived from a third-party source. Evidence from the witnesses' own senses is known as 'original evidence' or 'direct oral evidence'. At its strictest interpretation that would mean that if the witness did not see, hear, touch, taste or smell it, they may not speak about it or submit it in written form to the court. This would make certain situations unworkable if applied without any latitude, though. Confessions are an example of this.

Unless wrung from a defendant by cross-examination in open court (which is rare) confessions will always have been to a third party such as police officer, family member, friend or cell-mate. Naturally therefore the evidence would have to be given by the recipient of that information. What was said however, will still be a second-hand account of what happened but will nevertheless not be treated as hearsay.

There are other exceptions to the hearsay rule, largely due to practical issues, where someone else is allowed to give the evidence instead:

- If there is a deceased witness or at least too ill to testify.

- Expert evidence, under **Criminal Justice Act 2003 s. 118 and s.127** in some cases experts may present evidence of information received by them in the course of preparing the evidence.

- 'In the interests of justice for it to be admissible'. Under **Criminal Justice Act 2003 s. 114(1)(d)** the courts now have a general discretion to allow hearsay evidence (other than confessions obtained by oppression – see later).

- Previous inconsistent statements, under **Criminal Justice Act 2003 s. 120** if a defendant contradicts what he or she said in a previous statement, the court may ignore what was said to them. They may then take the previous statement (which would then possibly have to be read to them by a third party – hence its inclusion here) to be the more reliable.

- Records of business transactions, such as cash paid in or out of a bank account. This is third-party evidence but may well be allowed.

- Spontaneous exclamations (e.g. 'stop thief!!') or promptly reported complaints of offences (e.g. 'I've been raped, it was my ex-boyfriend') are also allowed to be repeated in court by a third party.

- Suicide notes can be read out in court.

- Threats – some situations in which witnesses are now too scared to present the witness evidence they originally gave to police can be overcome by a third party reading out the original complaint or statement.

Opinion

Generally speaking, opinion is not allowed to be given as evidence. The witnesses provide facts, the court or jury draws inferences and conclusions from that. For example, a man walks into a police station front counter area holding a blood-stained knife and says 'I've killed the bitch!'. The front counter clerk must give evidence of that alone and not add anything like 'and therefore in my opinion he must have killed the deceased' no matter how obvious that may be. Experts are of course by their very nature called upon to give their expert opinion so they are a notable exception to what has just been said. In point of fact, police officers almost never give expert evidence; their role is that of a professional factual witness. The long-held exception to this is drunkenness. A police officer may say that in his or her opinion the defendant was drunk. Apparently police officers are experts in the field of drunkenness!

Expert evidence

This type of evidence has courted a good deal of public scrutiny since the controversial convictions of several mothers for killing their babies. Expert evidence pointing away from these being cot deaths has since been thoroughly discredited, see **R v Cannings (2004)** in particular.

Expert evidence may not always be admitted. If the judge rules it is a matter that a jury can make a decision on without expert help, then they should do so. For instance in **R v Turner (1975)** the accused was not mentally ill but psychological evidence was to be adduced to show he was not the sort of person to murder. The judge disallowed the evidence. It is arguable that to allow such evidence could set a difficult precedent, one which could end in a psychologist giving evidence as to whether a person has the mindset which is capable of rape and so on. On a related note 'lie detector' machine evidence is never admissible as the law currently stands.

Conversely there are situations were expert evidence is mandatory such as in insanity and diminished responsibility cases. This is covered by **s. 1 Criminal Procedure (Insanity and Unfitness to Plead) Act 1991**.

Where an expert is used, he does not have to possess certain qualifications but the judge has the final say in whether he or she is suitably qualified. The expert must confine their evidence to their field of expertise and present fact. They must not, unless absolutely unavoidable, draw inferences from their work: that it is only proper for the court to do. The expert may for instance say that a piece of glass has a rare refractive index only found in 2 per cent of glass in the UK, some of which glass was found to have been fitted in windows in the victim's home. The expert may also say that a fragment was found on the accused's shoe. It would not be proper to go on to say that the glass fragment must have come from the victim's home, however. Certainly they must never say 'therefore the accused is guilty'.

Experts do not have a duty to those who pay for their services, they must disclose evidence that would help the other side's case (see **R v Maguire (1992)**). If they conceal it, they risk a prosecution for perjury.

Evidence of previous bad character

The general position is that evidence of a person's previous wrongdoing, including that of previous, highly relevant convictions, is not admissible. This is to prevent someone being damned by their reputation, perhaps after some years of 'going straight'. An important exception is the so called 'tit for tat' rule. If an accused makes allegations about the prosecution's conduct, most commonly of police brutality or entrapment for example, this means that the accused loses the protection otherwise enjoyed and previous relevant convictions may be read out.

In some cases, particularly sexual offences, it may be possible to adduce evidence of matters in the past even if they have not given rise to a conviction. This would be known as 'similar fact evidence'. For instance, consider the situation of a man had being charged, tried but acquitted of more than one instance of rape and in each case the alleged victim was tall and dark-haired. It may well be that evidence of these trials could be heard if he were charged with a later, very similar offence.

Illegally or unfairly obtained evidence

There is a general human rights principle under the **ECHR** (now largely enshrined in the **HRA 1998**) against the use of such evidence. This issue is largely covered by the **Police and Criminal Evidence Act (PACE) 1984**, in particular **s. 76** or **s.78**.

ACTIVITY

Covert intelligence gathering or undercover investigations are outside the scope of this volume. They are dealt with under the Regulation of Investigatory Powers Act 2000. Visit **www.homeoffice.gov.uk** and search under 'RIPA Codes' for more information.

The codes lay down principles of good practice that officers must follow. Some however are stipulations which, in essence can be found in statutes and case law already.

Breaches of the codes do not always lead to evidence being automatically excluded. There are usually repercussions of some sort for the officers in breach as we discussed in Chapter 3 but it may be that the case can proceed with the evidence. An example of where evidence must be excluded is the confession obtained by oppression under **s. 76(2) PACE 1984**. This may not be overt torture, it may be something more subtle than that, such as a refusal of breaks in the interview process or of adequate refreshments. It matters not whether the confession is true because, as we have said before, to allow such police behaviour to go unchecked would be to set a dangerous precedent. A summary of situations were evidence is inadmissible in all cases would be:

- Breath or blood samples taken from suspected drink drivers in breach of the procedures in the **Road Traffic Act 1988** and various statutory instruments under it.

- 'Bugging' – evidence obtained directly by intercepting postal services or telecommunications in the UK (**s. 17 Regulation of Investigatory Powers Act 2000**).

- Confessions obtained by oppression (**PACE s. 76(2)(a)**).

- Unreliable confessions – confessions obtained as a result of anything said or done that might have been likely to induce it (**PACE s. 76(2)(b)**).

The consequences of most breaches are the subject of the judge's discretion, however, **s. 78 PACE 1984** states:

In any proceedings the court may refuse to allow evidence on which the prosecution proposes to rely to be given if it appears to the court that, having regard to all the circumstances, including the circumstances in which the evidence was obtained, the admission of the evidence would have such an adverse effect on the fairness of the proceedings that the court ought not to admit it.

There is further guidance in case law, in **R v Walsh (1990)** the court held that:

If there are significant and substantial breaches of ...the Code, then prima facie the standards of fairness set by Parliament have not been met. ..to admit evidence against D in these circumstances cannot but have an adverse effect on the fairness of the proceedings. This does not mean that in every case...the evidence will automatically be excluded. Section 78 does not so provide. The task of the Court is not merely to consider whether there would be an adverse effect on the fairness of the proceedings, but such an adverse effect that justice requires the evidence to be excluded.

This does not by any means provide a villains' charter. In **Attorney-General's Reference (no 3 of 1999) (2001)** it was made very clear that the courts are prepared to favour the prosecution rather than adhere to some abstract notion of fairness. In this case the court considered the situation where a suspect had provided DNA samples for a previous offence for which he had been acquitted (and therefore should have been destroyed). These could be used at a later trial even though they were not destroyed, in breach of the rules then in force.

Entrapment by police officers is another controversial area; there is a fine line between undercover police officers setting a trap or 'sting' for criminals to fall into, it is another to cause the offence to happen in the first place.

An example of the former, quite proper, police tactic was found in **Williams v DPP (1993)** where cartons of cigarettes were left visible in the back of an unattended van for people to steal, they were then apprehended. Had they persuaded a perfectly law-abiding member of the public to commit the offence this would have been entrapment however. Police or even Trading Standards officers making purchases of stolen or counterfeit goods at say, a car boot sale would be perfectly lawful, though.

REVISION

The following will normally be inadmissible as evidence:
- ✓ irrelevant material;
- ✓ hearsay;
- ✓ opinion;
- ✓ evidence of previous bad character;
- ✓ illegally or unfairly obtained evidence.

There are limited exceptions to these rules, however.

Eye witness testimony, DNA and the right to silence

By the end of this section you will be able to

- explain the problems with eye witness testimony;

- evaluate the issues around DNA evidence;

- consider the status of the right to silence in the UK.

It merely remains for us to round up some other important issues in evidence law. These are unconnected but nevertheless are extremely important.

Eyewitness testimony

This type of evidence has come under increasing criticism in recent years. Studies have shown that it is not as reliable as it has long been popularly held to be. Even leaving aside the fact that people can be very self-absorbed and unobservant, the human brain will tend to focus on what it really needs to do in an emergency, i.e. react to it, either by 'fight or flight'. It will effectively shut down functions it does not need for self-preservation, including memory and associated abilities. In short, just when the law-enforcement process needs a reliable memory from a witness is just when he or she is least likely to have one.

ACTIVITY

The reliability of eyewitness testimony is easily tested. During a group activity, presentation or even social gathering, have someone only you know come in briefly and speak to you before leaving, do not warn the others that this is likely to happen. After a short while, ask those present to write a brief description of the person on a piece of paper. You may be surprised at how wildly inaccurate these turn out to be.

The notorious unreliability of this type of evidence came to the fore in a leading case, **R v Turnbull (1977)**. The court was not happy for eyewitness evidence to be accepted without question and required to know in what circumstances it was obtained. Police forces have developed a mnemonic: ADVOKATE, to help officers remember what they must record about this evidence:

- **A**mount of time under observation.

- **D**istance away from observer.

- **V**isibility at the time.

- **O**bstructions to the observers view.

- **K**nown or seen before.

- **A**ny reason for remembering the incident/person.

- **T**ime lapse between observation and later identification.

- **E**rror or material discrepancy in description.

These latter two points are designed to reassure the court that, where a suspect is later identified using an identification parade for example, no obvious reasons to doubt that identification have been overlooked.

DNA evidence

There is a widely held myth that DNA evidence is conclusive when in fact that is not the case. There are two reasons: one is that DNA is not unique to one individual, although the probability of finding someone with the same DNA may be extremely low indeed. The second is that, the trace at the scene or 'crime stain' may have DNA extracted from it that matches the accused. It remains to be proved beyond reasonable doubt however, that the crime stain got there because of the presence of the accused at the scene and not by some inadvertent transfer of material.

What is clear though, is that a complete mismatch between DNA profiles will prove that the samples came from two different persons. This may be conclusive proof of innocence. The reverse is not necessarily true however. A positive match between a stain and the accused does not provide proof of guilt, it may merely show that the odds are, say 10 million to one that this individual is not the person who left the stain. This is of course weighty evidence against the accused but should not be relied upon without other evidence to support it. In practice of course there is often other evidence to corroborate the DNA samples. A good way to look at this is to say that juries are expected to take the prior odds of guilt or innocence and combine them with the weight of the DNA evidence. In other words, the DNA and an eyewitness account placing the accused at the scene and a motive might be sufficient. Conversely if there are CCTV pictures of the accused in Barnsley at the exact time when the robbery took place in London then the prior odds of guilt are nonexistent and even a DNA match must be discounted.

As we have said, even if it conclusively matches that of the accused there must still be absolute certainty about how the sample came to be at the venue concerned. In more than one case it has been alleged that it got there carried on police officers' clothes as they searched the accused's home having just tended to the victim. Strict procedural rules are in place to try to prevent this happening, however.

Problems with evaluating the statistical significance of the evidence are not confined to DNA. For example in the Birmingham Six case it was said that the defendants had been tested for traces of explosives and that the tests were positive. It was stated that the test was 99 per cent accurate and therefore it was a 99 per cent certainty that the men had handled nitroglycerine. The problem was that the test was later found to give a positive result if the accused had handled soap or even playing cards as the same or similar chemical compounds were found on these items. More recently the case of Barry George, convicted of killing television personality Jill Dando has been referred back to the Court of Appeal as his conviction rested on a single speck of gunshot residue found in his pocket. It is now alleged the same mixture of chemicals can be found in a speck of household paint.

Knowledge Check 1

1. What is a 'court of first instance'?

2. Name two courts of appeal.

3. What is the difference between the 'burden of proof' and the 'standard of proof'?

4. How is a confession an exception to the hearsay rule?

5. What is 'entrapment'?

6. If proven, which section of **PACE 1984** would it fall under?

7. What does the mnemonic ADVOKATE stand for and from what case is it derived?

The right to silence

There is in fact no such thing as a 'right to silence' in the UK as exists in the USA, for example, under the fifth Amendment to the US Constitution. It is now possible to draw inferences of guilt from an accused's silence on arrest, during questioning or if they deliberately choose not to testify at court. This enshrined in **s.34 Criminal Justice and Public Order Act 1994**. There may be good reasons for the failure to answer questions and this does rather fly in the face of the guiding principle of being considered 'innocent until proven (by the prosecution) guilty'. In deference to this, judges adopt a particular form of words or 'model direction' to help the jury decide whether to draw an inference of guilt from silence. This was first used in **R v Cowan (1996)**:

The defendant has not given evidence. That is his right. But, as he has been told, the law is such that you may draw such inferences as appear proper from his failure to do so. Failure on its own cannot prove guilt, but depending on the circumstances, you may hold his failure against him when deciding whether he is guilty...If the only sensible explanation for his decision not to give evidence is that he has no answer to the case against him, or none that could have stood up to cross-examination, then it would be open to you to hold against him his failure to give evidence. It is for you to decide whether it is fair to do so.

The law of evidence is of course a vast topic and we can do little more than make some inroads into it here. There is considerable advanced reading that you could undertake should you wish to pursue the subject to a higher level. Some suggested titles are listed at the end of this chapter.

Suggested research

The rights of suspects vary greatly from jurisdiction to jurisdiction across the globe. Consider for example the so called Miranda rights of suspects in the US, meaning they must be 'read their rights' on arrest or the detention may be subject to legal challenge. Have a look on the web and see if you can find out what so called 'Rolling Miranda' rights are. Compare this approach with the fact that in France suspects are not necessarily entitled to a lawyer for the first nine hours of their questioning.

There was to be an attempt to standardise suspects' rights, at least across the countries of the EU in the proposed EU constitution. Look this up on the web and consider whether you think it is a workable solution or not.

Further reading

These works are useful for general reference on the law of evidence:

Allen, C (2004) *Practical guide to evidence* (2nd edn). London: Cavendish.

Cooper, S (1997) *Cases and materials on evidence*. London: Blackstone.

Dennis, IH (2002) *The law of evidence* (2nd edn). London: Sweet and Maxwell.

Hirst, M (2001) *Andrews and Hirst on criminal evidence* (4th edn). Bristol: Jordans.

McEwan, J (1998) *Evidence and the adversarial process* (2nd edn). Oxford: Blackwell.

May, R. *Criminal evidence* (5th edn). London. Sweet & Maxwell.

Munday, R (2005) *Evidence* (3rd edn). London. Butterworths.

Murphy, P (2005) *Murphy on evidence* (9th edn). Oxford: Oxford University Press.

Murphy, P (ed.) (2007) *Blackstone's criminal practice*. Oxford: Oxford University Press. Section F (evidence) and D12/D17 (juries)

Roberts, P and Zuckerman, A (2004) *Criminal evidence*. Oxford: Oxford University Press.

Specific works on forensic evidence include:

Balding, DJ and Donnelly, PJ (1994) The prosecutor's fallacy and DNA evidence. *Criminal Law Review*, 711

McEwan, J (1998) *Evidence and the adversarial process* (2nd edn). Oxford: Blackwell (especially pp. 156–165).

Useful websites

Legislation

www.opsi.gov.uk

Case law and legislation databases:

www.westlaw.com* (a legal database)

www.lexis-nexis.com* (a legal database)

www.pnld.co.uk* (a police service specific database of case law and statute)

* Likely to be available through the virtual learning environment (VLE) which supports your course/training.

Answers

Knowledge Check 1

1. A 'court of first instance' is where an offence is first tried, as opposed to where any appeal may be heard. The main courts of first instance in criminal law are the magistrates and Crown Courts.

2. The Court of Appeal, House of Lords or High Court (Queen's Bench).

3. The 'burden of proof' indicates which of the prosecution or defence must prove a particular point. The 'standard of proof' refers to the degree to which the point must be proven, in most instances this is 'beyond reasonable doubt' as the prosecution bears most of the burden of proving.

4. A confession is usually heard by a third party and then relayed to the court by that third party. Evidence of what one person told another is not normally admissible as hearsay. It

would not be possible to use any confession other than one made in the dock by the accused, if there were not such an exception.

5. Entrapment is where law enforcement officers go further than providing an opportunity for an offence to take place and then catch the offender. Entrapment is unlawful and would arise in circumstances were officers not only provided the opportunity but incited or procured the offence when the offender had no previous inclination to offend.

6. Entrapment would constitute evidence gathered unfairly and may breach **s. 78 PACE 1984**.

7. **A**mount of time under observation.

    Distance away from observer.

    Visibility at the time.

    Obstructions to the observers view.

    Known or seen before.

    Any reason for remembering the incident/person.

    Time lapse between observation and later identification.

    Error or material discrepancy in description.

15 Children, young persons and the mentally ill

(?) *Remember this symbol indicates that the material might be useful for your Student Officer Learning and Assessment Programme (SOLAP) portfolio or any attached reflective practice record you are required to make.*

Underpinning knowledge towards Patrol Officer NOS:

1A1, 1A2, 1A4, 1B9, 2C1, 2C3, 2C4, 2J1, 2J2, 2K2, 4C1

and PCSO NOS:

1A1, 1A4,1B11, 2C1, 2C3, 2C4, 2C5, 2J1,2J2, 4C1, 4C2

For further information on these NOS, which are also Policing Level 3 and 4 NVQ unit titles, refer to Appendix 1 to this volume.

The enforcement of law relating to children and young persons is shared to a degree between the police and the child services department of the local authority. Even to an extent the charity National Society for Prevention of Cruelty to Children (NSPCC) is involved in investigation and prosecution of abuse cases.

This volume is limited in its scope and merely hopes to explore the areas of children and young person law which it is likely that a student officer will need for general patrol duties. This chapter should be read in conjunction with Chapter 5, 'Police organisation', Chapter 7, 'Sexual offences', Chapter 11, 'Crime prevention', Chapter 17, 'Weapons' and Chapter 18, 'Alcohol', all of which touch on the law relating to those under 18 in their specific area.

The mentally ill are included in this chapter because, like children and young persons, the law deems that in the most extreme cases the mentally ill are not fully responsible for their actions. Like children, the law therefore allows for their liberty to be taken away when they perhaps have done nothing illegal but for their own protection or that of others. Children, young persons and the mentally ill are some of the most vulnerable groups in society and dealing with them requires a great deal of sensitivity and care. We turn now to the law on:

- children and young persons;
- the mentally ill.

Children and young persons

By the end of this section you will be able to:

- analyse the problem of defining children and young persons in law;
- describe in outline the legislation concerning police action and children and young persons;
- apply what you know to some multiple-choice questions.

Definitions

The **Children and Young Persons Act 1969** refers to a young person as someone aged between 14 and 18.

Defining a child is more problematic. One of the ongoing failures of English law is its general inability to consistently and precisely define the state of childhood. In civil law, such as tort, the concept is especially vague, talking in terms of the 'age of reason'. In criminal law the age of criminal responsibility is ten but a person may not consent to sexual activity or buy cigarettes for another six years by virtue of still being a child. A person is a child for the purposes of children and young persons law from the age of 14. This is so with the exception of the issue of compulsory education. The **Education Act 1996** refers to a person being a child until the age of 16. In contrast the **Children Act 1989** casts responsibility onto local authorities for the care of children to age 18 if they are without suitable parents or guardians. The only practical way forward is to ensure you know the relevant ages for each legal provision.

Police action

During general patrol duties police may need to take action or receive information to the following:

- abduction/kidnap;
- begging;
- cruelty;
- curfew;
- emergency removal;
- employment under age;
- reprimands and warnings;
- truancy.

There are of course many other occasions were specialist police officers may have to deal with more complex areas of child safety law and you may be called to assist them or social services. In those situations it will not be so important for you personally to be aware of the relevant law. This chapter hopes to equip you for situations you might meet and have to act on autonomously.

Abduction/kidnap

The Child Abduction Act ss. 1 and **2** create offences of abducting a child. This can even be by the father, mother or guardian if they do not have the appropriate consent. **Section 1** particularly focuses on sending the child out of the UK. The **Children Act 1989 s. 49** creates an offence if the abduction or inducement to run away is from local authority care or police protection.

The offence of kidnap is by contrast a common law one and may also apply to an adult. It involves:

- unlawfully
- taking or carrying away of one person
- by force or fraud
- without consent of the victim.

Begging

The **Children and Young Persons Act 1933 s. 4(1)** terms it an offence:

> If any person causes or procures any child or young person under the age of sixteen years or, having responsibility for such a child or young person, allows him to be in any street, premises, or place for the purpose of begging or receiving alms, or of inducing the giving of alms (whether or not there is any pretense of singing, playing, performing, offering anything for sale, or otherwise).

It should be remembered that some cultures do not see the use of young children to assist in begging as inherently wrong. Sensitivity and an awareness of diversity issues will be required when dealing with such incidents whilst nevertheless firmly applying the law as appropriate.

Cruelty

In common with domestic violence (see Chapter 6, 'Violence and intimidation') the circumstances of an assault should not be allowed to obscure the fact that a non-fatal offence against the person has occurred. If the child has suffered an injury such that his or her health or comfort has been affected then a charge under **s. 47 Offences Against the Person Act 1861** could be considered as well or instead of considering one of the following provisions. There are of course ways other than assault to neglect or be cruel to a child.

By the **Children and Young Persons Act 1933 s. 1(1)** if any person of 16 years and over and has responsibility for any child or young person under that age:

> ...wilfully assaults, ill-treated, neglects, abandons, or exposes him, or causes or procures him to be assaulted, ill-treated, neglected, abandoned, or exposed, in a manner likely to cause him unnecessary suffering or injury to health (including injury to or loss of sight, or hearing, or limb, or organ of the body, and any mental derangement), that person shall be guilty...

This creates an either-way offence with a maximum potential term of ten years. **Section 1(2)(a)** then gives examples of what might be termed neglect:

> *a parent or other person legally liable to maintain a child or young person, or the legal guardian of a child or young person, shall be deemed to have neglected him in a manner likely to cause injury to his health if he has failed to provide adequate food, clothing, medical aid or lodging for him, or if, having been unable otherwise to provide such food, clothing, medical aid or lodging, he has failed to take steps to procure it to be provided under the enactments applicable in that behalf;*

Under **s. 1(3)** there is also an example given of neglect which relates to very specific circumstances. That is of suffocating an infant under three which is in a bed with the accused whilst the accused was drunk.

Curfew

A curfew is an order which prohibits a person being out of doors after a certain time of day or before a certain time in the morning. These orders can be very useful in preventing a person disturbing the peace late at night or from committing offences which are easier in the hours of darkness, such as burglaries and damage. Such orders can be placed on an individual and usually come with a sentence of a court (see Chapter 13 generally).

Curfew orders covering not a person but a geographical location are also possible under the **Crime and Disorder Act 1998.** This is predominantly a crime-prevention-focused statute (see Chapter 11). **Section 14** allows the local authority to set up a child curfew scheme over a designated area for a specified period. A map posted locally is the usual method of advising residents of the order. By **s.15** a constable may remove a child in breach of this curfew to his or her residence.

Emergency removal

In certain circumstances, probably some of the most distressing you will ever witness or experience in your career, it is necessary to consider taking a child away from his or her parent, guardian or carer. **Section 46(1) Children Act 1989** empowers a constable to take a child into police protection:

> *Where a constable has reasonable cause to believe that a child would otherwise be likely to suffer significant harm, he may*
>
> (a) *remove the child to suitable accommodation and keep him there; or*
>
> (b) *take such steps as are reasonable to ensure that the child's removal from any hospital, or other place, in which he is then being accommodated is prevented.*

This situation can last for up to a maximum 72 hours but extensions can be applied for. There are certain steps that must be taken as soon as possible after the child has been taken into police protection:

- The local authority social services department must be informed.

- The designated police officer (designated to deal with such matters under the Act) must be informed.

- As far as possible the child must be informed of what is happening and his or her feelings ascertained.

- Parents, those who hold parental responsibility and the person with whom the child was living when taken into protection (if these are different people) must be informed of what has happened.

- Reasonable contact with the above and under any contact order must be allowed having regard to the best interests of the child.

- It must be ensured that the child is delivered to an appropriate refuge and/or local authority custody.

Employment under age

It is about two centuries since the legislative banned the use of children as factory labourers and so on. It is not uncommon however, to discover that children (sometimes under their own volition to supplement their pocket money) are working illegally. The rules are set out in **s. 18 Children and Young Persons Act 1933** but can be amended by local bye-law (as shown in brackets below), breach of these stipulations is an offence although there is a 'due diligence' defence in the statute for the employer. **Section 18(1)** as amended provides that it will be unlawful to employ anyone:

so long as he is under the age of fourteen years (local byelaws may specify 13); *or*

(aa) *to do any work other than light work (including occasional light agricultural or horticultural work for parent or guardian); or*

(b) *before the close of school hours on any day on which he is required to attend school (one hour before school may be allowed by byelaw); or*

(c) *before seven o'clock in the morning or after seven o'clock in the evening or any day; or*

(d) *for more than two hours on any day on which he is required to attend school; or*

(da) *for more than twelve hours in any week in which he is required to attend school; or*

(e) *for more than two hours on any Sunday; or*

(g) *for more than eight hours or, if he is under the age of fifteen years, for more than five hours in any day-*

(i) *on which he is not required to attend school, and*

(ii) *which is not a Sunday; or*

(h) *for more than thirty-five hours or, if he is under the age of fifteen years, for more than twenty-five hours in any week in which he is not required to attend school; or*

(i) *for more than four hours in any day without a rest break of one hour; or*

(j) at any time in a year unless at that time he has had, or could still have, during a period in the year in which he is not required to attend school, at least two consecutive weeks without employment.

It is most likely that process will be by way of summons unless the necessity requirement is met in the amended **s. 24 PACE 1984.**

Reprimands and warnings

The **Crime and Disorder Act 1998** made changes to the way that children and young people could be diverted from the criminal justice system and treated less formally. The idea was to create a more consistent system with an element of organised rehabilitation. **Section 65(1) Crime and Disorder Act 1998** lays out the circumstances where diversion may happen:

...where

(a) *a constable has evidence that a child or young person ("the offender") has committed an offence;*

(b) *the constable considers that the evidence is such that, if the offender were prosecuted for the offence, there would be a realistic prospect of his being convicted;*

(c) *the offender admits to the constable that he committed the offence;*

(d) *the offender has not previously been convicted of an offence; and*

(e) *the constable is satisfied that it would not be in the public interest for the offender to be prosecuted.*

There clearly has to be an offence and the offender must admit to it, rather like the requirements for an adult 'caution'. It would be a mistake therefore to use this diversion to deal with an offender informally because the chances of a conviction are slim. That is not what warnings and reprimands are intended for. The reprimand or warning can only take place if this is the first such occasion or at least the first within the last two years; **s. 65(2)-(4)**refer:

Subject to subsection (4) below, the constable may reprimand the offender if the offender has not previously been reprimanded or warned.

(3) *The constable may warn the offender if*

(a) *the offender has not previously been warned; or*

(b) *where the offender has previously been warned, the offence was committed more than two years after the date of the previous warning and the constable considers the offence to be not so serious as to require a charge to be brought;*

but no person may be warned under paragraph (b) above more than once.

(4) *Where the offender has not been previously reprimanded, the constable shall warn rather than reprimand the offender if he considers the offence to be so serious as to require a warning.*

An offender under 17 is entitled to an appropriate adult being present.

Clearly the terms reprimand and warning could be confused by the layman. There is a hierarchy however. A reprimand precedes a warning in terms of severity and a warning must result in the offender being referred to the local youth offending team (YOT). Both a reprimand and a warning should in practice take place at the police station.

ACTIVITY

If you have not already researched the area whilst reading another chapter, prepare a short briefing for your colleagues on the work of your local Youth Offending Team. Visit their website, an example from Nottinghamshire is provided here at **www.nottingham city.gov.uk**, and follow the links or search for Youth Offending Team. There will be an equivalent to cover the area you work in. Prepare a flipchart, or a set of electronic presentation slides, to deliver the information. It is always a good idea to practise with friends, family or colleagues first to make sure that you know your material, your voice is audible and you try to make eye contact with everyone in the room.

Truancy

You should also take a look at the relevant material in Chapter 5 as PCSOs (and therefore constables) are empowered, dependent on their chief officer's decision, to award fixed penalty notices to parents for failing to make sure their child attends school reasonably regularly and punctually. This power emanates originally from **s. 444A Education Act 1996**.

There are additional powers where a school has identified to police that it has a truancy problem. Under **s. 16 Crime and Disorder Act 1996** a child who will or who has attained the age of 16 during the final year of compulsory schooling (nowadays referred to as Year 10) can be removed from a public place by a constable, using reasonable force if necessary. The child should be delivered to the school and clearly this should only be done if the child has no legitimate reason for being absent from school. Although schools may grant exam leave towards the end of that year, in theory a child must attend school until the last school day of the academic year in which they become 16. The powers are only exercisable in public. Proceedings under **s. 444A** mentioned above could be considered however, if the child is discovered at home with no good reason on a regular basis. Bear in mind though that a surprisingly large number of children are schooled at home with the local authority's consent and that a child may be absent for reasons of religious observance, an issue which should be handled sensitively.

REVISION

✓ Abduction/kidnap – The Child Abduction Act s. 1 and 2/ s. 49 Children Act 1989/common law.
✓ Begging – s. 4(1) Children and Young Persons Act 1933.
✓ Cruelty – s. 1 Children and Young Persons Act 1933.
✓ Curfew – s. 14 Crime and Disorder Act 1998.
✓ Emergency removal – s. 46 Children Act 1989.
✓ Employment under age – s. 18 Children and Young Persons Act 1933.
✓ Reprimands and warnings – s. 65 Crime and Disorder Act 1998.
✓ Truancy – Crime and Disorder Act 1998/Education Act 1996.

The mentally ill

By the end of this section you will be able to:

- identify when a police constable can take action in respect of mental disorder;

- explain the extent of police action;

- apply your knowledge to some multiple-choice questions.

It may be that you are called upon to assist a mental health professional team to take a person into mental health care where the mental health practitioners have determined that they need to be placed in secure accommodation. This is often referred to being 'sectioned' under the **Mental Health Act 1983.** In those cases you are reliant on these professionals having satisfied the legal requirements of the Act and you are there simply to assist.

(?) *Despite advances there is still a great deal of discrimination against those with mental conditions. Society tends to view people as either sane or not. This is of course absurd as we do not label people as either sick or well in terms of physical ailments which in many cases come and go with varying levels of severity. We are not so precise in terms of the mentally ill. Fear and prejudice have generated terms of abuse like 'looney', 'mentallist' and 'wacko' where no equivalent exists for the physically sick. Readers of this volume may have a mental aberration and be completely unaware that this is the case. If you have an irrational fear of something, whether it be spiders, mice, snakes, enclosed spaces or even birds, you may have a neurosis. This is no more troublesome than a common cold in most situations but is nevertheless a mental condition – does that make you insane?*

In some cases you will encounter mental illness while going about general duties. In practice it is likely that you will simply be called to, or come across someone acting in a strange way. There could be many causes from drink or drugs, solvent abuse, even diabetes, that can cause a person to act abnormally. Care should be taken to try to eliminate these possible causes before treating the person concerned as mentally disordered. Once you have done this you may proceed under **s.136(1) Mental Health Act 1983** to remove that person. It is not simply that the person can be deemed mentally disordered however, the person must be found:

- in a place where the public have access; and

- appear to be suffering from a mental disorder and needs immediate care and control; and

- the constable must think removal necessary in that person's interests or for the protection of others.

Once those criteria have been met, the person may be removed to a place of safety for a period not exceeding 72 hours. This may not necessarily be a police station and it may be desirable to use a mental health facility if one is located within a reasonable distance.

Clearly a good deal of sensitivity and discretion is called for here. This must be weighed against the need to preserve public and personal safety.

Knowledge Check 1

1. PC McBride is on mobile patrol in the early hours of a Tuesday morning around the market area of Doolby, Mountfortshire. She notices a female apparently intoxicated. On approach however, there is no smell of intoxicating liquor. The female is cutting her arms with a small craft knife and muttering. There are no obvious signs of the misuse of any substance, legal or otherwise. McBride may:

   (a) Remove the female under s. 136 Mental Health Act 1983.

   (b) Arrest the female under s. 139 Criminal Justice Act 1988.

   (c) Issue an FPN for being found drunk.

   (d) Arrest for a public order offence.

2. The following day at 2pm McBride notices a boy of around 12 years old outside an amusement arcade in the town centre. It is a school day and the local school has raised concerns about truancy, if the boy has no lawful reason for being there McBride may:

   (a) Arrest the boy under s. 444A Education Act 1996.

   (b) Issue an FPN to the boy under s. 444A Education Act 1996.

   (c) Place the boy in police protection under s. 46 Children Act 1989.

   (d) Remove the boy to his school under s. 16 Crime and Disorder Act 1998.

3. It transpires later that the boy has not had a proper meal for two days and slept rough the previous night. His mother had locked him out of the house having come home drunk in the early evening. If this is a regular sequence of events police may:

   (a) Obtain a warrant and search the home address for signs of neglect.

   (b) Arrest the mother for being found drunk.

   (c) Inform the NSPCC but take no further action.

   (d) Consider action under s. 1 Children and Young Persons Act 1933.

The answers are at the end of the chapter.

Suggested research

Dealing with children and young persons most definitely requires a multi-agency approach. Visit the NSPCC website and look at what services they can offer should you need support in dealing with young people in your duties. This can be found at **www.nspcc.org.uk**

Further reading

More detailed coverage of the legal topics found in this chapter can be obtained by reading:

English, J, and Card, R (2005) *Police law* (9th edn). Oxford: Oxford University Press.

Although written with the social worker in mind, the following provide useful guides in a practical setting:

Dugmore, P, Pickford, J with Angus, S (2006) *Youth justice and social work*. Exeter: Learning Matters.

Brown, R (2006) *The approved social worker's guide to mental health law*. Exeter: Learning Matters.

Johns, R (2005) *Using the law in social work* (2nd edn). Exeter: Learning Matters.

Useful websites

Crown Prosecution Service:

www.cps.org.uk

NSPCC:

www.nspcc.org.uk

Home Office:

www.homeoffice.org.uk

Legislation:

www.opsi.gov.uk

Case law and legislation databases:

www.westlaw.com* (an educational case law and statute database)

www.lexis-nexis.com* (an educational case law and statute database)

www.pnld.co.uk* (a police service specific database of case law and statute)

* Likely to be available through the virtual learning environment (VLE) which supports your course/training.

Answers

Knowledge Check 1

1. (a) Remove the female under **s. 136 Mental Health Act 1983.**

2. (d) Remove the boy to his school under **s. 16 Crime and Disorder Act 1998**.

3. (d) Consider action under **s. 1 Children and Young Persons Act 1933**.

16 Conspiring, aiding, abetting and attempting to commit crime

(?) *Remember this symbol indicates that the material might be useful for your Student Officer Learning and Assessment Programme (SOLAP) portfolio or any attached reflective practice record you are required to make.*

Underpinning knowledge towards Patrol Officer NOS:

1A1, 2A1, 2C1, 2C3, 2G2, 2G4, 2H1, 2H2, 2I1, 2I2, 2J1, 2J2, 2K2, 4C1

and PCSO NOS:

1A1, 2A1, 2C1, 2C3, 2J1, 2J2, 4C1

For further information on these NOS, which are also Policing Level 3 and 4 NVQ unit titles, refer to Appendix 1 to this volume.

This chapter covers the law on the following matters:

- criminal attempts;
- aiding, abetting, counselling and procuring offences;
- conspiracy and incitement to commit offences.

Attempts and conspiracy are often referred to by lawyers as 'inchoate offences'. The dictionary definition of this word varies between 'at an initial or early stage' to 'just begun', alternatively 'imperfectly formed'. We are dealing here with criminal behaviour at a very early stage.

The order that we provide these topics is in roughly the order of descending moral blame-worthiness awarded by Parliament and the courts. In other words, the punishment handed out for attempting to commit a crime is often more or less the same as if the crime had been committed. This is logical as in many cases it is a matter of luck that the crime was not fully performed, such as when a bomb plot is foiled at the last moment by a sharp-eyed member of the public.

The other situations represent points on a journey towards committing a crime such as, in the bomb plot scenario, planning the target, through a third party buying the bomb-making materials, to the principal offender assembling them and placing the device at the target. These may attract lesser sentences.

Most of the case law is centred on the grey areas: how much hard action is required for the conspiracy to become an attempt? At what point does a criminal enterprise move from getting ready to commit the crime (which is not an offence provided there is no con-spiracy) to a criminal attempt or the offence itself? Much will depend on the construction of the offence. We have seen in Chapter 9 that burglary only requires a person to put any part of their body or even a tool of some kind into a building with the requisite *mens rea* and the offence is complete. The same level of preparation would not suffice for a **s. 18 Offences Against the Person Act (OAPA) 1861** GBH (see Chapter 6), however. The equiv-alent would be picking up the knife or knuckle duster intending to use it on the victim which in many circumstances would not lead to liability at that stage.

ACTIVITY

Go to **www.cps.gov.uk** for the links to the press release dated December 2006 relating to Maxine Carr. You may remember her from the news coverage of the Soham murders. Arising from that investigation you will see that she was to be separately prosecuted for 12 counts of deception. Look at how many are attempts at deception and what the details are, especially how the charges are framed. These crimes are relatively common but it is rare for them to receive such national prominence. They only do so here because of Ms Carr's prior conviction in relation to the murders.

Criminal attempts

By the end of this section you will be able to:

- define a criminal attempt;

- analyse the *mens rea* and *actus reus* elements of the offence;

- apply relevant case law and statute to a range of hypothetical situations.

Attempts to commit indictable and either-way offences (that are triable in England and Wales) are covered by **s. 1 Criminal Attempts Act 1981**. This provides at **s. 1**:

> *If, with intent to commit an offence to which this section applies, a person does an act which is **more than merely preparatory** to the commission of the offence, he is guilty of attempting to commit the offence.*

The emphasis is provided by the author and will be discussed a little later. Summary offences cannot be attempted unless that is provided for in the statute itself. Indeed some summary-only statutory offences cover the attempt and nothing else. An example is found in **s. 9 Criminal Attempts Act, 1981**:

A person is guilty of the offence of vehicle interference if he interferes with a motor vehicle or trailer or with anything carried in or on a motor vehicle or trailer with the intention that [theft or taking without owner's consent (TWOC) of the vehicle, trailer or anything in or on it] shall be committed by himself or some other person.

Going back to indictable and either-way offences, the question to be answered is whether the accused has gone beyond the preparatory stages of the offence. In **R v Jones (1990)** the accused had obtained a gun, shortened the barrel, loaded it, put on garments to disguise his appearance and driven to the point of intended murder in a car. These acts were considered by the court to be preparatory acts and not criminal. The tipping point was Jones getting out of the car and levelling the gun at the victim with the intention of killing him. This then became attempted murder. Where the courts draw the line may in some instances seem surprising and even inconsistent.

ACTIVITY

Look up **R v Tosti [1997]** Crim LR 746 and **R v Geddes [1996]** Crim LR 894 It is easiest to do this on **www.westlaw.com*** or **www.lexis-nexis.com***, both educational case law and statute databases. If you are unable to use an electronic source, any law library will normally allow you access for reference purposes. You may well be surprised at where the judges sometimes draw the line between an attempt and the commission of the offence itself.

*If the educational institution assisting with your training has subscribed to these resources.

The *mens rea* is always intent, never anything less, like recklessness. There is logic to this as well in that it would be rather nonsensical to recklessly attempt to commit, say **s. 47 OAPA 1861** ABH. The *actus reus* is of course that of attempting whatever the substantive offence is, killing, stealing, etc.

There is specific provision in the **Criminal Attempts Act** at **s. 1(2)** to the effect that it is a criminal offence to attempt an act which subsequently turns out to be impossible. This would occur for example if an offender shot his victim who was apparently asleep in an armchair but in fact was already dead. In a famous case, **R v Shivpuri (1986),** the accused carried what he thought was heroin through customs. It turned out to be harmless powder he had been conned into buying. He was nevertheless convicted of the attempt.

REVISION
- ✓ An attempt is 'more than merely preparatory' to the commission of the offence itself.
- ✓ The *mens rea* is always intent and the *actus reus* is the attempt to do the crime concerned.
- ✓ Attempts are covered by the Criminal Attempts Act 1981.

Aiding and abetting, counselling or procuring an offence

By the end of this section you will be able to:

- explain the importance of each of these terms;

- analyse the statutory basis of these offences;

- explain what is meant by a 'joint criminal enterprise'.

The **Accessories and Abettors Act 1861** brought this list of offences into existence in statutory form in 1861. Rather like the **OAPA 1861** the language is rather dated. Fortunately case law has determined that the terms all mean much the same thing. We need only concern ourselves with being an accessory to a crime or at most 'aiding and abetting'. **Section 8** of **the Aiders and Abettors Act 1861** states:

> *Whosoever shall aid, abet, counsel, or procure the commission of [any indictable offence*], whether the same be [an offence*] at common law or by virtue of any Act passed or to be passed, shall be liable to be tried, indicted, and punished as a principal offender.*

> *Inserted by later legislation.

This takes care of indictable offences. For offences tried at magistrates' court **s. 44(1) Magistrates' Courts Act 1980** provides:

> *A person who aids, abets, counsels or procures the commission by another person of a summary offence shall be guilty of the like offence and may be tried (whether or not he is charged as a principal)...*

This is often referred to as secondary participation. The *mens rea* is effectively knowledge of the proposed offence and intention to aid and abet. The essence is that assistance is given before or during the act. Assistance afterwards is not covered by this offence but would probably be perverting the course of justice.

The dividing line is a fine one between merely being present at the scene of a crime and not intervening and alternatively, encouraging that crime. Readers may be aware of the 1988 film *The Accused* starring Jodie Foster in which she plays a woman raped in a bar while others offered varying degrees of encouragement to the offenders. From a UK case with similar facts, **R v Clarkson (1971)**, it can be discerned that passive tolerance or watching an offence does not amount to secondary participation even if shouting encouragement would. It is possible for watching a crime take place to be an offence in itself of course, such as in child pornography cases. Allowing a child to witness a sexual act can be criminal too, under the **Sexual Offences Act 2003**. In **Wilcox v Jeffrey (1951)** clapping at an unlawful concert was considered aiding and abetting. In practice being present in support of an act committed by the principal offender, even if not participating, could tip the balance from being a passive observer to secondary participation.

(?) *Some cases involving drug addicts taking illegal drugs together have presented problems to the courts. If one person fills a syringe and passes it to another, who then injects and dies from an overdose, who is the principal offender and who is aiding and abetting? What offence is actually committed? See **R v Kennedy (No. 2) (2005)** for an example to help you reflect on this issue.*

A particularly thorny issue is that of a 'joint criminal enterprise'. In this situation both parties are equally guilty, such as when two people plant a bomb or mug a person on a tube train. The problem arises when one person goes beyond what had been implicitly or explicitly agreed. In this last hypothetical example that situation would occur if both planned to rob passengers on a particular tube train but, totally without warning, one of the offenders rapes a lone female passenger after robbing her. The other offender may be present but genuinely horrified. This is known as going beyond the joint criminal enterprise and would absolve the second offender of the rape.

This was affirmed in the case of **R v Perman (1996)**. In the conjoined appeals of **R v Powell; English (1997)** this principle was related to homicide when both agree to seriously injure but one goes on to murder. According to **R v Uddin (1998)** the crux is whether the 'acts of one participant can be said to be of a completely different type to those contemplated by the others'. If that is so there is no joint enterprise covering the ultimate offence. It should be borne in mind that some offences require many participants in themselves and therefore this concept would not apply, such as affray and riot, etc. (see Chapter 10). It should also be remembered that full participation is not necessary. If one person drives a car to a bank and the other runs inside with a gun and back out again with money, both will be guilty of robbery. This is so without the need for the getaway driver to fulfil any of the requirements of **s.8 Theft Act 1968** (see Chapter 9). This can even be when one offender cannot possibly commit the main offence, as Rose West found in the infamous Cromwell Street murder case. She was charged with rape merely because she restrained some of the victims for her husband Fred West.

REVISION

✓ The offence is covered by s. 8 Aiders and Abettors Act 1861 and s. 44 Magistrates Courts Act 1980.
✓ There is no practical difference between the terms, therefore accessory or aiding/abetting will suffice.
✓ A joint criminal enterprise occurs when two or more commit a crime together.

Conspiracy and incitement

By the end of this section you will be able to:

- explain the difference between these terms;

- analyse the statutory basis of these offences;

- explain what common law remains in this area.

There has long been a set of common law conspiracy offences, many are now effectively covered by legislation but one remains. There is one statutory offence and one common law offence to be concerned with.

- **S. 1** and **1A Criminal Law Act 1977** – Conspiracy to commit a criminal offence.

- Common law – conspiracy to defraud.

S. 1 and 1A Criminal Law Act 1977

Section 1 creates an offence in relation to conspiracy to commit a crime in England and Wales. It specifically provides:

> *...if a person agrees with any other person or persons that a course of conduct shall be pursued which, if the agreement is carried out in accordance with their intentions, either –*
>
> *(a) will necessarily amount to or involve the commission of any offence or offences by one or more of the parties to the agreement, or*
>
> *(b) would do so but for the existence of facts which render the commission of the offence or any of the offences impossible, he is guilty of conspiracy to commit the offence or offences in question.*

Section 1A merely extends that to a conspiracy in England and Wales to commit an offence in a foreign jurisdiction. This latter provision will be vital in relation to terror plots hatched here but to be carried out in foreign cities, etc. It will be noted that under this Act it is a crime to conspire to achieve the impossible.

Once agreement is reached the offence is complete. If a conspirator regrets their involvement and even reports the matter to police this will not absolve them of liability. For practical reasons though, it might be a consideration in whether the CPS decide to prosecute the informer or it might result in a more lenient sentence. Much will depend on the circumstances.

ACTIVITY

Have a look at the *Guardian* article 'Three men jailed over internet child rape plot' (5 February 2007) at **www.guardian.co.uk** Did the member of the conspiracy who 'ratted' on the others get any leniency from the courts?

There are circumstances where for public policy reasons there will be no conspiracy. A husband cannot conspire with a wife for example, and the intended victim cannot be one of the conspirators. So if a 14-year-old girl and a 25-year-old man agree to meet at a location for sex there will be no conspiracy.

Conspiracy to defraud

There could easily be an overlap here. A person who agrees with another to place reading devices on the front of cashpoint machines to obtain card details may well be conspiring to commit a deception offence now under **s. 2 Fraud Act 2006** (see Chapter 9). As such they could be charged under **s. 1 Criminal Law Act 1977**.

They are also committing the offence of conspiracy to defraud contrary to common law. The particularly useful part of the common law offence is that it does not require that an exact deception offence be made out by the prosecution. Thus if it were unclear precisely what the card details were to be used for but that the end result was that someone would be defrauded, then the common law offence could be used. It is, however, not possible to conspire to defraud if the fraud is impossible. This is in contrast to the other topics in this chapter.

Incitement

This offence involves encouraging others to commit a criminal offence. There have been some particularly high-profile cases recently about the religious sermons and protest chants of radical followers of the Muslim religion being an incitement to murder. Incitement has been a long-term part of English criminal law, however.

The basis of the offence is one of common law. It requires the accused to have been soliciting, persuading or encouraging another to commit a crime by words or deeds, explicitly or impliedly. This behaviour need not be successful as the *mens rea* required is only that intent to be successful is present. The accused cannot be guilty of incitement if the criminal act subsequently turns out to be impossible. Say, for example, A incites B to rob XYZ Stores not knowing that the Stores went into liquidation and closed the previous week. In this case there would be no offence.

REVISION

✓ s. 1 and 1A Criminal Law Act 1977 cover conspiracy.
✓ Common law conspiracy is limited for all practical purposes to conspiracy to defraud.
✓ Incitement is common law based and requires soliciting, persuading, or encouraging another to commit a crime.

Knowledge Check 1

1. On 11 January 2006 Clare drives to a children's home where children she is acquainted with live in local authority care. She has forged passports for them and herself, rope and tape. Is she guilty of attempted abduction when she acquires the things mentioned? Is she guilty when she drives to the home or when she hides in the grounds of the home?

2. Geoff Scott is a founder member of 'Vengeance', a radical white supremacist organisation with a racist agenda. During a speech and public rally one day he calls on all 'good believers' to attack 'the foreign scum' in their neighbourhoods and 'burn them out of their homes'. Part of his audience, Bob Godfery and his girlfriend Isla Swan, agree with each other to carry out Geoff's wishes. What offences, if any, have been committed?

3. Considering the scenario above, what would Bob and Isla have to do to commit a further offence if they know that this particular public gathering is unlawful?

Suggested research

So-called radicals Sheikh Abdullah el-Faisal and Abu Hamza have both been tried with offences which are dealt with in this chapter. Research the cases in the media and law reports. What charges were ultimately successful?

Further reading

Further detailed discussion of all the topics in this chapter can be found by reading:

Card, R, Cross, R and Jones, P (2005) *Criminal law*. London: Butterworths.

Elliott, C and Quinn, F (2006) *Criminal law* (6th edn). Harlow: Pearson.

English, J and Card, R (2005) *Police law* (9th edn). Oxford: Oxford University Press.

Heaton, R (2001) *Criminal law* (3rd edn). London: Butterworths.

Useful websites

The Crown Prosecution Service:

http://cps.gov.uk

Legislation:

www.opsi.gov.uk

Case law and legislation databases:

www.westlaw.com* (an educational case law and statute database)

www.lexis-nexis.com* (an educational case law and statute database)

www.pnld.co.uk* (a police service specific database of case law and statute)

* Likely to be available through the virtual learning environment (VLE) which supports your course/training.

Answers

Knowledge Check 1

1. Clare might be guilty of the attempt but the chances are slim. According to **R v Jones (1990)** these acts would be regarded as preparatory only even up to driving to the home. Even hiding in a school lavatory with similar implements was held to be merely preparatory in **R v Geddes (1996)**. Only if **R v Tosti (1997)** were followed could her actions at the point of hiding in the grounds be possibly considered an attempt.

2. Geoff Scott may well be inciting criminal damage contrary to the **Criminal Damage Act 1971**. He may also be inciting various assault, and public order offences including racially aggravated variants. Bob and Isla are conspiring to do the same, contrary to **s. 1 Criminal Law Act 1997**.

3. They may well be aiding and abetting the unlawful assembly. If they merely turn up and listen then according to **R v Clarkson (1971)** no offence is committed. According to **Wilcox v Jeffrey (1951)** however, if they applaud in any way that could constitute the **s. 8 Aiders and Abettors Act 1861** offence.

17 Weapons

(?) Remember this symbol indicates that the material might be useful for your Student Officer Learning and Assessment Programme (SOLAP) portfolio or any attached reflective practice record you are required to make.

Underpinning knowledge towards Patrol Officer NOS:

1A1, 1B9, 2A1, 2C1, 2C2, 2C3, 2I1, 2I2, 2J1, 2J2, 4C1, 4G2

and PCSO NOS:

1A1, 1B11, 2A1, 2C1, 2C2, 2C3, 2C5, 2J1, 2J2, 4C1, 4G2

For further information on these NOS, which are also Policing Level 3 and 4 NVQ unit titles, refer to Appendix 1 to this volume.

For good reason the law places restrictions on the ownership, sale and possession of weapons, particularly in public places. The restrictions on firearms in this country are some of the strictest in the world.

(?) The murder rate in the UK is at or around 850 per year at the moment. Our population is of the order of 60,000,000. The United States has a murder rate of around 20,000 per annum. It has a population only four or five times larger than our own despite its vast landmass, however. The US murder rate seems disproportionately large therefore. Can you make a connection between the content of this chapter and these figures? It might help to revisit Chapter 2, 'Human rights' to do so.

In this chapter the topics covered will be those most relevant to a student officer, those most likely to be encountered as a patrol officer:

- air weapons and crossbows;
- blades and points;
- firearms and shotguns;
- offensive weapons.

It is best not to treat this section in isolation, especially in relation to the stop-and-search provisions. When a person is searched, your suspicion may be aroused in relation to the misuse of drugs or stolen property. Drug dealers and thieves carry weapons as well of course and the search may reveal items which would give rise to say a charge of 'going equipped' (See Chapter 9) and an offensive weapon.

By the end of this section you will be able to:

- define an offensive weapon and 'blades and points' under legislation;

- differentiate between an air weapon, a dangerous air weapon, a crossbow, a shotgun and a firearm in law;

- apply what you know to some multiple-choice questions.

Air weapons and crossbows

Weapons in this category are defined in **s. 1(3)(b) Firearms Act 1968** (as amended) as:

> *an air weapon (that is to say, an air rifle, air gun or air pistol [which is not a prohibited weapon and] not of a type declared by rules made by the Secretary of State under* **sec-tion 53** *of this Act to be specially dangerous).*

This may not be of any help if you are unfamiliar with guns. An air weapon essentially is one that uses compressed gas to propel the bullet or pellet out of the muzzle instead of gunpowder. Most of these are subject to much fewer restrictions than true firearms and shotguns that do use gunpowder. They are not totally unrestricted, though.

An air weapon that can fire a pellet with more than 6ft/lb (12ft/lb in the case of an air pistol) is classified as a 'dangerous air weapon' and subject to the same restrictions as true firearms (see later). An air weapon that has been disguised to look like something else is also a dangerous air weapon in law.

Air weapons powered by compressed carbon dioxide are classified as firearms by the **Firearms (Amendment) Act 1997** although this does not appear to apply to weapons powered by a disposable carbon dioxide cartridge. If in doubt though, consult a force firearms officer.

Most of the restriction on (non-dangerous) air weapons are about possession and use rather than ownership. The relevant ages for these weapons are:

- under 14;

- 14–17;

- 21 and over.

An under-14-year-old can only use an air weapon whilst under the direct supervision of someone over 21 and only on private property providing they are not trespassing.

A person aged 14–17 years can use an air weapon unsupervised, however, on private property, again providing they are not trespassing.

The **Anti-Social Behaviour Act 2004** makes it an offence for someone in this age category to carry an air weapon or ammunition in a public place unless supervised by someone over 21, even if the gun is in a carrying case and unloaded.

Also by virtue of this Act, it is unlawful to fire pellets beyond the boundary of land which the young person has a right to be on, unless supervised by a 21-year-old or over.

In addition anyone will commit an offence if they have an air weapon in a public place without lawful authority or reasonable excuse. The same applies to an imitation firearm of any kind.

Air weapons should not be discharged within 50 feet of the centre of any public highway causing any member of the public to be 'injured, interrupted or endangered.'

A crossbow has the stock or shoulderpiece of a rifle but is fitted with a short bow and bowstring at right angles to that stock. There is a trigger mechanism, which releases a short arrow, or bolt, down a groove at the top of the weapon. These devices are extremely powerful over relatively short distances and can certainly kill in the wrong hands. Weapons with a draw weight (the power it takes to pull back the string) of at least 1.4 kg are however covered by the **Crossbows Act 1987.** In essence it is an offence:

- to sell or hire out such a weapon to a person under 17 years of age (reasonable belief of age would be a defence, however);

- for a person under 17 to possess a crossbow or a complete set of parts to make one unless supervised by a person 21 years or over.

Reasonable suspicion would permit a constable to search a person or vehicle to find the items described in these offences.

Blades and points

This legislation was introduced because the offensive weapons legislation (see later) may not easily apply to such as kitchen knives and screwdrivers, which can have innocent uses. They can of course, at a moment's notice become instruments of even murder. **Section 139(1) Criminal Justice Act 1988** makes it an offence for any person to have with them any article which has a blade or is sharply pointed in a public place without good reason or lawful authority. This excludes folding pocket-knives with blades less than 3 inches in length.

Because of the increase in media focus on stabbings in schools this legislation was amended and **s. 139A** inserted, which prohibits any person to have with them any article which has a blade or is sharply pointed or any offensive weapon on school premises without good reason or lawful authority.

The meaning of 'school' would exclude a caretaker's house in the grounds but would include the rest of any institution providing primary or secondary education. Further education colleges and universities would not appear to be covered here. A school would still be included in this provision though even if it provided further education in the evenings such as language evening classes.

Lawful authority would not tend to present a problem but whether the accused can provide a 'good reason' will be a question of fact in each case. The burden of proof is on the accused to provide the reason.

REVISION

✓ Ownership/possession of air weapons is not restricted unless:
  – over 6ft/lb or 12ft/lb(pistols) kinetic energy;
  – under 14 and unsupervised;
  – 14–17, in public and unsupervised.

✓ Unsupervised people under 17 cannot possess crossbows lawfully.

✓ Blades and points in public without lawful authority/reasonable excuse are unlawful except on a pocketknife with the blade not exceeding three inches.

Knowledge Check 1

1. PC Mohan is on mobile patrol when he sees a youth carrying what turns out to be a low-powered air rifle on an urban street. He says he is on his way to shoot rabbits at a farm mile away. This is lawful:

   (a) If the youth is over 17.

   (b) If the youth is over 21.

   (c) If the rifle is in a carrying case and he is over 17.

   (d) As there are no restrictions on air weapons.

2. Mohan next encounters a young woman showing something in her handbag to her friend; he sees it is a screwdriver. Mohan may act only if:

   (a) He can show by questioning that the woman intended to use it to protect herself by injuring any attacker.

   (b) The young woman is under 17.

   (c) The young woman is on school premises.

   (d) The young woman attacks him with the screwdriver.

The answers are at the end of the chapter.

Firearms

ACTIVITY

Research the 'Hungerford massacre' What types of weapons were outlawed as a result of that incident?

Find out all you can about the 'Dunblane massacre'. What was the 'Snowdrop Campaign' and what legislation did it lead to? Was it universally well received?

Legislation controlling firearms is mainly contained in the **Firearms Act 1968.** A firearm is a lethal barrelled weapon from which any shot, bullet or other missile can be discharged. It also includes all accessories like silencers and component parts like the stock (shoulder rest) or barrel. Firearm ammunition is also restricted. Note that the method of discharge does not have to by igniting gunpowder, thus as we have said all air weapons could be firearms; what exempts most of them is their relatively low power. Antiques and ornamental firearms are also excluded from the Act.

Home-made weapons, flare guns, starting pistols and even toys could be firearms if they are capable of inflicting a potentially fatal injury. It is possible to own and use a firearm with appropriate certification, as discussed later.

The following cannot be possessed legally without specific lawful authority. This in practice will almost certainly mean a police officer or member of Her Majesty's armed forces going about their lawful duty:

- automatic weapons;

- self-loading or pump action weapons unless with a calibre of less than .22 inches (about the width of a pencil);

- pistols and revolvers (handguns);

- shortened firearms (such as sawn-off weapons).

The first two of these categories were made unlawful after a man went on the rampage in Hungerford, Berkshire, in 1987 killing 14 with an array of automatic and semi-automatic weapons.

The **Firearms (Amendment) Act 1997** arrived in the wake of the equally infamous Dunblane incident in 1996 in which 16 primary school children and their teacher were gunned down by a former scoutmaster. By increments over a short period of time after the Act came into force, the private ownership and possession all handguns were outlawed in whatever circumstances.

Section 1 of the **Firearms Act 1968** provides the main restriction to which we have referred, **s .1(1)**:

Subject to any exemption under this Act, it is an offence for a person

(a) to have in his possession, or to purchase or acquire, a firearm to which this section applies without holding a firearm certificate in force at the time, or otherwise than as authorised by such a certificate;

(b) to have in his possession, or to purchase or acquire, any ammunition to which this section applies without holding a firearm certificate in force at the time, or otherwise than as authorised by such a certificate, or in quantities in excess of those so authorised.

The conditions imposed by a certificate, usually in terms of security of storage, etc., must be complied with also. The section goes on to explain which devices do not require a certificate, at **s. 3**:

(a) *a shot gun within the meaning of this Act, that is to say a smooth-bore gun (not being an air gun) which*

    (i) *has a barrel not less than 24 inches in length and does not have any barrel with a bore exceeding 2 inches in diameter;*

    (ii) *either has no [approved] magazine or has a non-detachable [approved] magazine incapable of holding more than two cartridges; and*

    (iii) *is not a revolver gun; and*

(b) *[a basic air weapon (see text above)]*

The Act also prohibits ammunition being held without a licence, **subsection 4** refers:

This section applies to any ammunition for a firearm, except the following articles, namely:

(a) *cartridges containing five or more shot, none of which exceeds .36 inches in diameter;*

(b) *ammunition for an air gun, air rifle or air pistol; and*

(c) *blank cartridges not more than one inch in diameter...*

The shotguns referred to above do not require a firearms certificate but they do require a shotgun certificate and may not be in the possession of anyone under 18 years old unsupervised. Shotguns are smooth-bore weapons that fire anything in excess of five shot or pellets from the same cartridge. They are used to kill small animals and birds at around 20–50 metre ranges. The shot spreads out on discharge giving a greater chance of hitting the target. At closer ranges they can and do easily deliver a shot fatal to a human target, however.

Section 48 Firearms Act 1968 empowers a constable to demand production of a relevant certificate from anyone the constable believes to be in possession of a firearm, ammunition or a shotgun.

Failing production of the certificate or an exemption under the Act, the constable may seize the firearm or ammunition and require the name and address of the person concerned to be given immediately. Failure to do so is an offence in itself.

There are considerable powers to stop and search under this legislation, contained in **s. 47 Firearms Act 1968**. **Section 47(1)** for example:

A constable may require any person whom he has reasonable cause to suspect

(a) *of having a firearm, with or without ammunition, with him in a public place; or*

(b) *to be committing or about to commit, elsewhere than in a public place, [the offences of having a firearm with intent to commit an indictable offence or to resist arrest (**s. 18(1)**) or trespassing with a firearm (**s. 20**)] to hand over the firearm or any ammunition for examination by the constable.*

Failure to do so on demand is an offence. **Section 47(3)** and **(4)** go further:

(3) *If a constable has reasonable cause to suspect a person of having a firearm with him in a public place, or to be committing or about to commit, elsewhere than in a* *public place, [the offences of having a firearm with intent to commit an indictable offence or to resist arrest (**s. 18(1)**) or trespassing with a firearm (**s. 20**)] the constable may search that person and may detain him for the purpose of doing so.*

Section 47(4) extends this power to stopping and searching vehicles and **s. 47(5)** gives a power of entry.

Offensive weapons

This topic covers any other type of device which can be used as a weapon whether it was originally designed to do so or not. The relevant legislation is **s. 1 Prevention of Crime Act 1953** as amended, **s. 1(1)**:

Any person who without lawful authority or reasonable excuse, the proof whereof shall lie on him, has with him in any public place any offensive weapon shall be guilty of an offence...

An order would normally be made for the destruction of the weapon on conviction.

The act defines a 'public place' as 'any highway and any other premises or place to which at the material time the public have or are permitted to have access, whether on payment or otherwise'.

Offensive weapon means 'any article made or adapted for use for causing injury to the person, or intended by the person having it with him for such use by him or by some other person'.

This means that anything from rice flails to knuckle-dusters, coshes, a pepper spray or even a plank with a nail through it would be prohibited in a public place unless carried with a reasonable excuse or lawful authority. This would be very hard for an ordinary member of the public to show with these examples. These items are 'made or adapted for use for causing injury'.

In contrast however, an array of items designed with innocent purposes in mind, from house bricks to golf clubs, could prove problematic for police. It is for this reason that a deliberate 'reverse burden of proof' is used in the Act to ensure that the onus is on the accused to show that they had a reasonable excuse or lawful authority to be carrying the item in public. These items would have to be deemed 'intended' for use for causing injury for a successful prosecution. Close and careful questioning of the accused is necessary here to nullify any assertion by a genuine offender that they are acting lawfully.

There is further legislation and case law in this general area of preventative legislation, which is outside the scope of this volume. Further reading suggestions are provided at the end of the chapter.

REVISION

✓ If it is a shotgun, firearm, ammunition or parts a certificate is required:
  – a firearm is lethal barrelled weapon from which any shot, bullet or other missile can be discharged;
  – pump action over .22 /automatic weapon banned outright;
  – handgun banned outright.
✓ Power to stop and search for firearms.

✓ Offensive weapons in public place:
  – made;
  – adapted or
  – intended for causing injury.

Knowledge Check 2

1. PC Smith attends an address in Letsby Avenue in the village of Little Lutonchester.

   i) Whilst on the street outside she sees a man openly placing a gun of some kind in the boot of his car; he is dressed for shooting. Smith may:

   (a) Not act, there is an exemption for hunting.

   (b) Having regard for personal safety, demand to see the man's firearms or shotgun certificate or reason under the Firearms Act 1968 that he does not need one.

   (c) Call an armed response unit.

   (d) Run away.

   ii) She attends the address she was originally called to, an elderly man has been bequeathed a service revolver by a World War 2 veteran friend. The man is seeking advice. The weapon will not legally be a firearm if:

   (a) It is of foreign manufacture.

   (b) It is an antique or curio.

   (c) It is less than .22 calibre.

   (d) It is a dangerous air weapon.

2. The man is thinking of selling his crossbow but does not want to be in breach of the law. He may sell it to:

   (a) Anyone as the Firearms Act 1968 does not apply.

   (b) Someone over 14.

   (c) Someone over 17.

   (d) Someone over 18.

The answers are at the end of the chapter.

Suggested research

The British Association of Shooting and Conservation (BASC) has its own website. Find out what you can about this enthusiasts' organisation and the shooting-related advice it can offer. Consult the firearms section of your own force's website also to see what advice is given to the public about owning firearms and certification.

Further reading

More detailed coverage of the topics found in this chapter can be obtained by reading:

Card, R, Cross, R and Jones, P (2005) *Criminal law*. London: Butterworths.

English, J and Card, R (2005) *Police law* (9th edn). Oxford: Oxford University Press.

Sampson, F (2007) *Blackstone's police manual, Volume 4 – General police duties* (9th edn). Oxford: Oxford University Press.

Useful websites

British Association for Shooting and Conservation:

www.basc.org.uk

Legislation:

www.opsi.gov.uk

Case law and legislation databases:

www.westlaw.com* (an educational case law and statute database)

www.lexis-nexis.com* (an educational case law and statute database)

www.pnld.co.uk* (a police service specific database of case law and statute)

* Likely to be available through the virtual learning environment (VLE) which supports your course/training.

Answers

Knowledge Check 1

1. (c) If the rifle is in a carrying case and he is over 17.

    NB The Anti-Social Behaviour Act 2004 prohibits the carrying of air weapons by anyone under 17 in public, covered or not.

2. (a) He can show by questioning that the woman intended to use it to protect herself by injuring any attacker.

NB The questioning would negate reasonable excuse/lawful authority. This is so even if ironically she may not incur liability for assault in the event of an actual serious attack as it could be self-defence. No such consideration is available here.

Knowledge Check 2

1. PC Smith attends an address in Letsby Avenue in the village of Little Lutonchester.

    i) (b) Having regard for personal safety, demand to see the man's firearms or shotgun certificate or reason under the **Firearms Act 1968** that he does not need one.

    ii) (b) It is an antique or curio.

    NB It is unlikely to be such a weapon in the final analysis as it cannot be more than 70 years old on the facts presented. This is not antique nor is it likely to be particularly rare.

2. (c) Someone over 17.

18 Alcohol, drunkenness and licensing

(?) *Remember this symbol indicates that the material might be useful for your Student Officer Learning and Assessment Programme (SOLAP) portfolio or any attached reflective practice record you are required to make.*

Underpinning knowledge towards Patrol Officer NOS:

1A1, 1B9, 2A1, 2C1, 2C2, 2C3, 2C4, 2J1, 2K2, 4C1

and PCSO NOS:

1A1, 1B11, 2A1, 2C1, 2C2, 2C3, 2C4, 2J1, 4C1

For further information on these NOS, which are also Policing Level 3 and 4 NVQ unit titles, refer to Appendix 1 to this volume.

The law on alcohol and licensing is a very large area. We touch on some of it elsewhere in the book, for example in the sections on PCSO powers (Chapter 5). We attempt here to provide an overview of the area at the level and breadth required for student officer training. We do not cover the licensing system for betting or taxis in this volume.

(?) *Alcohol or intoxicating liquor as it is best described in legal scenarios, is arguably responsible for a great many crimes from violence in the town centres to domestic abuse. Shoplifting sometimes happens to provide funds for alcohol-dependent people. It is sometimes referred to as 'our favourite drug'. The answer might lie in making alcohol an illegal substance as they do in some Middle Eastern nations. Reflect on whether prohibition would have the effect of cutting crime or simply create a black market for alcohol and thus actually increase crime. Why do you think a ban on alcohol in the Volstead Act of 1919 had such a criminogenic effect in the USA yet countries like Saudi Arabia seem to have accommodated such a ban into their culture without apparently so much difficulty? What lessons are there for the UK in this?*

The topics covered in this chapter are:

- the licensing framework;
- offences of public drunkenness.

The licensing framework

By the end of this section you will be able to:

- describe the legislation governing licensing;
- describe licensing authorities;
- apply what you know to some multiple-choice questions.

The old regime for the provision of licenses for the sale, etc., of alcohol was to be found under the **Licensing Act 1964**. Here the primacy was given to magistrates to decide, for example, who was a fit and proper person to hold a liquor licence. You will be familiar with the term 'Off Licence' to describe the local shop were you can go relatively late at night to buy alcoholic drink to take home or elsewhere to drink. In full, this is a term to describe premises where a licence has been granted to allow the sale of alcohol for consumption off the premises.

The **Licensing Act 2003** changed the regime significantly, placing responsibility for the granting of licenses in the hands of local authorities. **Section 3 (1)** states:

...In this Act 'licensing authority' means –

(a) the council of a district in England,

(b) the council of a county in England in which there are no district councils,

(c) the council of a county or county borough in Wales,

(d) the council of a London borough,

(e) the Common Council of the City of London,

(f) the Sub-Treasurer of the Inner Temple,

(g) the Under-Treasurer of the Middle Temple, or

(h) the Council of the Isles of Scilly.

For the vast majority of police areas this will mean that the licensing authority will be the local district or borough council rather than the county council. In some cities the city council has taken over the functions of the county council as well in their area, these are known as 'unitary authorities' and would be the licensing authority for that city. All the bodies listed in **s. 3(1)** will be responsible for liquor licensing in the geographical area for which they have general authority to act.

Section 1(1) Licensing Act 2003 delimits the alcohol-related activities for which a licence will be required:

...for the purposes of this Act the following are licensable activities

(a) *the sale by retail of alcohol,*

(b) *the supply of alcohol by or on behalf of a club to, or to the order of, a member of the club,*

(c) *the provision of regulated entertainment, and*

(d) *the provision of late night refreshment.*

ACTIVITY

The advent of the **Licensing Act 2003** brought in the potential for 24-hour drinking. Initial reaction from the police and press was that this would herald an era of greater public disorder in town centres. Having notified your supervisor of your purpose, visit the owners and staff of local pubs, clubs and entertainment venues. Speak also to colleagues who have policed town centres both before and after 24-hour licenses became a possibility. In all cases, ask questions about what changes if any to the atmosphere and drinking culture of these centres have come about. Form a view about whether 24-hour licensing has had any effect on the so-called 'binge drinking' culture of the UK.

The Act creates two types of licences:

- premises licences;
- personal licences.

These are fairly self-explanatory and you will have noticed as you pass into any drinking establishment that there is a notice above the door stipulating who it is within the premises who holds the liquor licence. This person is usually referred to as the landlord/lady of a pub. In a supermarket for instance, it would tend to be a member of the management team.

There are a number of offences created by the **Licensing Act 2003** and some enforcement powers, such as powers of entry, are set out as well. We do not provide detail of these here because as a student officer you would only need to be involved in, for example, the raiding of a premises acting in breach of its licence as part of a planned policing operation lead by a supervising officer. You could expect to be fully briefed at that time. Later in your career your force will be likely to provide further training on licensing as and when they deem necessary.

You can obtain an outline of some of the licensing and related offences by visiting the section on PCSO powers in Chapter 5. They are included there because PCSOs exercise constabulary powers in certain circumstances. In addition these offences can be proceeded against by way of a fixed penalty notice (FPN). A summary of the offences concerned is provided here, but see Chapter 5 for a more detailed discussion of:

- sale to person under 18;

- purchase for a person under 18;

- delivery to a person under 18;

- consumption or allowing consumption by a person under 18;

- buying or attempting to buy for under 18 including a power to search for and confiscate;

- selling or attempting to sell to person who is drunk;

- drinking in designated prohibited areas including a power to confiscate in a designated place.

REVISION

✓ The main legislation in this area is provided by the Licensing Act 2003.
✓ Licensing authorities are likely to be district, city or borough councils.
✓ The licensing authority, not magistrates, grants premises and personal licences.

Offences of public drunkenness

By the end of this section you will be able to:

- explain which legislation covers these remaining offences;

- explain the common requirement that the person is actually drunk and who can give evidence of this;

- apply this knowledge to some multiple-choice questions.

These offences are those in which the offender has to be actually 'drunk'.

This is of course a rather subjective opinion as no two people act in the same way when they are drunk. Neither is there a scientific definition for the condition. It is rather best described as a social 'construction' or concept, in other words. The courts take a fairly pragmatic view of this however and it is the only matter upon which the opinion of a police constable is accepted. All other evidence submitted by a non-specialist police officer must be fact only.

The offences covered here are:

- being found drunk;

- drunk in charge of other than a motor vehicle;

- drunk and disorderly.

Being found drunk

Seeing a person drunk in a public place is a fairly commonplace occurrence. Several euphemisms exist because since time immemorial a mild level of intoxication in public has been socially acceptable. We talk of a person being 'tipsy', 'merry', 'on the sauce', etc. Such people are not and never have been routinely carried off to the cells and the law reflects this reality.

Nevertheless a power exists to proceed against anyone in the magistrates' court who is found drunk in a 'highway or other public place, whether a building or not, or on any licensed premises' contrary to **s.12 Licensing Act 1872**. It is an offence to which an FPN can be applied. If all such offences which came to the notice of police were acted upon, the criminal justice system would be put to severe strain so a good deal of discretion is advised. Nevertheless if a person appears to be a danger to themselves (as opposed to others) then the power exists to take them into custody. Such a situation might arise if a person was found semi-conscious through drink lying on the pavement on a cold night. If he or she were unco-operative an advisable course of action might be to arrest and seek medical treatment but only if all other alternatives had been exhausted.

Drunk in charge of other than a motor vehicle

The offence of being drunk in charge of a motor vehicle is dealt with in Chapter 19, 'Roads policing'. It is a little-known fact however, that there are offences of being drunk in charge of other things. Perhaps most importantly it is an offence to be drunk in charge of a child. This is not unheard of in the summer months where garden barbecues and general drinking outside makes it more likely that children will be present when alcohol is drunk. When those who have drunk such alcohol proceed homeward, perhaps pushing a child in a buggy they put the child in a very vulnerable situation. **Section 2(1) Licensing Act 1902** as amended makes it an offence:

> *...If any person is found drunk in any highway or other public place, whether a building or not, or on any licensed premises, while having the charge of a child apparently under the age of seven years...*

There is a reverse burden of proof if there is any doubt as to the child's age. The accused must show that the child is over seven years to escape conviction.

In relation to other matters, **s.12 Licensing Act 1872** makes it an offence for:

> *Every person who is drunk while in charge on any highway or other public place of any carriage, horse, cattle, or steam engine, or who is drunk when in possession of any loaded firearms.*

The most likely application of this part of the section nowadays might be in relation to horseriding. It is most likely that the 'carriage', to use its general meaning, would be a bicycle. Other scenarios are encountered too infrequently or are sufficiently covered by other legislation and do not warrant further discussion here.

Drunk and disorderly

The **Criminal Justice Act 1967** makes it an offence at **s. 91(1)** for:

...Any person who in any public place is guilty, while drunk, of disorderly behaviour...

In contrast to the 'found drunk' provision, this is likely to be used when a person presents a danger to themselves and/or others. In practice many police forces exercise a great deal of discretion here also. Taking a pragmatic view, what is disorderly in the suburbs may be commonplace in a city centre on a Friday night.

It is also quite possible however, for the behaviour to contravene public order law irrespective of the fact that the person is drunk. That condition would not ordinarily afford any kind of defence (see Chapter 10).

REVISION

✓ Being found drunk – s. 12 Licensing Act 1872.

✓ Drunk in charge of other than a motor vehicle – s. 12 Licensing Act 1872.
   – of children – s. 2 licensing Act 1902.

✓ Drunk and disorderly – s. 91(1) Criminal Justice Act 1967.

Knowledge Check 1

1. PC Greenbaum is on foot patrol on the High Street, Grooby, Lechonshire, when he notices a male apparently intoxicated and smelling strongly of liquor repeatedly hitting his head on a lamp post. Greenbaum may:

    (a) Use his discretion and not act.

    (b) Arrest the man for being drunk and disorderly.

    (c) Issue an FPN for being found drunk.

    (d) Issue an FPN for a public order offence.

2. The male transpires to be 16. Greenbaum notices that he is carrying drink in a plastic bag bearing the name of the off licence down the street. Greenbaum may:

    (a) Use his discretion and warn the shop owner against selling to underage customers.

    (b) Issue an FPN for selling drink to someone under 18.

    (c) Arrest the shopkeeper for selling to someone under 18.

    (d) Arrest the 16-year-old for buying drink when under 18 years of age.

3. The organisation granting the licence to the shop in question would be the:

   (a) Magistrates under the Licensing Act 1964

   (b) Magistrates under the Licensing Act 2003

   (c) District Council under the Licensing Act 2003

   (d) District Council under the Licensing Act 1964.

The answers are at the end of the chapter.

Suggested research

Go to the BBC news website at: **http://news.bbc.co.uk** Follow the links or search for the news item 'Alcohol health warnings by 2008'. There is a proposal for drinks to carry voluntary warnings like those that are mandatory on cigarette packets under a code to be agreed between the government and the drinks industry. Carry out some informal primary research amongst friends, family and colleagues to see whether it is believed this idea may have any effect at all on people's drinking habits.

Further reading

More detailed coverage of the topics found in this chapter can be obtained by reading:

Card, R, Cross, R and Jones, P (2005) *Criminal law*. London: Butterworths.

English, J and Card, R (2005) *Police law* (9th edn). Oxford: Oxford University Press.

Sampson, F (2007) *Blackstone's police manual, Volume 4 – General police duties* (9th edn). Oxford: Oxford University Press.

Useful websites

Go to the local district, borough, city or county council website, follow the links to sections on applying for a liquor licence.

Legislation:

www.opsi.gov.uk

Case law and legislation databases:

www.westlaw.com* (an educational case law and statute database)

www.lexis-nexis.com* (an educational case law and statute database)

www.pnld.co.uk* (a police service specific database of case law and statute)

* Likely to be available through the virtual learning environment (VLE) which supports your course/training.

Answers

Knowledge Check 1

1. (b) Arrest the man for being drunk and disorderly.

    NB The man is too much of a danger to himself to proceed by any other way listed above.

2. (b) Issue an FPN for selling drink to someone under 18.

    NB This would of course depend on the result of Greenbaum's further investigations but would be more appropriate than an arrest in the circumstances. The 16-year-old is already under arrest.

3. (c) District Council under the **Licensing Act 2003**.

19 Roads policing

Underpinning knowledge towards Patrol Officer NOS:

2C1, 2C3, 2G2, 2G4, 2H1, 2H2, 2J1, 2J2, 2K2, 4C1, 4G2

and PCSO NOS:

2C1, 2C3, 1E5, 2C5, 2J1, 2J2, 4C1, 4G2

For further information on these NOS, which are also Policing Level 3 and 4 NVQ unit titles, refer to Appendix 1 to this volume.

It would be very difficult in a volume of this nature to cover all motor vehicle and driving law. The aim must be to equip the student officer with as much roads policing law as is needed for general patrol duties. Should a more complex area of traffic law present itself it may be prudent to call on the assistance of the traffic department of your force. For example, heavy goods vehicle (HGV) and passenger service vehicle (PSV) offences are only dealt with in passing here. Motorway offences and those which would normally require the assistance of a vehicle examiner to investigate, such as defective brakes or petrol tank maintenance, are also not examined in any depth.

In this chapter we are going to take a thematic approach. This means we are going to attempt to set out police action in a number of common situations and analyse the law which underpins that. The situations we are going to present are:

- a vehicle sighted in an apparently dangerous condition;

- a report of a motorcycle rider apparently unfit to drive;

- a road traffic collision.

A vehicle sighted in an apparently dangerous condition

By the end of this section you will be able to:

- describe the most important general road traffic and construction and use legislation;

- define some important terms and analyse how best to apply this information in a roads policing situation;

- apply what you know to some multiple-choice questions.

EXAMPLE

You notice a saloon car turn into a crescent as the driver sees you. You station yourself at the other end of the crescent and as the car approaches you notice that the female driver is not wearing a seatbelt. The car comes to a stop of the driver's own volition. On inspection of the vehicle you find that:

- *the seatbelt has been removed from the driver's side to facilitate the partially complete job of fitting a rally style seat;*

- *the vehicle's windscreen washers do not work due to another incomplete repair job;*

- *one of the tyres is bald;*

- *the vehicle is towing an open trailer with a load of fence panels which are not tied down in any way;*

- *there is a five-year-old child in the rear of the vehicle sitting on the car's rear seat.*

On completion of your investigation the driver, perhaps in frustration, gives four prolonged blasts on the car horn while the vehicle is at the kerbside and stationary.

Most 'construction and use' offences and indeed most road traffic offences generally are strict liability for policy reasons (see Chapter 1). There is therefore no need to show *mens rea* unless indicated in this chapter. The starting point for your investigation would be **s. 40A Road Traffic Act 1988** which renders unlawful the use of a motor vehicle on a road which is in a dangerous condition:

A person is guilty of an offence if he uses, or causes or permits another to use, a motor vehicle or trailer on a road when

(a) the condition of the motor vehicle or trailer, or of its accessories or equipment, or

(b) the purpose for which it is used, or

(c) the number of passengers carried by it, or the manner in which they are carried, or

(d) the weight, position or distribution of its load, or the manner in which it is secured, is such that the use of the motor vehicle or trailer involves a danger of injury to any person.

This, like most motor vehicle and driving offences is a summary one and you will be wishing to proceed by way of fixed penalty notice or summons. A Notice of Intended Prosecution (NIP) must be given when the following offences (per **Schedule 1 Road Traffic Act 1988**) are disclosed:

- dangerous, careless or inconsiderate driving/cycling or aiding and abetting the same;

- failing to conform to traffic signs or officer directing traffic;

- leaving a vehicle in a dangerous position;

- speeding.

The wording of this is:

You will be reported for the consideration of the question of prosecuting you for...

The offences here do not seem to fall within this list so no NIP need be given. A caution as per that used on arrest will ensure that any oral evidence that the driver gives will be admissible should they dispute matters later at court.

Before turning to the specific offences suspected it is necessary to deal with a few preliminary matters.

Having taken all regard for the safety of everyone concerned, the investigation should first establish who the owner of the vehicle is as some offences can only be committed by that person. The owner may not be the driver but they could have knowledge or be wilfully blind as to the dangerous condition of the vehicle. An employer could even order it to be used by the driver despite its condition. If this is so or the owner could have prevented it to be so used, they may be guilty of 'causing or permitting' the **s. 40A** offence above. For most practical purposes, the owner is the person who keeps the vehicle, irrespective of any hire purchase ownership issue or the like. It is possible to aid and abet a road traffic offence also under **s. 44(1) Magistrates' Courts Act 1980** (see Chapter 16). The word 'keeps' has a special definition as well. A person keeps a vehicle on a public road if they cause it to be there for any period when it is not in use.

ACTIVITY

Visit the Driver and Vehicle Licensing Agency website at **www.dvla.gov.uk** There is a mine of information there about driving and vehicle regulations. If you have a car or a member of your family or a colleague has one, look at the DVLA form V5 (also known as a log book), examine the wording and notes to familiarise yourself with this 'ownership' document.

The driver should be required to produce their documents if they do not have them with them. They will need to produce their driving licence, MOT certificate and insurance certificate at a nominated police station within seven days. A form 'Home Office Road Traffic 1' (HORT/1) should be used for this purpose. It is usually possible for the control room to be contacted by radio and a check made on the insurance database to establish the existence of a relevant policy of insurance. Under **s. 165(1) Road Traffic Act 1988** gives the relevant powers.

(a) *a person driving a motor vehicle (other than an invalid carriage) on a road, or*

(b) *a person whom a constable or vehicle examiner has reasonable cause to believe to have been the driver of a motor vehicle (other than an invalid carriage) at a time when an accident occurred owing to its presence on a road or other public place, or*

(c) *a person whom a constable or vehicle examiner has reasonable cause to believe to have committed an offence in relation to the use on a road of a motor vehicle (other than an invalid carriage), must, on being so required by a constable or vehicle examiner, give his name and address and the name and address of the owner of the vehicle and produce...*

an insurance or MOT certificate.

As stated in **s. 143(1) Road Traffic Act 1988**, there must be insurance in force:

(a) *a person must not use a motor vehicle on a road or other public place unless there is in force in relation to the use of the vehicle by that person such a policy of insurance or such a security in respect of third party risks as complies with the requirements of this Part of this Act.*

Some organisations have too many vehicles to insure economically so they are permitted to keep a sum of money as security against claims instead. Examples of this scheme include the Metropolitan Police and Armed Forces. It is also an offence to cause or permit a person to use a vehicle without cover of insurance or security.

Section 164(1) Road Traffic Act 1988 requires a person to produce their driving licence if they are a driver or supervisor of a learner in certain circumstances:

(a) *a person driving a motor vehicle on a road,*

(b) *a person whom a constable or vehicle examiner has reasonable cause to believe to have been the driver of a motor vehicle at a time when an accident occurred owing to its presence on a road,*

(c) *a person whom a constable or vehicle examiner has reasonable cause to believe to have committed an offence in relation to the use of a motor vehicle on a road, or*

(d) *a person*

(i) *who supervises the holder of a provisional licence while the holder is driving a motor vehicle on a road, or*

(ii) *whom a constable or vehicle examiner has reasonable cause to believe was supervising the holder of a provisional licence while driving, at a time when an accident [or offence] occurred...*

must produce their licence on demand.

The law uses different terms in different legislation. The main terms used are:

• motor car;

• mechanically propelled vehicle;

• motor vehicle.

A motor car is a mechanically propelled vehicle other than a motorcycle or an invalid carriage which is constructed to carry a load or (usually a maximum of seven) passengers and which is below 3,050 kg or 3,500 kg for LPG-powered vehicles, maximum 2,540 kg in all other cases. The maximum gross weight (MGW) is a vehicle's maximum weight plus maximum weight that it is allowed to carry or pull. The unladen weight includes the weight of the body of the vehicle excluding water, fuel and batteries used in electrically powered vehicles to supply propulsion power such as an electric milk float (but not batteries which supply power to lights, etc.) and loose tools/equipment. The manufacturer usually sets these figures.

A mechanically propelled vehicle is a vehicle driven by any kind of engine. By **s. 185 Road Traffic Act 1988** a motor vehicle is a mechanically propelled vehicle intended or adapted for use on roads. There are a number of cases where this definition has lead to disputes before the courts.

If there is any doubt it will be necessary to prove that a vehicle was 'intended or adapted' for use on roads. The general appearance of the vehicle will be a factor but not conclusive. In **Chief Constable of Avon and Somerset Police v Flemming (1987)** a motor cycle had been adapted for 'scrambling' on private land by the accused who was wheeling it along a road. Its registration plate, lights reflectors, and speedometer were missing. Flemming did not have a helmet as prescribed by the **Motor Cycle (Protective Helmets) Regulations 1998**, licence or insurance. He escaped conviction because the vehicle was held not to be intended for use on a road.

The legislation also uses different terms for what is commonly referred to as a road:

• road;

• highway;

• public road;

• public place.

A road is defined in **s. 192 Road Traffic Act 1988** as any highway and any other road to which the public has access and includes bridges over which a road passes. A highway however, is nowadays defined by reference to **s. 328(1)** and **(2) Highways Act 1980** to be the:

> *...whole or a part of a highway other than a ferry or waterway ... Where a highway passes over a bridge or through a tunnel, that bridge or tunnel is to be taken for the purposes of this Act to be a part of the highway.*

The term 'highway' has long been held to be all roads, bridges, carriageways, cartways, horseways, bridleways, footways, causeways, churchways, and pavements.

A public road is one repairable at public expense and a public place one to which the general public has access at the material time, whether by payment or otherwise.

ACTIVITY

Obtain an Ordnance Survey map of the area you are stationed in. Familiarise yourself with all the types of highways, roads and public spaces on it including bridleways and footpaths. You may find this research invaluable when you are on patrol and have to deal with motor vehicle offences.

REVISION
- ✓ A NIP is a Notice of Intended Prosecution.
- ✓ s. 40A RTA 1988 concerns dangerous vehicles.
- ✓ It is possible to cause, permit, aid and abet many of the construction and use offences.
- ✓ s. 143/165 RTA 1988 concerns insurance/production of insurance.
- ✓ Road, highway, public road, public place all have different definitions.

To turn now to the specific offences discovered in the example on page 280.

> *The seatbelt has been removed from the driver's side to facilitate the partially complete job of fitting a rally style seat.*

Under **Reg. 47 Road vehicle (Construction and Use) Regulations 1986** every vehicle first used after 1 April 1981 must have seatbelts for the drivers seat with three anchorage points, passenger seats must be fitted with an approved type as well. This applies to cars, light goods vehicles, small buses less than 3.5 tonnes unless with a design speed of 25 kilometres per hour or less. If one is fitted it must be worn.

Unless the vehicle here is over 16 years old a summary offence has been committed unless one of the seatbelt exemptions is applicable to the vehicle. The rules relating to children wearing seatbelts are linked to the issue of car seats and will be dealt with in relation to the five-year-old sitting in the rear later.

The seatbelt exemptions apply to:

- conducting a driving test if to wear one would be dangerous;
- Crown processions;
- delivery and collection persons, e.g. parcels;
- disabled person wearing an approved disabled person's belt;
- fire brigade – official purposes;
- inertia belt locked as vehicle on steep incline;
- medical exemption certificates (providing produced within seven days);
- police purposes;
- reversing including supervising learner reversing;
- taxi drivers plying for hire, answering call or with passengers (private hire drivers while carrying passengers for hire);
- trade-plate holder to investigate a fault.

Note that the commonly held belief that a pregnant woman does not need to wear a seat-belt has no substance. She would have to have a medical exemption certificate.

(?) *Many 'law-abiding' people have their first and often only encounters with police over road traffic matters. It is from these encounters that an impression of the police is often formed. In some cases a desire to help or hinder police germinates as a result of these meetings. Treat people who commit these road traffic infringements with courtesy and respect whilst applying the law with discretion and appropriateness. This is no matter how rude, irritated, ungrateful or untruthful they are to you. Your actions may make the difference later on between them deciding to come forward or not, having witnessed a serious matter. It is on this delicate police/public relationship that policing by consent depends.*

> **The vehicle's windscreen washers do not work due to another incomplete repair job.**

Reg. 34(1) Road Vehicle (Construction and Use) Regulations 1986 stipulates that windscreen wipers must be fitted and efficient. **34(6)** states that the wipers must be maintained adequately. The offence here is under **Reg. 34(2)** as the washers are fitted but are not capable of cleaning the window so that the driver can see adequately.

Exceptions to these offences are allowed for:

- agricultural vehicles:
  - used before 1 June 1986
  - driven at 20 mph or less;
- caterpillar-tracked vehicles such as diggers;
- vehicles where screen folds down;
- vehicles with maximum speed of 20 mph;
- vehicle providing a local service such as a bus.

None of these exemptions appears to apply, therefore an offence is disclosed.

> **One of the tyres is bald.**

The tyre is one of the most crucial parts of a vehicle as it is the only point of contact with the road, therefore a fault here seriously affects the ability of the driver to stop or steer and avoid a collision. The requirements for tyres are complex but this is unavoidable and they should be memorised. Pursuant to **Reg. 27 Road Vehicle (Construction and Use) Regulations 1986** a pneumatic tyre (one full of air) must:

- Be free from defect in a way which might cause damage to the road surface, persons in or on the vehicle or other road users.

- Be maintained in a condition fit for the use to which the vehicle or trailer is to be put.

- Be unsuitable with regard to the tyres fitted to the other wheels or to the vehicle's use. Usually this refers to the fact that in almost no circumstances can you put 'cross-ply' and 'radial' tyres on the same vehicle, the usual exception being temporary spares. The type should be written on the tyre in raised letters.

- Not be inflated so as to make it unfit for the use to which the vehicle is being put, i.e. flat or bulging with air.

- Not have a cut of more than 25 mm or 10 per cent of the width of the section of tyre (whichever is greater) and which is deep enough to reach the cord or ply (the material woven through the rubber for strength, usually a light colour and clearly visible if exposed).

- Not have a portion of the ply or cord exposed.

- Not have a separation or fracture of the tyres structure causing a lump, tear or bulge.

- Not have less than 1.6 mm depth of tread over the centre three-quarters of the tread breadth and around the entire circumference of the tyre if:

  - a passenger motor car adapted or constructed to carry eight or less seated passengers in addition to the driver;

  - a goods vehicle, or light trailer (with a maximum gross weight of 3,500 kgs or less).

- Other vehicles not pedestrian controlled must have a minimum of 1mm tread around the entire circumference over three-quarters of the tread breadth of the tyre and the remaining quarter to have a visible tread pattern at the base of the grooves.

- Unless a pedestrian-controlled vehicle (like a small road sweeper) have original tread pattern clearly visible at base of any groove, i.e. must not be smooth.

The temporary spare tyres referred to above are permitted on cars first used before 1 April 1987 constructed or adapted to carry up to eight passengers in addition to the driver. Vehicles which comply with European Community regulations on temporary spares may also use them. All such vehicles are restricted to a top speed of 50 mph and the correct tyre must be fitted as soon as possible. In practice you are unlikely to come across a vehicle that is using the temporary spare supplied with it but that is not the correct specification. If the spare belongs to another vehicle, further investigation might be warranted.

This is an ordinary family car so the offence is made out in relation to that one tyre unless one of the exemptions laid out below applies, i.e. with regard to:

- agricultural appliances and trailers;

- agricultural vehicles driven at or less than 20 mph;

- vehicles that are being towed by a motor vehicle at a speed not exceeding 20 mph and are broken down or going to a place to be scrapped.

None are exempt from the requirement that they be free from defect in a way which might cause damage to the road surface, persons in or on the vehicle or other road users. The last two exemptions are also not applicable to the requirement for 1.6 mm of tread.

No exemptions appear to apply to this vehicle so an offence can be prosecuted.

It is worth noting at this point that solid tyres, i.e. those not filled with air, may be fitted to some vehicles:

- locomotives;

- refuse disposal vehicles;

- street cleansing vehicles;

- tower wagons;

- tractors and certain other agricultural vehicles;

- vehicles:

  – fitted with a turntable fire escape;

  – first used before 1 January 1993;

  – mainly used for work on rough ground;

- works trucks.

It is quite possible to fit recut tyres, ones that have been worn down with use and have had the tread recut into them. This tends only to be possible with heavier vehicles with bigger tyres, however. Under **Reg. 27(5) Road Vehicle (Construction and Use) Regulations 1986** however, they may only be fitted to:

- Caravans with unladen weight exceeding 2,040 kg.

- Electrically propelled goods vehicles.

- Goods and dual purpose vehicles with unladen weight of 2,540 kg or more. With goods vehicles which are also cars, the diameter of the wheel rim must exceed 405 mm. This is related to the size of the vehicle generally as discussed in the paragraph above.

- Trailers:

  – with unladen weight exceeding 1,020 kg;

  – carrying plant and equipment with total weight exceeding 2,290 kgs

provided the cord is not exposed and the manufacturer's pattern is used.

Particular rules relate to HGV and PSV tyres. If your suspicions are aroused it may be advisable to call on the assistance of a traffic department officer.

> *The vehicle is towing an open trailer with a load of fence panels which are not tied down in any way.*

Trailers are defined by **s. 185(1) Road Traffic Act 1988** as a vehicle drawn by a motor vehicle. This definition does not normally, however, extend to another motor vehicle, such as one being towed by a towrope as it is broken down, etc.

Trailers are a particular source of confusion for the general public. For instance, it is not widely appreciated that if the driver passed his or her test after 1 January 1997 a separate test will need to be taken to enable the drawing of a trailer legally. Furthermore, the manufacturer in effect sets the weight of trailer that, say, a family car can lawfully pull. This information is in the handbook for the model of car concerned. It is quite surprising how low that figure is for most family saloons and even some smaller four-wheel-drive vehicles. It is always a good idea to check this information with the driver and advise them or proceed with prosecution as appropriate.

Reg. 100 Road Vehicle (Construction and Use) Regulations 1986 prohibits a person to use (or cause or permit it to be used) a motor vehicle or trailer for a purpose for which it was unsuitable so as to cause or be likely to cause danger or nuisance to persons. That is whether the persons are on the vehicle or trailer or are another road user. Furthermore, a load which was not secured by physical restraint other than its own weight or was in such a position that similar danger would be caused by it being blown or falling off would constitute an offence.

The trailer hitch should also be examined, as should the presence of a braking system. If there is any doubt on these matters the opinion of a member of the traffic department should be sought.

A relatively superficial examination should tell whether the load of fence panels in question was securely fastened or whether it might fall off. In many cases advice and a warning might be sufficient. Given the mounting number of offences this driver faces, that might not be appropriate here.

It is worth noting that relatively recently the law has changed with regard to motorcycles. These are now allowed to pull a trailer provided it is safe to do so. Trailers are now manufactured specifically for motorcycles.

> **There is a five-year-old child in the rear of the vehicle sitting on the car's rear seat.**

As from 18 September 2006, new regulations were introduced with regard to child restraints and booster seats. This child is not in a booster seat so the likelihood of an offence is quite high. The rules are:

- Up to 3 years of age

    - **Front seat** – a correct child restraint must be used at all times, i.e. a kite-marked booster seat.

    - **Rear seat** – a correct child restraint must be used but if one is not available in a taxi, travel unrestrained is lawful.

- Child from third birthday up to 135 cm in height (approx 4'5") (or 12th birthday, whichever they reach first)

    - **Front seat** – A correct child restraint must be used at all times, i.e. a kite-marked booster seat.

    - **Rear seat** – Where seatbelts fitted, correct child restraint must be used. They must use an adult belt if the correct child restraint is not available except:

        (I) for a short distance for reason of unexpected necessity; or

        (II) in a licensed taxi/private hire vehicle; or

(III) where two occupied child restraints prevent fitment of a third.

Unless seat belts are not available when travel in the rear seat is permissible.

- Child over 1.35 metres (approximately 4ft 5ins in height) or 12 or 13 years

  - **Front seat** – Seatbelt, if available must be worn.

  - **Rear seat** – Seatbelt, if available must be worn.

Note that the driver commits the offence in all cases above. An adult passenger without a seatbelt would commit the offence themselves however, not the driver.

Rear-facing baby seats must not be used in a seat protected by a functioning frontal air bag. There have been some horrific stories of babies being decapitated by the power of an inflating air bag.

On completion of your investigation the driver, perhaps in frustration, gives four prolonged blasts on the car horn while the vehicle is at the kerbside and stationary.

ACTIVITY

Obtain a copy of the *Highway Code*. Look up what it says about acceptable use of the horn generally. You may be aware that many people use their horn regularly for other purposes. What is the legal status of the *Highway Code*? Why are people not regularly prosecuted for breach of its provisions, including those on horns?

Reg. 37 Road Vehicle (Construction and Use) Regulations 1986 stipulate that a horn must be fitted. Horns which play a tune are prohibited unless they are part of an alarm system or announce goods are for sale, such as the familiar ice-cream van. **Reg. 99** lays down that an audible warning instrument must not be used when a vehicle is stationary except when in danger from another moving vehicle. Vehicles with approved reversing alarms are also exempt. The sounding of horns between 2330 hours and 0700 hours is also prohibited, even in motion on restricted roads, these are basically those with a speed limit of 30 mph. These often do not have a sign to that effect but are roads that have a system of streetlights no more than 182–88 metres apart and has been designated as restricted.

The use of a horn by this motorist is clearly unlawful but possibly warning and advice may suffice given the situation.

REVISION
✓ Construction and use:
  - Reg. 27 tyres
  - Reg. 34 washer/wiper
  - Reg. 37/99 horn
  - Reg. 47 seatbelts
  - Reg. 100 improper use of trailer.
✓ s. 185 RTA 1988 – definition of trailer.

Knowledge Check 1

1. A highway would include:

    (a) A railway bridge.

    (b) A bridle path.

    (c) A doctor's surgery car park.

    (d) A private driveway.

2. Rear-facing baby seats must:

    (a) Always be used in the front seat.

    (b) Never be used in the front seat.

    (c) Never be used in the front seat if there is a functioning airbag anywhere in the vehicle.

    (d) Never be used in the front seat if there is a functioning airbag on the front passenger side.

3. A trailer is defined by:

    (a) s. 185(1) Road Traffic Act 1988 as a vehicle drawn by a motor vehicle.

    (b) s. 158(1) Road Traffic Act 1988 as a vehicle drawn by a motor vehicle.

    (c) s. 185(1) Road Traffic Act 1988 as a vehicle drawn by any other vehicle.

    (d) s. 1 Road Traffic Act 1988 as any vehicle with a tow hitch.

The answers are at the end of the chapter.

A report of a motorcycle rider apparently unfit to drive

By the end of this section you will be able to:

- describe the most important legislation relating to drink drive and motorcycles;

- apply this information to a traffic stop;

- apply what you know to some multiple-choice questions.

EXAMPLE

You are on mobile patrol when you receive a report of a motorcyclist having consumed a large amount of alcohol and then driven off. You spot the vehicle and follow it. You note that it has a very loud exhaust and is creating a great deal of exhaust smoke. You signal for the motorcycle to stop, which it does.

The power to stop a motor vehicle or pedal cycle on a road comes from **s.163 Road Traffic Act 1988** provided, for safety reasons, the constable is in uniform. There is no random power to stop for breath testing, so the stop here is owing to information received or for a traffic offence committed whilst the vehicle is in motion. Under **s. 6(1) Road Traffic Act 1988** a constable in uniform can require a specimen of breath from a person who there are reasonable grounds to suspect is or has been:

- driving;

- attempting to drive;

- in charge of;

a motor vehicle on a road or other public place:

- with alcohol in his body;

- or has committed a traffic offence while the vehicle is in motion.

There are additional powers for a constable to require a breath test under **s. 6(2)** if an accident occurs owing to the presence of a motor vehicle on a road or other place. The test is required of a person where there are reasonable grounds to suspect they are or have been:

- driving;

- attempting to drive;

- in charge of;

the motor vehicle on a road or other public place at the time of the accident.

There are special procedures for the taking of samples other than breath which the custody officer will direct. Samples can be obtained at a hospital following an accident but special procedures apply here too and there is no power to arrest a hospital patient for drink-driving.

The priority will be to determine whether or not a drink/drive offence has occurred. The offences are driving or being in charge with excess alcohol contrary to **s. 5(1) Road Traffic Act 1988** if a person:

(a) *drives or attempts to drive a motor vehicle on a road or other public place, or*

(b) *is in charge of a motor vehicle on a road or other public place, after consuming so much alcohol that the proportion of it in his breath, blood or urine exceeds the prescribed limit he is guilty of an offence.*

In terms of the 'in charge' offence by **s. 5(1)(b)** it is a defence for a person to prove that at the time he is alleged to have committed the offence the circumstances were such that there was no likelihood of his driving the vehicle. This is another reverse burden of proof but would be satisfied by, for example, proving that someone else had all the keys to the vehicle.

The evidence for this offence would normally be from the lower of two intoximeter readings at the police station. The reasonable grounds for arrest come from the roadside breath test which, in this scenario, should be administered to the motorcyclist. If he fails it he can be arrested immediately under **s. 6**.

Should the motorcyclist pass the roadside test but still seem unfit to drive it may be that he is intoxicated through drugs. In the absence of a consistent national roadside test for drugs the officer's subjective opinion will effectively be enough for an arrest but all the evidence, such as the appearance of glazed eyes or unsteadiness, will need to be documented. The remaining offence (which could be also used for suspected drunk driving if no roadside test machine is available) is driving whilst unfit through drink or drugs contrary to **s. 4(1) Road Traffic Act 1988:**

> *A person who, when driving or attempting to drive a mechanically propelled vehicle on a road or other public place, is unfit to drive through drink or drugs is guilty of an offence.*

and may be arrested under that section.

Again there is a similar statutory defence as that in **s. 5**. A person shall be deemed not to have been in charge of a mechanically propelled vehicle if he proves that at the material time the circumstances were such that there was no likelihood of his driving it so long as he remained unfit to drive through drink or drugs.

Under **s. 5(5)** a person shall be taken to be unfit to drive if his ability to drive properly is for the time being impaired.

Should the motorcyclist refuse to be tested he may be arrested under **s. 6**. Should he make off and enter say a dwelling, there is a power of entry, as long as the constable reasonably expects them to be there, to arrest for a suspected **s. 4** offence.

A person who is driving whilst disqualified by a ban arising from a **s. 4** or **s. 5** conviction or indeed by virtue of say being too young, can be arrested.

It may be that you come across someone in the general vicinity of a car that you suspect they have been driving. There was an interesting human rights case in Scotland around just this scenario. The legislation required the person to admit whether or not they had been driving. In Scotland at least the judges ruled that such was contrary to the general presumption that the prosecution must prove its case. A comparable decision has not been made in the English courts, however.

In any event certain procedures are common to the preceding scenario around a dangerous vehicle. The motorcyclist can be required to produce his or her documents. Motorcycles in common with most motor vehicles must display a valid vehicle excise licence or 'tax disc'. Some motorcyclists do not fulfil this requirement for fear of the disc being stolen as it is harder to affix securely to a bike. That is no defence and if one is not present a witness statement in the prescribed form (currently a DVLA CLE2/6 form) can be submitted to DVLA for them to initiate any prosecution.

The further offences, which may need investigation, are the smoke and noise from the bike. It would also be prudent to check that the rider is qualified to ride the type of bike that is being ridden.

Reg. 61 Road Vehicle (Construction and Use) Regulations 1986 provide that it is unlawful for any smoke, visible vapour, grit, sparks or oily substance to emit from a motor vehicle exhaust on a road. Discretion might be appropriate in relation to minor smoking but large volumes can obscure the view for other drivers and should be acted upon.

Reg. 54 Road Vehicle (Construction and Use) Regulations 1986 require that every vehicle powered by an internal combustion engine must be fitted with an exhaust system including a silencer through which all the gases must pass. The exhaust system and silencer must be maintained in good and efficient working order and must not be altered to increase the noise.

Particularly young drivers and riders are sometimes tempted to add 'after-market' exhaust systems to make the vehicle sound more powerful. Whether or not this motorcyclist has done this or whether the noise is the result of poor maintenance, an offence would appear to have been committed.

The type of bike will be very important. By virtue of **s. 97(5) Road Traffic Act 1988** a learner rider may not ride a machine over 125cc capacity and limited to 11kW of power, known as 'restricted' machines. He must display an 'L' plate at the rear of the bike. The rider must be 21 before he can ride anything larger irrespective of whether he has a full licence and has passed a motorcycle test. If he has done so he may carry a pillion, however. In general a motorcycle is defined by **s. 185(1) Road Traffic Act** as a mechanically propelled vehicle other than an invalid carriage with three or fewer wheels and an unladen weight of no more than 410kg. Note that the protective headgear requirements do not apply to trikes but would apply to a motorcycle with a sidecar.

A moped no longer need have pedals at all. It is a motorcycle designed to go no faster than 30mph and weighing up to and including 250kg with an engine size of 50cc. If used first prior to 1 August 1977 the requirements are that the engine does not exceed 50cc and pedals be fitted.

In summary the engine size being 50cc is not sufficient for the law to deem the vehicle a moped. This is a source of some confusion amongst the general public. A rider aged 16 may only ride a moped. All motorcycle and moped learners must have passed a basic one-day course or 'CBT' before going on a public road for the first time.

REVISION

✓ Road Traffic Act 1988:
  – s. 4 Unfit through drink or drugs
  – s. 5 Excess alcohol
  – s. 6 Power to require breath test/arrest on failure or refusal
  – s. 97 Learner bike requirements
  – s. 163 Power to stop motor vehicle and pedal cycles
  – s. 185 Definition of motorcycle.
✓ Construction and use:
  – Reg. 61 exhaust smoke
  – Reg. 54 silencers.

A road traffic collision

By the end of this section you will be able to:

- define a road accident and identify a range of driver offences;

- describe the requirements for reporting of accidents;

- apply what you know to some multiple-choice questions.

EXAMPLE

You attend a reported road traffic collision. It appears that three vehicles were involved. It is 10pm and dark. Vehicle 1 is parked with its right-hand side against the kerb. Vehicle 2 has moved out to avoid it but his lights are not lit. Vehicle 3 has ignored a 'no entry' sign and, travelling very fast, has turned into the street colliding with vehicle 2. Vehicle 1 is unoccupied. The driver of vehicle 3 is injured and requires hospital treatment. A dog travelling in vehicle 2 is injured and has to be destroyed by a vet.

A road accident has its own definition in law as a term. By **s. 170(1) Road Traffic Act 1988** as amended it:

...applies in a case where, owing to the presence of a mechanically propelled vehicle on a road or other public place, an accident occurs by which

> (a) *personal injury is caused to a person other than the driver of that mechanically propelled vehicle, or*

> (b) *damage is caused*

>> (i) *to a vehicle other than that mechanically propelled vehicle or a trailer drawn by that mechanically propelled vehicle, or*

>> (ii) *to an animal other than an animal in or on that mechanically propelled vehicle or a trailer drawn by that mechanically propelled vehicle, or*

>> (iii) *to any other property constructed on, fixed to, growing in or otherwise forming part of the land on which the road or place in question is situated or land adjacent to such land.*

In general there are certain requirements placed on drivers involved in a road accident where the police are not called. It is worth exploring these first. In accidents where there are no injuries and the only damage is to the vehicles concerned and no offences have been alleged, there is no need for police involvement. The requirements are laid out in **s. 170 Road Traffic Act 1988**:

- Drivers involved must stop.

- Drivers must exchange personal details, owners' details and registration marks or give these details to anyone having reasonable grounds to request them. This is so that claims may be made as appropriate.

If there is an injury the driver must also produce a certificate of insurance to a constable or anyone with reasonable grounds to require production. In addition the person must report the accident to a constable or:

- must attend a police station and report the accident;

- as soon as reasonably practicable;

- in any case within 24 hours.

An offence of failing to stop and report an accident under this provision is arrestable subject to the amended **s. 24 PACE 1984**. This would in turn potentially give a power of entry under **s. 17 PACE 1984**.

A road accident involving damage to property would need to be reported. Property is anything:

- constructed on;

- fixed to;

- growing in;

- otherwise forming part of the land on which the road is situated, or the land adjacent to it.

Consequently an accident where a car veers off the road and is damaged by falling into a watercourse would not necessarily need to be reported. If the vehicle knocked over a lamp post or tree it should be reported, however.

An accident involving damage to a certain range of animals would also require a report. Interestingly this does not include cats despite the fact that they are routinely run over. The animals are:

- asses;

- cattle;

- dogs;

- goats;

- horses;

- mules;

- pigs;

- sheep.

The reasoning may be that these are the only common animals likely to attract a value.

It is clear from the above that the accident in the scenario will need to be reported as well as the relevant details exchanged between drivers and owners. We turn now to the offences apparent for each vehicle.

Vehicle 1

The potential offences in relation to this vehicle are relatively simple. **Reg. 101 Road Vehicle (Construction and Use) Regulations 1986** stipulates that, unless with the permission of a police officer, a vehicle must have its left-hand side as close as possible to the edge of the carriageway between sunrise and sunset. Emergency vehicles are exempt, as are taxis and buses at stops. The important exemption here is one-way streets. The 'no entry' sign mentioned at the end of the road suggests this is a one-way street. If that is the case no offence is committed.

The only other possibility is leaving the vehicle unattended with the engine running. It is an offence under **Reg. 107 Road Vehicle (Construction and Use) Regulations 1986** to leave or cause or permit to be left on a road a motor vehicle not attended by a person licensed to drive it unless the engine is stopped and parking brake set. There are the usual exemptions for emergency vehicles and vehicles used to supply power, etc., such as outside broadcast TV vans.

A quick check of the vehicle should determine if its engine is running or was recently, as the bonnet will be warm to the touch. An offence seems unlikely so it appears that the fault lies with either vehicle 2 or 3 or both.

Vehicle 2

Vehicle 2 appears to have performed a legal manoeuvre. Any offence will be in connection with the lack of functioning lights. **Reg. 25 Road Vehicle (Construction and Use) Regulations 1986** stipulates that a motor vehicle fitted with dipped beam headlights must keep them lit when driving in the hours of darkness or when visibility during the day is seriously reduced. Again the important exception is a restricted road (30 mph limit) with streetlights no more than 200 yards apart and illuminated. It is very likely that an urban one-way street is such a restricted road. Provided the streetlights are lit there may be no offence.

There is of course a multitude of regulations with respect to vehicle lighting that are too many to include here. The basic rule is that if a light is fitted to a vehicle it should work correctly. Further reading is suggested at the end of this chapter to assist more in depth research.

Vehicle 3

It is beginning to look as though vehicle 3 is the sole cause of the accident and may have committed several offences. Speeding and disobeying a traffic sign will be dealt with in a moment. The cumulative effect of the driver's actions may be said to be that danger was caused. **Section 1–3 Road Traffic Act 1988** stipulate:

S. 1: *A person who **causes the death** of another person by driving a mechanically propelled vehicle **dangerously** on a road or other public place is guilty of an offence.*

S. 2: *A person who drives a mechanically propelled vehicle **dangerously** on a road or other public place is guilty of an offence.*

S. 3: *If a person drives a mechanically propelled vehicle on a road or other public place without **due care and attention, or without reasonable consideration** for other persons using the road or place, he is guilty of an offence.*

The author's emphasis is added here for clarity but it is evident that as no human being has died (the death of the dog is in fact damage to property) the offence in **s.1** is not made out. If it were, arrest is highly likely subject to the amended **s. 24 PACE 1984**. The choice here is between dangerous driving and careless driving. It would appear that it would be easier to show dangerous driving in this situation as relatively serious injury and damage have resulted.

The vehicle may have been travelling at excess speed for a restricted road. The usual practice is for a trained officer to measure any tyre marks on the road and calculate the likely speed at the point of impact. The opinion evidence of two witnesses has been held to be sufficient in past cases where no other evidence that a driver has exceeded the speed limit exists. It is arguable that to rely on a court accepting this in the future may not be wise.

The prohibition on exceeding 30 mph in a restricted road is provided by **s. 81 Road Traffic Regulation Act 1984**. The offence of speeding, whether exceeding 30 mph in a restricted road or exceeding the speed limit on a road where a higher limit is specified by signs, is prosecuted under **s. 89**.

The driver also disobeyed a traffic sign. **Section 36 Road Traffic Act 1988** makes it an offence to disobey a traffic sign which indicates a statutory prohibition, restriction or requirement. This includes red traffic light. Note that there is no specific offence of contravening an amber traffic light but doing so will provide evidence of careless or dangerous driving. **Section 35** extends the s. 36 offence to disobeying a constable directing traffic.

Remember that these offences would require a NIP to be given (see page 281).

(?) *The prohibition on the use of mobile telephones whilst driving, even if the vehicle is stationary in traffic unless with the use of a 'hands free' kit, has received much publicity. Some police officers would like to see the use of even 'hands free' mobile phones banned because of the level of distraction they cause. Reflect on whether this is a good idea or not.*

The coverage of traffic legislation we can provide in a volume of this nature is limited. The aim of modern police training is to provide information but also signpost where more may be found through directed study. Through this approach we should have equipped you to tackle day-to-day traffic matters that arise whilst on general patrol. The further reading suggested at the end of the chapter will develop your knowledge as your career progresses.

REVISION

✓ All injury and damage to other than vehicles accidents must be reported within maximum 24 hours.
✓ Non-injury accidents drivers must exchange details.
✓ Construction and use:
  – Reg. 25 lights
  – Reg. 106 parking wrong way at night
  – Reg. 107 leaving unattended.
✓ s. 81 RTRA 1984 Speeding
✓ s. 1 RTA 1988 Death by dangerous driving
✓ s. 2 RTA 1988 Dangerous driving
✓ s. 3 RTA 1988 Careless driving

Knowledge Check 2

1. A learner may:

    (a) Ride any motorcycle provided he is displaying 'L' plates.

    (b) Ride any motorcycle of 250 cc and below provided he is displaying 'L' plates.

    (c) Ride any motorcycle of 250 cc and below.

    (d) None of the above.

2. Driving with excess alcohol is covered by:

    (a) s. 1 RTA 1988

    (b) s. 2 RTRA 1984

    (c) s. 5 RTA 1988

    (d) s. 4 RTA 1988.

3. Which accident would need to be reported to a constable or police station clerk?

    (a) One in which a cat was run over?

    (b) One in which a car clipped the kerb and overturned without injuring anyone?

    (c) One in which minor injury to a horse was sustained but the rider was unhurt?

    (d) One in which a traffic sign was ignored by either driver?

4. S. 1 RTA 1988 concerns:

    (a) Dangerous driving?

    (b) Drink driving?

    (c) Drunk in charge?

    (d) Death by dangerous driving?

The answers are at the end of the chapter.

Suggested research

The law on road traffic is constantly evolving. Often it responds to concerns by lobby groups. The Royal Society for the Prevention of Accidents is active in this area. Visit their website at **www.rospa.com/roadsafety** to find out more about ROSPA and what they are campaigning for.

Further reading

More detailed coverage of the driving offences such as death by dangerous driving can be obtained by reading:

Card, R, Cross, R and Jones, P (2005) *Criminal law*. London: Butterworths.

Heaton, R (2001) *Criminal law* (3rd edn). London: Butterworths.

In addition further information on the more technical aspects of roads policing law such as construction and use matters can be found in:

English, J and Card, R (2005) *Police law* (9th edn). Oxford: Oxford University Press.

Sampson, F (2007) *Blackstone's police manual, Volume 3 – Road policing* (9th edn). Oxford: Oxford University Press.

Useful websites

Crown Prosecution Service:

www.cps.org.uk

Driver and Vehicle Licensing Agency:

www.dvla.org.uk

Legislation:

www.opsi.gov.uk

Case law and legislation databases:

www.westlaw.com* (an educational case law and statute database)

www.lexis-nexis.com* (an educational case law and statute database)

www.pnld.co.uk* (a police service specific database of case law and statute)

* Likely to be available through the virtual learning environment (VLE) which supports your course/training.

Answers

Knowledge Check 1

1. (b) A bridle path.

2. (d) Never be used in the front seat if there is a functioning airbag on the front passenger side.

3. (a) **s. 185(1) Road Traffic Act 1988** as a vehicle drawn by a motor vehicle.

Knowledge Check 2

1. (d) None of the above.

   NB A learner may ride a restricted machine of no more than 125cc and displaying 'L' plates.

2. (c) **s. 5 RTA 1988**

3. (c) One in which minor injury to a horse was sustained but the rider was unhurt.

4. (d) Death by dangerous driving.

20 An understanding of civil law

(?) *Remember this symbol indicates that the material might be useful for your Student Officer Learning and Assessment Programme (SOLAP) portfolio or any attached reflective practice record you are required to make.*

Underpinning knowledge towards Patrol Officer NOS:

1A1, 1A2, 1A4, 1B9, 2C1, 2C3, 2C4, 2J1, 2J2, 4C1

and PCSO NOS:

1A1, 1A4, 1B11, 2C1, 2C3, 2C4, 2C5, 2J1, 2J2, 4C1

For further information on these NOS, which are also Policing Level 3 and 4 NVQ unit titles, refer to Appendix 1 to this volume.

The civil and criminal law: some differences

By the end of this section you will be able to:

- describe some fundamental differences between civil and criminal law;
- explain the purpose of civil law as distinct from criminal law;
- list the main subdivisions of civil jurisdiction.

The legal training of a police officer naturally is concerned almost exclusively with the criminal law. There are situations however, where a police officer will encounter civil law in the course of his duties. Some acts contain both civil and criminal remedies. The **Protection from Harassment Act 1997** is an example; arrests are possible under this Act but a civil injunction can also be sought.

You may also be called upon to assist in what is essentially a civil process. For example, the eviction of someone from their home may cause a breach of the peace which the police must use reasonable force to prevent. This chapter attempts to set out the basic framework of the civil law and highlight the areas that a patrol officer is likely to have to deal with.

The information in this chapter is provided so that you as a student officer can identify civil law when you see it. You should neither act under it nor give advice on it. Your remit is to ensure the criminal law is not breached even if you are assisting someone who is asserting his or her rights under the civil law. This could arise for example, if a parent were evicting their troublesome adolescent son from the home and sought your assistance. If a question of civil law is unresolved you should always advise the person concerned to consult a solicitor, Citizens Advice Bureau (CAB) or local volunteer law centre.

Civil law does not involve the state unless this happens to be one of the parties, such as a hospital, being sued for negligence. The system exists for individuals to be compensated for wrongs done to them. In some circumstances it is used to seek the protection of the courts. To do this an injunction is sought – a 'restraining order' is an American term for the same thing and should be avoided. An injunction tells the recipient not to do something, sometimes on pain of arrest and imprisonment. In a very few instances it compels someone to do something.

The parties are called the claimant (formerly called the plaintiff) and the defendant. The claimant sues the defendant, usually for a sum of money. The hearings take place most commonly in the local county court (small claims court in most cases for sums under £5,000) and failure to pay within 30 days results in a County Court Judgment (CCJ) being recorded against the loser. The losing party must pay both parties' legal costs also in cases involving a claim for more than £5,000. Very large numbers of civil claims are simple non-payment of bills such as credit cards or catalogue accounts, electricity or gas bills and the like. These cases take place in small claims courts. At the other extreme, complex and high-value claims are heard in the High Court. In neither case is a jury involved; a judge hears the case alone. The only exceptions to this are libel and slander cases (known together as defamation) and false imprisonment claims where a jury of eight people is still used.

It should be noted that the civil courts are not interested in punishment; the sole consideration is compensation in damages claims. This is not likely to reach the huge sums that are awarded in the USA. The reason is that in the US juries can be asked to award the figure of compensation whereas in the UK the judge uses predetermined figures in conjunction with recent case law to calculate a sum. That being said, many crimes have equivalents in the civil law. Assault, for example, is something an offender can be sued for and separately prosecuted for. A drink-driving charge arising from a road collision could result in a criminal penalty for the offender. It could also result in the other driver and passengers suing for their injuries sustained. This would happen separately in a civil trial.

The equivalence noted above has led to some high-profile instances of the victims using the civil courts as the next best thing when they are denied justice in the criminal courts. Lynn Siddons was murdered in Derby in April 1978, stabbed 43 times beside a canal. Lynn's grandmother took the killer of her granddaughter to civil court when prosecution of him failed to get underway. As a result of this civil action against Michael Brookes, the prosecution of him was reconsidered and he was eventually tried and convicted at Crown Court. The same principle exists in the USA and the actor and sports personality O.J. Simpson was acquitted of a grisly murder but subsequently successfully sued in a civil court for $25 million.

The criminal law is concerned with remedying wrongs but in that context the remedies are sentences (see Chapter 13). The damages (compensation) and injunctions already mentioned are the main remedies in civil law. There are other remedies but they need not concern us here.

The main subdivisions of civil law jurisdiction are:

- contract;

- tort;

- land law, equity and trusts;

- family;

- wills and probate.

You are unlikely to encounter wills and probate issues as a police officer but there is some discussion of the general principles under the section dealing with trusts below.

REVISION
- ✓ Civil law is for individuals to sue each other under, mostly for compensation.
- ✓ Civil law is not concerned with punishment, only recompense.
- ✓ The main areas of civil law are:
  - contract and tort
  - land law, equity and trusts
  - family, wills and probate.

Separate areas of civil jurisdiction

By the end of this section you will be able to:

- describe in very basic terms contract and tort, land law, equity and trusts family, wills and probate law;

- describe in very basic terms some common policing scenarios where civil law might be encountered;

- apply your knowledge to some short-answer questions.

Contract

This area of law is concerned with legally enforceable agreements. There are essentially five components that go to make up a legally binding contract. They are:

- offer;

- acceptance;

- 'consideration';

- intention to be legally bound;

- 'capacity'.

The best way to illustrate this is with an everyday example, buying a second-hand car from a friend or acquaintance. You arrive at the seller's address and he offers you the car. You look it over, test drive it then accept the offer. You give him consideration. This is a legal term which most commonly means money but could be anything of value; it could for example in this scenario be money and the buyer's old car in part-exchange. It could even be a promise to pay at a later date. It will be assumed, unless there is evidence to the contrary, that the parties intend to be legally bound by the agreement. Evidence to the contrary would be present, for example, if the sale was between mother and son. This might be seen as a domestic agreement and unenforceable. Finally, one of the parties could lack capacity if they were mentally ill or, most likely, if they were under 18. If all five components are present the car has been bought with a legally binding agreement.

This formula does not differ at all whether an apple is being bought on a market stall or a cruise liner is being built for a multinational shipping company. Only a very few contracts need to be in writing, most commonly those involving land and buildings. You could buy a £30,000 four-wheel-drive car with a verbal contract, for instance.

Most legal actions surround the breach of one of the parties' obligations. Either they do not deliver the goods or there is something wrong with them. Otherwise the buyer does not pay or at least not in full.

Employment disputes are essentially about breach of contract and so are many consumer law cases. There is a slight difference here though, as the law recognises one of the parties is weaker than the other one and there are statutes to protect that weaker party, that is the employee or consumer. It is for the parties to look after their own interests in most contract situations though. There is a saying *caveat emptor* in Latin, 'let the buyer beware'.

It is worth considering the topic of 'distraint' here. This is the removal of goods to satisfy a debt. With the exception of debts arising from unpaid taxes most goods are distrained upon because of non-payment of a debt arising out of unpaid sums due under a contract. For example, a large credit card or catalogue bill. This is very old law and probably long overdue for statutory clarification. In essence though, a debt collector can call and ask for the money due without having any special legal status. If the debt collector wants to remove goods and sell them at auction to satisfy the debt however, he must be a certificated bailiff, that is someone sworn before a judge. The only exceptions to this are the officials, called recovery officers, who remove goods and sell them for unpaid Council Tax. There is special dispensation in the relevant legislation for them to act without being certificated.

A bailiff or recovery officer can only enter a domestic dwelling if he or she has been invited in. There must also be an court order and a 'warrant of execution' in the case of county court judgments. Having entered as an invitee once however, he or she has taken goods therein, other than restricted items like livestock or tools of the trade, into 'walking possession'. If the debt is not paid within a further period, usually seven days, the goods may be removed, forcibly if necessary, and auctioned. This process is known as 'levying distraint'. There is considerable anecdotal evidence and some case law on bailiffs and debt collectors overstepping these boundaries. If called to assist these officials in the execution of their duty, the function of the police is to ensure the criminal law is adhered to and no breach of the peace occurs. It should be borne in mind to check that the debt recovery officials are acting lawfully themselves however; if not they may be breaching the criminal law as well.

REVISION

✓ Contracts consist of:
  – offer and acceptance
  – 'consideration'
  – intention to be legally bound and capacity.
✓ Distraint is sometimes used to remove goods and sell them if contractual debts are unpaid.
✓ In most cases only certificated bailiffs may distrain.

Tort

This part of the legal system deals with wrongs committed that are not breaches of contract. Common examples include:

- negligence;

- trespass;

- false imprisonment;

- libel and slander.

Negligence is probably the most commonly litigated tort, especially as people become more aware that they can be compensated for the lack of care of others that causes them loss. This is sometimes referred to as the 'compensation culture' by the media and politicians. The basic components of this tort are:

- duty of care;

- breach of duty;

- foreseeable loss.

To illustrate how this works in practice let us again look at a common example, a car accident. Freddy Choo leaves home in his car having consumed enough alcohol to make his blood alcohol level twice the legal limit. He hits and injures a pedestrian, Jatinderpal Singh, who is crossing the road legally on a pedestrian crossing. Choo may well be prosecuted but Jatinderpal can take a personal injury action in the county court for the trauma of his injuries, the damage to his person and some of the consequential loss he may have suffered but not without limit. He would have to show that Freddy owed him a duty of care. That would not be difficult, as case law has established that all drivers of motor vehicles owe a duty of care to pedestrians. The next task would be to show that Freddy was in breach of that duty. Again that should not present a problem, as the test in these sorts of cases is whether the standard of a 'reasonable man' has been met. It is unlikely that a 'reasonable man' would run over a pedestrian on a zebra crossing. The reference to a man here is a legal convention. The term also refers to 'reasonable woman'.

The last issue is that the actual quantity of loss that the defendant could have foreseen must be calculated and, if not agreed, a judge will decide. This means that any lost earnings would be payable but not necessarily, for example, the potential loss if Jatinderpal was on his way to a job interview which could have resulted in a much better-paid position for him. There remains then for the legal costs to be paid by the losing party, in practice this will be Freddy's insurer. The fact that the loser pays the reasonable costs of a legal action is the reason why 'no-win-no-fee schemes' can work, there is rarely if ever legal aid granted for these types of actions.

The same basic process is followed from a simple 'whiplash' claim from a traffic accident through to a multi-million pound claim between businesses over, say, the negligent installation of computer equipment.

Libel and slander, however, are rarely litigated, as they require an individual to have a reputation to protect. Libel is a false statement made in permanent form, usually writing or image; slander is the spoken form of the tort. In essence, the statement must be such that it will make most 'right thinking' members of the public think less of the victim. Jonathan Aitken, a former cabinet minister, Lord Jeffery Archer, novelist and former politician, singer Elton John and actor William Roach ('Ken Barlow' in the long running soap opera *Coronation Street*) have all taken libel actions against newspapers. One of the requirements of the tort is that the statement must actually be false. Maintaining it is false in court when it is in fact true is of course the criminal offence of perjury, as Aitken and Archer found to their cost.

Trespass could easily be something a police officer is called to deal with. Despite the prevalence of signs which say 'trespassers will be prosecuted', in its traditional form trespass to land is not a criminal offence any more and has not been so for a very long time. Criminal trespass is, however, committed by a number of people together in specific circumstances and is dealt with in Chapter 10, 'Public order'.

In terms of civil trespass, the police are there to assist the landowner and to ensure that no breach of the peace has occurred only, they do not act on the trespass itself. These situations might vary from helping the Sherriff to remove treetop protestors along a proposed road route to enabling an employer to remove a sacked employee who refuses to leave the premises. In England and Wales, the Sherriff is the equivalent of a bailiff but works for the High Court instead of the local county court.

'Trespass to the person' is a legal phrase for assault when it is the subject of a civil action rather than a prosecution. It is quite possible to sue for compensation if this happens. The police can be the subject of an action of this type if they act unlawfully. Examples would include those discussed in Chapter 3 such as an arrest or stop and search carried out without authority under warrant or **PACE 1984**. If such a breach of **PACE** or the **Codes** leads to a period of detention which is unjustifiable at law this could lead to a civil action for false imprisonment. Such actions have been taken against private security staff such as nightclub doormen in the past where a person has not been allowed to leave a premises despite the security staff being unaware that they could not do so. Acts to prevent the potential exit of a person, if unjustified, could be enough for a damages claim.

An action in trespass to goods might be used to recover very valuable items from someone who has no right to keep them, possibly because they stole them or they were obtained by fraud.

REVISION

✓ The main torts are:
  - negligence
  - trespass and false imprisonment
  - libel and slander.
✓ Negligence requires:
  - duty
  - breach of duty
  - foreseeable loss.
✓ Trespass is not a criminal offence.

Land law, equity and trusts

This is a vast area of highly complex law and, fortunately, police officers only encounter it in a very limited number of ways. These are:

- landlord and tenant disputes;

- evictions for mortgage arrears;

- domestic disputes over matrimonial property.

Landlord and tenant

You may be called to assist if a landlord and his or her tenant are in dispute. The landlord may be a private individual or company or a social housing provider. Nowadays both the local authority and housing associations provide this service. There is very little that you can do other than ensure there is no breach of the peace or any criminal offence committed. It would be prudent to check that the landlord has a copy of a court order or other legal document to support what is being done. This is particularly the case if he or she is attempting to gain entry or carry out an eviction in contested circumstances. Normally bailiffs will be on hand to assist. They should be 'certificated' by a judge and should be able produce identification if requested.

This chapter is about civil law but it should be mentioned at this point that a landlord attempting to enter premises or act in breach of the terms of the lease without a court order could be in breach of the **Protection from Eviction Act 1977**. This criminal statute creates an 'either way' offence that is committed by a landlord if they unlawfully evict or harass a residential tenant or unreasonably withhold services necessary for the enjoyment of the property, such as cut off the electricity supply. See Chapter 3 for powers of arrest for either way offences.

Evictions for mortgage arrears

A mortgage is not in fact the loan. In law a mortgage is a right that the purchaser signs over to the loan company. This right is to take over ownership and possession of the property if the loan payments fall a specified number of months in arrears, very often three months.

The term 'repossession' is a misnomer as on taking possession this will be the first time the company has possessed the property. They will then sell it to clear the defaulter's debts. In practice many defaulting homeowners will have vacated the property before eviction date but you may be called to assist bailiffs who are carrying out an eviction where the house-holder is unwilling to go. Much of what we have said about assisting at landlord and tenant evictions is true here as well. It is advisable to check that the bailiffs hold a copy of a court order and that they are 'certificated'. A team carrying out an eviction would normally consist of a representative of the lender, one or two bailiffs and a locksmith to assist in entry and change the locks. It is not uncommon however, for defaulters to be allowed back into a property after this event, under supervision, to collect personal belongings.

(?) *The removal of someone from their home by force is probably one of the most trau-matic things that can happen, even if carried out legally. Imagine if this happened to you. Consider how your attitudes and behaviours might help to escalate or de-escalate the stress of the situation.*

Domestic disputes over matrimonial property

Police can be called to a matrimonial home or a home shared by unmarried cohabitees where the relationship has broken down and there is a dispute over ownership of goods in the home or the home itself. In the absence of specific evidence proving ownership of any item it is most likely that a legal trust is in operation. In a trust there have to be:

- trustees;

- beneficiaries;

- trust property.

A trust is simply where there is property that is legally owned by the trustees but the ben-eficiaries receive the benefit of it. An example is in a simple will. Imagine you have left your house in your will to your children and then you and your partner die when the chil-dren are each still in their early teens. The house becomes the legal property of whomever you have chosen as your trustees; it is just that we commonly call such people 'executors' in this context. The executors may not treat the house as their own however, they must look after it until your children are 18 and then pass it to them or sell it and pass the money to a trust fund on their behalf.

What many people do not realise is that when people buy a home together they become 'joint tenants'. The use of the term 'tenant' is confusing and a legal oddity, you should not think that we are in any way talking about a let property here. What the term 'joint tenants' means is that each person holds the property 'jointly and severally'. In other words, each person holds the property as legal owner but also on trust for the other as beneficiary.

'Traditional' joint and several ownership of a house in joint names

They are both right and this stops one from selling the property without the other's consent.

Where this kind of situation exists, each does not own a discernible portion of the property. They each own all of it for the other's benefit. There are occasions when, after legal advice and often for tax or other financial reasons, couples choose to own their property as 'tenants in common'. Again ignore the use of the word 'tenant' here. In this situation, each party does own a distinct proportion of the value of the property.

This information is not provided so that you can advise the parties in any way should you be called to a dispute. It is merely that you should be able recognise the civil nature of the dispute and urge the parties to seek independent legal advice.

Issues of ownership can impact on the criminal law. If an allegation of criminal damage or theft is made, you would need to ascertain quite carefully that the property in question did in fact belong to someone other than the person damaging it or appropriating it. See Chapter 9 for further information on the **Theft Acts** and **Criminal Damage Act 1971**.

By way of completeness it should be noted that 'equity' is simply the name for a body of rules that have grown up outside the law but are nevertheless enforceable by the courts. These rules have perhaps the greatest application to land and property law, which is outside the scope of this volume.

REVISION
- ✓ Unlawful eviction of a residential tenant can be a criminal offence.
- ✓ Eviction requires a court order.
- ✓ Joint owners of a property each own all of it for the other's benefit. These are 'joint tenants'. 'Tenants in common' own a distinct proportion of the value of the property.

Family law

Family law concerns matters such as marriage, divorce, adoption and the residence of children or contact arrangements where the parents do not live together.

(?) *Disputes in this area can generate a great deal of emotion. When called to a dispute it is very important to ascertain who has the legal rights. Above all however, consider the needs, even the emotional ones, of the most vulnerable people present.*

One likely scenario is where there is a dispute over seeing the children after a relationship split. For instance, if a man calls police because his ex-partner has not returned the children after a weekend contact visit it will be necessary to ascertain if there was a formal court order spelling out contact arrangements or whether the arrangement is an informal one. If the latter is true, once police have ascertained that the children are safe and well, only advice to the parties to seek independent legal advice can be given. If there is a court order, and the mother is in breach of it, the children can legally be returned to the father. Great care should be exercised in this area because the welfare of the children is paramount, both emotional as well as physical. It will be extremely rare that the police will forcibly remove children in these circumstances and advice from a supervisor should always be sought.

It is worth noting here that the courts rarely if ever have any input into maintenance arrangements. The Child Support Agency or its successor organisation deals with these payments. Both are government agencies independent of the courts. You will be unable to get involved in disputes in these matters and, as always, the parties should be urged to seek legal advice.

Where there has been violence between parties, police may not be able to bring a case for a variety of reasons. In these circumstances or even if charges are brought, the injured party can seek an injunction against the aggressor. These are civil orders but often carry penalties of arrest and imprisonment for breach. These injunctions fall into two categories:

- occupation orders;

- non-molestation orders.

Occupation orders would normally be used when one party wants the other to leave the home they share. A common example might be where a battered spouse seeks the removal of the aggressor but wants to remain in the home as carer for the couple's children. An occupation order would be granted under **s. 33** to **s. 40 Family Law Act 1996** as amended by **Domestic Violence, Crime and Victims Act 2004**.

In this situation a non-molestation order would be used to keep the aggressor from revisiting the premises especially if the remaining spouse felt under threat of further violence. A non-molestation order would be granted under **s. 42** of the above Act as amended.

REVISION

✓ Family law is mainly concerned with:
  - marriage, divorce and civil partnership
  - adoption
  - the residence of children or contact arrangements.
✓ Occupation orders are used to eject a violent partner from the home.
✓ Non-molestation orders are used to prevent the violent partner from returning.

It is only possible to give a flavour of the civil law in this chapter but further reading is available at the end of the chapter on each of the main areas of law discussed.

Knowledge Check 1

1. What type of order is used to remove someone from an address because they have been violent to someone who lives there?

2. What is the law of 'distraint?

3. What is peculiar to land and real property bought in joint names in terms of ownership?

4. PC Davidson is called to an address. Two men have been seen removing another from the address by force. Davidson arrives on scene to see the three men scuffling in the front garden. Davidson is about to intervene when she notices a printed page taped to the window to the effect that the property has been taken into the possession of the Northshire Building Society. How should Davidson proceed?

The answers are at the end of the chapter.

Suggested research

Criminologists and legal scholars have noted for some time how more law is being enacted which is civil rather than criminal in nature, but is concerned with the maintenance of social order. Anti-social behaviour orders, dealt with elsewhere in this volume, are examples, the civil aspects of the Prevention of Harassment Act 1997, another. Consider the burdens of proof discussed in Chapter 14, 'Evidence' and the age of criminal responsibility encountered in Chapter 1, 'Legal concepts'. Consider why the civil law is being used in this way and whether it is desirable. You could look at: Hale, C, Hayward, K, Wahidin, A and Wincup, E (2005) *Criminology*. Oxford: Oxford University Press. Also the companion website at **www.oup.com/uk/booksites/content/0199270368/student**

Further reading

A general introduction to the legal system and its civil component might be found at:

Kelly, D and Slapper, G (2006) *The English legal system* (8th edn). London, Cavendish, especially Chapters 1, 3 and 7.

Specific basic reading on tort and contract law:

Elliott, C and Quinn, F (2005) *Tort law* (5th edn). Harlow: Pearson.

Elliott, C and Quinn, F (2005) *Contract law* (5th edn). Harlow: Pearson.

An introduction to some issues in family law:

Herring, J (2004) *Family law* (2nd edn). Harlow: Longman.

A basic guide to landlord and tenant issues could be found in:

Cole, G, Luxton, P, Morgan J and Wilkie, M (2006) *Landlord and tenant law*. Basingstoke: Palgrave Macmillian.

Useful websites

www.westlaw.com* (a legal database)

www.lexis-nexis.com* (a legal database)

www.pnld.co.uk* (a police service specific database of case law and statute)

* Likely to be available through the virtual learning environment (VLE) which supports your course/training.

Answers

Knowledge Check 1

1. An occupation order granted under **s. 33** to **s. 40 Family Law Act 1996**.

2. Distraint is the process by which a bailiff may take possession of goods to satisfy a debt owed. The operation can only take place if a court order exists and a 'warrant of execution' has been issued in the case of county court debts.

3. Both parties normally own land and buildings bought in joint names jointly and severally. This means that both own the property and act as reciprocal trustees for each other. It is possible for joint owners to rebut the presumption of being joint and several owners by electing to be 'tenants in common'. In this situation they own a distinct portion of the value of the property.

4. Davidson has potentially arrived at the scene of an eviction and should investigate this before making the assumption that a criminal act is taking place. She should attempt to speak to the man who was the householder if possible and warn him that further violence could result in arrest. When the situation is calm she should check that the two men who appear to have been trying to remove the third from the house are certificated bailiffs. She should also check that there is a court order in existence giving the company they are acting for the right to enter and take possession of the property. She should satisfy herself that the bailiffs have used reasonable force and no more in the execution of their function. If the previous occupier continues to resist the bailiffs, Davidson should consider arrest for breach of the peace or an appropriate assault or public order offence depending on the severity of his actions. She should bear in mind the relevant restrictions in **s. 24 PACE 1984** as amended by **s. 110 Serious Organised Crime and Police Act 2005**, however (see Chapter 3).

Appendix 1 National Occupational Standards (NOS)

A) Required for the Police Constable (Patrol Officer)

1A1	Use police actions in a fair and justified way
1A2	Communicate effectively with all members of the public and its communities
1A4	Foster people's equality, diversity and rights
1B9	Provide initial support to individuals affected by offending or anti-social behaviour and assess their needs for further support
2A1	Gather and submit information that has the potential to support policing objectives
2C1	Provide an initial response to incidents
2C2	Prepare for, and participate in, planned policing operations
2C3	Arrest, detain or report individuals
2C4	Minimise and deal with aggressive and abusive behaviour
2G2	Conduct investigations
2G4	Finalise investigations
2H1	Interview victims and witnesses
2H2	Interview suspects
2I1	Search individuals

2I2	Search vehicles, premises and land
2J1	Prepare and submit case files
2J2	Present evidence in court and at other hearings
2K1	Escort detained persons
2K2	Present detained persons to custody
4C1	Develop one's own knowledge and practice
4G2	Ensure your own actions reduce risks to health and safety
4G4	Administer First Aid

Note: These NOS also form the NVQ in Policing Level 3 and Level 4. For fuller details of the content of each unit you could visit these websites by an NVQ awarding body such as OCR: **www.ocr.org.uk/qualifications/OCRNVQLevel3inPolicing.html** and **www.ocr.org.uk/ qualifications/OCRNVQLevel4inPolicing.html**

B) Required for the Police Community Support Officer

1A1	Use police actions in a fair and justified way
1A4	Foster people's equality, diversity and rights
1B11	Contribute to resolving community issues
2A1	Gather and submit information that has the potential to support policing objectives
2C1	Provide an initial response to incidents
2C2	Prepare for, and participate in, planned policing operations
2C3	Arrest, detain or report individuals
2C4	Minimise and deal with aggressive and abusive behaviour
1E5	Contribute to road safety
2C5	Contribute to providing an initial response to incidents
SLP6	Maintain the security of property and premises through observation
2J1	Prepare and submit case files
2J2	Present evidence in court and at other hearings
2K1	Escort detained persons
4C1	Develop one's own knowledge and practice
4C2	Contribute to the development and effectiveness of work teams
4G2	Ensure your own actions reduce risks to health and safety
4G4	Administer First Aid

Index